I think that the conception of temporal organization as intrinsic to consciousness is a valuable one, and I plan to make use of it later in this essay. I shall
not, however, retain the model of perception, and I do not believe that it makes
sense to say that the consciousness that produces temporality is itself temporal.
More on this later. The next step in the unfolding of my argument is to
summarize my objections to Husserl's treatment of human temporality. If the
schema of intentionality is itself perceived, then it becomes a temporal object
that is subject to the dissolution imposed by the flow of temporality. We have
the "flowing stream" of the living present, but not its steadfastness, or *Ständ-
igkeit*. If it is not a temporal object, then it cannot be perceived, in which case it
must be a transcendental function or a theoretical *interpretation* of the phenomenon of temporality rather than an exact or evident description of the phenomenon itself. And this takes us outside the stream of consciousness, that is, away
from the domain of the description of what is present to the gaze of the
phenomenologist into the domain of what we might as well call metaphysics,
namely, theoretical speculation about the correct explanation of how we experience time in general and the present in particular.

Let me emphasize that it was not my intention to canvas the details of
Husserl's philosophy of time or to list every objection that could be or has been
made to it. I wanted only to indicate what I think is the most important defect
in Husserl's doctrine and what I regard as most helpful in pursuing the problem
of the lived present. Suffice it to say that Husserl does not seem to have
succeeded in describing the living present, and thus he has not explained the
steadfastness or enduring unity of the present as we human beings experience it.
A second model of human temporality has come to prominence in the twentieth century, thanks largely to Heidegger's revision of Husserlian phenomenology. This revision owes much to Aristotle's practical philosophy as well as to the
related anthropological doctrines of Augustine and other Christian thinkers,
but also, interestingly enough, to Nietzsche. Let us call this the model of praxis.
I use "praxis" more or less traditionally to refer to the human action that defines
our everyday life as the network of deeds and speeches by which we carry out
our purposes, strive to fulfill goals, and in general to determine the sense of our
lives; in particular, it is the activity of attempting to define who we are and what
counts as a life worth living.

I think that the model of praxis is more promising than that of perception
because it addresses the entire structure of activity, or, as one could also say, it
addresses the intentional character of human existence without reducing existence to the perception of objects. As this model is exemplified in Heidegger's

Being and Time, it has what is from my standpoint the defect of continuing the effort to explain temporality from within its own flow. I believe that the unsatisfactory nature of Heidegger's analysis can be illustrated effectively by considering his explanation of our experience of the present. This will serve as a transition to my own attempt to employ the model of praxis in a way that does not grant existential priority to temporality.

In *Being and Time,* Heidegger offers two distinct analyses of the structure of temporality as past, present, and future. The first account seems to treat time in a general and preliminary way as "anticipative resoluteness."[5] In the second, immediately following account, Heidegger gives a more elaborate analysis of the authentic and inauthentic modes of temporality.[6] I want to call attention to two features of these accounts. The first is that Heidegger identifies the originative unity of the structure of concern or care (*Sorge*) as temporality (327). Because the totality of the structure of human existence (*Dasein*) is identified as *Sorge* (231), this is an essential step in Heidegger's attempt to explain activity entirely from within the horizon of temporality. Let me underline this point. According to Heidegger, all fundamental structures of *Dasein* are to be grasped as modes of the *Zeitigung der Zeitlichkeit,* the "temporalizing of temporality" (304). This, of course, includes *Verstehen,* and so it must include ontology as well. Otherwise put, the sense or meaning (*Sinn*) of objects replaces these objects themselves; and the senses are defined as functions of human activity, which is itself at bottom the production of temporality.

The second point of interest in Heidegger's doctrine of time is the association of the fallen or inauthentic present with a concern for the tools and things of the everyday world (328).[7] As fallen or thrown into the world, human being (*Dasein*) is dispersed among these entities and is overcome with curiosity about them (338). This curiosity prevents it from seeking its appropriate possibility for existing. Such a possibility is a kind of unifying plan or interpretation, a capacity to give sense to life as a total enterprise rather than the piecemeal process of inspecting and manipulating, and so being manipulated by, things in the world.

Curiosity is inauthentically related to the future "because it is not present in the sense of waiting [*gewärtig*] for a possibility, but demands this already merely as something actual" (*Wirkliches:* 346). By "actual," Heidegger refers to the aforementioned things in the world and the uses to which they may be put. In an alternative formulation, Heidegger says that inauthentic understanding, that is, one grounded primarily in actualities, "temporalizes itself from within the inauthentic present" (*zeitigt sich aus dem Gegenwärtigen:* 338). On the other

In sum, whereas the gods are not to be vilified and are the source of all human excellence,[27] deception and concealment are intrinsic to divine action, that is to say, to the consequences for mortals of divine action. And human beings somehow resemble the gods.[28] It is against this background, of which I have provided a mere sketch, that I understand Pindar's statement in *Nemean* 7, "I even suspect that Odysseus' fame was greater than his worth, through the sweet words of Homer. For in his lies and in his winged devices there is an awesome power: wisdom is deceptive, seducing with its myths."[29]

This passage is not simply praise for poetry. Or rather it is praise for the wisdom of the poet, and hence of Pindar as well as of Homer, to respond to the greater power of the gods with the power of what Socrates will later call medicinal or noble lies or, in less shocking language, the seduction of myth. Human beings require to be seduced by the poets whose "fantasms" (to employ another Platonic expression) accommodate the deceptions of the gods to the human perspective. Myths or fantasms speak, but in such a way as also to be silent: it is not better for every truth to show its face, as Pindar warns us; silence is often wiser.[30]

When the Muses tell Hesiod, "We know how to tell many lies similar to the truth, but we also know how, when we wish, to proclaim the truth,"[31] they are making essentially the same point. The Muses convey to the poets the lies as well as the truths of the gods; that is to say, the wisdom of the poet is not a straightforward revelation of the truth. The origins are intrinsically ambiguous; poetic myth is from the outset an accommodation to or an interpretation of this ambiguity.

From our present standpoint, Hesiod, like Pindar, is a student of Homer. Let us therefore turn to the master, in our attempt to clarify the suggestion that the Greeks are distinguished by their recognition of what Nietzsche calls "Wahrheit und Lüge im aussermoralischen Sinne." It is not simply the appearances that deceive: the divine causes of the human significance of the appearances are also deceivers. Once this is recognized, it is the part of the wise man to deceive his fellow mortals, not simply to conceal himself from their own duplicity, but also to protect them from the deception of the gods.

The symbolic representation of the aforementioned recognition is the transition from Achilles to Odysseus. There is a detailed analysis of the difference between the heroic ethos personified by Achilles in the *Iliad* and the Ionian ethos of the *Odyssey*, as exemplified by Odysseus, in Wilhelm Luther's valuable study *"Wahrheit" und "Lüge" im ältesten Griechentum*.[32]

Luther shows that "*pseudos* contradicts the warrior Ideal of the *Iliad*" (84), in

which lying is reserved for cowardly and incompetent mortals, whereas the Olympian gods regularly lie and deceive (85). The situation changes fundamentally in the *Odyssey*: "The divine world of the *Iliad* in contrast inclines more to the human domain of the *Odyssey*" (95). Honesty, openness, absence of guile: these attributes of Achilles are not exemplified by Odysseus, who lies and deceives in common with beggars, merchants, and the lower orders, but who is no longer condemned for this behavior (87f.). "In the *Iliad*," Luther observes, "the behavior of the gods, in contrast to the heroic-aristocratic society of the warriors, is strikingly unheroic. Their attitude towards *pseudos, epiorkan, apatē, dolos,* and so on, is very close to that of the Ionians of the *Odyssey*, with the one difference that the gods behave in this respect much more arbitrarily than the mortals. On the other hand there is no essential deviation of the behavior of the gods in the *Iliad* from that in the *Odyssey*."

I restrict myself to one remark concerning Luther's inferences from the evidence he assembles. Luther says that the ancient bards presented an idealized conception of primitive man in the *Iliad*, whereas their portrait of the gods coincides with that of contemporary Ionian man (117). But he does not attempt to explain why the bards leave us with two distinct portraits of human nature, or what the common behavior of the gods is intended to signify in contrast with the difference in human behavior, humans who are furthermore presented poetically as in chronological continuity. Luther does say, in contrasting Homer with Hesiod, that whereas in Hesiod the *pseudos*-phenomenon is presented explicitly and self-consciously as a problem, there is no reflection in Homer upon lying and deception as problematic (138).

In my opinion, Luther's conclusion does not do justice to his own evidence of Homer's subtlety. What Homer actually shows is that the lying and deception of the gods is a poetic representation of the intrinsic structure of human experience. This fact is directly evident to the lower orders, who must live by their wits as well as their physical labor and who cannot afford to delude themselves about the nature of things.

In contrast, the earliest warrior-aristocrats, who are insulated by their class from the infinite labor of negativity (to use a Hegelian expression), may shape their lives, or more specifically the interpretation of their lives, in an aesthetic of nobility, one which extends to the sole negative activity of killing the enemy. Honesty, openness, and absence of guile thus constitute an inability to modify their conduct in the face of a reality which they reject as base and ugly, a reality which in due course will initiate the master-slave dialectic celebrated by Hegel. The heroes of the *Iliad*, and Achilles in particular, exhibit the simplicity of

innocence. In Odysseus, as it were, we see the world-historical transformation or synthesis of aristocratic strength and bravery with the cunning and duplicity of the lower orders.

No doubt it is true that Homer does not comment on the significance of the transition from Achilles to Odysseus. One might infer that in this respect Hesiod represents a decline in aesthetic and psychological subtlety. Even if Hesiod is a necessary step in the emergence of philosophy from poetry, we pay a certain price in the form of a reification of sensibility. Truth acquires its inner merit from a contrast with falsehood, but it does not follow that the contrast gains in precision and flexibility, in the domain of practice, by being rendered fully explicit. And as we have just noted, Hesiod's explicitness reveals the similarity of falsehood to truth, or the dependence of their distinctness upon the wishes of the Muses.

One should not mistake the simplicity of Achilles for that of Homer. The distinction, attributed to Antisthenes by Dio Chrysostom, between what Homer appeared to say (*doksei*) and what he said in truth (*alētheia*), is not at all anachronistic.[33] In any event, the difference between Achilles and Odysseus is unmistakable. This is already evident in the *Iliad,* in which Achilles says unequivocally of himself, "Hateful to me as the gates of Hades is he who hides one thing in his mind and says another" (9. 312). Odysseus's nature will be defined in the *Odyssey* by Nestor: "No one could match himself against Odysseus in wisdom, because the divine Odysseus triumphed entirely in all *dolois* [tricks]" (3. 120ff.).

It is to a radical or primordial version of this distinction that the Athenian Stranger refers in Plato's *Laws* (3. 679c2–7) when he says that the earliest mortals were good *dia tēn legomenēn euētheian* (through their so-called simplicity), by which he means that they were not wise enough, as are contemporary men, *pseudos huponoein* (to detect falsehood), but believed that whatever they heard about gods as well as mortals was true. A similar point underlies Herodotus's account of the Persians, with whom the Greeks contrasted themselves sharply. The Persians hold it to be unlawful to speak of what it is forbidden to do, and "they believe that the most shameful thing of all is to tell a lie" (1. 138).

This principle is illustrated, not contradicted, in the dialogue on the Persian revolution against the Medes, in which Darius is forced to introduce the need for deception: "There are many things impossible to reveal in speech but possible in deed. Some things can be spoken, but no noble deed is engendered. . . . When it is necessary to lie, one must do so" (3. 72). If space

permitted, it would be interesting to analyze Xenophon's portrait of the education of the Persian gentleman in the *Cyropaideia* and to contrast it with Socrates' account of the philosopher-king in the *Republic*. Here I will merely summarize the Greek perception of the difference between themselves and the Persians by citing Aeschylus's *Persians,* lines 361ff., in which Darius is said not to have understood the *dolos* of a Greek gentleman or the envy of the gods.

Throughout Plato's dialogues, one finds a continuous interest in falsehood, suspicion, deception, and concealment, an interest that is curiously unnoticed in the secondary literature. For an appreciation of this side of Plato, one must turn to Nietzsche, who is the first major thinker of my acquaintance to appreciate explicitly the connection between spiritual nobility and the mask.

The philosophical condemnation of the lie in the soul, or self-deception, is entirely compatible with the use of medicinal or noble lies.[34] Socrates' assertion that the worse lies are about gods and heroes, and his condemnation of the lying poets, in particular Homer and Hesiod,[35] must therefore mean that in the city under construction, the traditional falsehoods are not useful. In book 3, Socrates makes the interesting assertion that falsehood is not useful for the gods, whereas it is useful for mortals in the form of a medicine.[36] One wonders whether divine falsehood would be sanctioned if it were indeed useful.

According to Homer and his followers, the gods are deceitful. This is to say that the origins are bad or at the very least a mixture of the bad with the good. Hence the harshness of existence requires an accommodation on the part of nobility: the high must accommodate to the low, not for low motives but in order to survive. The existence of nobility depends upon the practice of Odyssean *dolos.*

In the account of the gods presented in the *Republic,* Socrates seems to repudiate this commonsensical understanding of life. In fact, however, the situation is more complex. To begin with, the account of the origins in the *Republic* is clearly political and designed to assist in the concealment of the medicinal lies of the philosopher-kings. When Plato turns to a straightforward account of the origins of civilization, as in the *Laws,* he clearly regards these origins as bad.[37]

In the *Republic,* the defective nature of reality is easily inferred from the elaborate precautions that are required to preserve the best city from destruction, in particular from the passions, with eros prominent among them, but also by the *thumos* (spiritedness) of the guardians, which reminds us of the heroic and straightforward Achilles. *Thumos* must be regulated by the *dianoia* (discursive intelligence); one part of nature must regulate the other. Those natural qualities upon which political existence depends are the same qualities

which, if left to themselves, would destroy the polis. This is what I called earlier the conjunction of presence and absence as the root of the relation between truth and falsehood.

The philosophical city is founded upon the *dolos* and *apatē* of the philosophers, and in the first instance by the *gennaion pseudos* (noble lie) of Socrates, the philosophical reincarnation of Odysseus. The city cannot be founded upon or preserved by the unmitigated truth because the "goodness" of the Ideas, and so too of the god of the philosophers, has nothing to do with everyday human existence. In particular, it has no bearing upon political life. At bottom, Socrates' understanding of political life is no different from that of Homer.

The difference between the two lies in their understanding of the divine. According to Homer, the gods are jealous, vindictive liars and deceivers who walk among mortals in concealed forms for the purpose of satisfying their desires, whether these bring happiness or misery to human beings. According to Socrates, the gods, for all practical purposes, do not exist. But the world of genesis behaves toward humankind exactly as though the tales of the poets, and of Homer in particular, were true.

Genesis is a magician, juggler, liar, deceiver, in a word, a sophist who continuously conceals himself under changing appearances. Let us assume here what is far from obvious, namely, that the philosopher is able to distinguish between the sophistical appearances of genesis and the theoretical vision of the true divinity of the Ideas. Whereas this may bring happiness to the soul of the philosopher, it changes nothing in the soul of the nonphilosopher. Political life in the comprehensive sense can be changed, if at all, only by the political *action* of the philosopher. And this action requires the philosopher to imitate the sophist, that is, the noble sophist Odysseus, by the use of *dolos* and concealment.

The least one can say is that the enactment of truth requires the mask of deception and concealment, almost exactly as we learn from the *Odyssey.* The one significant practical difference between Homer and Plato is that Odysseus wishes to return to the tranquil life of city and family, whereas the Socratic eros can be satisfied by neither. But the consequence of this difference is that Odysseus reveals his identity at the end of his adventures. There is, however, no end to the Socratic adventure, and as Nietzsche understood perfectly, the philosopher never relinquishes his masks.

As a final illustration of my thesis, I call attention to Plato's *Protagoras,* 316d3ff. The great sophist, in the presence of his assembled colleagues and students, reveals to Socrates and Hippocrates the surprising fact that the sophis-

tic *technē* is very old, but that those who practiced it before him "put forward a screen and concealed themselves, fearing the offensiveness of the *technē*." Among the concealed sophists of the past, Protagoras cites poets, initiates in the mysteries and oracles, gymnasts, and musicians, but not philosophers.

Protagoras goes on to say that he disagrees with his predecessors on the point of deception. They did not accomplish their intention, namely, to conceal themselves from those human beings who are capable of political action (*prattein*). These few who are by nature political leaders will see through the screens. As to the many, "they perceive nothing, so to speak."[38] I cannot study here in detail the implications of Protagorean frankness. The following brief remarks must serve as a promissory note for a more exhaustive analysis.

According to Protagoras, those who practice concealment of their wisdom are transparent to the men of *praxis*. There are, then, two different degrees of intelligence or, as we may say, of participation in the Greek miracle. The sophists are private citizens who withdraw behind their masks for prudential reasons: they surpass Achilles but fall short of Odysseus. Only in the case of the poets could one discern an indirect political or pedagogical role.

Protagoras, on the contrary, seeks a direct political influence. He is too wise to attempt what is beyond his gifts, namely, to try to gain power in his own name. But he is also too ambitious to restrict himself to the private station of the poet. His *dolos* is to combine elements from Achilles and Odysseus in a new mask that contains an anticipatory element of Machiavellian frankness.

Protagoras accepts the wisdom of the rulers, who are thoroughly aware of the deception required by the sophistical nature of genesis. To this extent he is a member of the aforementioned army whose general is Homer.[39] There is on this teaching no eternal domain of goodness, openness, or pure illumination behind the mask of genesis. For Homer and his troops, in the case of genesis, the mask is the ultimate truth, and so too it is the ultimate falsehood. Plato allies Socrates with Parmenides and is the actual author of the speech by which Protagoras unmasks himself and his predecessors.

By writing this speech, Plato does not deny the Homeric understanding of genesis, that is to say, of its human consequences. Instead, his rejection of Homer's mask is the negative side of the positive construction in the *Republic* of the city of philosopher-kings by means of lies, deception, and concealment. Plato reconstitutes Greek origins in the light of a profound reinterpretation of the Odyssean perception of the conjunction of truth and falsehood in the structure of things.

So far as nonphilosophical life goes, Homer is correct and continues to be an

authoritative text for Plato. As to the higher truth of the philosophical life, it has nothing intrinsic to do with political existence. If it is to be politically effective, it can be so only by means of the adoption of Odyssean practice. The essence of nonphilosophical life in Socrates' city is the same as the essence of nonphilosophical life in the actual Greek city. Plato thus repudiates Pythagorean frankness because he replaces the few who actually rule in the historical city with the few philosopher-kings.

More specifically, Pericles, as one could say, is replaced by Odysseus (the philosophers) and Achilles (the soldiers), but with Odysseus firmly in charge. This repudiation of Protagoras is thus at a deeper level a return to Homer. Protagoras is refuted or exposed, not because he is a disciple of Homer, but because he is a defective or renegade Homeric: a false philosopher.

Protagoras understands that Being is deceptive. This is not contested by Plato. The quarrel between Protagoras and Socrates is Plato's presentation of the quarrel between noble and base sophistry. And this, in passing, is why Socrates is amenable in the *Protagoras* to the identification of the good with the pleasant. The difference between the noble sophist and the philosopher is the vision of the Ideas, or, in another vocabulary, it is the supplementation of poetry by mathematics. But this vision or supplementation is politically, if not irrelevant, secondary.

I have suggested that one cannot understand the Greek account of the origins apart from the perception of the conjunction of truth and falsehood, that is to say, of the presentation of the truth in and through falsehood, or as the Eleatic Stranger puts it in the *Sophist,* of the necessity of fantasms as an accommodation to human vision.[40] In the expression of the Athenian Stranger, the perception of truth is not the simple openness to divine revelation but the manifestation of suspicion toward stories about the gods.

I am certainly not suggesting that the Greeks were the first to notice the harshness of human destiny. What characterizes the peculiarly Greek understanding of this destiny is that suspicion, which should be joined to wonder as the source of wisdom, leads to the perception of concealment as not simply a practical requirement in the face of the hostility of genesis, but as the intrinsic structure of genesis itself, and so as the key to the enigma of truth. This is why, as Marcel Detienne puts it, the "maître de vérité" is also a master of deception.[41]

No more than a brief word of conclusion is required. The question of Nietzsche's anti-Platonism has tended in our time to obscure his origins as a classical

philologist, more fundamentally, as a student whose philosophical nature was fecundated by the Greek understanding of genesis as dissimulation. Nietzsche's rhetoric of excess, which may be explained, following hints that he himself provides,[42] has tended to conceal that understanding.

We postmoderns, to vary a phrase of Nietzsche's, are no longer able to preserve the delicate interplay of frankness and dissimulation that Nietzsche exemplifies. The fanciful Being of art, and a fortiori of postphilosophy, has been sundered from the voice of science, and so of philology, with the net result that sobriety stands forth as ridiculous in the light of the patent richness of the texts of the masters. What we require is not anti-Platonism, and certainly not the Platonism of the philological academy, but the thoroughly Platonic *pharmakon* that consists of a mixture of sobriety and madness, in portions to be determined by the *esprit de finesse*. Only in this way will we be able to match the sinuosities of cosmogonic dissimulation.

Chapter 2 The Lived Present

This essay, previously unpublished, was written for delivery at Leuven University in February 1998, during my visit as Cardinal Mercier lecturer. It addresses a problem that I have long had with Heidegger's analysis of the structure of what I shall call human temporality, a problem that I found to underlie the ostensibly much different discussion of memory and anticipation in Plato's Philebus. The main intention of this essay is to suggest that the long-standing problem of how we experience the present cannot be solved by conceptual analyses of time, whether in the language of mathematical physics or ontology. But neither is it satisfactory to follow the traditional procedure of explaining the present as a synthesis of the past and the future. The first method abstracts immediately from human experience or lived time, whereas the second reduces the present to a combination of memory and anticipation, thereby apparently committing itself to the absurd, or at least counterintuitive, thesis that we live in the past and the future. I think that the second procedure is on the right track, but in order to account for the property of presence, without which we cannot explain the present, we must follow a clue given to us in quite different ways by Plato and Heidegger. I am referring to Platonic eros on the one hand and

Heideggerian care on the other. The present, I shall argue, is produced by the erotic (or caring) production of a cosmos (or world) that is constituted as a rank-ordering. That is, we experience the present neither as a moment or assemblage of moments, nor as a synthesis of the past and the future, but as an act of "opening" or world-constitution. This suggestion, stated baldly, seems to be Kantian rather than Platonic and to place me within the contemporary tradition of hermeneutical philosophy. But eros is also hermeneutical, as Diotima points out in the Symposium *(201E). The important question is whether there exists a basis for discriminating or rank-ordering interpretations. Plato's claim that there is such a basis is incorporated in the doctrine of the Ideas. This is an extraordinarily difficult doctrine in its own right, and it is not the subject of the present essay, which treats solely the question of how we can account for the integrity of the present within the flow of human temporality. This essay is closely related to chapter 11 of this book, which takes up the ambiguous status of the present, and so of the ontological role of temporality, in Gadamer's doctrine of universal hermeneutics.[1]*

In this essay, I shall be concerned with one aspect of the problem of human temporality. My question is this: How do we experience the present? Like the phenomenon of time, the question is itself at once familiar and obscure. We are all conversant with the experience of living in the present, as distinct from having existed in the past and being about to do so in the future, barring some unexpected accident. Let us say that the lived present has a certain thickness or what Bergson called *durée*. But to speak of the present as marked by duration is apparently to imply that it consists of the past and the future as well as itself. One can follow Bergson by claiming that "the moments of internal duration are not exterior to one another" and do not constitute a numerical multiplicity.[2] I find this both helpful and baffling. It is helpful in pointing to the fact that we do not experience the present as an instant. But I do not know what Bergson means by "the moments of internal duration." If they are not exterior to one another, then how can they be perceived or experienced as distinct? But if they are not distinct, then how does the enduring present retain the inner structure that preserves it from dissolution into chaos?

The problem can thus be put as follows: Apparently the present cannot be grasped in our experience as fully and actually distinct from the past and the future. But the past and the future are themselves distinguished, both empirically and conceptually, with respect to the present. When Hegel, for example, observes that the "Now" disappears as we attempt to grasp it, he is implying that the attempt to perceive the present, and so the structure of temporality,

from within the flow of time itself is a self-extinguishing procedure. At least this is what I wish to infer from his remark.

The question I am considering is not simply a psychological problem. I am not, for example, asking the question posed by William James about the specious present. James assumes in advance that the present is, strictly speaking, subjectively inaccessible, and that our impression of the present is an illusory perception of what is actually the recent past. I reply that it is the presentness of the experience of the ostensibly specious present that requires explanation. To put the point as simply as possible, the world must exist in a certain way if there is to be temporal experience, and this experience is itself impossible if it occurs in the past and the future or in memory and anticipation, but not in the present. My question is therefore ontological. Must not something be fully present to us in order to render intelligible absences of all kinds, including that of the past and the future?

And this brings me to the following general observation. At least since Locke, the most popular approach to the question of the experience of time has been to attempt to analyze what William James was apparently the first to call "the stream of consciousness." In this approach, the governing paradigm of the experience as well as the analysis is sense perception. This is as true of British empiricism as it is of the phenomenology of Edmund Husserl. I believe that this model is inadequate to the task for at least two fundamental reasons. The first is that perception constitutes only one aspect of our experience. And the second is that once we immerse ourselves entirely within the stream of consciousness, we are faced with the impossible task of accounting for its inner structure, and thus the structure of lived time, by means of the currents of that stream, or in other words with the aid of conceptual tools that are themselves temporal artifacts.

In his book *The Inordinance of Time,* Shaun Gallagher concurs with the statement by Aron Gurwitsch that Husserl "repeatedly expressed a preference, even a marked one, for Hume rather than Kant." Gallagher provides textual evidence from the various stages of Husserl's career to justify the following conclusion: like Hume, "Husserl . . . viewed the mind as a flow of consciousness, but without the need for a special faculty, external to the flow, to account for its unity—without either an imagination that, according to Hume, habitually but mistakenly construes consciousness as a unified identity or empirical self-consciousness, or a formally independent transcendental function that, by Kantian accounts, imposes phenomenal unity on empirical consciousness."[3]

Klaus Held derives an apparently different, or at least more complicated,

portrait of Husserl's later thought from his study of the B, C, and E manuscripts in the Husserl archives.[4] The main point of this study for my purposes is as follows. For the late Husserl, the transcendental constitution of objects is "temporalization" (*Zeitigung:* 8). In Husserl's words, "The Absolute is nothing other than absolute temporalization, and already its interpretation as Absolute, that I find in advance directly as my flowing originality [*Urtumlichkeit*], is temporalization" (90; Ms C 1, p. 16). On the other hand, there are numerous passages in which Husserl says that "the ego is not temporal" and even more strongly that "the ego in its most original originality is not in time" (117; Ms. E III, 2, p. 50 and Ms. C X, p. 21, dated 1920/22 and 1931, respectively).

It is not my intention to become involved in the details of Husserl philology. There seems to be some confusion in Husserl himself about the "original" temporality of the transcendental ego. As Held points out, if the ego is not in time, then what Husserl calls "the living presence," that is, the self-presentation and temporalization of the transcendental ego, within which all constitution of objects takes place as "presentation" *(Gegenwärtigung),* cannot itself be presented intuitively. It cannot be an object of perception. More precisely, we can grasp the flow of time from point to point as objectified at each place or we can grasp it as a totality of omnipresence that is, as it were, transtemporal or omnitemporal. But we cannot intuit, that is, perceive, the originatively self-presenting ego that is at once both the flowing and the standing presence of time (IX–X).

At least on the basis of this collection of passages, one must say that Husserl, even though he may have preferred Hume to Kant, has turned into a Kantian. But because he makes perception, that is, the description of perceptual objects, the paradigm of scientific epistemology, it would seem that the phenomenological description of the flow of time as it ostensibly appears from within the stream of consciousness is radically defective. On the other hand, we can say that the famous doctrine of horizontal and transverse intentionality provides us with a conceptual explanation of what Gallagher, in the previously cited passage, calls the unifying function built into the flow of consciousness itself. But this is still Kantian because we do not perceive the structure of intentionality; instead, it is the function of this ostensibly self-organizing capacity of the stream of consciousness that makes it possible for us to perceive temporal objects. In short, there are two questions here. First, is intentionality, the form of lived time, itself temporal? If it is itself a temporal event, then it seems to lose its formal status. Second, is intentionality as Husserl conceives it the correct version of the form of time?

Contents

Metaphysics in Ordinary Language

Stanley Rosen

Yale University Press

New Haven and London

Published with assistance from the Ernst Cassirer Publications Fund.

Printed in the United States of America.

Library of Congress Cataloging-in-Publication Data

Rosen, Stanley, 1929–
   Metaphysics in ordinary language / Stanley Rosen.
      p.   cm.
   Includes bibliographical references and index.
   ISBN 0-300-07478-6 (alk. paper)
   1. Philosophy. I. Title.
B945.R526M48   1999
191—dc21   98-26477
                                                                  CIP

A catalogue record for this book is available from the British Library.

The paper in this book meets the guidelines for permanence and durability of the
Committee on Production Guidelines for Book Longevity of the Council on
Library Resources.

10 9 8 7 6 5 4 3 2 1

To Jebediah

Chapter 1 Suspicion, Deception, and Concealment

—une croyance presque instinctive chez moi c'est que tout homme
puissant ment quand il parle, et à plus forte raison quand il écrit.
[—a belief that is almost instinctive with me is that every powerful man
lies when he speaks, and even more so when he writes.]
—*Stendhal*

*One of the many things I learned from the late Leo Strauss was the trad-
ition of esoteric writing. This tradition is discussed by representatives of
every major philosophical and literary age from the time of the Greeks to
the day before yesterday. The issue becomes entirely explicit at the time of
the Enlightenment, when it is widely held that, important as the concealment of dangerous views from the wider public may have been in the past,
it is now possible for the human race to enter the age of maturity. Accordingly, frankness on theoretical issues is now both possible and desirable. The
reader may consult Kant's* Critique of Pure Reason, B776. *The most
extensive discussion of esoteric writing before Strauss's may be found in
Nietzsche's* Beyond Good and Evil. *Nietzsche, however, analyzes two
distinct forms of esotericism without always making clear the difference*

between them. The first form is the intentional concealment of one's views for reasons of prudence, playfulness, or aristocratic pride. The second form is a reflection in human speech of the intrinsic deceptiveness of Becoming. This form underlies Heidegger's doctrine of the concealment of Being by the productions of the Being-process or, in slightly different terms, of the interplay between presence and absence. Whereas the first form of esotericism has not entirely disappeared, it is obvious that the second form is central in late-modern, and so in postmodern, thought. The main purpose of my essay is to show how the first form of esotericism is a response, not simply to political or prudential considerations, but to the very nature of human experience and, still more fundamentally, to the way things are. I wanted also to indicate that, very far from having been discovered by Heidegger or for that matter Nietzsche, the entire complex of issues is rooted in the earliest writings of classical Greece.

"Suspicion, Deception, and Concealment" was delivered at a conference entitled "Le miracle grec," held in Nice on May 18–20, 1989. The proceedings of the conference were published under the same name in 1992 by the Association des Publications de la Faculté des Lettres de Nice, 59–68. It later appeared in Arion *(Spring 1991): 112–27.*

The passage from Stendhal that serves as our motto is recorded by Nietzsche in a notebook entry dating from 1887–88.[1] It expresses a theme that fascinates Nietzsche at all stages of his productive life. The most powerful statement of that theme occurs in paragraph 30 of *Beyond Good and Evil*, as part of the climax of Nietzsche's account of the distance that separates the exceptional human being from the multitude (par. 26–30): "Our highest insights must—and should—sound like follies, perhaps like crimes, when in an impermissible manner they reach ears which are not suited or predetermined for them. The exoteric and the esoteric, as the philosophers formerly distinguished them, among the Indians as among the Greeks, Persians, and Musulmen, in short, wherever one believes in rank-ordering and not in equality and equal rights."[2] It is in this context that Nietzsche observes, ten paragraphs later, "Everything that is deep loves the mask; the deepest things have a hatred for image and likeness."[3]

One may easily multiply references in Nietzsche to the superior being's need for self-concealment. I restrict myself to two passages from the notebooks. First, "The necessary *concealment* of the wise man: his consciousness, to be unconditionally not understood."[4] Second, "What is noble? . . . always to be disguised; the higher his nature, the more does a man require an incognito. God, if there

were one, would be required on grounds of decency to show himself in the world only as a human being."5 These texts suggest two reasons for the practice of esotericism by the higher man: prudence and the exercise of an aristocratic natural right. A detailed analysis of these motives would be of independent interest, especially in the contemporary Anglo-Saxon intellectual community. In this essay, however, I prefer to take my bearings by a more fundamental stratum in Nietzsche's thought. As is exemplified by the insights incorporated in the early Greek poets and thinkers, deception and concealment are intrinsic to existence itself. Esotericism is thus the inevitable consequence of our warranted suspicion of nature.

It would be only partially correct and therefore misleading to say that for Nietzsche human existence is an illusion. We are put on the right track by the further statement that the dynamical structure of the illusion is intelligible. The key to Nietzsche's analysis is thus contained in his assertion that "the true essence of things is a fiction of *des vorstellenden Seins*."6 The German expression may be translated as "imaginative" or "representational Being." Scientific truth is for Nietzsche an artifact; like most modern philosophers, Nietzsche accepts the thesis that we know only what we make. Whereas Kant, for example, posits a transcendental process of world-constitution that is valid for all beings of our cognitive nature, Nietzsche substitutes a fanciful, random, intrinsically chaotic process of Becoming that expresses itself in a multiplicity of continuously shifting perspectives. Nietzsche traces this doctrine back to the earliest Greek thinkers: "The Greeks taught us gradually *to organize chaos*."7 And again: "To take possession of oneself, to organize the chaotic, to discard all fear of 'formation' [*Bildung*] and to be honest: summons to *gnōthi sauton*."8

Honesty here stands for philosophy as an existential requirement of the higher human type: a frank perception of the fanciful or invented status of natural order is the basis of concealment. To exist is to conceal chaos. And the higher man, who alone is capable of self-knowledge, *conceals this concealment*. Both levels of concealment underlie Nietzsche's famous invocation of art: "Art and nothing but art. It is art that is the great rendering possible of life, the great seductress to life, the great stimulus to life."9 When Nietzsche asserts from his own experience that "art is worth more than the truth,"10 he is referring to the poeticizing reason which in man is the expression of the fanciful Being that produces what we perceive as order.11 The "will to power as knowledge" is accordingly "not 'knowing' but schematizing, a superimposing of enough regularity and form onto chaos as will satisfy our practical needs."12

If science is the result of "a creative, formative constitutive power," or the

self-establishment of man within chaos,[13] so too is art. The higher value of art for life (and for the philosopher only as the legislator of a new type of human being) is that it encourages illusion and preserves the deception that is salutary for human existence. Science, on the other hand, tends to expose itself, the process of the dissipation of the illusion, as the deepest of illusions. One must not infer from this that art in the conventional sense of the term is for Nietzsche higher than philosophy—for the higher man. Nietzsche never deviates throughout his productive life from the view expressed in a letter to his sister dating from his twenty-first year: "In our researches, are we seeking tranquillity, peace, happiness? No; only the truth, even if it should be in the highest degree terrifying and hateful."[14] At the peak of his creative powers, Nietzsche expresses the same thought in his notebooks as follows: "We defend the artist and poet and whoever is a master, but as natures who are of the type higher than these who can only do something, than the merely 'productive men,' we do not confuse ourselves with them."[15]

The fundamental stratum of Nietzsche's teaching, in all of its ramifications, may therefore be traced back to the insights of his youthful reflections as a classical philologist. The earliest Greek thinkers teach us to derive the cosmos from chaos.[16] But mankind as a whole lives in tranquillity, security, and orderliness only when it forgets that truth is "a moving army of metaphors, metonymies, anthropomorphisms," when it forgets that the human being is an artist-creator.[17] We must distinguish here between two levels of truth in order to clarify Nietzsche's intention. Whereas the truth of the ordered cosmos is an artifact, the truth about cosmogony or fanciful Being is neither an illusion nor a perspective.

It is the latter truth about the artifactual nature of the former truth that necessitates dissimulation:

> The intellect, as a means to the preservation of the individual, develops its chief forces in dissimulation; for this is the means by which the weaker, less robust individuals preserve themselves, for which individuals the pursuit of a struggle for existence with horned creatures or the sharp bite of beasts of prey is excluded. This art of dissimulation reaches its peak in mankind. Here deception, flattery, lying and deluding, talking behind one's back, keeping up appearances, living within the concealed glance, masked existence, veiled convention, the stage-play before others and before oneself, in short, the continuous fluttering around the flame of vanity, is so much the rule and the law that it is almost inconceivable how an honest and pure drive for the truth could have arisen in human beings.[18]

Acknowledgments

I want to acknowledge the contribution of my research assistant, Lawrence Horsburgh, to the preparation of the manuscript of this book. I am once more indebted to my colleagues at Boston University, and to the editorial and production staffs of Yale University Press. I want in particular to thank John Silber for his support through the years. The book is dedicated to my grandson, who is just beginning his philosophical career.

In sum, human beings invent the distinction between truth and falsehood as a consequence of the emergence of language from society, which is itself a product of the need for peace.[19] But the entire process is precisely an invention of the fanciful Being or poeticizing reason. These in turn assume human shape and accommodate to human perspective, but the process of accommodation is not an artifact, not a perception. It is this which Nietzsche the philosopher describes in his analysis of dissimulation. The few conceal from the many what the many conceal from themselves. As reciprocal dissimulation, human activity exhibits rather than conceals the dynamic structure of Becoming. This concealment is extramoral because, to employ a non-Nietzschean term, it is ontological. When Heidegger speaks of the presence of Being as self-concealment, he transforms into ontological abstractions Nietzsche's vivid analysis of the cosmogonic production of perspectives. What shows itself achieves presence or visibility as a falsification of the continuous inner excitation of chaos, or of what Hegel refers to as the terrible power of negativity. It is not simply that human beings conceal their thoughts from one another. Thinking is *as such* concealment: to be is to dissimulate.

Hegel represents the attempt of German philosophy to master Greek genesis by the structure of its own activity, or, in other words, to interpret chaos as the formation process. This is in turn the result of an attempt to combine eternity with time, or what Kant calls the noumenal and the phenomenal. In Nietzsche, exactly the same attempt is visible, as may be indicated by a reference to the eternal return of the similar, Nietzsche's version of the Hegelian concept of totality. In Nietzsche, however, Hegel's synthesis of essence and appearance, or the identification of essence *as* what appears, is dissolved by the play of appearances themselves. We can describe the process of play, but as a metaphor or dissimulation, not as a quasi-mathematical or conceptually determinate structure. To conceptualize is for Nietzsche to suppress original dissimulation, but it is also to produce a world and thus to make life possible.

Nietzsche imitates the play of appearances in his texts, which are coherent but not systematic. I am suggesting that the key to the play of appearances is the distinction between philosophical truth and the philosophical production or world-creation that this truth necessitates. The truth or cosmogonic process always reveals itself in a disguise, namely, as this or that cosmos, this or that perspective. The process is always the same: it is, as it were, the eternal return of the similar; and the accessibility of this sameness enables us to "deconstruct" each manifestation as a dissimulation. For Nietzsche, however, there are only a

finite number of fundamental cosmic dissimulations or human types, which thus serve as Platonic Ideas in the sense that they allow us to organize and understand the unending production of perspectives *within* those types.

Nietzsche's self-professed "reversed Platonism" or replacement of the Ideas by "life within illusion"[20] could be shown to be Platonic in more than one sense; I restrict myself here to noting the nonillusory perception of life within illusion. "Within," not "as": the distinction is crucial. From the standpoint of the esotericist, who sees from above downward, life is visible as within, and so defined by, illusion, that is, by what I have called the cosmogonic process of dissimulation.

The question that interests me here is not so much whether Nietzsche's "anti-Platonism" has been correctly understood, by himself or his disciples, but rather what evidence we can find in the pre-Socratic poets and thinkers to sustain Nietzsche's account of the schematizing of chaos. I propose to devote the balance of this essay to the gathering of such evidence, a gathering that is, of course, far from exhaustive but that is sufficient to justify the thesis that the root of Nietzsche's thought is Greek. Nietzsche is one of the many modern captains in Homer's army.[21]

The Greek *phainomenon* is a conjunction of presence and absence. Let us turn first to Pindar. In the Olympian Odes he speaks on numerous occasions of the truth as being "spotted," "stained," or "veiled" by lies, which are again compared to an obscure cloud that drags away the correct path of things from men's minds.[22] These images sustain the insight that falsehoods, the lies told by things and events themselves, are an intrinsic property of the truth, and not an extrinsic covering that may be easily removed.

The intrinsic stain of falsehood prevents us from knowing whether what happens is for the best. We can, of course, often judge the desirability of an event by its future consequences. But apart from the fact that the future may be as ambiguous as the past, we live and act in the present. In a single *moira* (portion) of time, differing winds change rapidly.[23] One wind is a blessing, the other is not: a mortal who knows the ways of truth should prosper while he can.[24]

Wisdom, in other words, consists in moderating one's desires and ambitions in the face of present ambiguity. Men's hopes rise and fall, borne on falsehoods that tumble in the wind. No mortal has ever succeeded in discovering a *piston symbolon* (trustworthy token) about coming events from a god.[25] One should not, for example, sacrifice the present attainment for a future wish; who knows what will happen a year from now?[26]

Preface

The essays collected in this book originated for the most part as lectures for a variety of professional occasions. Three have not been previously published and two others are presented here in such radically altered form as to constitute new essays. Of the remainder, all but two have appeared in foreign languages or in publications that are not easily available. I am grateful to Yale University Press for allowing a larger audience to decide on their possible interest. The essays are united not by a common theme but by a common way of philosophizing. The reader will find here studies of abstract problems like that of negation and the relation between perception and judgment, but also discussions of eros, poetry, and freedom. A number of the essays are developments of a point made in previous publications, but some are attempts to break new ground. In some cases the analysis is associated with the interpretation of a particular text. In others, I take my bearings by a general problem. The collection closes with a memoir of my experience in the philosophical world of Paris in 1960–61.

In spite of this thematic diversity, I believe that the essays to follow are united in two ways. The first unifying element is my conviction

that philosophy must begin with a careful consideration of ordinary or every-day life as the context within which occur the dislocations and problems that demand extraordinary theoretical and analytical measures. I therefore share the views of many philosophers of our century, with one possible difference. It seems to me that phenomenologists and analysts alike are either too quick to transform ordinary experience into an artifact of technical discourse or too inclined, often because of the influence of modern scientific rationalism, to repudiate what they regard as outmoded ways of reflection. This inclination is conveniently represented as the rejection of metaphysics. In the attempt to position myself within the contemporary discussion, I have taken to using the expression "ordinary language metaphysics" to designate the procedures I favor.

The reference to metaphysics is not intended as a sign that I advocate a "reactionary" return to the prescientific dark ages of phantom substances and dancing angels. It is, however, meant to suggest that science is already an interpretation of ordinary experience, and even farther, that it is rooted in a metaphysical foundation. One may honor and even cherish science without falling prey to the full range of scientific ideologies, and especially those which render senseless and nonrational the very celebration of science. This brings me to the second unifying theme of this collection. It has to do with the relation in philosophy between theoretical or conceptual analysis and historical scholar-ship. In the past twenty years, the earlier tendency to distinguish sharply between scholarship and "original" philosophy has become muted if it has not altogether disappeared. The reason for this shift in fashion is easy to state. It reflects the very deep conviction that we are historical creatures, and so that truth is a historical artifact. As a direct consequence of this conviction, the belief in the possibility of philosophy in any but a purely technical sense, that is, as the production and analysis of artifacts, has steadily weakened.

Whereas a generation or two ago it was fashionable for the theoretically inclined to scorn specialists in the history of philosophy as mere scholars, such rejection of history on behalf of technical prowess had the ironical result of intensifying the power of the historical spirit itself. If philosophy in the honorific sense of the term consists in "theory construction" and if "originality" refers to novelty rather than to any sense of a return to the origins or first principles, then obviously enough each new philosophical theory is a finite creature, born to be falsified, as one might put it, and hence tainted with falsehood from the beginning. The origin is from this standpoint the womb of history, and today's philosophical prodigies are tomorrow's obstacles to progress.

A complete analysis of the contemporary belief in—perhaps one should say obsession with—the end of philosophy, which is hardly limited to postmodernists, would require a volume in itself. One would have to consider, for example, the strongest currents in twentieth-century philosophy of mathematics, including such issues as the historicist implications of formalism, of constructivism, and, more generally, of a pure axiomatic approach. And a similar analysis would have to be made of the philosophy of science. When we avert our gaze from history, it has a tendency to stab us in the back. This is obvious in the results of our fascination with technique. Having passed through the valley of positivism, we have emerged onto the plains of nihilism.

Twenty years ago, it seemed that all analytically oriented philosophers were studying theories of reference. Today the fashion is without doubt being set by cognitive science. Metaphysicians (as well as their cousins, the postmetaphysicians) live slightly longer generations. Thirty years ago, they were immersed in ontology; today, Being is out (except in the persona of Becoming) and difference is in. If human beings are machines and sameness is a simulacrum of otherness, then the context for cognitive science and postmodernism cannot be supplied by philosophy in its old sense as love of wisdom. And so we turn to history, not in order to discover the truth, but precisely because we no longer believe in truth and are left with nothing but the investigation of how we arrived at the present impasse.

This is, of course, a sketch, intended to indicate the most pervasive lineaments of contemporary tendencies that I oppose. More precisely, the view of the relation between theory and history to which I adhere is quite different from the one I have just described. To begin with, I agree that it is necessary to know history in order to avoid being hoodwinked by illusions of our originality. I also accept the Husserlian conception of "desedimentation," or the need to uncover the roots of theoretical problems in the world of everyday life, a process that requires us to strip away the layers of history that have concealed those roots. This last expression is perhaps misleading; the stripping away must be performed with the proper tools and care, not by brute force.

To say this in another way, we have to conduct two analyses conjointly, one devoted to everyday life and the other to its historical costume. Everyday life is not itself a historical creature; the term "everyday," like its conceptual partner "ordinary," implies a certain regularity that provides us with a basis for assessing the different interpretations, however "extraordinary," that we give to our speeches and deeds. What is today called hermeneutics, or the act of interpretation, is one manifestation of everyday life that arises in response to the more

general love of truth, and still more generally, to the love of the good. These forms of love may take on historical postures of various kinds, but they are rooted in human nature. Stated again with maximum brevity, I subscribe to the Socratic thesis that the human being is the philosophical animal, and that everyday life is itself an expression of the love of truth and wisdom that in its fully developed form is nothing other than philosophy. We may decide that we no longer wish to be human beings, but wishing will not make it so. As history itself has demonstrated, it is much easier to become sub- than superhuman. This in turn shows us the limited utility of appeals to natural laws and to oversimple conceptions of nature as a standard. Whereas we are by nature the philosophical animal, we are also naturally disobedient. It is therefore of great importance to study the arguments and protestations of the antiphilosophers. A thorough knowledge of sin is unfortunately a necessary prerequisite to confidence in virtue. It needs to be shown that the affirmation of historicism is itself a distorted version of the love of wisdom.

Thus far I could be taken to have spoken of history as a detritus that we need to know in order to discount it. But this is only a part of the picture. We are indeed temporal beings who live in history in the literal sense of that term: We conduct inquiries and we tell tales about what we have discovered. There is no human life, and so no philosophical life, that transpires *sub specie aeternitatis*. Life, and so too philosophizing, takes place in particular ways; it is conducted at particular times, each with its own prevailing standpoints. The attempt to rank-order these ways and their standpoints is not a denial of our historicity but the very manifestation of its significance. This attempt brings us into contact with our fellow philosophers of the past and makes us accessible to philosophers of the future. We are all engaged in a common venture, and it is this venture that raises us above, but does not detach us entirely from, our historical environment.

In short, if we cannot rise, we shall sink. The attempt to rise is easy to caricature as a form of speculative levitation. Those who sink, however, provide their own caricature in the celebration of insignificance, however ironically expressed. The following essays are attempts to strike a happy balance between an excessive lightness of being and the kind of hard-headedness that runs the risk of spiritual sclerosis.

Metaphysics in Ordinary Language

hand, "the future has priority in the ecstatic unity of original and authentic temporality" and again, "the primary phenomenon of original and authentic temporality is the future" (329). "The authentic present [*Augenblick*] . . . temporalizes itself from within the authentic future" (338).

This will suffice as a basis for the following observation. Although Heidegger denies that the distinction between authenticity and inauthenticity is a rank-ordering or value judgment, it is obvious that authenticity is to be preferred to inauthenticity. And it is very striking that inauthenticity is closely connected with the actual, whereas authenticity is equally or even more closely connected to the future. Differently stated, the genuine sense of actual things in the world must be derived from the future, and furthermore, from a future that manifests itself as a possibility for interpreting, rather than as the eventual actualization of this or that possibility. This is in keeping with Heidegger's assertion that possibility is higher than actuality (38) and that "*Dasein* is essentially its possibility" (42). Heidegger, in a silent but unmistakable rebuke of Husserl, replaces his living present with an inauthentic concern for actual entities. To this, he adds the ontologically superior authentic present as a *Seinkönnen*. The authentic present is marked by resoluteness, but the sense of resoluteness comes primarily from the future or inactual. In sum, the authentic present derives its significance or meaning (*Sinn*) from the future, not from the "standing opposite" (*Gegenwärtigen*) of presence. Otherwise put, the present is "living" (*lebendige*) as open to the choice of possible modes of action that are enjoined by what one truly is. Perception is no longer central to the analysis of inner time-consciousness.

The defect of this account becomes clear when we ask ourselves how we will know which possibilities represent our genuine selves, or in what sense we can be said to constitute a self. In the first case, we are referred to such evasive resources as the silent voice of conscience; in the second, we are said to be defined by our radical negativity or anxiety before death. At no point in Heidegger's brilliant articulation of a future-centered temporality is there any reference to the presence of an actual criterion for decision or choice. As to the self-definition through radical negativity, this cannot provide me with evidence of my uniqueness or particular identity; one nullity is indistinguishable from another. But all factors leading toward self-identification are themselves possibilities. Differently stated, only inauthentic temporality has actual content. Authentic temporality is a concatenation of possibilities. Merleau-Ponty is right to insist that the present is the place in which we decide, that is, choose resolutely.[8] And the present is defined by presences or actualities, not by vacancies waiting to be filled. Or rather, the vacancies are themselves present within the temporal present, and we fill them with the assistance of what we already are.

I want to make one more critical remark. If the present is defined by the past and the future, the future by the past and the present, and the past by the present and the future, then we seem to have returned to Bergson's *durée,* in which no element of temporality is external to the others. Surely the ecstatic unity of past, present, and future is itself visible within the present, not as an object of perception and not as possibility or *Seinkönnen,* but as the ontological sense of time. If this sense is itself temporal, not only will it pass away like any temporal event, but the question arises as to how it can be conceived as an actual truth for the present epoch of historicity. Is not possibility higher than actuality? In sum, to say that the present is a possibility is to say either that it is not experienced as actual or else that our awareness of that possibility is grounded in an extratemporal sense of presence.

This concludes my sketch of the context within which I situate my own efforts to understand the lived present. I now turn more directly to that task. In so doing, I take my bearings from everyday speeches and activities because it is everyday life that first introduces us to what Robert Sokolowski calls the theater of the living present.[9]

I suggest that there are two primary ways in which we refer to ourselves as present. I can say of myself both that I am "in the present" and that I am "present before" something. In the first case, I speak of myself as a member of the present generation of Americans, or as absorbed in contemporary events, or as living for the moment, and so on. In the second case, I say that I am present to a person or before a building, or that I am "present and accounted for" or "ready for action" or that my presence makes a difference, and so on. To begin with the first case, it is easy although certainly unsatisfactory to think of the present as a place that I have entered. The problem with this image is that it leaves unexplained how I got here. I certainly did not enter the present from the past or the future. On the contrary, to the extent that I am in the past, it is in the form of lapsed presents, and the analogous truth with respect to the future is that I am "present" within it as an indefinite series of possibilities. The past is somewhere I end up, not a place from which I emerge.

One can say that I emerge from the future, but this is not very helpful because to be in the future is not yet to be in the present, and this means not to exist. For even though existing may include the future as a component, it does so only in the sense that the future is operative within the present. If I am entirely in the future, then I can be said to exist only as a possibility. But this is not existence in the genuine sense of the term, even in the sense according to which it is the same as or is rooted in the ecstatic unity of past, present, and future. In short, as within the future, I do not exist yet or now. How can a non-existent me move from one place to another? In Heideggerian terminology, we are "thrown into" the present, which expression seems to be a kind of metaphor for saying that we find ourselves as already within it. I take this to be Heidegger's way of acknowledging that we do not move from the future or the past into the present, but that we are, as existing, always in the present, albeit in a way that includes or, let us say, overlaps with the past and the future.

To summarize: Wherever I am, then, that is, whatever the place that I occupy, I am always in the present with respect to myself, and this is true of my recollection of the past and anticipation of the future as well. Both take place in the present. It is true that our lives depend upon memory for their continuity and hope for their directedness.[10] But this does not mean that we live in the past and the future or that the present is nothing but a unity or synthesis of the past and the future. Since to exist is to be situated temporally or, in Heidegger's terminology, to be *there* and thus to have a point of reference with which to relate to the modes of time, the question is whether that point or "there" can be anything other than the present. But what we mean by the present is that we are now situating ourselves temporally. That is why we are thrown or fall into the present or are always already there, that is, as soon as we become aware of ourselves. The present is *where* we are when we appropriate aspects of the past and the future in the temporalization process. For this reason it is misleading to say, as Heidegger does, that the present is surrounded in or enclosed by the future and the past in original time.[11] The reverse is the case. We live in the present, and life is such as to express itself thanks to the assistance of memories and hopes. In other words, whereas what we remember took place in the past, and what we hope for will take place in the future, we who remember and hope are in the present. It would be much better to say that the future and the past are surrounded by the present. Stated more concretely, the range of future possibilities is always determined by present actualities, even though these actualities may be subjected to subsequent modification by the choices we make. Similarly, our access to the past is always through the present, even and indeed precisely if the present is the surface of the past.

I infer from this preliminary reflection that if the present is like a place, then it must be a place that we are always in. We neither enter from some other place nor leave it for yet another place. To exit from the present is, in other words, to cease to be. The present is not a place like that of spatial location but is instead more like our own skin. It is a "place" that we always carry around with us. But perhaps it is not a place at all. Let us try another hypothesis. What if the present is something that we secrete by the very activity of existing? In other words, what if to exist is to be engaged in activities that produce past, present, and future?

I begin by considering a metaphor or model of the "secretion" theory of temporality. The model is defective, but in an instructive manner. We can speak of the secretion of temporality as analogous to the spinning of a spiderweb. On this interpretation, human beings have purposes, and they take action to fulfill these purposes in such a way as to transform possible lines of action into present realities on the basis of their genetic heritage and past experience. No one could deny that without the heritage and experience on the one hand, and the openness of the future on the other, that is, the possibility that present actions can determine future events, nothing would happen; there would be no present. But once again, the purpose of the spiderweb is to allow the spider to reach the fly, that is, to be present before it and to eat it presently.

At this point a defect in the image of the spider comes into view. This may be preliminarily described as the problem of the temporal location of the web or, more generally, of the spinning process. It is the fly that shifts unambiguously into the past by being eaten, not the spider who eats. The fly disappears from the web by being eaten. This disappearance is equivalent to a transfer from the present into the past. But the past is a strand on the web and it endures; in fact, it can be traversed and retraversed by the spider or serve as the prison for subsequent generations of insects. The absence of the fly is thus not the same as the production of the past. And the continued presence of the spider on its web is not the same as the web understood as the secretion of temporality. The situation is something like this. The spiderweb represents the ecstatic unity of past, present, and future. The motions or changes of position as well as the activities of the spider on the web represent the interpretation of life as an ecstatic unity of past, present, and future. But the living is distinct from the spiderweb, which is not life but the structure of time.

Let me now shift from spiders to human beings. Our position in time is analogous to that of the spider on its web. The temporal coordinates of the web are not the same as those of the events that transpired on or in that web. For example, the event in which the spider eats the fly moves into the spider's past, but the spider does not move with it. The fly is *out of* the web, whereas the spider may somehow remember it as a good dinner consumed on strand number 9 of the northwest portion of the web. Less facetiously, if I secrete the web of time, I do not also secrete the beings, processes, or events that transpire on or in the web. Again, these events move into the past, not by changing positions on the web, now understood as the ecstatic structure of time, but by departing from the web. I can remember the Vietnam War, but I cannot now participate in it. I recollect happy days passed with old friends, but they are no longer here to share new experiences with me. And so too with the future.

But there is a still more fundamental problem with the doctrine that human being produces time. If we secrete time, then we cannot ourselves be "in" the present. That is a form of conceptualization that belongs to the previously inspected and rejected hypothesis. Where then are we? What are we to say about the situatedness of the process of time-production that will not return us to the conception of time as a container or empty space? The spiderweb is on my windowsill or in a nearby tree or a corner of my garden. The temporalization process, however, is not in the past, present, or future, regardless of what sense we give to "in," because this would make the process a temporal event, whereas it is stipulated to be the form or nature of temporality.[12] "Form" and "nature" are good Platonist terms, and the Heideggerian may wish to use Germanic expressions to bring out the temporality of temporality, such as *Wësen* or *Er-eignen,* but this is verbal trickery. Heidegger would like to have his cake and eat it too. I mean by this that he would like to speak of the essence of temporality even while attributing temporality to the essence. Otherwise stated, if one level of temporality is the ground of another, then the latter stands to the former in a nontemporal relation of priority.

To repeat the previous conclusion: If human activity produces time rather than filling or occupying it like a place or structure of places that already exists, then it makes no sense to ask for the temporal location of this activity. More precisely, it makes no sense to locate it in the present, as for example by saying that I (= anyone) am now, that is, presently, and so in the present, producing time, including the present. But neither does it make sense to locate this activity in the past or future. In short, if I produce time, then the activity of production must be atemporal. As so producing, I do not merely attain to the ecstatic unity of the three modes of temporality. Or rather, in so attaining, I exemplify the atemporality of existence as understood or conceptualized, however much it may be the case that my experience or actual living of my life is always within the three-dimensional penumbra of time.

It may be useful to give a Platonic example of this point that is not sufficiently appreciated. In the *Phaedrus* (247B-C), Socrates describes in mythical
terms the ascent of the soul to the vision of the hyperuranian beings, that is, the
Ideas, which lie outside the cosmos and therefore beyond time. But the soul,
here represented as a charioteer driving a team of horses, is continuously jostled
by the horses of competing souls as it struggles to rise to the surface of the
cosmos. This double motion reduces to the one comprehensive motion of
the rotating cosmos on which the philosophical souls are standing; it is thus the
motion in which they share even as they are viewing the Ideas. In other words,
life itself is an obstacle to as well as an occasion for philosophical or erotic
ascent. But even if we overcome the obstacle, we cannot ourselves leave the
moving cosmos and rise to the atemporal being of the Ideas.

So Plato. The relevance to the hypothesis of existence as time-production is
as follows. Even though we are ourselves "moving" within or undergoing the
flow of temporality, this in itself does not mean that we have no access to the
atemporal. On the contrary, our constitution of temporality, which amounts
finally to self-production, is itself the counterpart to or necessary correlative of a
Platonic Idea or atemporal truth. In a word, it is eros. I will come back to this
point in my conclusion. Let the reference to eros serve here as an illustration of
the assertion that if I produce time, then time-production is not temporal.
If I do not produce time, then I occupy it. Each alternative has its characteristic disadvantages. A disadvantage that is common to both is the difficulty of
defining the present.

In sum, we cannot understand human time unless we can explain what we
mean by "the present." But this explanation will not be found by invoking the
past and the future. Neither is it satisfactory to say that the present is what
happens "now" because "now" is relative to my personal temporal experience,
and hence to my already being in the present. In other words, "now" means
"present to me." But this cannot be a definition of the present. If there is an
explanation, it depends upon an antecedent understanding of what it is to be
present. It may look initially like the idle spinning of wheels, but I suggest that
we refer to the defining property of the present as *presence*. The temporal
present must possess an identity that is not simply a product or artifact of the
blending of past and future, for if it does not, then life becomes unintelligible.
In this case, the direct intuitive understanding of the present as the horizon of
actual and self-conscious existence supervenes, and in fact makes thoroughly
unacceptable, all philosophical doctrines about human time.

Without pretending to have exhausted the subject, I hope to have said enough about the obscurities of the present understood as "present within" to justify the inference that we need to look in another direction. I therefore now shift to a discussion of the present as "present before," and I propose to arrive at some clarification of what is meant by "presence" by following this second road.

I begin with the simple observation that there is more than one way to refer to the fact that someone or something is not present. Let us consider just two words, "absent" and "missing," in some of their many uses. The senses of these terms overlap in numerous contexts, but they often convey distinct shades of meaning. In general, we say that someone or something is absent or missing if we expect to find that person or thing in a particular location but fail to do so. Which term we use, however, depends upon the context, the nature of the item, and our intentional relation to it.

If I go to a party at the home of John Smith and he is not there, then I am allowed to say, "John Smith is absent from the party." But it would be odd for me to say that John Stuart Mill is absent from the party because he was not and could never have been expected to attend. Odd, but not impossible. More likely, but still not very likely, would be a statement about currently living persons who were not in attendance: "Jacques Derrida and Jürgen Habermas were absent from the party" is a possible locution, but not a very likely one unless the host is personally acquainted with these distinguished philosophers, has invited them to his party, and they have failed to appear, or if other well-known philosophers are present but not these.

In these cases, the term "absent" can be replaced with its near relative "missing," in order to make the same point. Whatever is missing is not where we expected to find it, and therefore it is absent. This is the sense underlying the expression "the missing link." If we wish to say that something is not in a certain place or relation, without implying that it ought to be, then we have to make use of simple negation: "There were no metaphysicians at John Smith's party" or "There were no elephants at that party," and so on. If I modify this very slightly, for example, by saying, "There were simply no metaphysicians at John Smith's party," I am already implying that I expected that there would be some metaphysicians in attendance or that there might have been.

To come back to "absent," one might say, "John Smith's sofa was absent from the party because he loaned it to a friend." But this would not mean the same as the statement that Smith's friend was absent from the party. The absence of the friend might have been voluntary or involuntary. But the absence of the sofa depends upon the will of John Smith or some robber, not upon the sofa. To give just one more example: "in the absence of mitigating circumstances" does not mean that the circumstances decided to leave, but that the criminal decided to act or not act in a certain way. So there are different senses of "absent," depending very roughly upon the role of intention. Note that all senses depend upon the presence of something, even if it is something as trivial as a room in which we would expect to find a sofa.

If you ask me, "Where is your sofa?" I will normally reply that it is missing, not that it is absent. Now of course persons can also be missing; that is why police departments have the "missing persons bureau." But they do not have an "absent persons bureau" because absence in itself is not enough to initiate an inquiry into the whereabouts of someone. Absence must deepen into "being missed" before concern arises. If Jacques Derrida is absent from my party, I do not call the police. I do so only if he is missing, that is to say, absent under suspicious circumstances. On the other hand, if I am separated from my wife for a period of time and tell someone, "I miss her," I do not mean to say that I have called in the police to determine her whereabouts.

These simple examples show that "absent" and "missing" are not pure synonyms. If I am not mistaken, this is reflected in the fact that when philosophers talk about being, they refer to presence and absence but do not say that being is missing. And the same point holds with respect to the past and the future. The past is not missing from the present unless I expect it to be there. That none of this is precise should be obvious. But that is my point. "Absent" and "missing" are synonyms only at a level so general as to be useless for a discourse that makes accurate or fine distinctions.

Now it seems entirely reasonable to say that, however we finally define "presence," if anything is present to someone or something else, then it is neither absent nor missing. Conversely, if it is absent or missing, then it is not present. But since "present to" is a necessary property of anything that is "in the present" (however we define "in"), it seems fair to conclude that nothing is absent or missing from the present in the same sense that it is present. Something can be present even though it lacks a property or relation, but the absence of that property or relation is determined by the presence of a set of properties or the perception of an individual that lacks the item in question. All this applies to our experience of time. The past and the future are lacking in the present, but this does not mean that the present qua present is lacking. In general, absence is not only defined by what is present, but is itself present, and especially when we notice it.

These small linguistic considerations help us to see the bigger picture. There is no single sense of "presence" because different kinds of beings can be present in different ways. As we have just seen, they can be present rather than absent or they can be present rather than missing, but finally (at least as far as we have carried our analysis), they can be present in some neutral sense that is difficult to specify precisely because it is neutral. If these presences were removed, or disappeared, it would make no difference to us. In other words, what we mean by "presence" is a function of our intentions toward the being in question. In this sense, I am an advocate of the "equivocity" of presence.

I draw the following tentative inference from the preceding discussion. We can make a bit of progress in the definition of presence, but only because we start with an intuitive understanding of what it is for one thing to be present to another. One of the problems with Husserl's treatment of inner time-consciousness is that he tries to state this intuitive truth in technical terms which, at least in English, are extremely clumsy and assume for their intelligibility what they are ostensibly defining. Nevertheless, Husserl is correct on the central point. All cognitive activity originates in presence. Hegel claims that Being and Nothing are the same, but it is not by chance that he begins his dialectical presentation with Being. Heidegger's famous and often ridiculed statement, "The nothing itself nothings" becomes intelligible, if still problematical, only in contrast with what he elsewhere expresses as *es gibt Sein,* an expression that is impossible to translate literally in English but that invokes the presence of Being.

To come back to everyday occurrences, we can understand what it is to be absent (or missing) only because we understand what it is to be present. A friend is present in quite a different way from the presence of a stranger. The presence of the expected is again quite different from the presence of the unexpected. Our pet dog or cat is present to us in a way that is derivative from the presence of a friend, but which is at the same time the presence of a possession. It is this intermediate status of the presence of "pets" that causes so much difficulty in our analysis of their rights. The furniture in my apartment is present, if that is the right word, in a way quite different from that of human beings or pet animals. And so, too, with the apartment building next door, which is present differently from my home or from the trees on the street where my house is located, which have a presence that is lacking to the trees on the next street or on the hill that I can just make out from my living room window.

I can take two different stances toward the differences that I have just registered. The first stance is to say that the differences are irrelevant and that what I wish to know is what is common to the presence of all things whatsoever.

But just as Aristotle, in his pursuit of being qua being, arrived at a diverse list of categories or ways of being, not to mention different words like *einai, ousia,* and *on,* or the problem of the difference between divine and natural being, so too Heidegger abandoned the attempt to carry out a discursive account of the sense of Being, in favor of a variety of pathways toward the equally various self-manifestations of Being, manifestations that include the dimension of conceal-ment or absence. Not only are there different senses of "presence," but it is extremely dubious that the term can be applied to inanimate objects life sofas, trees, and stones on the path through a forest, in order to designate their brute existence.

I illustrate this point as follows. We can say that stones are present on the path or that bacteria are present in meat, and even that an opportunity presents itself, when "present" means either directly or indirectly "present to intelligent beings" in a way that affects their attention or interests. If no one is watching, then stones do not present themselves; they simply are or exist. It is, I think, correct to say that "presence" implies an audience to which the presentation is made; but it is not correct, or at least it seems to be dubious, to argue that simply because anything can become a presence to an intelligent observer, therefore "to be" is to be a presence. This would be so if there were one and only one universal sense of "to be." But that is not the case.

Does this mean that the second and correct stance is the abandonment of the pursuit of unity and the celebration of difference? I do not believe that this can be correct. The point is that we should not be so confused by the diversity in the senses of "presence" that we forget they are unified, not by concepts, but by life itself. And this remark provides the bridge back to the original question of the temporal present. But before crossing that bridge, I want to take another step in my discussion of the senses of presence.

The different senses constitute a series of diminishing degrees of what we can call initially, with much hesitation, our personal interest in the present (or absent) item. We started with friends and worked our way down through strangers, pets, possessions, and so on, to neutral presences which may be simply affirmed or denied. Our classification was, of course, restricted to the most common relations of everyday life. It would have to be supplemented by more sophisti-cated examples, such as our rank-orderings or views on a choiceworthy life. The important and common element here is that the list itself is drawn up in each case, not by an appeal to a universally applicable and hence absolutely correct categorial scheme, but by what Plato calls eros and Heidegger "care" or "con-cern" (*Sorge*).

As previously cited, Heidegger himself says that "the original unity of the structure of care lies in temporality" (327). But what if the truth is the reverse, namely, that the original unity of the structure of temporality lies in care? I have suggested and offered at least some evidence to support my suggestion that the analysis of temporality falters with respect to the present. The possibility of removing this difficulty by the reversal just suggested is already visible in Heidegger's assertion that *Das Sein-bei . . . wird ermöglicht im Gegenwärtigen,* "'Being-by' or 'next to' is rendered possible in the present" (ibid.). But we have to reverse this statement as well and say rather that the present is rendered possible through being by or next to "innerworldly encountered entities" (317).

How can we spell out the consequences of this suggested *Kehre?* Stated very generally, here is the main point. I note parenthetically that I find it in Plato and Nietzsche, and in that sense I certainly agree with the later Heidegger's judgment that Nietzsche was a Platonist. Human existence is fundamentally a rank-ordering, as Plato shows most vividly in the *Symposium* and *Phaedrus*. There is, of course, a great difference between Plato and Nietzsche. With his strange hypothesis of the Ideas, Plato makes it possible to claim that some rank-orderings are better than others, or in other words that there is a rank-ordering intrinsic in the kinds of beings, and that the order of excellence of the human souls is determined by their choice of a rank-ordering. This possibility is not available to Nietzsche, who accordingly fluctuates between intuitive appeals to the tastes of superior souls and the admission that the power of the will is the only basis for estimating one rank-ordering as superior to another.

I repeat: human existence is fundamentally a rank-ordering or what we can call an attunement of erotic ascent. The present of human temporality is defined as the horizon of the erotic desire that articulates itself into a cosmos. We produce the lived present, not as a synthesis of temporal points, but as the self-orientation of erotic striving. Incidentally, I believe that this is also the horizon of intentionality, as is expressed mythically by Plato when he speaks of the love of the Ideas. Intentionality fixes the excitation of eros or care. But the primary or original act of erotic desire is not toward this or that intentional object. It is toward what has been variously called immortality, completeness, satisfaction, and self-authentication. In Heideggerian jargon, it is the opening of the horizon of the world. One could object that "striving toward" gives preeminence to the future, but this is a mistake. The means to the achievement of the goal, and so the sense of the future, are for the Platonist presence itself, not temporality. Thus, whereas for Heidegger the horizon is itself temporality, for the Platonist, the opening of the horizon is the act by which temporality is produced.

This "opening" is not temporal in itself; it is neither the present, the past, nor the future. Instead, we should think of it as the founding of presence as the atemporal condition that makes possible the articulation of past, present, and future. Otherwise put, we cannot synthesize presence out of past, present, and future. In fact, presence is not so much a synthesis as a unity, and in that sense it is like the Kantian synthetic unity of apperception. Unlike the Kantian conception, however, it is stamped from the outset by eros or care rather than by rules, categories, and concepts.

It is essential to remember throughout that I am speaking of human or lived time and not of clock time or the time of mathematical physics. The problem, again, is how to explain our immediate intuition that we live in the present and, even more strongly, that the state of presence that characterizes consciousness in general and self-consciousness in particular cannot be an illusion or a derivative of our "presence" in the past and the future. Self-consciousness cannot be an illusion because one must be self-conscious in order to undergo it. It cannot be primarily occurring in the past or future because we would then have to be *present* in the past and future, in such a way as to make our location there (our *Da-Sein*) the focal point of our recollection of what occurred prior to it, and our anticipation of what might occur afterward but has not yet done so. And this would simply reposition the present, thereby moving the past "backward" and the future "forward," relative to the displaced present.

The only way to deal with this problem is to accept that it cannot be resolved in abstract temporal language. We begin with human experience; we do not derive our experience of time from subhuman motions or ontological analyses. As to phenomenological descriptions, these must be in the first instance of everyday language and therefore of praxis, not of perception. And this beginning is our sense of the present. Paradox arises when we try to grasp the present as a point or instant that has arrived from the future but not yet slipped into the past. Since this is impossible, we are inclined to try to resolve the paradox by referring to memory and anticipation as the sources of continuity. The result is that the present disappears or is confused with the past and the future. Our sense of the present becomes displaced, and even placeless. And this leads to the dissolution of human temporality or its reduction to natural time, in which there is no room for human life because there is no present other than that of the instant or moment.

In sum, we cannot arrive from the future or pass away into the past without occupying the present. The present just is our awareness of temporal passage. The passing of time is *present to* us, and it is this presence that allows us to speculate upon its nature, for example, whether we secrete it or occupy it or whether some other account is required. I say that we occupy the present. But this is not to say that we are simply standing there, like a passenger on a train, looking out the window at the flow of human temporality. Such an image is entirely inappropriate, and I believe that it is encouraged, even if unintentionally, by the claim that the inner unity of the structure of concern lies in temporality.

We do not feel concern because we are in time; on the contrary, we are in time because we are concerned. Concern or, in my preferred term, the erotic nature of the soul, transforms natural time into existence. It produces an ordered continuum out of mathematical points, and objects of desire out of the random motions of points of force. The objects are present in various ways; as we saw previously, there is no univocal sense of "presence." Some objects cannot properly be said to be present at all. We would have to find some other way of speaking about the being of a stone or a tree. "Presence," then, is not a characteristic of objects, things, or Platonic Ideas. It is the pulsation of eros, that is, the rank-ordering and world-constituting force of the human soul. But it is not a transcendental ego; or at least it is not something that cannot be experienced as immediately present, and this is, again, because it is not an object of perception but praxis itself.

In this last section of my essay, I want to summarize my argument in such a way as to provide further clarification of my suggestion that we reverse the priorities of eros and temporality. The general problem that concerns us is the coherence of the lived present. How do we experience the present as a series of past and future moments, if there is no part of that series that corresponds to the present itself? It is relatively easy to define the future as the not-yet and the past as the no-longer. But why is this easy? What is it that renders the distinction between past and future intelligible? The natural answer that springs to one's lips is surely that whatever else they may mean, "not yet" and "no longer" are two different ways of saying "not now." But "not now" is itself intelligible only if we understand what it is to be "now." So the future and the past are privations of the present. The now stands to the not-yet and the no-longer as an actuality to distinct privations. The now is not absent but present; the present is now. We arrive at a circle. But is this surprising? If the now is primitive or fundamental, there is no reason it should be definable in terms of something else, that is, in terms of some simpler constituent.

Of course, we can clarify or expand the circle. "Now" is a characteristic tense of temporal flow, but it cannot be defined exclusively through temporality. The tenses of time are intelligible only with respect to temporal events or content. If nothing happened, the past and the future would not merely be identical with the present, but the tripartition would be inaccessible. But this is not enough to resolve our problem. In fact, it simply poses the problem. For how can anything happen in the present? If time is continuous flow, the present happening flows away as it occurs. It is true that the flow of temporality is from the future into the past, and that this path goes through the present; but the flowing content does not pause for the present. The process of "going through" the present seems to take no time. For suppose it took time, let us say one second. In the first place, the second would itself be flowing and therefore would not be the now. Or else it would not flow, in which case it would not be temporal. A flowing second is not present for a second but is continuously disappearing into the past as it emerges from the future. A static second cannot be measured as a unit of temporality, so temporal flow must be restricted to the past and the future. In other words, on this alternative not only is time discontinuous, but it cannot be passing *now*.

We have to distinguish between time and the experience of time. I suggest that if we restrict ourselves to temporal flow, there is no way in which to grasp the present or now. The experience of the present is not accessible as a synthesis of passing moments because this synthesis, as itself a temporal unity, is subject to the same disappearance into the past and emergence from the future that we just saw in the case of the isolated second or moment. If this is right, then our experience of the present must be produced by something that is not just temporal flow, or the impression of temporal flow, or a construction of flowing temporal moments. Something other than time must produce the experience of the present.

This statement can be generalized. Time is not a substance, an entity, an independent object of perception analogous to a physical body or cognitive experience. We do not perceive time as we do flowers, trees, persons, the starry sky, and so on. But neither do we perceive time as a property of an individual event or perception, in the way that we perceive the color of a flower as red. Furthermore, we don't perceive individual events or things as totally independent. Perception or cognition is itself an event within a process, which we call variously consciousness, experience, awareness, or apperception. We perceive a flower as present in a field, blowing in the wind, exuding a distinctive odor, attracting insects, and so on. The field, the wind, the odor, and the insects are each part of the background to the perception of the flower, and this background in turn is not static but is an ingredient in our experience; for example, we distinguish the field from the nearby buildings, the wind as changing direction, rising and falling, and so too with each aspect of the general segment of the environment to which we turn our attention. "Turning one's attention" is, in other words, not a single static and independent event, but a process of our openness to the whole. This openness is not like standing still and peering through an aperture at a motionless object. It is a process that takes place as a well-ordering of before and after, in which our attention shifts from one discernible aspect of the process to another. The accessibility of the entire process to our perceptual and cognitive awareness is an integrated set of changes through which we proceed cognitively, focusing on this or that event or object, but always within a horizon of awareness that is itself graded in various changing zones of precision.

Only now are we in a position to say something about the experience of time. I don't watch time passing; I perceive the wind starting and stopping, insects coming and going, flowers moving and standing still; I see myself moving from one destination to another, the sky lighting up and darkening, my thoughts changing in a variety of ways, some of them ordered and some not, and all of these events are related or relatable to one another in a unity of consciousness that I interpret reflexively as my experience, but not of a "me" that is isolated from everything else. My experience is experience of the unity of possible and actual experiences, that is, of the world as available for experience. I can insert my well-ordering of experiences of before and after into a more general framework that includes your well-ordering of experiences, and this framework is public or clock time. This can itself be inserted into a conceptual generalization, defined by natural processes such as the motion of the stars or, at the other end of the spectrum, by atomic decay, but our experience of this time is attenuated. We experience cosmological time only through the experiencing of before and after of such small-scale phenomena as the position of the dial of a chronometer or some process in the laboratory.

Now let us move in the other direction, from clock time to individual temporality. Just as we do not directly experience cosmological time, neither do we directly experience clock time, or what we can call rather awkwardly local public time. If I feel that time is passing while I type this essay, it is because my muscles are getting tired, my attention is wandering, I feel the pangs of hunger, and so on. I glance at my wristwatch, go back to typing, vaguely aware that it is taking time, look at my watch again, and in this way I fit the act of typing the essay into an intentional sequence of events: my schedule for the day. And this schedule is part of my schedule for the week, which in turn is a unit in my plans for the semester, and so on outward, as far as I have made plans for my life.

I can sit in my chair and meditate on the passage of time, but there is no substance or entity called time about which I am thinking. What I am thinking about is a set of processes, marked by before and after, which set is thinkable only because it is made up of events that can themselves be cognized, such as my hair turning gray, my teeth falling out, my knees aching, my children growing up, the house beginning to rot, and so on. I can focus on any one or several of these processes, or I can represent them in general as me getting older, or still more generally as the passage of time. But in no case is time walking through the room or moving along inexorably, side by side with the processes I have mentioned. Neither is it like a screen or filter through which the processes are secreted in such a way as to constitute my experience.

I can also experience any one, several, or all of these processes as occurring at different rates. I may feel myself to be aging rapidly or slowly, depending upon how old I am, how I feel, with whom I am comparing myself, and so on. Any single experience may seem to be instantaneous, dragging on endlessly, or moving along at a good pace. I might suppose that there are multiple time-streams, all of them set at different and even varying speeds, but it soon becomes impossible to account for the unity of my life on this hypothesis. The reason I can perceive events as quick or slow, dragging on or disappearing, and the like is that I measure them against a standard perception of time, namely, my accumulated sense of who I am, how old I am, the circumstances of my life, and so how my life fits into the pace of the world.

In other words, I measure what I will call subjective time-rates with respect to my general sense of public or clock time, a general sense that is modifiable by various factors but not dissolvable into them. And this in turn is possible because it is the nature of human experience to occur in accord with what I shall call standard rates of change. These standards are of course experienced, but with respect to the different kinds of things, events, and processes that make up our lives. I know directly how fast my inner awareness should move and what constitutes a "speeding up" or "slowing down" because of excitement, fear, illness, or hallucination. Equally important, "how fast," "too fast," and "too slow" are themselves rendered intelligible because they are measured with respect to perceptions and cognitions of things, relations, and events that have stable identities, whether or not they are themselves moving spatially and temporally.

From considerations of this sort, I infer that the experience of time is a function of changes and motions, which in turn are the necessary consequence of the sequential nature of life. Still more generally, in order for anything at all to exist, it must be "spread out" or possess dimensionality, that is, it must have a series of aspects or parts that are arranged in a well-ordering that constitutes the identity of that thing and which is perceived through a movement of awareness from one aspect to another. Perception is therefore dual in nature. It is true that I do not perceive, say, a rose as a static item in a frozen or even vacuous universe. My perception of the rose is an integration of the relevant sensations, together with various concepts about the flower, plants, filling up space, moving in the wind, and so on. But the items that are integrated are themselves identifiable as a rose, a flower, a petal, a color, and these identities are not temporal events like a second, a minute, or an hour. They are the fixed points that articulate into an intelligible structure the set of changes constituting my experience, into a well-ordering of before and after. More generally, I don't perceive anything as something of a certain sort except on the basis of an awareness of the categorial structure of existence, through which I relate items of various kinds into objects and events of various sorts.

I suggest that our experience of time is constructed from the steps by which our awareness develops into an openness to the totality of life as an ongoing process of many levels, all of them integrated into a self-differentiating unity, to borrow an expression from Plato that is applied to eros in the *Symposium* (187a5). And that is why I reverse Heidegger's thesis that temporality is the ground of care. Heidegger cannot be right because without care, intentionality, or eros, there would be no human experience of time. The flow of primordial temporality would not possess inner articulation, directedness, or what one could call an interpretation of change into a paradigm of before and after. But then it would be impossible to refer to this primordial flow as human temporality.

I further suggest that our experience of the lived present is at bottom the spontaneous manifestation of consciousness that Kant seems to have in mind by the expression "synthetic unity of apperception." This unity is spontaneous in the sense that it cannot be derived from or reduced to the corporeal or neurophysiological conditions of its manifestation, or from a miraculous creation by a higher intelligence, or out of any simpler or more fundamental stratum, whether empirical or ontological. But more important in the present context is the fact that each of us defines the lived present on the basis of our intentional or (in Kant's term) purposive awareness of a focus of attention. And this means that *something is present*. Contrary to the critics of *parousia* and the champions of decentering and *differance,* presence is the nontemporal foundation of the temporal present.

The mistake made by doctrines of this sort is that they all start from the primacy of the flow of consciousness. In other words, they begin with the assumption of the primordiality of temporal flow and then explain the constitution of beings (in all senses of that term) as though they were rates of change of subcurrents of that stream of temporal flow. But the resultant explanations are all of temporal items. The beings are constituted by a flow that is already passing away or not yet in existence. Otherwise put, the structural elements of temporal beings are themselves temporal beings, as we saw previously in the case of Husserl and Heidegger. The puzzle of deriving the present from the past and the future is thus relocated at the heart of the structures that are supposed to account for human temporality itself.

Our experience of the present is "specious" only in the sense that it cannot be measured by public or clock time. This is because it is not a unit of temporal flow. It is rather the point of organization for all experience of temporal flow. And the organization of that flow, as I have tried to explain here, is a synthesis of a multiplicity of rates of change, each of which is grounded in its own set of characteristic identities, together with a lived awareness of how fast life proceeds under various psychic attunements. This awareness in turn is the synthetic unity of temporal apperception. Plato's eros is thus not so different from Kant's synthetic unity of apperception, once we see that the latter cannot produce human experience merely through the opening of a unified field of consciousness. That "openness" must be ordered by desire at the very outset of conscious life. If it is not, we may be unified, but we are nowhere. Nowhere, however, is where we would be, if it were true that temporality were the ground of apperception.

Chapter 3 Erotic Ascent

This chapter is an extract from what was originally intended to be a reconsideration of the Platonic doctrine of eros. For various reasons, I have decided not to complete the project. I have been discussing the topic in print since the midsixties, rather before it became fashionable among English-speaking classicists and philosophers. My decision to abstain is not due to any illusion that I have exhausted the subject, but, if anything, to the ever-deepening realization that it is inexhaustible. Perhaps the main reason for the current popularity of the topic is the gay liberation, one of the more striking elements in the congeries of social issues that have influenced public discourse since 1968. I believe that the results have not been happy for our understanding of Plato: The contemporary interest is largely political, whereas the Platonic doctrine of eros has only secondarily to do with politics; it is in the first instance a doctrine of what might be called the ontology of human being. Eros perplexes us because it manifests itself with violence as well as subtlety, and the violence is likely to overwhelm and thus to coarsen the subtlety.

I want to add at once that the expression "ontology of human being" is an expression of convenience and should not be taken too seriously. As the present essay is intended to show, we approach eros through the everyday details of life, not through the construction of abstract psychological, neurophysiological, or ontological structures. My essay is intended as a very modest contribution to the accumulation of the relevant details.

"Erotic Ascent" first appeared in Graduate Faculty Philosophy Journal *17, no. 1–2 (1994): 37–58, in honor of the late David R. Lachterman.*

ASCENT AND DESCENT

In all three Platonic accounts of Eros, to be found in the *Symposium, Phaedrus,* and *Republic,* there is an ascent from the city to the domain of the Ideas. But this ascent is not uniform in all cases; and, contrary to Heracleitus's assurance, the way up is not the same as the way down. I begin with a comparison of the *Symposium* and the *Phaedrus.* In the *Symposium,* Diotima tells Socrates that Eros is a daimon; she goes on to explain that "every *daimonion* is in between god and mortal" (202d13f). The Greek term is used elsewhere by Socrates to describe the voice that restrains him from certain actions; I shall refer to this as the separative power of the daimonic. According to Diotima, the function of the daimonic is binding: to pass back and forth as interpreter between gods and mortals. These two species are separate in advance of the daimonic activity; the separation is overcome, not by unity, whether sexual or intellectual, but by a political hermeneutic of master and slave. The *daimonion* explains human needs and sacrifices to the gods, and divine commands as well as recompense for sacrifice to the humans.

Diotima's teaching has the curious consequence that the cosmos, or All (*to pan:* 202e3ff), is not divine, as in the traditional view, but daimonic. The gods and mortals need each other; the cosmos is the result of the satisfaction of that mutual need by the daimonic, of which Eros is merely a single element. Just as Eros multiplies as it unites, so one might say that the daimonic preserves the initial separation as it binds. The Socratic *daimonion* is, then, a special case of the general rule; it separates Socrates from the impious or unphilosophical, and so from the merely human, but without attaching him to the divine. The philosopher is the exemplification of the intermediate status of the daimonic: he is not bound to anything but instead provides interpretations of heaven and earth that bind them into a totality.

To say this in a slightly different way, "god and human cannot mix; all intercourse and discussion on the part of the gods with the mortals is by way of the daimonic" (203a1–3). The All, or cosmos, is constituted discursively, but by a language that is neither human nor divine because it somehow participates in both dimensions. In this sense the daimonic is something like a Kantian schematism. It is as such not merely discursive; Diotima does not teach that the All is a linguistic production or horizon in the contemporary sense. The daimonic is a force that issues (or may issue) in speech. Daimonic speech is revelatory: the horizon that it opens is not itself a consequence of syntactic rules but the space within which discourse occurs, as well as the light that illuminates our speech.

Eros, as a daimon, comes from above and hence outside the human sphere. The descent of Eros is, as it were, by a different path than his joint ascent with the human soul. And the path of ascent is, of course, not the same for every soul; or if it is the same, there are "stages on life's way" corresponding to the different fundamental needs or objects of desire. The highest stage for a human being is to discern beauty itself, or what we may call the Idea of Beauty, but not to possess or unite with it. As we shall see, the separation between gods and mortals is preserved when Ideas are substituted for gods.

It is a striking difference between the *Symposium* and the *Phaedrus* that in Diotima's teaching, the gods, after her initial reference to them in the passage just analyzed, play no further role. In the urban and nocturnal account of Eros, the desire for the good, although its penultimate stage is the vision of pure Beauty, makes use of the daimonic in order to gratify the personal or private longing for immortality. This longing has nothing to do with the gods, as we shall see that it clearly does in the *Phaedrus*. To anticipate, in that dialogue, Socrates tells how the soul, prior to its incarnation, belongs to a heavenly band that is led by one of the Olympian gods; after incarnation, our erotic desire is inflected in accordance with the nature of the god to whose band we belonged in the previous stage of existence.

Socrates' myth of the winged charioteer is not fully compatible with the central thesis of Diotima's teaching in the *Symposium*. There is no formal contradiction, inasmuch as the *homilia,* or intercourse, between human souls and the gods does not take place on earth, during our historical lives. But Socrates establishes a close and enduring relationship between the human and the divine soul that is entirely missing in his teacher's account. As we shall see, the crucial element of that relationship is political rather than private or personal. In the *Symposium,* one could almost say, Diotima attributes to the vision of pure Beauty a function that makes the Olympian gods superfluous. The initial political relation of master and slave is thus abolished in the case of the philosopher.

To return to Diotima, there is some ambiguity in her explanation of the nature of the object of erotic love. She says categorically that human beings may be called lovers (*erastai:* 205d6) if and only if they love (*eran*) the good and wish to possess it forever (205d1–206a13). In this case, the name is misapplied to the great majority of human beings, as is evident from the fact that, as Diotima points out, we normally reserve the name "lovers" for those who are erotically attracted to human beings and, in the first instance, to their bodies. But there is a more fundamental ambiguity. Whatever may be true of ordinary usage, the young Socrates himself believes, prior to instruction by Diotima, that Eros directs us toward the beautiful (*tou kalou*). She corrects this belief; the lover actually longs for "reproduction and birth in the beautiful" because this is the only form of immortality accessible to human beings (206e5–8).

Socrates indicates that, as a youth, he had some reservations about this doctrine of his teacher; hence his reply to her at this point: "It may be" (*eien*), to which she peremptorily replies, "It certainly is!" (*panu men oun:* 206e6f). The most obvious difficulty with Diotima's contention is that few if any are aware of what she calls the genuine nature of their longing. Whereas one may mistakenly believe that what is false is true, or that what is true is false, it is hard to see how we could be mistaken about what we desire. Elsewhere, the mature Socrates is inclined to argue that desires and their associated pleasures are false if they are connected with false beliefs or judgments (for example, *Philebus* 37d2ff, 41b11ff). No doubt this loss of early doubt on the matter is due to the influence of Diotima. But we may perhaps sympathize with the young Socrates.

The problem can be sharpened in terms of Diotima's own teaching. Her initial conclusion is as follows: "It is necessary by this reasoning [*ek toutou tou logou*] that Eros is for the immortal" (207a3f). In this case, the attraction to pure Beauty is instrumental, not final. The good, which lovers long to possess forever, would seem to be nothing other than deathlessness itself. The confusion of the many on this point, expressed prosaically, is that they are immediately distracted by the violence of the means which nature has provided to gratify their deeper desire. We thus require a prophetess rather than a biologist or neurophysiologist to interpret the "intentions" of our natural instincts.

This is not, however, Diotima's last word on the matter. She goes on to describe the erotic ascent as a progress toward ever purer degrees of beauty, culminating in the vision by the adept of Beauty itself (207a5ff, 210e5ff). In this ultimate stage of ascent, Diotima says cryptically, the lover is able "to generate, not images of excellence [*eidōla aretēs*] but true excellence" (*alēthē:*, 212a3–5). It is unclear whether the good is now to be understood as the act of generation, which is the surrogate for immortality, the excellence that we generate, or the Beauty that is instantiated in our excellent productions. The longing to possess the good forever, if it is not merely the desire for immortality, must be the desire to be or to be in the presence of the good forever.

Diotima does not resolve this ambiguity. In a slightly different formulation, we are not told whether Beauty is the same as the good, and hence the original excellence (*aretē*) that is not copied but contained within the productions of the erotic adept, or whether Beauty is rather the instrument or mediate object of desire, by which we are led to the good. And on this latter alternative, we do not know whether the good is immortality or something else that we desire to possess forever.

In my opinion, the general tendency of Diotima's teaching is to suggest that Beauty and the good are the same and that the good productions of the erotic initiate are good because they are beautiful. If this is indeed Diotima's intention, then Socrates was not wrong to believe that Eros longs for Beauty. His mistake must have been in failing to understand the need to reproduce in the beautiful as the only type of immortality available to mortals. Apparently Socrates never succeeded in fully assimilating Diotima's revelation, and in particular the highest stage of the erotic mysteries. Or else his natural barrenness prevented him from the generation of truth.

What needs to be emphasized here is that lovers require instruction in, that is, initiation into, the erotic mysteries. In more precise terms, human desire must be not only modified by the daimonic Eros but interpreted by a prophetess like Diotima or by one of her students. This is plain both from the poetical and the discursive contents of Diotima's teaching. Human beings do not understand what they desire; alternatively expressed, Eros is the illumination of desire, but only a prophetess can see by its daimonic light. There is a crucial consequence: whereas the erotic vision of Beauty may make philosophy possible, it is not the philosopher but the prophetess who explains the conditions for the possibility of philosophy. As a discursive account of the whole, philosophy is dependent upon revelation; discursivity is dependent upon poetry.

I want to make one additional point about erotic ascent in the *Symposium*. The descent of Eros is itself motivated by need, in the first instance by the need of the gods to command and to reward their mortal worshipers. Whereas human beings may desire immortality, the need of Eros is to bind the elements of the mortal and the immortal into a cosmos. Since Eros is continuously changing its shape, hence both dying and coming into existence, the cosmos is not immortal, except as the consequence of a recurring *dunamis*. This *dunamis* transforms desire into Eros; little wonder that the modern epoch, which begins by reversing this transformation, dissolves the cosmos into the universe.

Turning to the *Phaedrus*, I direct the reader's attention to the point in the dialogue at which Socrates has just concluded his speech, under compulsion from Phaedrus, in defense of the nonlover, who is in fact a concealed lover, just as Socrates delivers the speech with his head concealed by his cloak. Socrates completes only that part of the speech which is devoted to criticism of the lover; he refuses to deliver the part in which the nonlover is actually praised (241d4ff). He is about to cross over the Ilissus and to depart before Phaedrus can exercise a further compulsion on him. Socrates claims that he has been speaking in hexameters and wishes to avoid being possessed by nymphs, or, in other words, to undergo transformation into a prophetess or one who speaks as a woman possessed (241e1–5).

Phaedrus urges Socrates to remain, noting that it is now high noon and so too hot to walk. He wishes to continue the conversation until it becomes cooler. Socrates replies that Phaedrus is divine and an extraordinary marvel at generating speeches, whether by himself or by compelling others to do so; perhaps he has been excelled in this only by Simmias the Theban, who incidentally is a principal interlocutor in the *Phaedo* (242a3ff). The implication is that Phaedrus's physical beauty has compelled his lovers to speak, in order to satisfy his appetite for oratory.

Phaedrus is not himself erotic but a "philologist" like Socrates (236e4), although one could not say that he shares Socrates' love of learning (230d3). The man who is called "the father of the *logos*" in the *Symposium* (177d4f) is also the main instigator of the Socratic speeches on Eros in the dialogue to which he gives his name. Yet his own understanding of Eros is of that which is useful, rather than of something that induces ecstasy or transcendence, as is evident from his speech in the *Symposium* as well as in his extravagant praise for the speech of Lysias, who celebrates the utility of nonerotic sexual gratification.

In both dialogues, Phaedrus is closely associated with physicians: Eryximachus in the *Symposium* (177a3ff) and Acumenus in the *Phaedrus* (227a4ff). Phaedrus is by nature a valetudinarian, a man of low erotic energy and equally low tastes in rhetoric, a beloved rather than a lover who sees his own beauty as a useful property rather than as an occasion for spiritual ascent. It is Phaedrus who responds to Socrates' myth of the winged charioteer by returning to the question of political rhetoric (257c2ff). Phaedrus is plainly earthbound. Why then should he be the father of the *logos* in both dialogues dedicated to erotic ascent?

We may distinguish Phaedrus's function as a pretentious follower of contemporary rhetorical fashion from his "metaphysical" significance. The nonlover in Lysias's speech is a caricature of the sober element in the philosophical nature, which is able to calculate the true utility of speeches and deeds to the satisfaction of human desires, without being misled by those desires or by the rhetoric of edification. But Phaedrus, despite his utilitarian tendency, is not a man of sober calculation. He uses his beauty to compel others, such as Eryximachus, to calculate on his behalf.

I believe that we come closer to the heart of the matter by observing that Phaedrus is a passive homosexual rather than an active pederast. As the object of desire who does not himself desire in return, Phaedrus is a caricature, not of the philosopher, but of the Ideas, and in particular of the Idea of Beauty. This is why Phaedrus excels everyone but Simmias as a cause of the generation of speeches. At a still more fundamental level, Phaedrus the earthbound is the negative pole of erotic descent. If we take our bearings by Phaedrus, no ascent is possible, as is clear from the failure of Socrates to redirect his companion's attention to higher things, despite an accommodation of his rhetoric to Phaedrus's vulgar tastes (257a4–6).

Erotic ascent requires not simply a retuning of corporeal desire in the sense that a physician might give instructions for improving one's physical constitution, but a separation from the earth. We should not confuse this daimonic separation, which is represented in the present context by the Socratic *daimonion*, with the link within philosophical discourse between rhetoric and medicine (270b1ff). Philosophy must understand the body, and more generally the earth and the other heavenly bodies; but it can do so only if it perceives them as components within a cosmos of which the bond is the daimonic, in which Eros is a peculiarly active element. Phaedrus's concern with the body is for the sake of life in this world, not because of love of knowledge.

To come back now to the scene at high noon by the banks of the Ilissus, Socrates is about to depart when he is prevented by his *daimonion*. He has sinned against the divine in criticizing Eros, for Eros is a god in the *Phaedrus*, and the son of Aphrodite, although his father is not mentioned (242d9). This sin was ostensibly compelled by Phaedrus, who is thereby the occasion for Socrates' recantation. Piety requires that Socrates separate himself from Phaedrus's utilitarianism, although we must not forget that the language of the recantation is accommodated to Phaedrus for what may be called political reasons: to prepare a bridge between the true description of erotic ascent and its dissemination among fashionable intellectuals. It is a complication in the structure of the *Phaedrus* that Plato combines the metaphysical and the political or pedagogical in the figure of Phaedrus, and so the double need on Socrates' part to separate himself from Phaedrus while at the same time attempting to educate and so influence him. But those who dislike such complications should not address themselves to Plato, let alone to Eros.

In submitting to the *daimonion,* Socrates emphasizes his own mantic capacity and that generally of the human soul (242c3–7). Socrates, as it were, plays Diotima to Phaedrus's young Socrates. In this connection, it should be noted that Socrates regularly refers to himself in terms suitable for a woman. He speaks of Phaedrus and himself as co-corybants (228b7), or priestesses of Dionysus, an identification that is repeated later with the verb *sunebakcheusa* (234d5), "I joined you in Bacchic frenzy." At 238d1 Socrates describes himself as *numpholēptos,* "possessed by a nymph," and at 241e3–5 he worries lest he become *numpholēptos* under the compulsion of Phaedrus. At 259a7, Socrates compares Phaedrus and himself to the Sirens. One should also consider Socrates' use of the woman's oath "By Hera!" at 230b2.

Let me put to one side the extension by courtesy of the role of priestess or prophetess to Phaedrus. The cited passages give substance to the implied substitution of Socrates for Diotima; more fundamentally, they bring out the fact that the philosophical nature must include the female as well as the male, and, equally important, that the teaching of Eros is associated with the former rather than with the latter component of the human soul. This theme will surface once more when I turn later to the Socratic art of midwifery. Also of note, erotic instruction is associated with the female component of the soul but is not necessarily restricted to women.

The role of the priestess (whether incarnated as male or female) is to illuminate erotic intoxication but not to be intoxicated herself. In slightly different terms, the interpreter of madness is not mad but sober. This is true of both Diotima in the *Symposium* and Socrates in the *Phaedrus.* A speech or image of Eros substitutes for the manifestation of the original. This is not to deny Socrates' assertion that "the greatest of goods comes to us through madness when it is a gift from the gods" (244a3–8). There is no reason to assume that the speeches about Eros, rather than the visitation of and possession by Eros, are the greatest of goods.

In fact, by attributing his speech about erotic ascent to the poet Stesichorus, Socrates implies that it is inspired by the Muses and so belongs to the third kind of madness, rather than to the fourth, in which the sight of beauty on earth leads to the recollection of true beauty and thereby to the growth of the soul's wings as well as of the desire to fly toward the hyperuranian beings, a desire that cannot be gratified because of the body (245a1ff, 249d4ff). As noted, Socrates' madness is quite calculated; he retains the sobriety of the nonlover in singing the praises of Eros.

Not even those who are possessed by the fourth kind of madness can ascend to the roof of the cosmos; a direct view of the hyperuranian beings, however blurred and discontinuous, is possible only for disembodied souls which most resemble the gods (248a1ff). The incarnate lover who is bound to the earth can only mimic psychic ascent in his erotic response to a beautiful youth. These responses correspond in each case to the nature of the god in whose train the soul served prior to incarnation (252c3ff, 253e5ff). The best souls, which resemble Zeus, may obtain a recollection of the hyperuranian beings by the mediation of icons that are accessible to the dim organs of sense perception (250b3ff). Such a lover lives with his beloved in a chaste philosophical communion that Socrates describes as *homonoētikon,* or "same-mindedness" (256b1). In an earlier passage, Socrates refers to this life as a "practicing of pederasty with philosophy" (249a2).

This brings me back to the role of the gods in the erotic life as described in the *Phaedrus.* The paradigm is the care taken of the cosmos by disembodied soul: "Soul altogether [*psuchē pasa:* cf. 245c5] has the management of the All" (*pantos:* 246b6; cf. *to pan* in the *Symposium* 202e6). The souls of the gods are forever discarnate and winged; as such, they travel through the air and govern the cosmos (246b7-c2). Human souls lose their wings and become attached to a body. There are eleven squadrons of deities, one for each of the Olympians with the exception of Hestia. "Zeus, the great leader in the heavens, goes first, driving a winged chariot, ordering and taking care of everything" (246e4–6). The other ten gods follow in an unspecified order, each with his or her band of souls, fulfilling some part of the divine government as assigned by Zeus.

The ascent to the roof of the cosmos to view the hyperuranian beings is not part of the movement through the heavens by which soul governs the All. Instead, it is associated with a feast and banquet which only the gods can attend because the horses of their chariots are equally balanced and obey the rein (246d6ff). They can therefore ascend to the roof and there obtain a secure view of the hyperuranian beings. The other souls, which will subsequently become attached to bodies, are even here pulled downward by "the horse of evil" (*ho tēs kakēs hippos:* 247b3). In other words, the principle of what is subsequently identified as the base horse of sexual desire in the human soul is already present in the disembodied stage.

Of the various details associated with this section of Socrates' speech, I note the following: First, Zeus, and presumably the other Olympians, drives a winged chariot. In the description of the human soul as a winged charioteer, nothing is said of a chariot. Second, the best human souls see the hyperuranian beings only with difficulty, thanks to the confusion of the horses (248a1ff). Third, the distinction between the work of care or cosmic management is distinguished from feasting and banqueting in the activities of the gods and their attendant souls; nothing is said of erotic attraction, which presumably does not exist in the absence of bodies. In the case of human beings, however, erotic attraction, which is the direct impetus to our imitation of divine ascent or feasting and banqueting, is itself modulated by the ordering or managing function of the soul during its disembodied phase.

In sum, it is the absence of Eros, who, although a god, is not one of the twelve Olympians and hence does not lead a heavenly host, that allows for the separation of care and feasting, that is, of work and play. In human existence, this separation is impossible because of the presence of Eros. Without the continued effect of the cosmic order, namely, of divine care (*epimeleia*) for the All, there would be no philosophical pederasty and, at least within the perspective of Socrates' speech, no philosophy. The base horse, or sexual desire, would triumph over the noble horse. Eros could not perform its task of leading the soul in an ascent to the recollection of the hyperuranian beings.

This point is closely related to the assertion by Socrates that, among human souls, only the discursive intellect (*dianoia*) of the philosopher is winged (249c4ff). In the nonphilosophical souls, the two horses possess wings, but not the intellect. The wing, more than any other bodily part, partakes of the nature of the divine attributes: beauty, wisdom, goodness, and so on (246d6ff). These are the attributes that make the wings of the soul to grow and flourish. The wings of the gods are clearly not of an erotic nature, and neither is the wing of the philosophical intellect. This raises the possibility that there may be an ascent to the hyperuranian beings that is not erotic in the specific sense that it is not connected with or stimulated by attraction to physical beauty.

In conclusion: In the *Symposium*, Aristophanes says, "Eros is the name for the desire and pursuit of the whole." For this reason, Eros is our "guide and commander"; whoever opposes him is also opposed to and hated by the gods (193b1ff). Aristophanes, as it were, combines the mediating function of the daimonic Eros of Diotima with the political or caring function of the Zeus of the Socrates of the *Phaedrus*. Socrates, on the other hand, separates the functions of Zeus and Eros and makes Eros subordinate to Zeus. The promotion of

Eros from the daimonic to the divine is in fact a demotion; Eros is no longer the bond of heaven and earth. The loss of the role of cosmic interpreter is represented by the silence of the soul during its erotic ascent in the *Phaedrus,* with the sole exception of a dispute between the noble and the base horse as to whether or not to have sexual intercourse with the beautiful boy (254c5ff, 255e4ff).

VIEWING ETERNITY

The *Symposium* and the *Phaedrus* suggest two different replies to the question of how we are to view, and in that sense participate in, eternity. In the *Symposium,* the pure intellectual vision of Beauty itself gives rise directly to the production of beautiful and fitting speeches and thoughts (*dianoēmata*) in unstinting philosophy "so that, strengthened and augmented thereby, [the lover] may observe a certain single knowledge, which is of the Beauty in question" (210d3-e1). This reference to production is repeated at the end of Diotima's instruction when she speaks of the generating of true excellence as opposed to images (212a1–5). The emphasis is entirely on viewing and generating; the reference to observation of the science of Beauty does not state that the lover knows this science discursively. On the contrary, the production of speeches and thoughts leads up to the view of the science of Beauty. Similarly, the second reference to generation is of instances of true excellence, not of true *logoi.* But the point is not entirely clear.

In the *Phaedrus,* there is no reference in the description of disembodied ascent to speech and none to generating. The hyperuranian beings are accessible to the divine *dianoia,* which is nourished on intellect and science (*nō te kai epistēmē*) and so is able to view for a time (*idousa dia chronou*) and rejoice in the gazing upon what is true (*theorousa talēthē*). This vision includes the sight of Justice, Temperance, and "knowledge that resides in what genuinely is" (*tēn en tō ho estin on ontōs epistēmēn:* 247c1-e2). Despite the appearance of the word "knowledge," the entire weight of the passage is plainly upon vision or observation rather than upon discursive thinking. As is plain from 250b1ff, the content of the vision vouchsafed the human intellect is the same, albeit of a much lower degree of clarity. This vision is neither preceded by nor does it culminate in the generating of speeches or any other instance of true excellence. In the case of the gods, it is followed by rest and the feasting upon ambrosia and nectar (247e2–6). As to the mortal souls, their view of eternity is followed by a meal of opinion (*trophēi doksastē:* 248b5).

So much for the visions of the disembodied souls. The incarnated souls of the philosophers must rise to a recollection of the hyperuranian domain by arriving through the bond of calculation (*logismos*) at a form (*eidos*) or unity derived from many instances of sense perception (249b6ff). Here one could say that the usual discursive intelligence is at work; there is accordingly a production of what we would today call "concepts." Despite the use of the term *eidos*, the form in question is clearly a "recollection" or image of eternity, and in that sense an artifact. *Logismos* binds together what in the world of genesis exists separately as individual sense perceptions. The hyperuranian being itself could never be produced by the binding function of calculative intelligence.

In brief, the pure theoretical vision of eternity, as described in the *Phaedrus*, occurs prior to ordinary or incarnated human existence; in the *Symposium*, this vision is the highest episode of human existence itself. It should be carefully noted that in both accounts, the soul, whether divine or mortal, acquires its glimpse of eternity *through time*. There is no eternal vision of eternity; even the souls of the gods view eternity while standing on the back of the moving cosmos. In both accounts of erotic ascent, but especially in the *Phaedrus*, we see a convergence of Platonism and anti-Platonism on this critical point. The view of eternity is that of a temporal perspective. We may observe a science of eternity, but we do not cognitively possess it.

The view of eternity in the *Phaedrus* is heterogeneous in comparison with that in the *Symposium*, in which Diotima refers to no other candidate for the title "Platonic Idea" than Beauty itself. In the *Phaedrus*, as we have just seen, Socrates not only speaks in the plural of hyperuranian "beings" but cites three instances other than Beauty. As is appropriate in the context of a discussion of Eros, however, Beauty is given a special role. Beauty shines most brightly among its eternal companions and those who saw it while in the train of Zeus "were initiated into mysteries which it is lawful [*themis*] to call the happiest" (250b5ff). We who dwell on the surface of the earth are thus best able to recall Beauty in memory. It shines most brightly on earth thanks to vision, the sharpest of our senses, which is not, however, able to see *phronēsis*, or "wisdom," as I believe the term should be translated here (250c7-d4).

The sight of beauty in the body of the beloved is the clearest and most powerful stimulant to the erotic excitation of the soul in this life. This is illustrated in the account, famous for its sexual imagery, of the stimulation of the wings of the soul (251b1ff). In its disembodied state, the soul is led upward to the roof of the cosmos by Zeus, not by Eros. As attached to a human body, the soul stirs its wings under the influence of pederastic desire. This desire, however, is modulated by the need to seek a beloved whose soul resembles the god in whose train the lover served prior to incarnation.

In the *Phaedrus* more clearly than in the *Symposium,* the lover (*erastēs*) is defined as one who longs for (*eran*) true beauty (249d4-e4). Because it is Zeus rather than Eros who leads the way to the hyperuranian beings, erotic need, paradoxical as it may sound, is not the state of being possessed by Eros so much as it is a recollection of the heavenly train of the gods, of which Zeus is the leader. This recollection is weakened as one moves downward in the hierarchy of souls. Those which lack a sufficient perception of beauty and the other beings that are "honored by the soul" (250b1ff) turn through their bodies to pleasure and sexual reproduction (250e1ff). There follows the aforementioned account of the stimulation of the feathers and the sexual stimulation of the wings. Human beings refer to this *pathos* as Eros, but the gods, according to Socrates, call it the Winged One (252b1ff). Thus far in the description of the soul's response to beauty, the words "lover" and "loves" recur, but Eros himself is mentioned only in the passage just cited. The theoretical effect of the replacement of the name "Eros" by "Winged One" is to demote sexual desire in favor of the Olympian property, exemplified by Zeus, of rising toward the hyperuranian beings. A few lines later Socrates speaks of being "seized by Eros" (252c3–6), but here again the determining factor in erotic activity is the god in whose squadron the soul previously served. "The desire of the true lovers and their initiation" or practice brings beauty and happiness "from the friend who is maddened by Eros [*di' erōta*] to the one who is befriended, if he should be captured" (253c2–6). We thus have two main types of love: the bestial or sexual and the divine or chaste.

This distinction is developed in terms of the simile of the two winged horses, which I do not need to study in detail. The main point is that throughout this description, the difference between the noble and the base horse corresponds in general to that between the Olympian, or Zeuslike, component in the soul and the component of sexual desire. I say "in general" because the noble horse is also clearly subject to sexual excitation (for example, 254c3ff). After all, Zeus himself was in love with Ganymede (255c1f). But the noble horse, in conjunction with the charioteer, or intellect, opposes all surrender to this excitation with shame and *logos* (256aa3–6). One must infer that Socrates' standards of chastity are higher than those of Zeus himself.

The noble and chaste life is that of philosophy (256a6ff); but it is quite plain that this life is "correct pederasty," as Diotima calls it in the *Symposium* (211d5).

Socrates' speech may thus be understood as the attempt to moderate the sexual desire of those who "engage in pederasty together with philosophy" (*Phaedrus* 249a2). His rhetoric is dedicated to the attempt to transform the longing of sexual desire into the longing for Beauty. This attempt, however, may be understood in a commonplace or in a deeper sense. Those who read Socrates' speech as a kind of tacit confession on Plato's part of his own pederastic nature and his struggle to master his erotic desires by philosophical purification have succumbed to the rhetoric which is addressed to Phaedrus, and through him to the well-to-do, leisured youths of the Athenian upper class.

I do not mean by this to deny that Plato was a pederast. This is of no interest in the present context. If our intention is to understand Platonism as metaphysics, then we must move from the sociological and biographical to the metaphysical level of interpretation. Such a shift is, of course, impossible if we ignore the textual details. As those details make entirely clear, Platonist metaphysics is not simply about ontology or the Ideas; it is a comprehensive account of the philosophical way of life. I have immersed the reader in textual detail, not because I have mistaken literature or drama for philosophy, but because philosophy, as a way of life, is closer to drama than to logical or conceptual analysis. Logical and conceptual analyses are essential ingredients of philosophy, but for the Platonist their roots lie in the nature of human existence. The roots may be exposed by analysis, but this exposure tears them from the soil that gives them life.

The *Symposium* and *Phaedrus,* despite numerous differences between them, are not devoted to the analysis of the aforementioned roots and certainly not of the soil itself. It is the special mark of Plato's genius that he provides us with two complementary paradigms of the philosopher: one is that of the lover and the other may be at least initially characterized as that of the nonlover. In slightly different terms, the first paradigm is that of the philosophical life. The second paradigm describes the philosophical life as a preparation for dying.

We are presently immersed in the study of the first paradigm. In what I am calling the metaphysical understanding of this paradigm, there is no disregard of the pervasive features of everyday human existence, but neither can we rest content with an everyday interpretation. As is always the case in a sound hermeneutics, the textual details provide us with the evidence, but the work of understanding the evidence is left to the reader. The evidence of the *Phaedrus* leads us to the following general inference: The closer we come to philosophy, the more clearly is Eros subordinated to Zeus. This subordination is not the same as elimination; Zeus too is a lover. Whatever lives must love.

Otherwise put, life is need for life; in Diotima's account, gods and mortals need one another but are unable to communicate without the mediation of Eros. Diotima soon abstracts from the political implications of this need in order to emphasize the nature of individual Eros as the longing for blessedness or the eternal possession of eternity. The production of speeches and of true instances of excellence is a consequence of the unsatisfiability of this longing. Philosophy is a surrogate for godhood. In the *Phaedrus,* the subordination of Eros to Zeus, or of sexuality to the hierarchy of the Olympian gods, is an indication of the limitations of Diotima's teaching. By making Eros the son of Aphrodite, Socrates "politicizes" sexual desire.

I put the term in scare-quotes in order to bring out that it is itself a metaphor. Philosophy is a way of life, but it is not the way that owes primary obedience to the polis. The transformation of the rule of Eros into the rule of Zeus is the translation from the polis to the cosmos. The philosopher retains his obligation to the polis because he is primarily concerned with the order of the cosmos. Eros, the son of Aphrodite, thus continues to mediate between the divine and the human. The polis is the human expression of mortal residence within the cosmos. One could therefore say that whereas Zeus rules the cosmos, it is Eros who binds it into a totality. No doubt this is why Zeus himself is not immune to the *dunamis* of Eros.

The theme of pederasty plays a variety of roles in the Platonic economy, one of which is to represent the partial detachment of the philosophical life from the polis. Pederasty cannot result in sexual reproduction; it turns Eros away from the family hearth. That it is an insufficient metaphor for the philosophical life is indicated by the female elements in Plato's presentation, not merely of Eros, but of Socrates as well. The emphasis is upon production of children of the soul rather than of the body. Plato also assigns different functions to the male and female components of the soul, which is to say that he gives a metaphysical interpretation of sexuality rather than a sexual interpretation of metaphysics.

Eros multiplies; Zeus unites. Eros descends; Zeus ascends. But these are tendencies implicit in one and the same cosmos, and so too in each soul or microcosmos. The cosmos is "alive" as the manifestation of forces that constitute a beautiful order through a harmony of opposites. This harmony itself "desires" or strives toward the perfection of the lifeless Ideas, the hyperuranian or transcosmic beings. But the cosmos is separated from eternity by the boundary of time. On this point the difference between Plato and Heidegger is very slight, although extremely important. The metaphysics of Platonism stands or falls on the claim that eternity is visible in the order of the temporal cosmos. The claim is that order, although accessible in an image, is the same as the original.

A painting of a human being is not itself a human being. But the beauty of the painting is the same as the beauty of the human being. The original beauty is both presented in and obscured by the inert materials of the painting, but when the observer comments on the beauty of the person portrayed, he is not referring to some property other than beauty itself. Plato may be said to extend a property of mathematical entities to all entities: formal properties are visible in their material exhibitions. The number of elements in a collection is visible in that collection as distinct from its elements. The definition of a geometrical shape is visible in some instance as distinct from that instance.

"Visibility" and "distinctness" are the critical terms here, not "separation" in the sense of Aristotle's criticism of Plato's doctrine of Ideas. The so-called Platonism of those who believe in the separate existence of mathematical and other "abstract" objects has nothing to do with the Platonist metaphysics of the hyperuranian beings. These beings are separate from the cosmos in the sense that they constitute the structure of temporality. But that structure is for Plato "concrete" or particular: beauty, justice, temperance, and knowledge are not, as properties, different in the hyperuranian domain from their temporal manifestation. An instance of beauty is not, as this particular instance, Beauty; but Beauty shows itself within the beautiful instance.

This, I believe, is more or less the most that can be said about the Ideas on the basis of Socrates' speech on Eros. I must restrict myself here to the suggestion that the content of that speech is entirely compatible with the later discussion of knowledge and the method of division and collection. The first discussion (270c9ff) more or less repeats what Socrates has already stated at 249b5ff. In the second of these two discussions (273d2ff is prepared by 265d3ff), the emphasis is upon the discovery of likenesses as central to the pursuit of truth.

In order to divide entities in accordance with their form (*kat' eidē*), we must be able to perceive that they are like each other. This likeness cannot be anything other than the "single Idea" (*mia Idea*) under which we place them. More precisely, the single Idea is the visible core of the likeness; if it were not, likeness would reduce to unlikeness or difference, exactly as results in the postmodernist repudiation of the Platonic Ideas. The discovery of likenesses is, then, the construction of concepts by the method of division and collection; but likenesses can be discovered only through a perception of the single Idea that illuminates them.

The description of eternity in the *Symposium* is, as it were, monoeidetic in contrast to that in the *Phaedrus*. There is also nothing in Diotima's teaching to correspond to what Socrates describes in the *Phaedrus* as the unification of sense particulars by calculative thinking (*logismos*); accordingly, there is no direct equivalent to what Socrates refers to as his Eros for division and collection in accordance with forms or kinds (266b3). There is instead a sudden or instantaneous (*eksaiphnēs*) vision of Beauty itself (210e4), to which Diotima refers as knowledge (*mathēma*: 211c8).

"Knowledge" here means coming to know that something exists; since Beauty itself is nothing definite but is compared by Diotima to a sea (210d4), it does not show itself as a *logos or epistēmē* (211a5–7). The adept may recognize Beauty, but he cannot translate this recognition into determinate conceptual cognition. The sea of beauty has no definite properties and is described by Diotima in negative terms (211a1ff). The lover is suddenly overwhelmed by and entirely absorbed into it (211d1–2); Diotima seems to be describing a psychic encounter rather than a discursive science, despite her reference to a single science at 210d7. To repeat an earlier formulation: We can see that such a science exists and that Eros is monoeidetic (211e4), or homogeneous, but that is not the same as being able to give a scientific analysis of the form of Beauty.

ASCENT IN THE *REPUBLIC*

The topic of Eros is first introduced in the *Republic* by Cephalus, the father of Polemarchus and Lysias, the orator whom Phaedrus admires so highly. Cephalus is living with Polemarchus; it is in their home that the main conversation takes place. According to Cephalus, old age brings peace and freedom from sexual desire (1. 329b8–c7). He cites Sophocles in asserting that when these desires cease, we are rid of many mad masters (329d1). This is the first of several associations in the *Republic* between Eros and tyranny as well as madness (cf. c3–4 and especially 9. 573b6ff).

The first extensive discussion of Eros is contained in book 3. The topic is now the musical education of the guardians in the just or beautiful city. Socrates and Glaucon have just agreed that we will not become musical until we know the forms (*eidē*) of temperance, courage, freedom, magnificence, and so on (402b9ff). When there is a coincidence of psychic and corporeal beauty, this is the "most beautiful sight for whoever is able to see it"; in addition, "the most beautiful is the most lovable" (*to ge kalliston erasmiōtaton*: 402d1–7).

Glaucon goes on to say that whereas the truly musical man will not tolerate defects in the soul, if they are in the body he will be prepared to overlook them and continue to cling to the person. Socrates notes that Glaucon is known to have had sweethearts of this sort. Glaucon's eroticism is further clarified when he says that he knows of no pleasure that is greater, sharper, and more manic than that of Eros. Socrates immediately counters that the correct Eros is by nature of the orderly and noble and is temperate and musical. Glaucon agrees to this and also to the contention that nothing manic should be allowed to come near the correct Eros. He thus accepts Socrates' discipline with the same vehemence that Cephalus employed in referring to the tyrannical grip of Eros on those who are not yet old (402d8–403a12).

Cephalus was freed from the mad tyranny of Eros by old age; Glaucon is prepared to submit to the liberating discourse of Socrates, at least while the conversation is sustained. We rise from the infirmity of the body to the influence of music upon the soul: "One must complete music in the erotics of the beautiful" (403c6–7). Thus far, the teaching is more or less the same as that of the *Symposium* and *Phaedrus:* erotic ascent is from the beauty of the body to that of the soul. There is, however, this difference. Whereas Socrates distinguished in the *Phaedrus* between divine or salutary and merely human or harmful madness and so included Eros in the category of divine madness, in the *Republic* he condemns both Eros and madness. Furthermore, Cephalus represents the initial abstraction from the body in nonphilosophers; no such stage is included in any descriptions of the potential or actual philosopher.

One would expect the next stage to be the ascent from the soul to the Ideas. But the topic of marriage and reproduction is interposed at the insistence of Polemarchus and Adeimantus (5. 449a7ff). The treatment of women and children, and so of sexual love, constitutes together with the discussion of the philosophical education of the guardians a digression in the main flow of the conversation about the just city (see 6. 503a8, and 7. 536c1ff). The main purpose of this digression is clearly to transform sexual into philosophical Eros. But there is a complication. The guardian class is to be divided into two groups, warriors and philosopher-kings, who are marked, respectively, by spiritedness and intelligence. It is, of course, impossible that the warriors lack intelligence and the philosophers courage; by the same token, both subclasses are also marked by sexual Eros. This raises problems about the relation between Eros and spiritedness (*thumos*) that I will explore in a sequel to the present study.

The private pleasures of Eros are an obstacle to patriotism as well as to philosophy. One could object that the family depends upon the privacy of Eros, and the city, in turn, upon the structure of the family. But Socrates' intention is to replace the family by the city for the class of guardians (that is, warriors and philosopher-kings). In carrying out this intention, Socrates assimilates the discussion of women to the guiding principle of *technē* or the division of labor in accord with natural aptitude. This abstraction from sexual differences is based upon the assumption that psychic gifts are neutral with respect to sex. There is a tension, if not an outright contradiction, between this assumption and the treatment of the sexes in the *Symposium* and *Phaedrus*. To mention only one example, in these two dialogues, it is evident that the nature of the philosopher must include both the female and the male components. But this is because psychic attributes do exhibit sexual differences, even if the exceptional individual may combine the male and female attributes in equal or appropriately proportional degrees.

The abstraction from sexual differences is, of course, in the first instance an abstraction from the body. But it has the net effect of contributing to the homogenization of the souls of the two groups of the guardian class. The guardians as a whole, but, as one may infer, the warriors in particular, are all marked by a common love of the city and a common understanding of how to protect it. The philosophers are subjected to a further abstraction from difference by a lengthy mathematical education. Even more important, as Socrates describes them, they all hold to the same views; there are no philosophical sects or schools in the just city. Interestingly enough, this is facilitated by Socrates' reinterpretation of Eros as itself general or universal.

Earlier in the dialogue, Socrates observes that we care best for what we love (*philōn*), and we love that whose interests we suppose to coincide with our own (3. 412d2ff). Most people love themselves, their children, their wives, and their private property as well as their personal productions because they identify the first with the other items in the list. In order to ensure love of the city in the guardian class, Socrates deprives them of family, property, and also private production, since the warriors' work is not productive but military; furthermore, it is entirely on behalf of the city rather than on behalf of one's family in addition to the city. Similarly, the philosopher-kings produce nothing but engage in mathematics and dialectic, or the theoretical contemplation of common forms.

In the case of the warriors, it is tacitly assumed that spiritedness (*thumos*) will dominate over Eros and thereby universalize it or render it homogeneous. One might suppose that the same task is assigned to the intellect in the case of the philosophers. But Socrates uses the same, or a very similar, erotic terminology in the *Republic* when speaking of the philosophical nature as he employs in the

Symposium and *Phaedrus.* There is no discussion of the daimonic or divine Eros, and the emphasis is on mathematics and dialectic rather than on poetry and rhetoric; but the philosopher is said to be motivated by an Eros for truth.

In discussing this point, Socrates uses *philein, epithumein,* and *eran* interchangeably. We note the following stages of that discussion. Whoever loves something (*philein*), loves all of it. The main example is that of the erotic man (*andri erōtikō*) who loves all youths, not some of them; Socrates is referring here to Glaucon himself (5. 474c8ff). In general, whoever desires something, desires (*epithumein*) the entire species (*eidous*). So the philosopher is he who desires (*epithumētēn*) all of wisdom (475b4–10). This is the philosophical counterpart to the love of the warrior, which must be directed to all of the city. This raises a difficulty, incidentally, since the guardian cannot possibly have the same feeling for the farmers and workers that he has for the warriors and philosophers. By analogous reasoning, we may infer that the philosopher cannot love the city as much as he loves the *eidos* of wisdom.

Important as these problems are to a comprehensive understanding of the *Republic,* I cannot pause here to consider them further. The crucial point is that the love of the entire species of wisdom is further generalized into a love of the Platonic Ideas. Because these, like mathematical forms, can be "possessed" by all those who are capable of thinking them, the Eros of the philosopher is rendered homogeneous in the sense that all philosophers love the same entities. In addition, because this love is contemplative rather than productive or practical, it has no divisive political consequences. The philosopher is the person who by nature loves the Ideas, and this love is gratified by pure thought. There is, then, no reason to produce philosophical sects or, in other words, to politicize philosophy.

The discussion of the philosophical nature in erotic terms is continued in book 6. For example, we are told at 485a10ff that the philosophical natures love (*erōsin*) that kind of knowledge which reveals something of the *ousia* that exists forever (*tēs aei ousēs*). In general, the philosopher desires (*oregesthai*) all of truth (485b4); his desires (*epithumiai*) are directed toward wisdom and truth (485d4); he yearns for (*eporeksesthai*) the whole and all of the divine and mortal (486a5f). That is to say, the philosopher desires the Whole or the All, not in its spatiotemporal detail or in its political manifestation, but in its eidetic structure. The philosophical Eros is the Eros for the Ideas.

By a rather different route, we arrive at a conclusion that resembles what we have discovered in the *Symposium* and *Phaedrus.* Despite the political responsibilities of the philosopher in the *Republic,* however, he generates no speeches or instances of true excellence as a direct consequence of his longing for immortality. The most he could be said to do is to reproduce, or guarantee the survival, of the city as generated by Socrates, with the assistance of Glaucon and Adeimantus; the founders of the city are like painters (*zōgraphoi*) who draw it by copying the divine paradigm (6. 500e2–4; 500d4–501a7; 501b1–c3). Perhaps this is what Socrates means when he speaks of the genuine philosopher in contrast to the imposter who claims that name; he who truly strives for being in the city as it currently exists will generate intellect and truth (6. 490b5). He will do so in opposition to the madness of the multitude, attending to his own calculations (*logismoi*) and minding his own business (496c6ff).

But the philosopher-king, who is a figure in the drawing of the just city, does not himself draw or innovate. And unlike the philosopher of the *Phaedrus,* he is not under the supervision of Zeus as he rises to the domain of the hyperuranian beings. Perhaps most strikingly, the philosopher-king is not said to be moved initially by the erotic longing for beautiful boys, as is apparently true of Glaucon, for example, but rather for wisdom. It is mathematics that mediates between everyday life and philosophical dialectic, not sexuality, and not even the love of the beautiful.

The philosophical nature loves (*erastas*) being and truth (501d2); this asexual Eros leads in turn to the vision of the Ideas and finally to the knowledge (*mathēma*) of the Idea of the Good (505a2). In a famous passage, Socrates compares the Idea of the Good to the sun, which furnishes visibility, genesis, growth, and nourishment to all living things; so the Good furnishes intelligibility, being, and essence (*to einai te kai tēn ousian*), although it is not itself an *ousia* but "beyond *ousia* and excels it in dignity and power" (509b2–10). Dialectical knowledge of the Ideas itself depends upon knowledge or cognition (*noēsis*) of the good as it is itself (511b8ff; 7. 532b1ff, d8). This is the highest point of erotic ascent in the *Republic.*

Let me now summarize the stages of this ascent. We move from everyday experience of natural phenomena to the apprehension of relations, ratios, and harmonies or to mathematics both applied and pure, and from there to the Ideas, culminating in the vision of the Idea of the Good. On the whole, it can be said that the philosophical nature, despite the terminology of Eros and desire, is defined in opposition to the human, and in particular to sexual or political encounters and activities. The passage concerning the divided line is a summary of the ontic and epistemic situation (6. 511d6ff). Nothing is said about the knowledge of human beings or political institutions. It is taken for granted that the philosopher in actual cities will separate himself from the tyrannical sexual

Eros and the madness of the multitude and of political life. It is also taken for granted that the musical education of his early years, together with the mathematical training of his maturity and the culminating study of dialectic, will prepare the philosopher within the painted city for his royal duties.

The question must finally be posed: Is there a genuine erotic ascent in the *Republic?* In one sense, the answer is no, since the entire education of the potential philosopher-king, as well as the nature of the potential philosopher in actual cities, serves to separate him from sexual desire or the love of beautiful bodies. In another sense, the answer must be affirmative, since Socrates speaks as usual about the philosophical Eros as directed toward truth, being, and the Ideas. Socrates takes no notice of any conflict between his criticism of sexual Eros and his use of the language of Eros and desire to characterize the typically philosophical longing.

One could well be tempted to infer from this silence that there is no conflict, or that Socrates simply assumes a sublimation of the sexual into the intellectual Eros in the philosophical nature. Despite the tripartition of the soul into the intellect, spiritedness, and desire, of which the strongest is sexual Eros, we have seen that Eros recurs in the two highest parts as well as in the lowest.

Furthermore, the sexual Eros requires the strictest supervision in the guardian class, and so necessarily among the potential philosophers if not among the mature philosopher-kings. The need for this restraint is sufficient testimony to the highly erotic natures of the guardians, and does not support the thesis that the potential philosopher is by nature attracted, not toward other living bodies, but only toward mathematical forms and Platonic Ideas. Eros is a tyrant and madman to whom all human beings are by nature subjected; the use of these pejorative epithets, as well as the extraordinary restrictive measures taken by Socrates as founding father of a just city, measures which cannot succeed in preserving the city from eventual destruction through their violation (7. 546a2ff), all combine to enforce our doubt concerning the bond or separation between the intellectual and the appetitive Eros, to say nothing for the moment about spiritedness.

The *Republic,* then, may be described as an erotic ascent which abstracts, not merely from the body but from Eros itself. I mean by this that the intellectual Eros ascends in actual cities by disregarding the bodily Eros; in the just city it ascends by suppressing the bodily Eros through the temperance of music and the health of gymnastic (3. 404e4f). In order to free philosophy from the tyranny of Eros, Socrates subjects Eros to the tyranny of intellect or spiritedness or both. But this is to subject one form of Eros to the tyranny of two other forms of Eros. Eros continues to multiply. What looks like the precision, appropriate to the mathematical atmosphere of the *Republic,* of the tripartition of the soul, in fact supports the conclusion that the soul cannot be mathematicized. It has no parts that preserve a definite and independent existence so as to be amenable to counting by standard integers.

In book 4, at 436a8ff, Socrates says that it is hard to know whether the soul does everything as a whole or whether it does each deed with a separate part of itself. He answers this question, in accord with the principle of justice or the division of labor, in favor of the second alternative. But the analysis of the soul, and in particular of Eros, shows that this answer is incorrect. One cannot use the paradigm of *technē* to arrive at an understanding of the soul; hence it is impossible to resolve the political problem in accord with this paradigm. Eros must be subordinated to Zeus, but even Zeus is erotic.

Chapter 4 The Golden Apple

This essay first appeared in Arion *(Winter 1990): 187–207. It contains a detailed review of G. R. F. Ferrari's* Listening to the Cicadas, *an extremely valuable study of Plato's* Phaedrus. *Ferrari's book was of special interest to me because it was the first example in my experience of an approach to Plato by a member of the Anglo-Saxon establishment that employed the methods of Leo Strauss. Whereas many other writers of this school now duplicate the approach of Strauss without deigning to notice his existence, Ferrari explicitly distinguishes himself from Strauss on the ground that he does not attribute insincerity or the concealment of his true opinions to Plato. I have no intention of engaging in polemics with Ferrari, whose work I admire and whom I count as a friend. On the point at issue, however, he is mistaken. Strauss never accuses Plato of duplicity. The distinction between the surface and the deeper meaning of a Platonic dialogue is on Strauss's view explained by Maimonides' image in* The Guide of the Perplexed *of a golden apple that is covered by a silver filigree with very small interstices. The silver covering is valuable in itself; to those with sufficiently keen eyesight, there is an even more valuable vision contained within the filigree. There is a second point to be made in this context. All dramas, and more comprehensively, all works of art, necessarily contain a surface, namely, the explicit action, poetical discourse, or symbolic representation of spiritual states, and a deeper interior consisting equally of the artist's fuller intentions as well as the responses of the audience. It is intrinsic to the nature of things that the surface conceals the depths, not because of the insincerity or duplicitousness of the artist, but because depths reveal themselves only through the specificities of surfaces. This is the theme of the first essay in the present book. To make the point as simply as possible, when I meet a man for the first time and engage in an initial conversation with him, I see only the external appearance of my interlocutor. It takes time to get to know anyone who is worth knowing. And even if my new friend is unusually frank, his speech is still ambiguous until I can establish the context of familiarity with his character, intentions, and previous experience, a context that is indispensable for competent interpretation. Whoever does not know this knows nothing of human beings. Of course, my new friend can give voice to a series of arguments, which I may check for validity or conceptual coherence, but this tells me nothing of the speaker's motives. One might hold that the task of understanding a philosophical document is precisely to verify the validity of the arguments and their conceptual coherence. The obtuseness of such a reply is especially evident in the case of a dramatic dialogue, but it should be clear with respect to the interpretation of any text in which the author wishes not simply to produce valid arguments, like an animated Turing machine, but to persuade us of something. In this sense, Kant is as much a rhetorician as Plato.*

The verbal intercourse of human beings is swathed in rhetoric, from the constantly reiterated "Have a good day" and the still more obnoxious "Enjoy!" to the subtlest debate about the ontological foundations of mathematics. It is not the canons of logic or the doctrine of predication that penetrates and evaluates this rhetorical covering, but the living intelligence. To make a related point, it is the equivocity of language that enables us to express the shades of meaning by which we render more rather than less precise our categorial assertions. It would be worth considering in some detail whether communication is possible at all without equivocation. One might wish for a methodical training in the intelligence of equivocation, but unfortunately the situation here is the same as in the case of eros. There is nothing but detail. One can learn to read Greek as well as the techniques of elementary logic, but one cannot learn how to be intelligent. The merits of Ferrari's book stem from his natural subtlety; even when his insights cannot be sustained, they point us in the right direction.

Almost fifty years ago, as a young student at the University of Chicago, I received my preliminary initiation into the erotic mysteries of the Platonic dialogues from an ambiguous foreign prophet named Leo Strauss. As I was no Socrates and Strauss no Diotima, this initiation could not be entirely satisfactory. I had no difficulty in accepting Strauss's central hermeneutical principle that the key to Plato's teaching is the dialogue-form itself. What could be more self-evident than that Plato wrote dramas rather than treatises (albeit somewhat eccentric, not to say occasionally boring dramas like the *Parmenides* and *Timaeus*) and so that he concealed his views within the dramatic action and the masks of his protagonists? The unsatisfactory aspect of my initiation lay in the consequences of Strauss's extraordinarily subtle application of his hermeneutical principle. It would be easy, but in my opinion insufficient and misleading, to say that Strauss withheld the final mysteries from his youthful auditors. The problem lies rather in what Strauss revealed. On the one hand, he taught us that the philosophical life is the highest form of human existence, a life that is available in its purity to a handful of persons who are blessed with the divine madness of theoretical lucidity as well as the sobriety of the well-regulated soul. On the other hand, whereas Strauss exhibited a striking combination of cunning and probity, there was little if any display of divine madness. The upshot of his stimulating exegeses was an unmistakable hint, not of a higher revelation awaiting older and wiser adepts but of what might be called Hebraic Averroism.

In the introduction to the first part of *The Guide of the Perplexed*, Maimonides illustrates the method he has employed by means of a citation from Proverbs 25.11:

> The Sage has said: "a word fitly spoken is like apples of gold in settings [*maskiyyoth*] of silver." . . . The term *maskiyyoth* denotes filigree traceries; I mean to say traceries in which there are apertures with very small eyelets, like the handiwork of silversmiths. They are so called because a glance penetrates through them. . . . The Sage accordingly said that a saying uttered with a view to two meanings is like an apple of gold overlaid with silver-filigree work having very small holes. Now see how this dictum describes a well-constructed parable. For he says that in a saying that has two meanings—he means an external and an internal one—the external meaning ought to be as beautiful as silver, while its internal meaning ought to be more beautiful than the external one. . . . When looked at from a distance or with imperfect attention, it is deemed to be an apple of silver; but when a keen-sighted observer looks at it with full attention, its interior becomes clear to him and he knows that it is of gold.[1]

I have cited this passage at length not simply for the light it casts upon Straussian hermeneutics, but because it sets the scene for the following reflections on Plato. As I may restate Strauss's method in Maimonidean terms, the silver filigree or external meaning of the Platonic dialogues contains a valuable teaching for the unphilosophical many, whereas the golden apple is the meaning reserved for the philosophical adept. Strauss's ambiguity consisted in directing our glances through the small holes in the silver filigree, but in such a way as to give the distinct impression that there was no golden apple within. Inside the silver, as it were, was more silver, perhaps of a purer alloy than the exterior, but in no sense the promised gold.

In nonmetaphorical language, Strauss's complex teaching pointed toward the inference not only that wisdom is impossible for human beings, but that philosophy, as described in the silver exterior of the Platonic dialogues, is also impossible. As an alternative school of prophets emanating from the Schwarzwald and the École normale was announcing the death of philosophy, Strauss was preparing his disciples to defend the truth of classical antiquity with what could seem like a much harsher thesis, namely, that philosophy had never been born.

Whereas the Straussian doctrine in its full elaboration has been resisted stoutly by the English-speaking academic establishment, the more explicit revelations from the Continent have made their mark in unexpected quarters. One consequence of the continental influence is the paradoxical adoption of Strauss's hermeneutical methods by the new generation of the very school of Plato scholars that has been most adamant in its criticism of Strauss's teachings.

Let me summarize a long story by saying that analysts, phenomenologists, and (to use a convenient portmanteau term) postmodernists have either accepted enthusiastically or are in the process of accepting Nietzsche's dictum that art is worth more than the truth. I cannot here discuss whether that dictum has been understood in its genuinely Nietzschean sense. Suffice it to say that as confidence in the objective validity of formal analysis wanes and acceptance of doctrines of relativism and perspectivalism increases, Strauss's hermeneutical thesis becomes more attractive.

This thesis must, however, be detached from Strauss's comprehensive teaching, which is conservative and so directly counter to the dominating political views of the Anglo-Saxon academy. The problem is reminiscent of, but not identical to, the difficulties faced by the disciples of the prophet of the Schwarzwald by recent attention to his Nazi past. One major difference here is that Heidegger's views have been politically sanitized by their assimilation into postmodernism, which is grounded in the invention of a radical left-wing Nietzsche.

This is all I need to say about an indispensable component in the constellation of contemporary intellectual attitudes. The balance of my discussion will be concentrated on the issue of the golden apple, that is to say, the possibility of philosophy, as this issue arises in the study of Plato. I want to consider in close detail a recent book on Plato's *Phaedrus,* Giovanni R. F. Ferrari's *Listening to the Cicadas.* The book is of interest in itself, but also as a sign of the times. Hegel says that modern man prays by reading the morning newspaper. As postmoderns, we should not scruple to keep our finger on the pulse of current ideological developments, even when these developments are reported not in the morning newspaper but in the *New York Review of Books.*

Ferrari's book is in my opinion the best consequence of the new look in English Plato studies. Its merits are not restricted to its silver exterior; one seems to discern a golden apple lurking within, not necessarily the apple of philosophy, but an apple of peculiarly Straussian contours. One does not wish, as they say in espionage circles, to "blow his cover," but the interests of philological precision require a certain frankness on my part. Ferrari emerges from a school of Plato scholarship that has for some decades distinguished between philosophical argument and literary ornamentation, to the detriment of the latter. We should therefore expect some accommodations to the stricter Muses of Oxbridge and the Ivy League. At the same time, as will soon become apparent, the substance of Ferrari's interpretation is very much qualified by the relaxed Muses of postmodernism.

If we understand the term *Straussian* to apply to the doctrine rather than to official academic allegiance, then Ferrari is a Straussian in two senses. First and foremost, he accepts the hermeneutical principle that the dramatic form of the Platonic dialogue is not only an essential element in, but the key that unlocks, Platonic teaching. This is evident on the first page of Ferrari's study, where he tells us that he "will argue that by considering how Socrates and Phaedrus orient themselves in their physical environment, and by recognizing what this reveals of their characters, the reader is oriented to the dialogue's major concerns" (1–2).

This principle is enacted throughout the study. Ferrari pays very close attention to dramatic detail, such as the connection between Socrates' response to the countryside in the opening scene of the dialogue and the main distinction drawn in the rhetorical speeches between the nonlover and the lover (2, 16). In an especially suggestive section, he relates the dramatic setting to an illuminating discussion of the "background" to philosophical discourse (22–25). The significance of the title to Ferrari's study lies in his view that the singing of the cicadas functions as a warning to us to distinguish between types of speeches (27).

More generally, Ferrari says that "the emblematic charge of the dramatic action . . . empowers an interpretation of how the dialogue itself is to be read" (26). Ferrari tells us that he will "part company from the majority of commentators" by holding that for Plato, if rhetoric must become philosophical, then "philosophy must acknowledge the extent to which it is rhetoric" (38). Accordingly, he holds that "'philosophy' . . . lies in both halves of the dialogue and, just as crucially, in the articulation between them" (30).[2] The speeches and the analysis of rhetoric are both, Ferrari says, philosophical performances (68). As a final example, I note his wise remark on page 212 that the action of the dialogue qualifies Socrates' extreme words on writing.

So far, clear sailing. But the waters become troubled by the fact that, very far from crediting Strauss or his students as his own predecessors, Ferrari dissociates himself from Straussian methodology in a footnote. The footnote comes in the midst of a critical discussion of Jacques Derrida's reading of *Phaedrus*. Ferrari grants as "a simple truth" that "writing, with its capacity to capture words in a permanent form external to and potentially independent of their user, is especially prone to encourage that fetishizing of words which Phaedrus exemplifies and which is the antithesis of genuine communicative art" (221).[3] The attached note (n. 28) contains the assurance that the admission in the text in no way commits Ferrari to "the 'ironic' mode of interpretation" as "the genre appropriate to the reading of all Platonic dialogues."

Ferrari is not himself insensitive to the role of irony in Plato. One need consider here only his reference to the "dizzy irony" of the opening section of the dialogue, and his more general comment on the role of irony in advancing the "serious" Socratic (and Platonic) teaching on page 213 (a comment to which I shall return below). Unfortunately, when it comes to the "Straussian" method, Ferrari is (or pretends to be) under the impression that, according to the Straussian "ironic" mode of interpretation, Plato has committed to writing "the exact opposite of his genuine opinions" (see the previously cited note). The note concludes, "For a general critique of the 'ironic' method, as practiced by Leo Strauss, see Burnyeat 1985a and 1985b."[4]

Ferrari's treatment of Leo Strauss could give the impression that he is himself a master of the esoteric method. The only mention of Strauss comes in a footnote to a passage that is concerned not with Strauss but with Derrida. The "simple truth" that occasions the note is so simple as to be useless in bringing Leo Strauss to our attention; it reminds me more of T. S. Eliot, who comments somewhere (I think in *Four Quartets*) that when one sits down to write, the words that emerge from the pen are not those one had initially in mind.

Fetishism is one thing, furthermore; stating always the opposite of what one thinks is something else again. We normally refer to such behavior as pathological lying. It has nothing to do with the medicinal or noble lies sanctioned by Socrates on more than one occasion in the *Republic,* and certainly nothing to do with Strauss's approach to Plato, which depends upon the shape of the silver covering to guide us toward the golden apple within. This remains true even if there is no golden apple because in this case the silver exterior assumes a still greater importance.

In sum, not a single utterance by Leo Strauss is mentioned in this book (although the conventional English scholarly literature is piously surveyed). Instead, Ferrari illustrates the ironical method by a brief criticism of a book on *Phaedrus* by Ronna Burger, the student of a student of Strauss, and his most eccentric student at that.[5] One has heard somewhere that the sins of the father shall be visited upon the children and the children's children. But surely it is a bit perverse to visit the sins of the children's children upon the grandfather?

I turn now to the second sense in which Ferrari is a Straussian. If the golden apple is not a myth but a logos, it must among other things establish the possibility of the philosophical life. Ferrari states plainly (and correctly) that "Plato equates the practice of philosophy with the right way to live" (121). There must accordingly be a clear distinction between the right and the wrong way of life, even if the former should be accessible only to a small number of exceptional persons. Ferrari, like Strauss, sees that this way of life is not simply equivalent to dialectic, the art of dividing and collecting in accordance with kinds. He understands Plato's message to be this: "Don't use [dialectic]; live it" (62).

We must therefore establish what it means to "live" dialectic. One of Ferrari's crucial points is that "the dialogue is out to vindicate the philosophic life against a life that merely seeks its effects" (223). Dialectic, when taken by itself, is a device of "a bag of formal tricks" (32) which could also be employed by the nonphilosophical orator (69). In a distinction not drawn by Ferrari, but which seems to express his general thesis, philosophy is not simply theory but also practice; indeed, practice is higher or more comprehensive than theory. Thus the mythical portions of the dialogue, together with its dramatic action, provide us with the necessary background to philosophical discourse or dialectic.

The background to philosophy fulfills more than one function. First, it provides the tacit component to all competence and hence also to explicit philosophical speech (33). Second, it furnishes the presuppositions (or conditions for the possibility) of philosophical argument, which cannot themselves be demonstrated in a noncircular manner (45, 56). Third, it furnishes the basis for a dramatic exhibition of those presuppositions (32, 35, 58, 65, 67). It is thus closely connected to rhetoric, which, as we saw previously, Ferrari regards as a part of philosophy (38). Fourth and perhaps most important, the expression "living well" (20) clearly has an ethical sense. The philosophical life is ethical (91, 121, 137, 213), and this dimension is also furnished by the background.

Philosophy, the art that examines all arts, including itself (32), employs both myth and dialectic, which are equally serious components of the philosophical life (64). Perhaps we could describe this life as the activity of achieving clarity about the tacit implications of the background, which itself seems to be something like doxa or the *Lebenswelt,* although Ferrari does not say this. The closest he comes to it is in an early passage on page 20, where he distinguishes between the philosophical art and the professions: "The doctor and rhetorician can take time off from their professional duties to enjoy the pleasures of the layman. The philosopher, on the other hand, never seems more a philosopher than when immersed in the everyday."

If it is fair to say that Ferrari's portrait gives precedence to praxis, one must immediately qualify this statement by noting that, in distinguishing between the life of philosophy and a life that uses the effects of philosophy for some other purpose, Ferrari appeals to the pursuit of truth for its own sake (45: I will return to this passage in a moment). To anticipate: The philosophical life, understood (as it is in the *Phaedrus*) as a life of philosophical love and friendship, is entirely contingent (Ferrari's own term) to the genuinely philosophical activity of grasping the truth for its own sake. From this standpoint, practice is altogether subordinate to theory. There is no theory without practice, but it is a matter of accident, of our physical natures, for example, in which practice we are (given the contingent circumstances) obliged to engage (129).

The apparent tension between theory and practice might be resolved as follows: The acquisition of truth depends upon contingent factors or alternative patterns of the philosophical life (230). In this case, Ferrari must establish two results. First, he must show that the pattern of the philosophical lover leads to the successful apprehension of truth. Second, because there are alternative patterns, Ferrari must provide a criterion for distinguishing between philosophical and nonphilosophical lives. He cannot simply point to the pursuit of truth for its own sake unless he can tell us what truth is and how it is apprehended.

If Ferrari says that it is the core of Plato's golden apple that we cannot demonstrate the apprehension of truth, but only our devotion to it, he is obviously begging the question. Any life, including that of the poet or the orator, may claim that it is dedicated to the pursuit of the truth for its own sake, while providing an idiosyncratic and self-serving definition of "truth." This is precisely why Platonism gave way to epistemology and ontology; it is also the basis for Hegel's attempt to fulfill the claim of Platonism by demonstrating his own possession of wisdom. Post-Hegelian and in particular postmodern anti-Platonism may then be seen as a return to Platonism, namely, to the admission (granting the aforementioned assumption) that the truth is inaccessible.

No one could blame Ferrari for failing to solve the problem that has baffled the finest intellects of the race. But one may, I think, expect him to state the problem consistently or, in other words, to recognize its existence. Here, I think, Ferrari falls short; and this is the second sense in which he may be called a Straussian. In my opinion, Strauss was aware of the problem and intentionally obscured its formulation, although he gave very explicit hints about it when speaking, for example, of the quarrel between faith and reason. I find no evidence in Ferrari's book that he is aware of the inconsistency of his portrait of the philosophical life. However this may be, he states the nature of that life in such a way as to make it in principle equivalent to any life whatsoever. The net result is to leave the reflective reader with the impression that there is no golden apple within the silver filigree.

At first glance, Ferrari's interpretation may seem to be very far removed from Strauss's "elitist" understanding of the philosophical life. One must also say that it is rather distant from the outermost surface of Plato's silver filigree. Even if, however, Strauss is right to say that the depths are contained only via the surfaces, it does not follow that the depths are the same as the surfaces. Neither, as I have just suggested, is it necessary that Ferrari sees clearly the implications of his own analysis. I call Ferrari a Straussian here not out of perversity and not ironically, but in a sense closely related to Nietzsche's observation that his philosophy is reversed Platonism.

This reference to Nietzsche is critical for the "background" of our discussion, to employ Ferrari's excellent term. Ferrari's understanding of the philosophical life is, or leads directly to, a "reversed Straussianism." And the two conceptions of the philosophical life are, in my opinion, the result, whether directly or indirectly, of two opposing interpretations of Nietzsche.

I have argued elsewhere in some detail that Nietzsche's account of the philosophical life (as distinct from his repudiation of "Platonism" understood as the "two-worlds" doctrine) is markedly Platonic.[6] Perhaps the nub of the matter is this. For Nietzsche, the philosopher is a superior being of exalted spiritual and intellectual powers who necessarily practices esotericism and whose principal occupation is to produce a new race of human beings, whom he will rule by virtue of having promulgated their laws and values. Nietzsche's philosopher is not an ontologist but a political artist. Because chaos is at the core of apparent order, which is itself an artifact of human perspective, if there is a golden apple within the silver filigree of Nietzsche's writings, it must be a concealed or artistically adorned perception of the impossibility of philosophy understood as the pursuit of an independently existing order.

The creation of new values is then very much like Socrates' activity in the *Republic:* the imaginative production of a myth of the golden apple. This is to say that it is reserved for the very few extraordinary individuals at the level of a Plato or a Nietzsche. Only someone who has misunderstood or been misled by the silver filigree would commit the egregious error of applying doctrines of the celebration of creativity and radical individuality to the nonphilosophical multitude. This is exactly what has transpired in the past thirty years, thanks to the various social and political developments that culminated in a repudiation, or vulgarization, of the European high tradition. Nietzsche's aristocratic doctrine of *Geist,* which constitutes his genuine Platonism, has been replaced by a bogus, but politically compelling, left-wing Nietzscheanism.

The prophet of the transvaluation of values has himself been devalued, not, to be sure, without textual support from Nietzsche himself, but through the simple expedient of ignoring his own distinction between the esoteric and the exoteric. Authenticity replaces the "pure and moderate life" (*Phaedo* 108c3–4) of the Platonic philosopher; a rage for fairness replaces the love of truth. Instead of philosophical friendship, we are offered decency (to everyone except "Straussians" or "ironists"). By a series of historical steps we move from German speculative extremes to Anglo-Saxon platitudes.

Ferrari cannot be simply positioned on either the German or the Anglo-Saxon end of the spectrum of late modernity. It can, however, be shown that his conception of the philosophical life, as he finds it in Phaedrus, is one, as I suggested above, that has no determinate content. In slightly different terms, it is a life that virtually anyone can claim to lead; in that sense, it is accessible to all, or let us say to many, rather than to a small number of elite persons. This is Ferrari's reversed Straussianism.

I introduce the analysis of Ferrari's treatment of the philosophical life by noting his assertion that Phaedrus is not "a hopeless case" but that "the action of the dialogue is built around the possibility of his rescue" for philosophy (39).

Phaedrus is described by Ferrari as an intellectual or cultural impresario (4ff.) who admires the rhetoric of Lysias. His "inadequacy is a spring-board for exploration of how the talk of the true philosopher is indeed appropriate just to the extent that it is good" (9), as will be revealed in the course of the dialogue. We may fairly say that Phaedrus is, if not quite Everyman, certainly a paradigm for Ferrari of how even a dull intellectual of low tastes may be converted to the philosophical life.

This conversion is to take place by means of rhetorical persuasion. The rhetoric to be employed for the conversion of the reader must be that of the dialogue itself, in its entirety. In a very good passage, Ferrari says, "Plato accepts and acts upon rhetoric's insistence that truth is impotent without persuasion. Plato is out to dissuade us from one way of life—the rhetorical—and turn us to another—the philosophical. . . . To be truly persuaded, we must in addition be presented with examples of those opposing lives, and simply find them attractive or unattractive." Hence Plato's "painstaking care" with his dramatic figures: "so that we can know who we will be" (58).

In itself, this is well said. Unfortunately, we may well be Lysias or Phaedrus rather than Socrates. Does it make any difference? In the context of Ferrari's comprehensive account of the philosophical life, I am not sure that it does, if by "difference" one means that it is better by an objective standard to be Socrates. We begin our consideration of this question by returning to Ferrari's understanding of contingency, which will lead us in turn to the central theme of Eros.

Ferrari indicates this connection in the following general statement: "Socrates in his mythic hymn examines not only the nature of the soul but also the nature of the phenomenon itself: what happens to the philosophers when they look into the soul; for he wants to stress the subjective effects of the investigation on the investigators, as well as its objective results" (122). It should be mentioned at once that Ferrari pays very little attention to Socrates' attribution of this myth to Stesichorus. He addresses the point by noting that "as a philosopher, Socrates is naturally wary of the capacity of poetry to hinder as well as help his pursuit of truth" (111). He concludes his brief development of this remark with the assurance that "Socrates does not in retrospect disavow the content of the speech, but only its lack of integration into a larger perspective" (112).

If Ferrari had thought more carefully about irony, he would have noticed that Socrates' wariness toward poetry, together with the attribution to Stesichorus, suggests at the least a reservation about the content of the myth of the soul. If Socrates has an ironic reason for introducing the myth, it would be counterproductive for him to disown it subsequently. The lack of such a disclaimer accordingly becomes part of the irony. What has to be done, then, is to determine Socrates' attitude toward his myth. Ferrari, I suggest, is not in a position to make this determination, because he is too much concerned to establish Socrates' (and Plato's) underlying "seriousness" or, to employ a fashionable term, sincerity. In his eagerness to establish that Socrates says what he means and not the opposite, Ferrari is selective in his attention to what Socrates in fact says. On a decisive point, Ferrari has misunderstood Straussian hermeneutics, which is to say that he has fallen short on a cardinal rule of hermeneutics in general, or what Schleiermacher called *subtilitas legendi,* and Boeckh *der richtige Takt.*[7]

I can establish my objection to Ferrari's interpretation without rehashing the question of irony, as Ferrari, following Burnyeat, seems to understand that term. Internal evidence will suffice. Ferrari holds that Plato attributes a complex structure to soul "because he wants to show that his gods, no less than mythmaking mortals, must cope with contingency" (127). The divine souls are concerned with ordering and controlling the inanimate, not because it is essential to the vision of the Forms, "which the charioteer alone enjoys," but because the environment or physical cosmos, although it is ultimately contingent, is, as existing, subject to the desire of the soul to administer (128).

Ferrari connects this desire to contemplation of the Forms, "the sustaining condition of the gods' concern for a cosmos the sensible element of which is alien to them" (129). The activity of the gods, Ferrari says, is a kind of mythical projection onto "the cosmic screen of questions arising from the philosophic life" (ibid.) The myth shows that "goods such as intellectual friendship and the thrill of discovery" belong, but are external, to the philosophical life; it shows further "what philosophers must do if they are to approach these peculiar goods of the philosophic life with the appropriate attitude" (128-29).

Friendship, or the philosophical transformation of Eros, is thus not an end in itself but may be properly enjoyed as a "contingent function" of the free play of the philosophical impulse. Ferrari says, "It is, ultimately, only accidental that the philosophers care for friendship (and not some other thing) yet also recognize that that recognition is intrinsic to their way of life" (129). In other words, just as ruling the divine cosmos is contingent to the divine desire to view the Forms, so friendship, but hence also the philosophical life, is contingent to that same desire in human beings. Eros, after all, is not the possession or vision of, but the longing for, the Forms: the desire for what it lacks. The vision is necessary; how one obtains it is contingent.

This is no doubt why Ferrari says that there is more than one pattern for the philosophical life (230). The myth of the erotic soul and the pattern of the philosophical life it exhibits are contingent; the love of philosophical lovers is not the whole of philosophy. But given that pattern, the relationship between the lovers "is no mere allegory of philosophic discussion. . . . It's love that Socrates is talking about in that speech; and for those philosophic lovers of his, philosophy and love must struggle to come to terms" (ibid.). It is "blessed luck" (ibid.) to find such love, but once found, "the beautiful boy is no mere instrument of the philosophic lover's self-development" (224).

In sum, "Plato invents his cosmic myth in order to illuminate—make us recognize—what happens when philosophers cope with contingency by attempting to gain the cosmic or impersonal perspective while maintaining their personal sense of who they are and why they are making the attempt" (129). This particular attempt requires genuine love of a beautiful boy, and at least friendship in the boy for the older lover. Some other way of coping with contingency would presumably have no such requirement.

I postpone for the moment the question of an alternative pattern for the philosophical life. We note that Ferrari takes the myth literally on the central issue of pederasty—not its carnal fulfillment, but its function as a reminder of the beauty of the eternal Forms. Of crucial importance, whether in this pattern or in some other, is the actual vision of the eternal Forms. But the myth in *Phaedrus* makes it quite clear, as Ferrari recognizes, that this vision is capable of nothing more than intermittent and unsatisfactory fulfillment:

> Even for the best human soul the vision of the place beyond the heavens was stressful. Not only did the unbalanced chariot-team make the aerial climb a struggle (247b3-6), but even at the sky's rim continually harassed the charioteer, who could barely keep his head above heavenly water, craning for his glimpse of hyperuranian space (248a1-5). Plato here puts at the pinnacle of human achievement, in his eschatological myth of the greatest prize for human soul, not a mystic union with the divine, but a full confrontation with our human limits—and a soberingly farcical picture it is.(151)

As Ferrari's analysis shows, Phaedrus, on the crucial point of the essential moment of human psychic existence, depicts "a struggle and a comedy," which "is then obscured behind the solemn halo of beauty's mystic revelation" (ibid.). This could not have been better said by Leo Strauss. Yet Ferrari seems to have no clue as to the meaning of his own words. The philosophical life, and so too the entire account of philosophical Eros, as a contingent preparation for that essential moment, must surely be something even worse, that is, more depressing than a comedy. I can think of no better term than tragedy. As to the obscuring solemn halo, we are entitled to suppose that Ferrari has penetrated the silver filigree and perceived the absence of an inner golden apple, but that his tongue refuses to acknowledge what his eyes have seen.

Ferrari may well be correct when he says that "for Plato our moral lives are not led in spite of contingency (in Kantian fashion), but become complete through proper dealings with contingency" (137). But Ferrari does not see, or gives no signal of having seen, that in this case human life, the "philosophical life" included, is what Kant calls a *Possenspiel,* or farce.[8] Ferrari seems inadvertently to have outstripped Leo Strauss in exposing the myth of the golden apple. The erotic life, as Ferrari illuminatingly analyzes it, is presented by Socrates, even in the case of divine love, "as an 'impure' mixture of pleasure and pain" (166). This is "the mark of contingency" in which the pleasure of love is balanced by the pain of the burden of embodiment and ignorance, or in other words of human nature. "It is an experience that keeps [the philosophic lover] from the complete spiritual integration of a god. And thus his love is actually fueled by a measure of hostility and resistance . . . to the mixed pleasure of soul that love is" (166–67).

What Ferrari calls "the blessed luck" (230) of philosophical love is in fact the attempt to ascend from corporeal existence to a pure intellectual cognition of the hyperuranian beings or Forms. It is the erotic vision of what Socrates calls in the *Theaetetus* the need to flee from earthly existence and to become "as much like the god as possible" (176a8-b2). Ferrari shows us plainly that, even in the best case, this attempt is a failure. I mean by this not that there are no Forms to see but that we cannot see them with the steadiness and purity required by philosophical logos. The Socratic philosopher strives to become a god; this striving, on Ferrari's plausible analysis, results in comedy.

If we consider carefully the flawed nature of Eros, there is good reason for us to approach Lysias's initial defense of the nonlover with renewed interest. Ferrari rightly insists that the speech is not without merit, but in my opinion he fails to see why this is so. On his account, the nonlover plays upon the ambiguous nature of love and exaggerates its "unsettleability" by offering in its stead a "business-like attainment" of love's desirable effects. The Lysian orator "offers society the seductive promise of a decision. His talent is for making the audience settle. But the price to be paid for security is opting out of the search for truth" (51).

Ferrari is under the impression that Plato has allowed Socrates "to miss the subtlety of Lysias' speech." Socrates lacks "sophistication" on this point; he is "naive" in not seeing that Lysias is following current oratorical practice in producing "an effect of haphazardness and spontaneity" (52–53). Here I think that it is Ferrari who is naive, not Socrates. The subtlety of the Lysian speech lies not in its oratorical spontaneity but in its very detailed demonstration, albeit in the coarse terms of everyday life, or as it were in silver filigree, of the very dangers of the erotic life that emerge with various degrees of clarity from Ferrari's own analysis.

In a dialogue devoted to the praise of Eros, Socrates is right to object to Lysias's speech, and he is right to do so in terms that will be persuasive to Phaedrus. But this does not invalidate the merits of that speech as a spur to a second reading of the dialogue, a reading that is stimulated by the patent inadequacies of Socrates' Stesichorean myth. Let us assume that Ferrari is right to say that the myth teaches us the pinnacle of human achievement, "a full confrontation with our human limits" (151). This limit is inadvertently pointed out by Ferrari himself: "Only through the agency of the bad horse does the charioteer come into full re-possession of his birthright; for he would not otherwise have come close enough [to the beautiful boy] to be dazzled" (191).

Let me be blunt for the sake of clarity. Are we to suppose that for the Socrates of *Phaedrus* (and by extension of *Symposium*), philosophy is sublimated buggery (see 249a2: *paiderastēsantos meta philosophias*)? Or are we dealing here with something much deeper and much more complex, an "irony" that is revealed by Alcibiades in *Symposium* and, much more allusively but with sufficient explicitness for the "sophisticated" reader, by Socrates himself in *Phaedrus*? And by "irony" I do not mean "saying the opposite of what one means." Socrates says explicitly that the conquest of sexual Eros is greater than any achievement of human temperance and divine madness (256b5ff.). If that conquest is impossible (as even the *Republic* makes clear),[9] then it makes good sense to neutralize Eros as much as possible by assimilating it into a myth of the philosophical life.

Stated more comprehensively, the evidence uncovered by Ferrari himself seems to me to support the following hypothesis about the general sense of *Phaedrus*. If the philosophical life depends upon a secure intellectual grasp of the pure Forms, sufficient to generate true speeches and to provide a basis for justice that is both correct and accessible to human beings, then that life is impossible. Philosophy is divine madness because it rests upon the soul's "prophetic" nature or "recollection" of an original vision of the pure Forms, a recollection that is sufficient to guide some persons toward the attempt to capture it in discourse. This attempt in turn requires a "temperate" style of life and, as a corollary, the advocacy of temperance and justice for nonphilosophers.

Myth is then the instrument by which the philosopher accommodates the paradoxical and indeed dangerous nature of philosophy to the understanding of the nonphilosopher.

Nothing in this brief summary is unconventional, nor is any of it the "opposite" of what Plato says. It does, however, require us to take a rather different view of Phaedrus from that offered by Ferrari, for all the excellence of his analyses. Socrates' regular characterization of his myth, and of the entire conversation, as a game or joke, duly noted by Ferrari (213), must be related to the comic portrayal of the peak of erotic madness and to the soundness of much of what the nonlover has to say about love. This does not require us to repudiate the doctrine of Eros in its entirety, or in effect to join ranks with Lysias and Phaedrus.

I cannot therefore agree with Ferrari's thesis that the action of the dialogue is built around the possibility of rescuing Phaedrus for the philosophical life (39). This contention would be implausible even if we were to agree that Socrates is completely "serious" about his hymn to his love. Ferrari's account of Phaedrus points in exactly the opposite direction and makes unintelligible why Plato should have made him the auditor of a "serious" paean to philosophical love. On the other hand, Ferrari himself provides us with a clue to the answer to this puzzle. Phaedrus is an "intellectual impresario" (4ff.) and lover of oratory. Socrates engages in an effort to convert Phaedrus into an "impresario" for philosophy: not, of course, for the golden apple, but for the silver filigree.

This effort is not doomed to failure by Phaedrus's vulgarity. We should judge Socrates' (or better, Plato's) success not by the effects of Socrates' speech on Phaedrus but by the historical influence of the dialogue. And this, incidentally, enables us to sustain Ferrari's objection to Derrida on the supposedly paradoxical criticism of writing within a writing. The paradox is a necessary feature of philosophical rhetoric, the purpose of which is pedagogical or political, not ontological or for that matter postontological (cf. Ferrari, 222). This is why, immediately following Socrates' inspiring hymn, the poetic language of which is an accommodation to Phaedrus, the lover of Lysias (257a4-b5), his auditor turns directly not to a flight to the roof of the cosmos but to political oratory (257c1ff.).

By way of conclusion, consider one final aspect of the problem of the philosophical life. Ferrari suggests, with all due qualification, that Socrates' "ethos" is that of the philosophical lover. Here are two supporting citations: (1) With respect to the hymn to love, "it is apparent that [Socrates] is no longer elaborating a set theme, but moulding an ideal for himself and other philosophers; so that in the figure of the philosophic lover we naturally look to find traces of Socrates himself" (87). (2) Socrates, says Ferrari, integrates his first speech with that of Lysias "into his polyphonic song of the charioteer's success. . . . Socrates' philosophic ethos shows through his speeches much as Lysias' rhetorical ethos shows through his. In particular, we can now see why it matters that Socrates should come into full voice only gradually: because his is the ethos of the charioteer who learns through struggle" (200).[10]

There is an important dramatic consideration that casts doubt on this conclusion with respect to Socrates' ethos. Ferrari has noticed it, but he mutes it by relegating the crucial point to a footnote. After emphasizing that "it's love that Socrates is talking about" as an exhibition of Plato's acknowledgment of "the blessed luck of those who find [love]," Ferrari goes on to say, "Socrates' speech is not the whole dialogue, nor is the love of philosophic lovers the whole of philosophy, or the only pattern for the philosophic life" (230).

A few lines later, the following footnote is appended to the text: "Socrates in this dialogue is no philosophic lover—in the simple but crucial sense that he and Phaedrus are not represented as being in love" (note 42). This is a crucial point, and one of which Ferrari makes no use whatsoever. I suspect that this lapse is caused by his unwillingness to question Socrates' sincerity. We for our part will want to connect the portrait of a sober and unerotic Socrates praising erotic divine madness with that of the sober Socrates of the *Symposium,* who drinks his companions under the table and then goes about his everyday affairs.

This observation needs to be sharpened. Again we start with a claim by Ferrari. There is more than one pattern for the philosophic life. Ferrari does not tell us what the other patterns are; he also seems to regard the erotic pattern as unusually lucky or blessed (230, 232). In any event, if Socrates reflects the ethos of the charioteer, then he must be a philosopher who is marked by the psychological trait of those who are "lucky enough to find philosophic love" (232).

Who, then, is Socrates' beloved? Certainly not Phaedrus, as we have just seen. The answer is in fact notorious to every reader of Plato: Socrates claims to love Alcibiades. I note in passing that it would be profitable to study the *Greater Alcibiades* closely in this connection, a dialogue in which Socrates temporarily persuades the young Alcibiades to pursue *dikaiosunē* (135 6e5ff.). For the sake of brevity, I restrict myself to reminding the reader that, in *Symposium,* the intoxicated Alcibiades reveals the truth about Socrates' hybris and hidden nature (215a5ff.). Socrates, says Alcibiades, pretends to be erotically attracted to beautiful youths[11] but is in fact immune to their physical charms. "Socrates," says Alcibiades, "lives his whole life among mortals practicing irony and playing" (216e4).

I note that Alcibiades challenges Socrates to contradict him if he is not telling the truth; no such contradiction occurs. If Alcibiades is lying or mistaken, then certainly Plato is engaging in an irony of a sort that Ferrari wishes to exclude. But Alcibiades' account is sustained by the evidence of the dialogues themselves. Socrates is regularly presented as living not the pattern of the philosophical lover of Phaedrus, victim to "a state of mind that he cannot control, nor remove" (163), but that of the entirely unerotic philosopher who is praised in *Theaetetus* and *Phaedo*.

In *Theaetetus*, Socrates says that the genuine philosopher does not know his way to any place of public assembly, has no political knowledge, and engages in no political activity, and certainly not in banquets or in carousing with flute-girls; in sum, the philosopher has no knowledge of or concern with human affairs. Only his body resides within the city; his *dianoia* dwells below the earth and beyond the heavens (*ouranou te huper*), "as Pindar says." The philosopher pays no attention to his neighbor and hardly knows whether he is a human being or some other animal (173c8ff.). There is nothing here of coming to terms with contingency, erotic attraction, concern with the welfare of the beloved (Ferrari, 183), or the desire to produce something jointly with any human being (cf. Ferrari, 184).

This "pattern" of the philosophical life is plainly not a life at all, certainly not in any sense that is compatible with the life described, as Ferrari understands it, in *Phaedrus*. The pattern of *Theaetetus* conforms instead with what Socrates says under quite different circumstances in *Phaedo*. We are told there that philosophers should desire to die as soon as possible (61b7ff.), and that those who correctly grasp philosophy occupy themselves with nothing but dying and being dead (64a7ff.). The true philosopher despises the body and wants only to approach what each thing is in itself (*auto kath' hauto*) by means of his intelligence alone (65e6ff.).

I have no doubt that Socrates accommodates this pattern of the philosophical life in the first instance to the nature of the sober mathematician Theaetetus and in the second to Simmias and Cebes, or more broadly, to all those who fear death. But this does not alter the problem facing Ferrari; it rather emphasizes that problem. For is it not likely, to say the least, that Socrates is accommodating his portrait of the erotic version of philosophical life to the nature of Phaedrus? Does he not in fact say so, as we have seen?

Ferrari cannot finesse this problem by saying that there are different patterns of the philosophical life for persons of different natures. Socrates never says this; the inference is therefore inescapable that he practices irony in a sense much deeper than that allowed by Ferrari. By giving two extreme and opposing patterns of the philosophical life, which correspond to the lover and the non-lover, respectively, without telling us which one he prefers or whether either is of any use to human beings, Socrates, and more fundamentally Plato, does far more than say the opposite of what he means. He says nothing.

Or rather, what he actually says is this: Of the two extreme paradigms of the philosophical life, one is a comedy and the other is, if not a tragedy, death. One might reasonably respond: Our job is to balance these two patterns or arrive at a reasonable middle way. But what is the middle way? Is it not the comprehensive portrait of the philosophical life in the Platonic dialogues, a portrait that contradicts itself by pointing in two extreme and opposite directions simultaneously? Everything is left to the reader, who will interpret the dialogues in accordance with his or her nature.

On balance, I conclude that Ferrari's study is of great value in assisting us to conclusions which are other than his: the myth of the philosophical lover seems to be a myth of the golden apple. No doubt one could infer that the resolution of the aforementioned contradiction is the life that combines the attributes of the lover with those of the nonlover in the correct proportion. But what is the correct proportion? Are we merely, like bemused positivists, to read the dialogues aloud to one another, in order to enunciate Plato's meaning? We return to the silver filigree, peering into its interstices, not, as the postmoderns would have it, at the *parousia* of Being, but at its apparent absence.

Chapter 5 The Problem of Sense Perception in Plato's *Philebus*

An earlier version of this essay was delivered as a lecture at the Catholic University of America in September 1993 and was published in 1997 by Catholic University Press in a volume edited by Johannes M. Van Ophuijsen, who made some helpful comments about the manuscript. The present version has been revised and expanded to include unpublished material presented to my graduate seminars of 1994 and 1997 on the Philebus. *The main theme is the incipient Kantianism of Plato's treatment of sense perception in the* Theaetetus *and* Philebus. *The question is whether it is possible to distinguish between the two ostensibly opposing positions. There is also a discussion of the Kantian doctrine in chapter 9 of this book. Just as chapter 2 deals with lived rather than clock time, so this essay is concerned with the experience of sense perception, not with the neurophysiological machinery that plays so important a role in generating it. I might note that Plato's metaphor of a writer in the soul is vaguely reminiscent of what the neurophysiologist Michael Gazzaniga calls the interpreter in the left-brain-based system who monitors the effects of the modules of brain organization "and immediately constructs a hypothesis as to why particular actions occurred" ("Brain Modularity: Toward a Philosophy of Conscious*

Experience," *in* Consciousness in Contemporary Science, *edited by A. J. Marcel and E. Bisiach [Oxford: Clarendon Press, 1988], 219).*

The main part of this essay will consist of a detailed analysis of a short but dense and puzzling passage on sense perception in Plato's *Philebus* (38c5 to 39c6 in the Stephanus pagination). As a preface to this analysis, I shall refer briefly to a passage in the *Theaetetus.* Although I shall give as precise an analysis as I can of the Platonic text, my goal is neither philological nor historical, but theoretical. I want to study the text in question for the light it sheds on the general problem of how to explain our ability to distinguish between true and false perceptual judgments. In particular, I want to show that the analysis of sense perception in the *Theaetetus* and *Philebus* reveals a surprisingly Kantian component. This raises the question of what is required to prevent Platonism from turning into Kantianism.

At 185c4ff and again at 186e1ff of the *Theaetetus,* Socrates contends, with the assistance of the young mathematician, that perception does not "share in" (μετέστιν) truth because it does not share in being (οὐσία) or not-being (τὸ μὴ εἶναι). It is the soul, "itself by itself" (αὐτὴ δι' αὑτῆς), as Theaetetus puts it, that arrives at the truth about perceived entities (185d7ff). As Socrates clarifies the process, the soul speaks to itself or engages in discursive thinking about the οὐσία it has apprehended; and so it arrives at a judgment (δοξάζειν) about the perceived entity (189e6ff).

I interject a philological remark. The Greek words δόξα and δοξάζειν may be translated variously by the appropriate English expressions of belief, opinion, or judgment. The opinion with which we are concerned in both the *Theaetetus* and the *Philebus* arises from the choice between opposing or distinct identifications of a perceptual entity. In the *Philebus* (38c6), Socrates uses the verb κρίνειν, to decide, choose, or judge, to express the first step in this process. To form an opinion is thus to come to a judgment. The terms δόξα and δοξάζειν refer to the result or process of coming to a judgment, not to the scientific or philosophical certitude of that judgment. Even a true δόξα lacks the veridical status of epistemic knowledge or a true λόγος. With these qualifications in mind, I translate δόξα and δοξάζειν throughout as "judgment" and "to judge."

For my present purposes, the upshot of the passage in the *Theaetetus* is as follows. Because the soul arrives at truth about the perceived entity entirely apart from sense perception, it is, to say the least, unclear what role that process plays in the formation of true judgments about the aforementioned entity. One could say that the sensory construction serves as a framework or basis upon which to add the dimension of truth. But this leaves entirely unexplained the procedure by which the soul, through communion with itself about the being and other common properties of any perceptual entity whatsoever, should license a true judgment about the sensed properties of this entity in particular. It should be added that "being" (οὐσία) is here a general property, and not a Platonic Idea or paradigm of perceived entities of such and such a kind. We cannot therefore invoke the doctrine of Ideas, which is absent from the *Theaetetus,* to account for the "synthesis" (I employ this Kantian term intentionally) of common and particular properties in the entity about which we formulate a judgment.

At least in the passages under inspection, it looks as though the Socrates of the *Theaetetus* accounts for true perceptual judgments by way neither of sense perception per se nor of the noetic apprehension of pure forms or Ideas. The most likely inference from his quite tentative and generally aporetic analysis is that the soul "somehow" (as Aristotle would say) constitutes what can properly be called an object of perception, by way of an oddly anachronistic-looking process of synthesis that is anticipative of Kant, or, still more generally, of the modern doctrine of the projection of the object by the subject. The common properties correspond to the Kantian categories and conceptual rules for object-construction, whereas the sensed properties correspond to what Kant calls "sensation" (*Empfindung*). Socrates turns out to be a proto-Kantian in this passage.

In short, Socrates and Theaetetus take it for granted that we do of course apprehend the unified entity that includes, but is not cognized via, its perceived properties. As Socrates puts it, it would be strange if we contained within ourselves many separate senses that did not unite in one *idea* or form, "whether we call it soul or something else," by which we perceive through the instruments of the senses (184d1ff). Not only would it be strange, but there would be no experience to analyze. Nevertheless, Socrates does not explain how experience is possible, and he certainly never alludes to the doctrine of Platonic Ideas as playing a role in this possibility. In another proto-Kantian touch, the word *idea* in the passage just cited refers to the unifying power of the soul, not to the form of the unified entity.

In this brief inspection of the *Theaetetus,* it is not my intention to suggest that Plato had a unified doctrine of sense perception of any kind, let alone of the Kantian variety. No doubt Plato's analysis of the problem of sense perception varies from dialogue to dialogue. The passage in the *Theaetetus* suffices, however, to show us that the problem of Kantianism is already visible in the Platonic texts. I shall refer to the traditional doctrine of Ideas as "Platonism" and use the name "Kantianism" to designate the doctrine of the constitution of the form of the perceived object as a synthesis of concepts and sensations. The question that concerns me is whether it is possible to mount a plausible defense of Platonism. As a corollary, I want to consider the consequences of the failure of Platonism. Kantian synthesis is in my opinion the most attractive and successful of the alternatives to Platonism. If this too is defective, then the object of perception deteriorates steadily back into the chaos of sensations from which Kant rescued it; or else the constructive powers of the will and the imagination, first invoked by British empiricists like Locke and Hume, are once more assigned the role of producing experience, and we lose all touch with a common reality. The failure of Platonism and Kantianism, I suggest, leads directly to postmodernism.

So much by way of motivation. Coming to closer grips with the *Philebus,* I begin with a brief account of the context within which the problem of perceptual judgments is broached. There are in Plato, as in Aristotle after him, two main senses of "true." The first refers to propositions or assertions that what is, is, or that what is not, is not. The second refers to beings and says of them that they are genuine instances of such and such a kind. It is also helpful to notice the distinction between "true" and "correct." "Correct" refers to types of reasoning, such as arithmetical calculations, but it can also stand in for propositional truth. Normally "correct" does not mean "genuine." For example, a genuine diamond is not a correct diamond, although our statement that this diamond is genuine may be a correct statement, namely, a true one. Today we speak of "politically correct views." This means that it is correct in the sense of conforming to a certain criterion of what is appropriate and what is not. It does not mean that the view is true, or even that it is a genuine view. I might be pretending to hold a certain view in order to gain favor with the ruling standpoint.

These distinctions were introduced in the section of the *Philebus* directly preceding the passage that concerns us. Socrates and Protarchus were considering whether pleasures can be subordinated to standards like those of truth, genuineness, or correctness. The position of Protarchus is roughly as follows. A pleasure is never correctly identified as false, although there can be opinions about pleasures that are false. If I am pleased, I cannot be mistaken about this; but I can be mistaken about the cause of the pleasure and also about whether the pleasure is good or bad with respect to a given standard of judgment, for example, the standard of morality that is dominant in a community. Socrates' position is that pleasures can be, and are, subordinated to standards like good and evil, and that an evil pleasure is a false pleasure. Note that Socrates does not actually deny that an evil pleasure is pleasant. At bottom, there is no difference between him and Protarchus on this point. What Socrates denies is that pleasure is "the" good, since goodness is something independent of pleasure. So much by way of a review.

Socrates now begins a new stage of the discussion by establishing that some judgments are true and others false, and that both kinds of judgment are often followed by pleasure or pain (38b6–11). Less trivially, he gains Protarchus's agreement to the assertion that judgment together with the process of forming a judgment is undertaken by us on each occasion on the basis of memory and sense perception (αἴσθησις: 38b12–c2). Because memory was itself defined as the preservation of sense perception, Socrates must be referring here to judgments about bodies or bodily experience. Αἴσθησις is the initiating activity in the sequence that terminates in judgment; it must contain a component of awareness or the taking note of something and thus be part of, or itself contain, what we call consciousness. It is this taking note of that is preserved by memory. I use the expression "taking note of" to explicate what Socrates calls "not being unaware" (33d9) or the joint pathos of the body and soul with respect to an agitation or change (34a3–5). The participation of the soul in the agitation is what distinguishes it from the ἀναίσθησις, or unawareness of mere bodily agitation. This agitation of the soul cannot itself be the functioning of memory because in that case we could not distinguish between experience and memory. Even more drastically, αἴσθησις would be indistinguishable from memory. We would not experience but only remember that we experienced.

It sounds unintelligible to say that we do not experience but only remember that we have experienced. If one insists, however, that the present is an instant of clock time, then the assertion can be defended as follows.[1] An experience takes more than an instant. It is actually a sequence of instants. But this sequence is composed of just one present instant; all the rest must belong to the past. Experience is in fact holding together or synthesizing this sequence, virtually all of which is retained by memory. The argument would probably have to be modified to include anticipation of the future within the producing of an experience. But the diminishing of the present to a virtual nullity remains the consequence. My inclination is to say that the present is indeed different from if related to clock time or a measurable sequence of instants. Or perhaps it would be better to say that there are two senses of "the present," one corresponding to chronometric time and the other to lived time. In lived time, the present is an indefinite state defined as "taking note of." The chronometric present, on the other hand, is whatever unit of duration we are able, and choose, to measure with respect to our external environment and the appropriate instruments.

It would be false to say that Socrates does not allude to this situation. But he does so in such a way as to leave unexamined the nature of the present, as well as the act of consciousness that is characteristic of the present. Of course, he calls our attention to memory and anticipation, both of which take place in the present. But neither is directed toward the present, that is, toward what is within the present, namely, *presence* or παρουσία. Nor does Socrates emphasize that memory and anticipation occur within the present. He comes very close to allowing the present to disappear into the past and the future. This also makes it easier for Aristotle to speak of the present as "the now," which is not itself a part of time but a conceptual artifact with respect to which we attempt to divide the temporal flow. This use of an artifact for division is, however, a surrogate for the actual problem of how to locate the lived present. In other words, we ignore the actual problem and replace it with a theoretical construction. That this construction does not resolve the problem is obvious from the fact that no one lives in the "now" or "moment." Otherwise stated, the division of temporal flow results in the disappearance of the lived present, not in its capture or preservation in a concept. We cannot "live for the moment," although it is somewhat easier to carpe diem.

In our actual experience, we do not distinguish the present from the other tenses as a point of any kind. I have suggested that our awareness of the present can be initially described as a continuum or duration of time that is different from the moments of analyzed or clock time. It is as though we are living simultaneously in two different but related dimensions. One dimension is the measurable time of a flow of moments that can be counted with a degree of precision that is relative to our instruments. The basis-step is, of course, just the human soul that says, "now, now, now . . ." and in this way acquires the most rudimentary analysis of temporal flow. From an empirical standpoint, however, it would be false to say that each "now" is for us the present. Instead, we are within a present through which the stream of "now's" is passing. Neither is there any precise point at which the present disappears into the past or can be said to emerge from the future.

In my opinion, there is no temporal analysis of the lived present because all such analyses replace it with points, instances, or extratemporal references like "the now." We can describe the characteristics of the lived present, but this is because it has a complexity and duration that is entirely different from the punctuality of measured time. None of this appears in the *Philebus* or anywhere else in Plato. Instead, we have dramatic or mythical time or a kind of poetical timelessness such as that experienced when one is attending a play or the cinema. In the simplest case, we experience this time when someone is telling us a fascinating story. But so far as I can see, whereas Plato, as it were, immerses us within lived time in its dramatic, mythical, or poetic manifestation, he nowhere provides an account of its nature. The past is explicated by reference to memory and recollection, and the future by reference to expectation and hope. The present is represented by αἴσθησις, but this is almost immediately assimilated into the memory. Socrates does not explain even *which* function of the soul is agitated together with the body in the pathos of sense perception, although he implies that it is memory.

I have introduced these reflections on lived time because the discussion of memory and anticipation, and so of the three modes of temporality, are relevant to the story that Socrates is about to tell. To return to the text, Socrates is about to offer an account of how false judgments occur. As we shall see, this account is much more complicated than its counterpart in the *Theaetetus*. Socrates wishes here to establish the nature of false pleasure, and this will require the mediation of judgment, that is, of assertions to the effect that a certain pleasure is false. On the basis of the preceding part of the dialogue, it would seem to be better for Socrates to show that by "false pleasure" he means "a nongenuine or inauthentic pleasure." The judgments in question are those that originate in, or are associated with, sense perception. Socrates is not concerned here with judgments about purely intellectual pleasures, although there was a very brief reference, not developed, to the pleasure arising in the soul alone from the recollection of learning. The focus is upon pleasures that are plausibly identifiable as false in the sense of discreditable, that is, as evil or ugly. It is these judgments that directly concern the question of the good life.

Let us remind ourselves of the difference between the text we are now studying and the previous parts of the *Philebus*. In the analysis of pleasure, we are directly involved with the most important dimension of the question of the good life. The investigation of the good life is not the same as the analysis of the structure of pure form. From an ontological standpoint, it may be appropriate to refer to life as a mixture, but as lived, life is a unity. This is why Socrates begins with a story or dramatic representation of a man who is engaged in the effort to arrive at a correct judgment about sense perception. Otherwise put, we have to discover a way of analyzing human existence that does not destroy it or, let us say, conceal the very nature of what we are attempting to understand. The problem is not entirely different from that of the analysis of pure forms. Even in the latter analysis, we have to pick out the parts or constitutive elements without dissolving the whole. Still, there is a much better chance of reassembling the whole of a complex form from its detached elements than there is of reproducing human life from a collection of fragments or parts called memory, anticipation, pleasure, judgment, and so on. With all due acknowledgment of the need to understand through analysis, there is a deep sense in which life is understood in the living.

This difference between formal and existential analysis is related to the difference between the structural analysis of time, which is finally mathematical, and the qualitative description of human time. I do not mean to say that we should never analyze the faculties of the soul or the characteristics of life. The point is rather that these analyses must be controlled by the priority of the unity of life. We should therefore not lose sight of the dramatic personage whose experience Socrates is about to analyze. We are to imagine a man who frequently sees something at a distance and not at all clearly, and who wishes to decide what it is that he sees (38c5–7). The word translated as "decide," κρίνειν, means not merely to pick out or choose, but also to judge in the sense of separating the right from the wrong. The nouns "judge" and "critic" are thus related to one another. This is of considerable importance because it reveals a basis within the function of everyday cognition for the unity of reason and a sense of goodness or excellence. Even the opinions or beliefs of everyday life are expressions of a fundamental conviction that the correct identification of sensations is better than an incorrect identification, just as the successful resolution of an aporia is better than failure or a mistaken choice.

In sum, to the extent that reasoning is discerning or identifying or for that matter attempting to remove obstacles to our intentions—in other words, whether it is a primitive form of theory or practice—reason is choosing, and we choose on the basis of our desire to be correct or successful. The man we are observing is not interested in remaining in doubt about the identity of the object he sees unclearly, and he does not wish to misidentify it. This is not a trivial fact. When it is fully grasped, it provides us with a basis for overcoming the so-called fact-value distinction or the view that formal reasoning yields no implications for the nature of the good life. Even if this is accepted, however, there remains a further obstacle. We must be in a position to choose correctly, and this in turn depends upon our ability in fact to identify objects, or in other words upon their independence from as well as accessibility to the cognitive process by which we apprehend them. Even the Kantian must insist that although we construct the objects of experience from a transcendental standpoint, experience itself consists in the successful acquisition of scientific knowledge. And such knowledge depends upon the "objectivity" of the objects of perception.

The preceding remarks will suffice to sketch the general context within which Socrates studies the nature of perceptual judgment. In the first step of his account, the perceiver is alone and speaks to himself about his uncertainty concerning what he sees. It should at least be mentioned that Socrates begins this account with the temporary breakdown of perception, not with its ordinary successes. So long as there is no problem in identifying what we see, no questions about perception arise. The situation is quite different here from the wonder that is instilled in us by the regular and unceasing order of the heavens. Although we are immeasurably closer to ourselves than to the stars, the heavenly order is in a way more accessible. As so accessible, of course, it raises the question of the nature of the heavenly beings, and this question sooner or later unites with the problem of perception that we are now examining. Whether we turn initially outward toward the stars or inward within ourselves, the destination is aporia.

The hero of Socrates' story is perplexed about the identity of something he sees. Normally, we say that we see something when we can identify it. Even if we see colors or a pattern of light and shadow, we can identify these phenomena as sensations of such and such a sort. But we can also see *that* as well as *what*. I mean by this that we can see that something, we know not what, is within our visual field. If we are close enough to the object, we begin to distinguish what it might be from what it probably or even certainly is not. The sequence in our reasoning seems to be this. First, we ask ourselves, "Is there anything there?" And next we ask, "What is it?" In other words, even if we are startled by an unexpected sensation and ask, "What is that?" we are actually asking whether the sensation corresponds to anything that possesses an identity. The What is X? question cannot be asked or makes no sense until we have ascertained *that* there is something about which to ask it.

I can restate the previous point by observing that sense perception is coextensive with human awareness. There is no way to be aware of or to take note of something entirely apart from perception unless we are detached from our bodies. But in this case we are no longer alive, or, more cautiously, we are no longer living human beings. In the ordinary course of things, perception and so awareness means the process of noting that there are identifiable objects, of which we are familiar with a sufficient number to carry out our normal activities. Any kind of disruption in this process, unless it is momentary, shifts our attention from the acts we are performing to the unfamiliar object. We first attempt to identify the object by going through the "that/what" procedure. After a sufficient number of experiences of this sort, our attention is drawn to the faculty of perception itself.

The perceiver in Socrates' story has not reached that stage of reflection. He is presented to us in a familiar setting of everyday life. There is something just beyond the range of his ability to identify adequately what he is looking at. This obstacle causes him to speak. In other words, had there been no problem of identification, it is obvious that the man would not have asked, "What is it?" Nor do we normally identify to ourselves with explicitly formulated statements the objects that constitute the flow of our experience. Either we know what they are and thus identify them tacitly or we have no need to know what they are. When a certain object is required for a certain act and does not function properly, or when an unidentified object interferes with the regular flow of experience, we are stopped short, and the "that/what" sequence is generated.

This is reminiscent of, yet importantly different from, Heidegger's analysis of the tool world in *Being and Time* and his emphasis on the importance of a break in the web of relations constituting that world. For Heidegger, the decisive moment in human experience is when our practical activities are interrupted by a gap. Something we need in order to carry out a familiar activity, for example, a hammer, is missing. In the *Philebus* passage, the situation is different. The perceiver does not require to know either where he has put a tool or, so far as the story tells us, to identify the object that concerns him in order to effectuate some end. His interest in the identity of the object is theoretical. He wants to know, not where some absent object may be, but *what* it is at which he is looking. Heidegger's question, so to speak, is, "Where is it?" Socrates' question is, "What is it?" To this extent at least, we can see Socrates' emphasis upon presence and Heidegger's upon absence. But Socrates would say that we can ask, "Where is it?" only of something whose presence is familiar to us, something whose look we know and can identify. This identification is not compromised by, but is the basis for the fulfillment of, the desire to identify correctly, and so for the preference of truth over falsehood.

Our hero is then said to ask himself, "What is that thing that appears to be standing next to the rock under a tree?" (38c12-d3). I note first that the question about the unidentified object makes use of objects that are identifiable. Questions of perceptual identification occur within a field of familiar objects. The as-yet-unknown thing is standing; it is not walking or flying, and this already limits the range of possible identities, as does its location next to a rock and underneath a tree. The rock and the tree serve to fix our attention and to delimit the area of uncertainty. Furthermore, the participial τὸ φανταζόμενον, "the thing that appears," conveys two points. First, something shows itself or is a "phenomenon" in the positive sense of the term. Second, what shows itself is a phantasm (φάντασμα). That which shows itself does so in an illusory manner. It does not clearly identify itself. In this case, one should not say that the phantasm shows itself as something other than what it actually is because the perceiver has not yet mistaken the identity of the object. He has not yet identified it; there is an aporia, but not an error.

The perceiver may reply to his own question by saying that the phantasm is in fact a man, and in so doing, Socrates says, he "hits the mark" (ἐπιτυχῶς). Alternatively, he may move in the wrong direction, or be turned aside (παρενεχθείς) like an arrow that misses the target, and take the appearance to be an image of a man, a statue of some sort (ἄγαλμα) constructed by shepherds (38d5–10). The connection between perception and judgment has now been illustrated. There is a joint agitation of the body and the soul, to employ Socrates' previous terminology. The result of this agitation is that something that shows itself to be present produces in the perceiver a phantasm which he tries to identify. Nothing is said here about the memory. The perceiver is in direct contact with the phenomenon, even though he cannot identify it. But he has already identified the rock and the tree, and this would have been impossible if he had not remembered the looks of rocks and trees from previous experience. The memory is not mentioned because, when actually attempting to formulate a correct perceptual judgment, we do not invoke it. If I cannot see clearly what something is, I do not call upon my memory (or my recollection) to identify the object. The memory comes into play only after I have seen the look clearly and still cannot say what it is. This shows that there is a third stage besides seeing clearly and identifying correctly or incorrectly. It is possible for us to see clearly and still not know what we see.

In short, Socrates leaves unexplained, here and previously, how perception originates. The drama of the perceiver begins in medias res, with all faculties fully developed and experience itself already constituted through successful identifications of phenomena. Our story casts no light on the first identification. How could we identify anything unless we could speak, and how is it possible to speak if one does not already know a language, that is, unless one has already spoken? Socrates does not present a Chomskyan account of the genesis of language or any other account, for that matter. Even Theuth, who first sorted out sounds, must already have been able to formulate to himself the "What is that?" question as he examined what he was about to call vowels, consonants, and so on. Had the perceiver been unable to ask himself, "What is that?" or to request from himself a perceptual judgment, there would have been no perception. The analysis of perception in which αἴσθησις is placed prior to δόξα is thus misleading. The two can no more be separated or ordered temporally than can αἴσθησις and memory. The analysis of the faculties takes place in what might be called theoretical time, not in lived time. Eventually this leads to the misrepresentation of life by the analytical intelligence.

What is called in the story of the perceiver "hitting the mark" corresponds to the previous "taking note of" that must be an element of perception and that is the necessary precondition for the perception's being retained in the memory. I cannot repeat too frequently: *Perception does not begin as memory alone, understood as memorizing.* We remember things of which we were antecedently aware or things that are occurring now, but which can be memorized because they are independent of the act of memorizing. We must not, however, make the mistake of saying that "passing by" or "being averted from" corresponds to ἀναίσθησις. Strictly speaking, this would be true if in passing by, the perceiver had failed to observe the phantasm and thus came to no judgment at all rather than an erroneous one. Misidentification or erroneous perceptual judgment is like taking one thing for another. But because, as Socrates points out in the *Theaetetus,* we can mistake one thing for another only if we know both things, it is difficult if not impossible to explain how we confuse them.

So there is a disanalogy between the story and the immediately preceding account of sense perception, memory, and recollection. Curiously enough, the situation in Plato, at least so far, is the same as in Kant: neither philosopher can supply us with a successful explanation of false perceptual judgment. There is a second feature of the opening part of the story that is very suggestive. I call attention to the fact that Socrates speaks of "hitting the mark" and "passing by" instead of truth and falsehood or correctness and incorrectness. The question of the truth of the judgment will come up soon, but in a different stage of the story. Meanwhile, we can say that truth or correctness depends upon our hitting the mark in the sense of apprehending the object of perception in such a way that a judgment of identity or predication is possible. In order to say correctly that something is an instance of such and such a kind or that it possesses a certain property, we must grasp it in advance of picking out the identity or the property and not just by way of making the identification or attributing the property. If this were not so, then we could produce true judgments simply by asserting them. Correlatively, every judgment we asserted would have to be true.

In other words, the judgment is not true in a vacuum or by itself; it is true of an object. And a judgment is false if it does not fit the object. But we cannot determine whether the judgment is false simply by looking at the judgment itself. Instead, we have to see the object which the judgment misses or passes by. This viewing or hitting upon the object must not be prevented by the falseness of the judgment. Otherwise we could not know that the judgment is indeed false. There is no way in which to explain how we apprehend objects prior to formulating judgments about them, as is clear from the fact that what hits the mark or passes it by is itself a judgment. But perhaps we can distinguish between two kinds of judging, one of which is successful when it apprehends the object and thereby makes it accessible to judgments of the second kind. I admit at once that the distinction is extremely vague and that it may not be possible to sustain it. If Socrates had spoken of seeing the object or not seeing it, this would have been easier to understand. We could then have taken this as a reference to a kind of noetic intuition that hits or does not hit the object by grasping or not grasping its look or form. We cannot, however, rewrite the text to suit our convenience. I therefore leave it at noting a possible hint, in the terms just mentioned, of the prelinguistic component of perception, thanks to which we are able to make judgments about objects without first or at the same time producing those objects by the judgments themselves.

There is a parallel passage in the *Theaetetus* in which Socrates employs the same metaphor to describe false judgments. He speaks of the case in which a man knows both Theaetetus and Theodorus and is also perceiving them both but fails to connect his memory of their identities with the corresponding perception: "But like a bad archer, he shoots beyond the target and makes an error, and this is called "'false'"; that is, a false δόξα arises from the transposition of the two perceptions (193e6–194a4).

The cases in the two dialogues are not identical. In the *Philebus,* the problem is not to distinguish between the identities of two recognized persons, but to establish whether something is a person or not. Furthermore, the distinction in the *Theaetetus* between true and false perceptual judgment depends upon the memory (195c6ff), just as it does in the *Philebus*. It must nevertheless be granted that this passage allows for the identification of hitting the target with formulating a true judgment. In the *Theaetetus*, Socrates is simply too cryptic for us to find room for a completely satisfying interpretation. In the *Philebus,* Socrates goes into much more vivid detail, but this leads to the more nuanced presentation of difficulties, not to a satisfactory resolution of the underlying problem. The *Philebus*, for all its peculiarities, makes a space between the apprehension of the perceived entity and true or false judgments about that entity. In the *Theaetetus*, there is no such space. As a result, Socrates is more like Kant in the *Theaetetus* than he is in the *Philebus*. But he is very far in this dialogue also from being a traditional Platonist.

The problem I have just described is sometimes raised with respect to the correspondence theory of knowledge. According to this theory, a proposition is true if and only if it corresponds to the nature of the object. "Corresponds" means here something like "correctly expresses the identity or a certain property of the object." "Expresses" can be variously interpreted, for example, in a picture-theory of meaning. The structure of the proposition is then supposed to be a picture of the structure of the object. There is an obvious flaw in this theory. In order to determine whether the proposition corresponds to its object, we should have to apprehend the object independently of the proposition. In this case we would know the truth about the object without needing to invoke the proposition.

The reason this is a flaw is that the correspondence theory of truth identifies truth with a proposition. If one does not make this identification, then the consequence of the correspondence theory is that propositional or discursive truth is rooted in a deeper, prediscursive truth. I believe that the problem of false perceptual judgments strongly supports this way of viewing truth. But that does not mean that anyone, including me, is in a position to explain discursively the nondiscursive sense of truth. The best one can do is to defend that sense by *reductio* arguments showing the disastrous consequences of its not being accepted. If we do not accept it, we are left with a coherence theory of truth, which is unfortunately unable to prove that truth and coherence are the same or, in other words, that a coherent account is also true. This problem soon leads to conventional definitions of truth, or "true within a formal language," or something of that sort, that is, to the rejection of truth in its only interesting sense, namely, as the expression of what things are, regardless of whether or how we speak about them. As soon as we reject this sense of truth, we are left with art, as Nietzsche rightly saw.

One other point in the *Philebus* text adds to the confusion in that it seems to cut in two directions. Socrates has introduced the story about the phantasm in order to illustrate his contention that opinion or judgment and the act of forming a judgment, and so the distinction between true and false judgment, "arise in each case from memory and perception" (38b12–c1). Memory is not introduced into our story until after the perceiver has departed from the scene of the phantasm. This gives some support to the distinction between hitting or missing the mark and forming true or false judgments. On the other hand, immediately after describing the isolated perceiver's reaction to the phantasm, Socrates asks whether—and Protarchus confirms that—had someone been with the man, "he might speak aloud, thereby repeating to his companion what he had initially said to himself. And so arises a λόγος from what we had previously called δόξα" (38e1–5). By "previously," Socrates presumably refers to the immediate antecedent, in which the perceiver speaks to himself and thereby hits or misses the mark. In this case, "hitting or missing" must be synonymous with "making a true or a false judgment." I do not believe that it is possible to reconcile all the passages in our text into one coherent interpretation. Whether Plato is simply confused or is rather attempting to show us the inner intractability of the problem is irrelevant to its general philosophical implications.

In the first stage of Socrates' story, the perceiver is in the immediate presence of the phantasm, either by himself or with a companion. In the second stage, he is alone and retains for some time his account (διανοούμενος) to himself of the appearance. That is, he has been separated from the phantasm but retains it in his memory (38e6–8). As the participles ῥηθέντα and διανοούμενος show, discursive thinking is associated with sense perception at both stages. The difference between the two stages is that, during direct perception, there is no reference to the memory. We hit or miss the mark through the medium of speech, and we do so by identifying, not predicating. Let us suggest that this is a case of existential judgment that serves as the basis for predication, or what I previously called the that/what structure. Furthermore, in the first stage, there is no analysis of perception because it is like νόησις; the identification is that of a form. Analysis occurs only later, in the predicating stage.

A phantasm is what we may call an incomplete perception; it requires something further in order to shift from appearance to manifestation, namely, a correct identification. I suggest that something has been omitted in Socrates' account, namely, how we shift from the incomplete phantasm to the manifest and correctly identified perception. Platonism (as I am calling it) depends upon perceptual contact with the identity of a being that is not itself the product of vision or discursive speech. If the identity is produced by the combination of visual sensations and the judgment of identity, the result is proto-Kantianism. The metaphor of overshooting the target provides a hermeneutical space for us to infer the need for contact with a form that is not constructed by perceptual judgment, but it does not supply an explanation of how that takes place, let alone assert that it does.

We turn now to the second stage, in which the hero of our story is considering to himself what he has just seen (38e6–7). Although it is not explicitly stated, we may assume that this consideration involves the memory of the initial perception. Socrates asks Protarchus whether he agrees that the soul in this situation resembles a book (literally, a strip of parchment with writing on it: 38e9–14). At this point, Socrates shifts from a story, or an account of perception as it is experienced in everyday life, to a rudimentary version of what philosophers of science would today call a *model.* The root of the model is a simile: this is like that, in which "like" means "has a common structure." We shift from this to that because we believe that the latter will bring out more perspicuously the structure or function of the former, whether altogether or in part. It goes without saying that in most ways the soul is nothing like a book, any more than it is a structure of mathematical or chemical relations. There is, however, a crucial difference between a scientific model and a simile like the one Socrates employs. The scientific model makes the structure of the original more visible by freeing it from a particular physical realization, whereas a simile highlights a characteristic of the original by exhibiting the same characteristic in an unexpected context. The poet says to his beloved, "Thou art like a flower." Again, it is unnecessary to emphasize that girls are in almost all ways *unlike* flowers. But the bloom of a flower, its freshness, even its fragility may serve to accentuate analogous features in a girl, and all the more so because girls and flowers are otherwise so different.

Furthermore, the mathematical model takes us from the concrete realization with which we began to an abstract structure or set of abstract relationships, whereas the simile takes us from one concrete realization of a property or relation to another concrete realization. A flower is a flower, not a girl, and a book is a book, not the soul. But the relations in the mathematical model are intended to be the same in every relevant realization. More precisely, a realization is relevant if and only if it possesses the structure of the model. The structure is the same in all cases. But a simile is not an identity statement, and this affects the point of comparison. The properties being compared are *similar,* not identical. The simile works, not by persuading us that, say, a girl really is like a flower, but by suggesting that something about flowers illuminates in a psychologically effective manner something about girls. In some cases the simile may mislead us dangerously into exaggerating or overextending the sense in which one thing is like another, although there is little chance of that happening in the example of the flower.

How does the soul resemble a book? Unfortunately, Socrates' formulation is difficult to translate; one editor (Badham) has secluded a phrase in order to make things smoother, but Gosling retains the manuscript reading, and as a matter of principle, I follow him: "Memory falling together with perceptions into the same [thing] together with the affections (τὰ παθήματα) that occur in connection with these seems to me very much like writing statements (λόγους) into our souls. And when this affection (τοῦτο τὸ πάθημα: secluded by Badham) writes the truth, the result in us is true judgment and true statements. But when the writer within us writes falsely, the opposite to truth is the result" (39a1–7).

In the first place, a book is an artifact in two senses, both as a physical object and with respect to the writing it contains. In the simile, the λόγοι are artifacts of the part of the soul represented by the scribe. Λόγος means here "statement in a natural language," not ratio or ontological truth. Next, Socrates says that memory "falls together with" perceptions εἰς ταῦτὸν "into the same thing." This is in line with the previous interpretation of the memory as inseparable from the conscious element in sense perception; it also leaves unclear whether the memory *is* the conscious element of perception or acts in addition to the function by which perception takes note of something. Memory is the writer, that is, the function by which the soul records the παθήματα or agitations it undergoes together with the body. The written statement is thus not merely an artifact, but it must correspond to a natural condition or pathos of the soul, which in turn is the result of an external or bodily agitation.

In the second part of his simile, Socrates says that "this πάθημα" writes truly or falsely. The expression has caused confusion because the πάθος in question is now the writer, and so presumably it is the memory, whereas the previous παθήματα were the recorded agitations or the writings. We can perhaps understand Socrates to be calling attention here to the passive aspect of memory, which is a receiving or recording, and in this sense the undergoing of an imprint. As that part of the soul which receives bodily agitation, the memory is passive. As the part of the soul that records these agitations and so preserves them, it is active. What is especially interesting here is that perceptual judgments are both natural and artificial. In other words, whereas perception occurs through contact with rather than solely by the construction of objects, this "natural" apprehension must be mediated by the discursive act of the construction of a judgment that is either true or false. At this point, the language that we speak and through which we express our articulation of experience plays a role in the judging of the perception. And what linguists call natural languages are in fact historical or artificial. This is, so to speak, the window in Socrates' account of perception through which philosophers of language are able to gain entrance.

I will restate this point with an eye to the relation between Plato and Kant, who is the grandfather of the philosophy of language. On the one hand, the remembered impression must actually be occurring as it is being memorized, and indeed, it must exist independently of the operation of the memory. If this is not so, then perceiving is remembering and nothing more. In other words, the agitations or impressions are then themselves produced by the memory. On the other hand, the writer is a personification of the joint function of memory and perception or of the undergoing of agitations and the recording of them into true or false judgments. And this seems to make the process of discursive judgment coextensive with that of perception as agitation. The Socratic model or simile seems to be very similar itself to the Kantian model, according to which discursive rules or categories not only participate, but take the leading role, in the process of constituting objects, which act of constitution makes perception coextensive with, and inseparable from, a judgment.

In my opinion, the difference between Plato and Kant on this point is very small but nevertheless crucial. For Kant, truth is a predicate of judgments; it is not a real predicate. In my previous terminology, this means that "true" in Kant is synonymous with "correct" and does not extend to the ontological sense of "genuine" or "genuinely the case." This is obviously connected with the doctrine of the constitution of objects. Sensations or impressions in themselves lack all cognitive content for Kant. A perception differs from a sensation in that it is a judgment about the nature of an object, and an object is constituted from rules or categories imposing themselves onto sensations. Whereas one could say that the sensations somehow put us into contact with things in themselves, they do not do so in a cognitively significant way. There is no way in Kant to hit the mark of the object so as to allow us to formulate a judgment about it. To hit the mark is already to formulate a judgment. Unless there is a judgment, there is no mark to hit. Since to judge is to constitute the object, there is no explanation of false perceptual judgments. There are no explanations of false perceptual judgments in Plato either, or for that matter of true perceptual judgments, if by "explanation" one means a complete, consistent conceptual analysis of the structure of perceptual judgment. The most one could say is that in Plato stories and animated cartoons help us to formulate what must be the case if we are to account for experience as we actually live it.

To continue with the simile, the recorder or writer is now joined by another demiurge, the painter, who comes into existence in our souls at that time and who draws in our souls icons of what the writer has recorded (39b3–7). The writing is the process of memorizing the agitation that has entered the soul from the body. The picture is not, as one might have expected, the image of the perceived object but is rather of the statement or *logos,* in other words, the judgment about the object. I take this to mean that there is no preliminary intellectual apprehension of the look in the sense of the εἶδος or Idea that serves to ground sense perception and to allow for the difference between true and false judgments. Perception, so to speak, is on its own. And this makes the memorization process of central importance. The merely physical agitations are as meaningless in themselves as are sensations in Kant's doctrine. The soul gives significance to these agitations through the activity of the memory, which must include awareness or taking note of what it is recording. The writer, after all, is not scribbling; he is producing intelligible judgments that are either true or false.

One could say that a judgment is true if it hits the mark, but unfortunately, there seems to be no way independent of perception itself to know whether the mark has been hit. At 39b9ff, Socrates says that the perceiver (presumably the same person to whom he previously referred) can separate what was judged and said from sight or from any of the senses and can see icons of these in the inner eye. This again seems to mean that the icons are pictures of the discursive faculty of the soul, not of the senses. But it also implies that the senses are contributing something to the perception by themselves, namely, the agitations of the body. In sum, these agitations become part of a judgment and subsequently the originals of images only by passing through the memory. The images are like recollections, oddly enough, in that they bring to our attention memories rather than original sensations or agitations.

If Socrates had invoked the theory of Ideas at this point, he could have argued that sense perception occurs together with intellectual intuition of form. This intuition is sometimes obscured by the agitations of perception (as in the myth of the winged charioteer in the *Phaedrus*), and in these cases we formulate erroneous judgments about the object whose form we cannot accurately grasp. As it happens, he does not take this line of argument. The best one can do under these circumstances is to employ a *reductio* argument or try to show that unless we are in touch with objects in advance of the constructive activity of forming judgments about them, Platonism turns into Kantianism. Socrates employs no such argument. Instead, he gives us a story and a simile or protomodel, which the reader, who at least has more leisure than poor Protarchus, is left to interpret.

The painter produces images (εἰκόνας), not originals. To the extent that an original is present, it is the content of our memories or the sublated physical agitations or sensations. I mean by "sublated" that the content is immediately transformed into a judgment and is accessible to the perceiver—that is, the man who is the hero of the previous story—only in and as that judgment. In a formulation that reminds us of Derrida, and yet differs from him, writing is not prior to speech but rather *is* speech. Thinking is talking to oneself; hence the equation of thinking with writing does not establish a priority of writing over speech. Nevertheless, the Derridean can maintain that there is no priority of speech over writing and that what one says (the λόγος or δόξα) *is* a writing (the recording by the memory). On this basis, the two positions are one and the same. The only difference between them is which element of the identity we stress. Or perhaps we could say that there is also a speech with oneself in which one tries to decide what it would be best to write. This would be the awareness by which the memory takes note of what it records.

In the story of the perceiver, the man initially says to himself, "What is it that seems to be standing under the tree?" The verb, once more, is φανταζόμενον; the man is looking directly at the object under the tree, not, as in the simile, at icons of the recorded memory of the tree. This is an important difference. It also calls our attention to the fact that Socrates does not give a complete account of perception. Most important, he gives no account of a successful perceptual act. The perceiver looks at the object but sees a phantasm rather than the object itself. We are not told how he shifts from a phantasm to an identification via a true judgment. Nothing is said, apart from the cryptic hint in "hitting the mark," that would allow us to determine Socrates' position on the very heart of perception. As to the simile, it seems to tell us that the senses themselves, such as sight, are the original source of the apprehension of the object about which we judge or write (39b9-c1). The sequence is thus as follows: sense perception / memory / judgment / painting of icons.

One last point needs to be made about the simile. An icon is true or false depending upon whether it is of a true or a false judgment. So the truth or falsehood of the judgments is independent of and antecedent to that of the icons, which, to repeat, look like recollections, whereas the judgments are rooted in if not identical to memories. Icons either do or do not correctly portray judgments. But what do judgments portray, such that we can compare the copy with the original and say the copy is a true or false one, that is, correct or incorrect? There is no genuine response to this question in the *Philebus,* as we have now seen at length. It is not an answer to say that the judgments refer to sensations because at the level of sensation there is no object present, oddly enough, just as is the case for Kant.

So much for the analysis of perception. In closing, I want to emphasize the connection between that analysis and the theme of human temporality. The key link is the impossibility of presenting a structural analysis of the initiation of perception. To paraphrase Aristotle, in order to perceive, we must already have perceived. I am referring here to the accessibility of the object to the process of judgment (including identification), which accessibility must not itself be produced by that process. Otherwise stated, the most important step in the analysis of perception is memory. Socrates speaks as if memory is both taking note of, and hence in some sense identifying or judging, and recording material for the subsequent production of judgments that are themselves icons of the remembered agitation.

The act of viewing an object cannot take place in the past or the future; such "views" are called instead memory or recollection (making allowances for Socrates' distinction) on the one hand and imagination or expectation in the other. Furthermore, as Socrates' story brings out clearly, some present viewings are unsuccessful or result in phantasms. At this point, we do not memorize our uncertainty in such a way as to make a judgment; we are in a state of "willing suspension of belief" while we try to clarify our perception. But this attempt is itself characterized by the process of rational deliberation, that is, we make judgments in one sense, for example, about the context of the phantasm, and test judgments in another, that is, about the identity of the phantasm. No doubt the memory is involved in these complex operations, but it cannot be the same as or identical with all of them. In other words, Socrates defines the memory as both present awareness and preservation of the past. Judging is then left to recollection. But recollection recalls memories of past events. The net result is that judgment about the present is in fact judgment about the past. The present as present is rendered inaccessible by the very processes that are supposed to interpret it.

Chapter 6 Forms, Elements, and Categories

One of the curious features of analytical philosophy in the middle and late decades of the twentieth century was the widespread conviction that Wittgenstein had performed an original and epoch-making task by demonstrating (if that is not too strong a word) the impossibility of systematic philosophy, and indeed, of philosophy itself in any but a destructive sense. This enterprise is as old as philosophy itself. Actually there are two enterprises here, since the repudiation of systematic philosophy is not the same as the repudiation of philosophy. This is apparent from the Platonic dialogues, in which Socrates argues simultaneously that philosophy depends upon knowledge of the pure forms known ever since as Platonic Ideas, and that knowledge of these Ideas, in the proper sense of the term, is impossible. Yet he never rejects the possibility of philosophy itself. It follows that he must accept knowledge of Ideas in some improper or unusual sense of the term. This is again obvious from the dramatic form of the dialogues as well as from the importance of myths in the case of the three great unities or totalities of cosmos, city, and soul.

The correct interpretation of Wittgenstein is as much a matter of dispute as that of Plato. I am not a specialist in Wittgenstein and mention him only to put into a contemporary context the main points of the present essay, which originated as a talk delivered at an international conference on categories, sponsored by the Centre National de Recherches Scientifiques of France and the Basque University in San Sebastián, Spain, in 1993. The official occasion was the awarding of an honorary doctorate to René Thom, the great mathematician and systematizer of catastrophe theory. Speakers from many countries and with a wide range of specialties were invited to talk about the question of categorial explanation. I defended the view that it is impossible to devise a table of categories adequate to articulate the structure of the totality of experience. It goes without saying that the topic is in no way commensurate with the brevity of the essay, but I wished to make a general point, in however introductory a manner, about the main theme of the conference. The point is that the impossibility of systematic philosophy has nothing to do with the impossibility of philosophy, or for that matter with the construction of ad hoc categories useful for a wide range of purposes.

The proceedings of the conference were published in a volume entitled Actas del Primer Congreso Internacional de Ontología, *edited by Victor Gómez Pin (Bellaterra: Publicaciones de la Universidad Autónoma de Barcelona, 1994). My essay is on pages 357–62.*

My thesis is quite simple: However useful the development of categorial schemata may be on an ad hoc basis, it is a philosophical error to attempt to impose a table of categories onto the totality of experience. As a corollary to this thesis, I would suggest that the discovery of order is to a certain extent a consequence of production and is therefore at least partly relative to human intention. An excessive insistence upon the comprehensive adequacy of this or that categorial table leads invariably to disappointment, whether through internal difficulties or the discovery of new modes of order, often through a change in intentions. The consequence of this disappointment is a tendency to exaggerate the subjective or perspectival nature of order, an exaggeration that culminates in the ultimately vitiating reduction of discovery altogether to production or, in a contemporary idiom, in the reduction of identity to difference.

From this standpoint, the informal procedure of Aristotle, who does not provide us with a rigorous justification of his categories, is preferable to the illusory arithmetical precision of Kant or to Hegel's ostensibly comprehensive dialectico-speculative development of the totality of conceptual structure. Aristotle's rather casual enumeration of his categories does not weaken but instead strengthens their plausibility as an articulation of everyday experience. They are elicted from a commonsensical inspection of the accessible structure of independent entities, and we are free to add to their number if we happen to find others that he has overlooked.

In the German tradition, on the other hand, one encounters a transcendental adaptation of the axiomatic method that is at the same time a generalized version of the Cartesian attempt to master nature by rule-governed thinking. But rules are abolished as well as passed, and alternative axiomatizations of intelligible structure are always possible. The fundamental difficulty is to be found in Kant's doctrine of the autonomy and spontaneity of pure reason and categorial understanding. Kant insists that rational thought actualizes spontaneously as the rules of necessity, whether Ideal, categorial, or conceptual. But by rendering necessity spontaneous, Kant makes it indistinguishable from possibility.

I suggest that the origin of historical ontology in German Idealism can be understood precisely as the attempt to articulate the inner identity between necessity and possibility, and that the fullest statement of this attempt is to be found in Hegel's *Wissenschaft der Logik*. The collapse of Hegel's claim to absolute knowledge in the historicisms of the left-Hegelians, Dilthey, and Nietzsche constitutes the admission of the unsustainability of the concept of spontaneous necessity, although this same claim, in more than one way, was made again in our own century by Heidegger and was again repudiated by the postmodernists, deconstructors, and hermeneuticists of the past generation.

The history of category theory in Western philosophy is thus something like a parabola that emerges from the action-centered thinking of everyday life and moves upward toward increasing conceptual rigor, only to begin its gradual descent into the chaos of what Heidegger, citing Hölderlin, calls "*dieser dürftiger Zeit.*" I cannot resist mentioning, although mathematics is not my specialty, that the repudiation of the Hilbert program by Gödel's limitation theorems led to an explosion of technical genius in the foundational disciplines of mathematics, but an explosion that is based upon the triumph of contingency over necessity, and thus to a tacit rejection of the grand philosophical schemes of the founding fathers of mathematical logic and set theory. Just as in the earlier but parallel case of Hegel, the collapse of an excessive claim on behalf of pure reason led to the celebration of technical multiplicity, and so to the death of philosophy.

So much for my general thesis. I want to go back now to certain fundamental aspects of Greek thought and to show how the seeds of what I have called the parabolical path of category theory are to be found in the origins of Western philosophy. Once again I can state the main point in a rather simple manner.

Of the two greatest ancient philosophers, Plato is closer to everyday experience and farther from the development of technical terminology than is Aristotle. There is accordingly no doctrine of categories in Plato; what is normally regarded as the decisive technical aspect of Platonic thinking, the doctrine of Ideas, takes us in quite a different direction.

Unfortunately, or so it seemed to Aristotle, this direction is one of silence rather than of discursive knowledge. The doctrine of categories is a generalization on the preliminary discussions of predication to be found in the Platonic dialogues, a generalization intended to render articulate the Platonic Idea by transferring its ontological location from the mythical hyperuranian domain of Platonism to its actualization within the intellect that becomes all things.[1] Aristotle assumes that as so present within thinking, the form is now accessible to discursive determination.

As I am about to suggest, however, Aristotle does not succeed in overcoming the inner silence of Platonism; instead, he replaces the unity of the species-form, which is given via perception or definition or by some other, never identified method,[2] with the discursively accessible structure of the combination of form and matter he calls primary *ousia* in chapter 5 of the *Categories*. In a word, Aristotle never succeeds in applying his categories to Being in the genuine sense of the species-*eidos,* the successor to the Platonic Idea. The Being of secondary ousia or the species-eidos is not at all being qua being in the sense of the categorial schematism exemplified by a primary ousia as bearer of values from the remaining categories. The Platonic Idea is like the Aristotelian species-eidos insofar as it is given to intellectual perception, and not by way of predicative or analytical reasoning. The unity of the eidetic elements of the Platonic Idea is thus like the "belonging" (*huparchein*) of the *kath' hauta* elements of an Aristotelian ousia or species-eidos. Curiously enough, "being" in this sense, and not in the sense of the scheme of predication, is "given," in a way quite reminiscent of the Heideggerian "es gibt" or "Er-eignis."

I turn now to the elaboration of these suggestions. The classical Greek words "eidos" and "*katēgoria,*" which stand at the foundation of the Western tradition of metaphysics and ontology, may be translated literally as "look" and "accusation," respectively. These words point out two distinguishable but closely related responses to the items of our everyday life. More precisely, they suggest that metaphysics and ontology are rooted in our responses to those items that can be identified as self-subsistent, alive, and fully or partly responsible for their actions. The same general inference seems to follow from the word "*genos,*" literally "race," "family," or "offspring." Things belong to the same genos if they can breed together. Things possessing the same look or eidos may be said to belong to the same genos; the terms "eidos" and "genos" are used inter-changeably in Plato. The logical distinction between genus and species is a later sense and no longer implies interbreeding.

In sum, the look or family of a living being determines its *phusis*, not simply "nature" but, in keeping with the old etymologies, its "growth" or "emergence" into the light of visibility. This emergence is in the primary sense generation. What happens is determined by, and in that sense relative to, the family look, which in turn enables us to determine whether beings of that look may be held responsible for their actions, and so whether it is legitimate to level accusations against them when these actions violate custom, law, or, more simply, our welfare, whether common or individual. Accusation or guilt is subsequent upon identification.

If we take together *phusis,* eidos, genos, and katēgoria it seems that the root conceptions of philosophy are derived from the activity of living beings, and in the first instance, of human beings and their gods. This in no way contradicts the thesis that philosophy in its mature form extends these conceptions to the apprehension and analysis of the structure of any being whatsoever. In response to the thesis that philosophy begins in wonder at the heavenly motions, in other words, at the order and beauty of the cosmos, I reply as follows.

The order, beauty, and purposiveness of the cosmos are taken initially as evidence that it is a living being who is responsible or cares for us; the subse-quent distinction between the practical and the theoretical life, even in Aris-totle's relatively sharp version, nevertheless defines theory as the highest form of *praksis,* or as what we can call its limit-case, in which our desire to live a divine life and thus to approximate to the divine *noēsis tēs noēseōs* is an expression of the goodness or blessedness of theory.[3] In this specific sense, there is a unity between theory and practice, a unity not of categorial structure but of truth and excellence. Human desire and human intentions thus play a shaping role in the determination of order, the act that underlies the development of categories.

Praksis is impossible without reflexivity. We cannot recognize beings whose looks are the same as or other than our own unless we have already recognized ourselves. On the other hand, to point out the obvious origin of classificatory terms in reflection upon divine and human activity, and primarily of generative activity, is not the same as to attribute a doctrine of protosubjectivity to the first philosophers, or, in closely related terminology, to deny the distinction between philosophy and poetry.

There is no reason to assume in advance that we cannot distinguish between

genuine and deceiving looks; the very notion of deceit or error is itself dependent upon genuine identifications and sound accusations. Human beings do
not look like horses or oxen, and we can say that a mistake has been made in
counting the elements of a collection only because we know how to arrive at the
correct sum. To say that principles of order are relative to the ordering intelligence is no more relativism than to say, with Aristotle, that method is relative
to the nature of the investigation. There is no order without intelligence.

To come back now to "eidos" and "katēgoria," eidos or its close relative
idea is the central theoretical term for Plato, whereas Aristotle supplements
his teacher's doctrine of eidos with his own doctrine of katēgoria, that is, of
categories and predication. In the Platonic dialogues, the initially apprehended look or eidos is given two principal and quite different senses. For
purposes of convenience, I will distinguish these as the phenomenological
and the ontological sense. By the phenomenological sense I refer to the look
that permits us to identify distinct entities of experience such as a man, a
woman, a horse, a cow, a tree, but also properties of these entities such as
beauty, justice, or temperance, as well as relations like largeness and small-
ness. By the ontological sense I mean the looks of elements of looks, such as
one, many, same, other, but also of states or relations of looks, such as rest,
motion, being, and nonbeing.

This very general distinction shows that instead of categorial analysis, Plato
emphasizes the sensible or intellectual perception of paradigms and their structural elements. Same and other, for example, are not categories but distinct
elements or beings. A category or predicate is a concept or interpretation of
something; there is thus a link between the existing element or property and
discursive thinking. But the constituent elements of Platonic forms are not
concepts, and their only link with discourse, so long as we restrict ourselves to
grasping them as independent entities, is in the act of naming them. This is
apparent, for example, in the account of eidetic arithmetic in the *Philebus*
(16c5ff), where we are told to analyze an Idea into its finite number of eidetic
components; no methodological instruction is provided other than to look at
the Idea.

This is not predicative or analytical discourse but something like Cartesian
intuition of the parts of a whole. Analytical discourse about formal elements is
impossible except through their *koinōnia* or *sumplokē,* in other words, through
their combination. But if they combine, then they are no longer eidetic elements. The weaving together of concepts by means of language is not the same
as the interwovenness of the formal elements about which we are attempting to

speak. And if the elements are not themselves woven together, then our speech is inaccurate.

Let me emphasize the main point. The phenomenological looks do not direct us toward a doctrine of categories in the sense of a list of general types or properties coextensive with the structure of being and intelligibility. The Idea of the ox may be responsible for the existence of the oxen grazing in the fields, but we learn nothing more about the general properties of beings, or of Being altogether, from the apprehension of phenomenological Ideas than we do from the perception of instances of each phenomenological type. The ontological looks or elements of phenomenological Ideas, although they are not categories and certainly not concepts, do achieve a higher level of generality, but there is no way to draw them into language except by transforming them, to adapt a Platonic metaphor, from letters into syllables and words.

This can also be expressed as the transformation of Plato into Hegel. The elements of looks as looks, such as being, same, other, rest, and motion, may be intuitable and nameable, but as I have just noted, they cannot be discursively described in themselves, that is, each as separate from the others. To give only a single example, being, as itself, is the same as itself and other than the other elements. We can of course refer by name to one or another of these ontological elements, but naming is not the same as describing the nature underlying the name. Every analysis of the element "being" depends upon sameness and otherness as ingredient within that element, not as attached to it by predicative discourse.

It does not follow from these considerations, however, that Hegelianism contains the solution to our problems. Hegel overcomes the separation of the formal elements by assuming in advance that they are modes or categories of a single, comprehensive concept. Every attempt to describe a mode or category in isolation from the others leads to the endless and circular process by which we describe the transformation of one element into another, with the progressive accumulation of structure, in such a way that to attempt to describe any element is in fact to describe the whole, which is not itself a category but a process of category formation.

In Hegel's technical terminology, the key point is the identity of the thing *an sich* and *für uns*. This goes entirely beyond the Aristotelian linkage between intuited formal structure and its discursive analysis; it is a synthesis of Aristotle and Kant. Such a synthesis, as I noted earlier in this essay, carries with it the aporia of spontaneity or the requirement that freedom be defined as the identity of necessity and possibility. In more accessible language, it requires a self-exhibition of completeness or circularity, in order to guarantee that the transformation of one category into another is not the substitution of one historical perspective for another.

A failure to solve this aporia leads to the doctrine that every articulation of categorial structure is a tentative or temporary conceptual "carving up" of experience, to employ a Wittgensteinian expression, an articulation that depends upon our angle of perception if not upon our life-forms and linguistic conventions. I am not the only person who has noticed a certain similarity between Wittgenstein and Heidegger with respect to the linguistic perspectivism of the former and the latter's doctrine of historicity or the event of Being. One of the main purposes of this essay is to suggest that late modern historicism in both its ontological and linguistic versions is prepared unintentionally by Aristotle's doctrine of categorial predication.

And this brings me back to Plato, whose doctrine of forms leads us toward the silence of intellectual perception at the level of the ontological looks, and to the relativity and contingency of sensuous perception at the level of the phenomenological looks, but certainly not toward a conceptual articulation of the categorial structure of the whole. Aristotle attempts to overcome silence and contingency by bringing the intuited form into direct contact with discursive thinking. In so doing, however, he is led to introduce, whether intentionally or not, an implicit distinction between being as indeterminate and inaccessible to discursive or predicational discourse, and the being qua being of the doctrine of the categories.

In Aristotle, the perception or intellectual apprehension of the eidos, or family look, is of course also fundamental.[4] But the eidos is subordinated for analytical purposes to the katēgoria, or types of accusation that one may level against self-subsistent entities. The eidos itself becomes an accusation. In more accessible language, it is "predicated of" but does not itself admit of predication. To katēgorein is to say something of something, and the "something" in the first of these cases is classified under one or another of the terms constituting the table of categories.[5] Corresponding to the subject is the combination of form and matter, or primary ousia, namely, the self-subsistent entity.[6] A species-eidos or secondary ousia is said of the primary ousia or combination of form and matter.[7] The other categories contain predicates or the discursive or conceptual expression corresponding to a property of the primary ousia.

In sum, from the standpoint of predication, the species-eidos is silently present exactly like the Platonic Idea; it is both entirely familiar and entirely inaccessible to demonstrative knowledge. The classification of the eidos as belonging to a primary ousia or subject (for example, "This is a man") must precede, and cannot be determined by, the subsequent identification of the properties or predicates of which the ousia is accused. As Aristotle insists, there is no predication in the definition of the ousia, no before and after, that is, no relation of owner and property.[8] This amounts to the assertion that there is no predication within the act of grasping the species-ousia. The genus and the difference that constitute the ousia must therefore be given in advance to the discursive intelligence. Afterward, of course, one may predicate the elements of the species-ousia to the subject or primary ousia, for example, "animal" of man.[9]

Otherwise put, we have a tripartite structure of the species-ousia, the primary ousia and essential properties, and the accidents. But the unity of the structure, although presumably exhibited or given to *nous,* is not captured in the discursive articulation of the parts of the structure. Aristotle introduces the schema of owner and properties as the basis of a supposed clarification of the Platonic doctrine of eidos, but in such a way as to leave unanalyzed, no doubt because it is unanalyzable, the underlying sense of "belonging" by which the structure of owner and properties is defined. The relation of belonging is grounded in the unity of the intuition of the eidetic ousia as given to prediscursive thinking. There is thus a discontinuity that remains between the repudiation of the Platonic Ideas as "mere sound" or else as irrelevant to apodictic predication, and predication itself.[10] Occupying the space of that discontinuity is the unity of the elements of the *ti esti,* or species-form.

This unity is the silent presence of Being understood as the prepredicative *hupokeimenon,* or as one could say the origin, of ousia and *sumbebēkota,* whether essential or accidental. And this is the ancestor of the Heideggerian Being that presents itself as absent or as veiled over by the entities or beings whose structure is accessible to predicative discourse. But this also gives rise to the linguistic or nominalistic tradition of emphasis, whether positive or negative, upon predication, in view of the invisibility or inaccessibility to discursive speech of the substance (which Locke calls a "je ne sais quoi"). Both branches of this tradition may be said to culminate in various nineteenth-century doctrines of historicism and perspectivism, of which the teachings of Nietzsche and the later Wittgenstein constitute the currently most influential varieties.

We can now see that the original emphasis upon reflexivity or, in other words, the original tendency to devise schemas of classification on the basis of *praksis,* that is, intentional activity, as exhibited in the literal meanings of words like "eidos," "genos," "katēgoria," and so on, combined with the natural desire to render as determinate as possible our discursive grasp of the structure of intelligibility, resulted in the separation of Being from beings on the one hand and, on the other, the gradual triumph of linguistic nominalism and conventionalism over all forms of metaphysics and transcendental philosophies.

To conclude, there is an intrinsic instability in the primordial unity of theory and practice, which instability I symbolize by the term "production." The active dimension of thinking leads it to devise artifacts for the fulfillment of human intentions, which artifacts inevitably replace the initial beings toward which our intentions or desires were directed; and this in turn leads to the modification of our intentions and desires. The correlative attempt to master silence by speech, which is a necessary aspect of human activity, produces a world-structure, often derived from or represented as a table or schema of categories, that exhibits order at the price of cutting us off from the source of our creativity. The necessity of limitation, like Kant's spontaneous rules, is thus at the mercy of chaos.

Chapter 7   *Technē* and
the Origins of Modernity

This essay was written for the Symposium on Science, Reason, and Modern Democracy, held at Michigan State University during the academic year 1989–90. The proceedings were published by Cornell University Press in 1993 under the title Technology in the Western Political Tradition, *edited by Arthur M. Melzer, Jerry Weinberger, and M. Richard Zinman. My essay is to be found on pages 69–84. In the traditional account of the origins of the modern worldview reference is regularly made to the Platonic influence on the great mathematician philosophers of the Renaissance and early modern epoch, for whom the universe was a book written in the language of mathematics. Without wishing to deny or even to qualify this account, I wanted to add another important dimension to the discussion. There is a strong element of constructivism in Plato's thought and, in particular, in his political philosophy. This element is closely connected to the ambiguous relation between human beings and nature. In this essay, I make the point that is developed at length in my book* Plato's Statesman: The Web of Politics *(New Haven: Yale University Press, 1995). The city is a human construction having as its primary purpose the defense of human beings against a nature that is very far from being entirely friendly to our survival. Whereas human beings possess natures, the citizen, that is to say, the city, is a work of human art. It is of course true that the city answers to a natural need; in that sense, Plato would accept the Aristotelian definition of human beings as the political animal. But the expression of this nature is already a manifestation of what Hegel calls the "inner tear" (innere Zerrissenheit) in human self-consciousness. The Platonic image for the political art is weaving; webs are artifacts designed to protect the body against the rigors of nature. This is the basis for the subsequent application of* technē *by early modern thinkers, not simply to "produce" citizens by weaving together natural types that are separate by nature, but to apply* technē *to the task of preserving us from the hostile dimension of the cosmos.*

In this essay, I make a suggestion about the role of Platonism in the development of the modern epoch. It has become quite common to find in the scholarly literature the claim that such originators of modernity as Copernicus, Kepler, Galileo, and Descartes were influenced by Plato's geometrical cosmology. According to this view, the mythical description of the cosmos as constructed from a variety of pure geometrical figures, which Plato records in the *Timaeus,* is the prototype for the late Renaissance and early modern conviction that philosophy is written in the book of nature in the languages of mathematics.

This language, as Galileo puts it, consists in characters that are triangles, circles, and other geometrical figures.[1] Those who, like Ernst Cassirer, Alexandre Koyré, and E. A. Burtt, see in this and similar texts the influence of Platonic metaphysics on the founders of modernity take the passage just cited to refer to the presupposition of a mathematical ontology. The ontological thesis has been challenged by other scholars, among them Stillman Drake and, more recently, Gary Hatfield.

Drake denies that Galileo's science owes anything to the philosophers: "All the documents from his early years at Padua indicate his interest in technological rather than philosophical questions."[2] Hatfield contends that Galileo alludes not to a mathematical ontology but to those properties of natural beings that lend themselves to scientific knowledge: "Mathematics is the language, not of the universe, but of philosophy."[3] Hatfield buttresses his interpretation by citing the *Letter on Sunspots,* in which Galileo tells us to "forsake essences and focus on geometrical properties."[4]

This disagreement between the two sets of scholars suggests that Galileo was either a theoretical Platonist or a practical engineer and scientist for whom philosophy was of interest, if at all, from an epistemological rather than a Platonist standpoint. This disagreement may be generalized over most if not all of the founders of modernity.[5] The alternative is theoretical Platonism or an apparently un-Platonic empiricism, with the latter connected to a mathematical epistemology.

My suggestion leaves this controversy unresolved. It is designed instead to broaden the perspective within which we attempt to account for the origins of modernity. The suggestion is this: Whether or not Galileo and the other founders of modernity were theoretical Platonists, their emphasis on production is entirely compatible with the Platonic dialogues. In a somewhat more elaborate form, I suggest that the difference between Plato and Aristotle with respect to the classification of the arts and sciences has a role to play in the background to the emergence of the modern epoch.

This course leads me to deny, or at least to qualify, the customary opposition, as stated by Koyré, that whereas mathematical physics finds its ancestry in Plato, the claim that physics is built directly upon experience and sense perception is Aristotelian.[6] I am not proposing to deny the link between Aristotle and scientific empiricism. The difference between Plato and Aristotle that interests me here does not concern the role of experience in natural science but rather the relation of production to practice.

In the Platonic dialogues, we regularly find classifications of the arts and sciences in terms of whether or not they issue in the production of a separate artifact. Such sciences as arithmetic and geometry produce nothing but discover the natures of mathematical beings; following Plato's terminology, let me call these the theoretical or "acquisitive" sciences. Other forms of knowledge lead to the production of artifacts, as in the case of such arts as carpentry and shoemaking. Plato calls these the "productive" *technai.*

As is obvious from the distinction between theory and production, the Platonic dialogues do not distinguish a third group of practical arts and sciences. Plato does not group ethics and politics as a distinct family that is neither theoretical nor productive. Strictly speaking, there is no ethical virtue in Plato, as is evident from the *Republic.* I here limit myself to the citation of two crucial passages.

In 6. 500d4–8, Socrates says that the philosopher "makes" or "fashions" (*plattein*) not only himself but "temperance, justice, and all of demotic virtue" as copies of the Ideas. In 7. 518d9ff., he explains that, with one exception, what are called virtues are closer to the body than to the soul and are produced by custom and exercise (*ethesi kai askēsesin*). The exception is the virtue of *phronēsis,* or intelligence, which is altogether more divine than the others.

The distinction between the genuine or philosophical virtue and the demo-tic or vulgar virtues is equivalent to the distinction between intelligence and what Aristotle calls the ethical or practical virtues. Plato makes no distinction between theoretical and practical intelligence at the level of philosophy. Instead, he distinguishes between theoretical and productive uses of intelligence. In the light of this distinction, politics is a productive rather than a purely theoretical art.

I say that politics is not "purely" theoretical in order to capture an ambiguity in the Platonic texts. This ambiguity may be illustrated by a reference to the dialogue *Statesman*. The main spokesman of this dialogue, the Eleatic Stranger, engages in a long, extremely tangled discussion full of obscure divisions and containing an equally obscure myth, the upshot of which is to treat politics as both theoretical and productive. The initial distinction of the sciences and arts is between the practical and the gnostic. The gnostic technai are stripped of *praxis;* they produce nothing, neither *pragmata* nor *erga,* that is, neither things nor deeds. The practical technai such as carpentry and the handicrafts help to complete bodies that did not previously exist (258d4-e7).

The following question now arises: Where does Plato classify politics? According to the official diaeresis of the *Statesman,* it lies within the gnostic branch, although the Stranger contradicts himself by placing it first within the purely critical or discriminatory subbranch (260b3) and later in the *epitactic* subbranch, that is, among such arts as architecture, which command or arrange in an order (292b9).

Commanding arts like architecture do not themselves produce but rather give orders for production. Politics is such an art and therefore exemplifies what one may call the intersection between theory and production, but not at all what Aristotle is the first to call practice. This is why the art of weaving plays a central role as a paradigm of the art of the statesman (for example, 305e2ff.). But weaving is a productive, not a theoretical art. We could say that weaving is instrumental to *phronēsis,* which is identified as the royal or political art par excellence (293c5ff.). But we should note that the concluding summary of the dialogue begins with the assertion that we are speaking of the "synthetic sciences" and their *pragmata,* that is, their practical productions (308b1off.).

These practical productions are, of course, both the city and its citizens. The materials from which the statesman weaves the web of the city are human beings (308d1). It belongs exclusively to the statesman and good lawgiver, acting on behalf of the Muse of the royal art, to produce (*empoiein*) within the souls of correctly blended citizens of diverse natures the true doxa (309d1ff.). And this is also the doctrine of Plato's most famous and comprehensive discussion of the relation between philosophy and politics, namely, the *Republic*.

It would take me too far afield to illustrate with detailed citations the productive nature of philosophical politics in the *Republic*. Having already done this elsewhere,[7] I restrict myself here to the general statement that in the *Republic* Socrates regularly refers to the activity of the philosopher-kings as poetic or demiurgic (for example, 3. 394b9-c1: the guardians are restricted to being demiurges of the freedom of the city). The productive nature of politics also follows from the sickness of the human soul (*Gorgias* 505a6ff.), that is, the rule by nature of desire over spiritedness and intelligence, in the terms of the *Republic*, which must be corrected by the medicinal art of philosophy.[8] The city, in other words, particularly the healthy city, does not exist by nature. It must be produced by a theoretico-productive art whose paradigms include weaving and medicine.

The true statesman does not produce directly, but indirectly, either by formulating laws and customs (as in the *Republic*) or by ruling over those who are capable of producing a city of virtuous citizens (as in the *Statesman*). The reason it is necessary to produce the city is that man is naturally defective, even sick; this defect or illness can be cured, or else contained, by the art of weaving together human beings whose natural differences correspond to the warp and woof of a cloak, blanket, or other woven artifact.

In the *Statesman*, theoretical production is not addressed to the mastery of the cosmos but rather to the therapy or care (*therapeia, epimeleia*) of human beings. This care is illustrated by the paradigm of weaving, particularly the weaving of wool into various shelters or garments for protecting the body against the rigors of nature (279c7). In sum, politics is a theoretico-productive art that corrects nature or supplements it with artifacts for the protection of human beings. Politics is both productive and defensive. I can now express the fundamental difference between the ancients and the moderns in political terms. The ancients construct tools as a defense against nature; the moderns subscribe to the thesis that the best defense is a powerful offense.

By putting the point in this way, I do not at all intend to overlook or minimize the importance of radical new discoveries in mathematics, physics, engineering, and the other natural sciences. But even if these discoveries were all made independently of more general philosophical reflection, which I doubt, it remains true that the coordinated plan to employ them for the safety and increased comfort of the human race, and still more fundamentally to make humankind the master and possessor of nature, is political in the comprehensive sense of that term.

In this light, one may suggest that the incomplete separation of theory from production in Plato, as well as the absence of a distinct buffer zone of the practical, makes it easy to conceive of the fundamental paradigm of the modern revolution: a theoretically articulated project, initiated by the human will, to transform human life through the instrumental mastery of nature. This is much closer to the Platonic paradigm of philosophy as the unity of theory and practico-production, which culminates in the prophetic or lawgiving activity of the philosopher, than it is to the Aristotelian paradigm of theoretical philosophy as independent from practice, and of both as independent from production.

The modern epoch does not originate in a shift from Aristotelian theory to a production that is equally Aristotelian in its distinctness from practice. It would be more accurate to say that modernity originates in a shift from the Aristotelian tripartition of the arts and sciences to a revision of the Platonic model in which, despite the fundamental distinction between knowing and making, the lines separating theory, action, and production are tangled and blurred. The tangled state of these lines thus constitutes a genuinely Platonic presupposition for the eventual assimilation of theory into practico-production in the modern epoch.

Let me emphasize that I am not attempting the anachronistic task of making Plato into a modern, and I have not forgotten the differences between Platonic *theōria* and modern constructive theory. My suggestion is intended to broaden the terms within which discussion of the origin of modernity takes place. Hitherto it has been popular, even in the face of recent criticism, to present the origin of modernity as a renaissance of Plato's mathematical *theōria*. I leave this claim as it stands, suggesting instead that the deeper influence of Platonism on early modernity is practico-productive.

One more reference to the *Republic* may serve as an effort to clarify and sharpen this suggestion. In book 10, Socrates observes that there are three technai that pertain to all other arts: using, making, and imitating. Of these three, it is the technē of the user that determines the excellence, beauty, and rightness of everything that is made or that exists by nature (601d1ff.). The user is, of course, man, and the useful is relative to human intentions, which are independent of the mathematical or eidetic structures of things even if conditioned by them.

The subordination of making and imitating to usefulness is the core of the union between production and practice. It is no doubt true that in Plato human intentions are subordinated to the natures of things, and also to human nature. But this in itself does not constitute a difference between Platonism and modernity. It will take several centuries for the subordination of form and essence to mathematics, and of mathematics to the human will, to dissolve the Platonist assumption of the founders of modernity that science discovers rather than makes the natural order.

One of the crucial steps in this process, in my opinion, is a shift in the understanding of happiness. Here again I believe that I see the subterranean influence of Platonism at work. According to Aristotle, happiness is possible not only for the theoretical man but also for the practical man, albeit in two distinct senses. In Plato the possibility of happiness is considerably more obscure. Because there is no ethical or practical virtue apart from theoretical virtue, and if happiness depends upon perfection, that is, upon the possession of virtue, then the happiness of the nonphilosopher must be specious at best. One might object that it is guaranteed by the rule of the philosopher, but this rule will occur, if ever, only in the beautiful city of speech that is constructed in the *Republic,* and the possibility of this city is, to say the least, dubious.

As to the philosopher himself, there is good reason to suspect that he also cannot be truly happy in the imperfect city; to the extent that such happiness is available, it seems to be associated with a radical detachment from political or communal existence, and so with assimilation into a pure intellectual contemplation of eternal forms. On balance, one must say that the Platonic dialogues lean toward the teaching that human life is unhappy. The sickness and restlessness of the desires are amenable only to a perception of the good or, as one may also express this, to a perception of the goodness of reason.

When reason becomes separated from the good, as happens in early modernity under the influence of an un-Platonic reliance upon the exclusive paradigm of mathematics, the desires are no longer subject to rational restriction. Geometrical structure and algebraic ratio carry no sense of temperance or of the nobility of reason. There is no longer any reason to restrict the desires, not even the desire to conquer, and thus change, geometrical and algebraic order. Happiness is then reinterpreted as the satisfaction of desire, and satisfaction is shifted into the future. As Leo Strauss once said of John Locke's doctrine of man, life is the joyless quest for joy. To which I would add, How dangerously close to Plato!

So much for my sketch of the suggestion that the practico-productive dimension of Platonism has an important role to play in the origin of modernity. I now turn to a corollary thesis, namely, that the modern view of the unending perfectibility of technē was accessible to the ancients as well. We have just seen that in the Platonic dialogues, technē, whether productive or imitative, is subordinated to human intentions on the one hand and to *phronēsis,* or sound judgment, on the other. This is quite different from the claim that technē is subordinated to the Ideas, and, in fact, I know of no occurrence of that claim in the Platonic dialogues.

The Ideas serve as the *telos* of philosophical Eros or, in an alternative formulation, of pure theoretical cognition. They may be said to determine what is truly, and so what can be known, but they do not directly determine what we ought to do or make. This determination depends entirely upon the mediation of the philosopher-king and thus upon theoretical rather than practico-productive excellence.

Even here, it is not so much the direct apprehension of pure forms that guides the political activity of the philosopher as it is his intellectual judgment concerning how human beings ought to live if those who cannot see the Ideas are to be preserved in an orderly and temperate community. As to the excellence of such a community, it is determined in the final analysis by the degree to which the philosophical life can take place within it. As I have already noted, the nonphilosophical or demotic justice is associated with the body, not the soul. In the case of the soul, justice is equivalent to *phronēsis,* or intelligence, the same term that occurs in the *Statesman* to designate the perfect form of the royal art.

All this being so, it follows that the intentions of the philosopher, who is for Plato the highest type of human being, ought to direct all of the arts and sciences. This direction should be in the light of the Ideas, or what Socrates calls the light of the highest Idea or principle of the Ideas, the Good (518d9ff.). The Good is not itself an Idea in the sense of a form of this or that kind of being; Socrates compares it to the sun that illuminates all things on the face of the earth and thereby causes them to grow as well as to be visible.

It would not be easy to show that the Good serves a political or ethical role in addition to what we may call its ontological function as the principle of beingness, or *ousia.* Stated as sharply as possible, the Good does not tell us what to do. What it does is to illuminate the Ideas toward which we, that is to say, in the first instance the philosophers among us, are directed by Eros. From all points of view, I believe, one arrives at the conclusion that human activity, on Plato's analysis, ought to be regulated by the philosopher, who is in turn guided in his intentions by the love of wisdom. The philosopher is guided in his intentions by philosophy.

To return to the case of technē, it is not difficult to understand the sense in which it is to be regulated by philosophy. In the *Republic,* for example, technē is regulated in order to preserve the rule of the philosophers, which in turn is required if the city is to be just. But why do we require a just city? In order to be happy, which in turn depends upon a well-regulated soul. And this can be acquired only if philosophers are kings and kings philosophers.

Strictly speaking, it is false to say that justice, except as a synonym for philosophy, is for Plato a good in itself. The most that could be claimed is that happiness or blessedness is a good in itself, and that this requires us to be just. This amounts to saying that philosophy and happiness are synonymous, or, more narrowly, that they are synonymous in the city that allows the perfect philosopher to exist.

In actual or historical cities, the reasons for restricting the progress of technē are not so compelling. I do not mean by this that Plato was in favor of unlimited technical progress as a principle of his ordinary political doctrine. No doubt he was quite conservative on this point, as on many others. But if the philosopher does not rule, then the city cannot, as it were, be abstracted from history. In all actual cities the happiness available to the philosopher must be entirely private, as I have noted previously.

This is not contradicted by the extraordinary emphasis on politics in the Platonic dialogues. That emphasis is due in the last analysis to the conflict between philosophy and politics, or to the inexpungable conflict between philosophical and nonphilosophical conceptions of happiness. It is this conflict that leads us to doubt whether happiness is available to human beings of any kind, whether philosophical or not, given Plato's understanding of our natures.

One might therefore listen to the conversations of Socrates, or somewhat later read the Platonic dialogues, and come away with the feeling that philosophy is irrelevant to human well-being, let alone to human happiness. And this doubt places the question of technē in quite a different light. Or rather, it shifts us back to the light of ordinary political experience, as that light is cast upon the pages of Thucydides' *History of the Peloponnesian War.*

Thucydides is silent about philosophy in his great inquiry; the word appears only once, in the speech of Pericles, where it does not carry the Platonic sense but means something like *paideia,* or musical and verbal cultivation. If the fundamental fact about human life is war, then it is impossible to restrict the development of technē. This problem is not discussed by Socrates in the *Republic;* despite the crucial role of the guardians, we are given the impression that war may be limited if not entirely avoided, together with what is today called international relations.

Thucydides presents us with the actual political situation in book 1, chapter 71, section 3. The context is the debate between the Corinthian and Athenian representatives before the Spartan authorities in the preliminary stages of the outbreak of the war. The Corinthians contrast the daring and innovative nature of the Athenians with the slow, cautious, excessively traditional nature of the Lacedaimonians and warn that the necessities of political change require technical innovation. It is necessary in politics "just as in technē always to master what comes next."

Should one not then say that it is Thucydides rather than Plato who provides us with the classical antecedent of the modern unleashing of technē? Perhaps so, but this is a corollary to my original thesis, not its contradiction. My suggestion was not that Plato unleashes technē, but that he does not, in fact, distinguish as sharply as he seems to do between the theoretical and the practico-productive technai. As soon as Thucydidean realism triumphs over Platonic madness, Plato's own tangling of the lines separating politics from theory on the one side and production on the other serves as a philosophical basis for the articulation of realism into a comprehensive program in which politics and philosophy are married by experimental and mathematical science.

As I see it, in the passage cited above Thucydides expresses what is implied or implicitly guaranteed by Plato's attempt to subordinate politics to philosophy, an attempt that is, for Thucydides, impossible and not even worth considering. He silently rules out the possibility of the regulation of desire by intelligence. This being so, and regardless of whether his personal political preferences are conservative or progressive, the subordination of technē to political control must be rejected as impolitic. Add to this the Platonic notion of politics as a productive art, and at least part of the stage is set for the advent of modernity.

Given what I call the Thucydidean inflection of Platonism, the intentions of the philosopher are directed away from imaginary principalities toward the actual task of defending humankind in its war with nature. In other words, nature is war, not peace. In ontological terms, the mathematical structure of nature is subject to the will of humankind in its pursuit of comfortable security. Ethics is replaced by physiology, and happiness gives way to the unending effort to satisfy desire.

The union of the view that life is fundamentally war with the Platonic understanding of politics as a productive technē gives birth to the decisively modern conception that human beings are, or may become, the masters of their destiny. As a crucial text to illustrate this conception, I cite a well-known passage from Machiavelli's *Prince:* "It is better to be impetuous than respectful, because fortune is a woman, and it is necessary, if you wish to keep her quiet, to beat her and hit her. It is evident that she lets herself rather be conquered by such men than by those who proceed coldly. Therefore, like a woman, she is always the friend of the young, because they are less cautious, more ferocious, and command her with more audacity."[9]

Machiavelli is speaking here of politics, not of natural science. But my point is precisely that there is a political presupposition or context for the extension of the productive model of technē that is found within the natural sciences. Perhaps it would be more accurate to say that the political and scientific senses of technical production modify and stimulate each other so as to lead to the development of a comprehensive philosophical program of revolution, a revolution that can no longer be designated as either theoretical, practical, or productive because it is all three in one.

This passage from Machiavelli should be read together with Descartes' *Passions of the Soul,* in which, as one could say, ethics and politics are united with natural science through the medium of physiology. Descartes instructs men of strong or great souls (what the ancients called *megalopsuchia,* which he reinterprets as *generosité*) to destroy the belief in fortune by reflecting upon divine providence as equivalent to the natural order.[10] This order is both necessary and accessible to human intelligence. It cannot itself be changed but may be understood and so mastered in the sense that it may serve as the basis for supplementary constructions that will safeguard and improve the quality of human existence.

There is, then, no "mathematical ontology" in Descartes; mathematics is the language constructed by humankind to further the intentions of the will of the philosopher. It would also be a distortion of Plato's thought to infer from the geometrical cosmology of the *Timaeus* that he held to a mathematical ontology. At the same time, I know of no compelling evidence in the Platonic dialogues to sustain the thesis that the Platonic Ideas are arranged in a hierarchy of excellence, or what Nietzsche called a *Rangordnung.* There is no obvious sense in which the various accounts of the Platonic Ideas are connected with a doctrine of teleology. On the contrary, the order of excellence in the cosmos is usually attributed by Plato's interlocutors to the *epimeleia* of the ranked Olympian gods, led by Zeus, who order and care for the cosmos.[11]

This attribution means that the intentions of the philosopher, despite his

Eros for the Ideas, are determined directly not by them, but by the philosopher's *phronēsis*, or judgment, as to what action best serves the interest of philosophy. Such a view comes much closer than the Aristotelian teleology to the modern doctrine of the freedom of thought from regulation by natural ends, even while respecting the natural order. One has only to replace the Platonic Ideas with the geometrical structures of the *Timaeus* or, more radically, with the symbolical beings of modern mathematics, and the philosopher is transformed into a mathematical physicist free to do whatever he believes will satisfy his desire for the truth. And this is a step away from the desire to satisfy desire.

That Aristotle is not so close to modernity on this point may be suggested by the following citation from the *Politics*. In book I, at 1257b25ff, Aristotle says, "The art of medicine pursues health without limit, and each of the arts pursues its end in an unlimited way (for they wish to accomplish this to the greatest possible extent); although with respect to the end they do not proceed in an unlimited way (for the end is a limit to all the arts)."

In other words, technē has no intrinsic limit with respect to the development and perfection of means to the accomplishment of its end. This is especially plain in the case of war, in which each stage in the development of weaponry forces the opponent to match and surpass it. But according to Aristotle, there is an external limit to the progress of technē, namely, the end toward which it is directed. Peace is the natural limit to war, and health is the natural limit to medicine. What does this argument amount to? It seems to license unending technical perfection, with the nominal qualification that such perfection is always in the service of an unchanging end or limit.

This is a fragile argument for more than one reason. If technical progress is allowed to continue endlessly, a time will come, as we have reason to know, when the ends will themselves be dissolved by an unending process of interpretation. In addition, progress in the development of weaponry may come to a temporary end with the conclusion of one war, yet it starts up again with the outbreak of new hostilities, to say nothing of secret research during periods of ostensible peace. And an analogous argument may be constructed in the case of medicine. For all practical purposes, this means that the ends do not serve to limit technical progress but at the most to identify it as progress of such-and-such a type. As we also have reason to know, these types are not so easy to distinguish; the line between medicinal and military research cannot be drawn cleanly on the basis of a view toward the telos of health.

For a text from the Aristotelian school, if not directly from the master himself, that is closer in keeping with the origins of modernity, we may cite the opening lines of the treatise called *Mechanical Problems (Mēchanika),* usually attributed to the post-Aristotelian peripatetic school. This text begins by distinguishing between "marvelous events that occur in accordance with nature, of which we do not know the cause, and those that occur contrary to nature, which come to be through technē for the benefit of mortals. For in many cases nature makes something that is contrary to our benefit. For nature always acts in the same way and simply; but what is beneficial changes frequently."

This is extraordinarily modern in spirit. The author goes on to say that we must have recourse to technē in order to produce a "device" (*mēchanē*) that will enable us to act contrary to nature. "For as the poet Antiphon wrote, and as is true, 'we master by technē those things in which we are conquered by nature'" (847a11–21).[12] It reminds us of the Cartesian radicalization of Bacon's New Instauration, or the turn to a practico-productive theory with the power to make men the masters and possessors of nature.[13] I have been suggesting that the middle term between Antiphon and Descartes is Plato rather than Aristotle.

According to Sir Francis Bacon, the greatest obstacle to progress in the sciences lies "in the despair of mankind and in the supposition of its impossibility."[14] A parallel remark is to be found in Descartes' *Passions of the Soul.* In speaking of desires that depend upon ourselves for fulfillment, Descartes says, "The fault that one is accustomed to commit here, is never to desire too much; it is only that one desires too little."[15] The possibility of scientific progress is implicit in technē, that is, in the proceedings of the artisans, which we must employ to discover the force and the actions of the elements and the heavens.[16] This is an example of activity that depends upon ourselves.

What one could call Platonic pessimism, or a despair of the possibility of happiness, lightly disguised by the salutary equanimity of a Socrates "grown beautiful and young,"[17] is transformed into the optimism of the founding fathers of modernity by a series of steps, some of which, paradoxical though it may sound at first hearing, have been furnished by Plato himself.

Unlike the analogous situation in Aristotle, the cosmos of genesis is, according to Plato, not eternal but transient and cyclic. This has to do with the famous and obscure "separation" of the Platonic forms from their generated copies or instances, as well as with the reduction of virtue to wisdom and the correlative assimilation of practico-production into the domain of philosophical *phronēsis.*

None of this is intended to suggest that modernity is a direct consequence of, or even that it is somehow at bottom fully compatible with, Platonism. Perhaps I could summarize this essay by saying that I sense in Plato a poetical discontent with the place of human beings in the cosmos that I do not find in Aristotle. From this standpoint, I would not regard the aporetic nature of so many of the Socratic conversations, or the reliance upon myth in the decisive cases of the soul, the city, and the cosmos, as concealing a deeper positive teaching but rather as presenting a lightly masked representation, couched in the tones of Attic urbanity, of the incipient spirit of modernity.

I close with a prudent reminder: As these terms are normally employed, Plato was an ancient, not a modern. I mean by this something more than the obvious chronological or historical remark. The practico-productive nature of Plato's philosophy is restrained by the Ideas on the one hand and the radical difference between the philosopher and the nonphilosopher on the other. There is no point in speculating upon what Plato would have said, had he been aware of modern mathematics and natural science. Yet I cannot entirely restrain the impression that he would have aligned himself with the founders of modernity, less because of the spirit of philanthropy than because of his deeply poetical soul.

To say this in one more way, the "dialectic" of the dialogues, understood as the aporetic effort to grasp the visible yet illusive Ideas, and as distinct from the (in my opinion) imaginary dialectic of pure Ideas that Socrates wishes for in the *Republic,* is closer to what Hegel called "the peculiar restlessness and dispersion of our modern consciousness"[18] than is the Aristotelian effort to imitate the "thought thinking itself" of the god of the philosophers. I say this despite Hegel's own marked preference for Aristotle, upon whom he clearly modeled himself, and also despite what is to my mind the finally unconvincing portrait in Plato of philosophical *Heiterkeit,* or "beyondness," a portrait that is contradicted by the actual description of human existence, including the destiny of the philosopher, for whom life is a preparation for dying.

Whether this impression is right or wrong, however, has no bearing upon the soundness of the suggestion that I have outlined in this essay. Plato's contribution to the origin of modernity is closer to technē or *poiēsis* than it is to mathematics.

Chapter 8 Sad Reason

This essay contains material that was presented in various forms as the Priestley Lectures for 1997 at University College, the University of Toronto; the John U. Nef Lecture for 1997 at the University of Chicago; and the Cardinal Mercier Public Lecture at the Catholic University of Louvain in 1998. It will be published in the Tijdschrift voor filosofie *IV (60) (December 1998) as part of my stay at Louvain. I am extremely grateful to all three institutions for generous hospitality and a sympathetic audience.*

The essay is devoted to the question of what I take to be one of the two salient defects of the Enlightenment, namely, reliance upon an excessively attenuated if extremely powerful paradigm of rationality. (The other defect, which I hope to address elsewhere, is the attempt to define virtue in terms of comfort.) My intention is not to repudiate the Enlightenment but to preserve and strengthen its best features. It should be, but apparently is not, superfluous for me to assert that my long-standing concern with the quarrel between the ancients and the moderns has always been characterized by my loyalty to the modern epoch. I refer the interested reader to an earlier essay, "A Modest Proposal to Rethink Enlightenment," in The Ancients and the Moderns *(New Haven: Yale University Press, 1989).*

I trust that the title I have chosen is not too melancholy. The topic is a large one, but it is certainly familiar to all of us, and it is difficult to see how anything could be of greater concern to thoughtful human beings. The question before us is whether the life of reason is happy or sad. Those who dislike large topics might be inclined to reply, "Sometimes sad, sometimes happy," and I suppose they would mean by this that happiness depends upon something other than our degree of rationality. In one sense, I agree with this sober reply. It is by no means obvious that all rational persons are happy, and perhaps even less that the most rational among us have been the happiest. But this observation does not quite go to the heart of my topic.

I take my bearings by an interesting historical phenomenon. According to the traditional view that is at least as old as Socrates, philosophy, understood as the life of reason, is the source of the highest and most genuine form of human happiness. It is a corollary of this view that philosophy is available only to a small minority. An important change takes place at the beginning of the modern age. The life of reason, and so too philosophy, is redefined in accord with the model of the mathematical and experimental sciences. It remains true that mastery of these sciences is reserved for the few, but now we are assured that the fruits of science will be made available to the entire human race.

This assurance reaches fever pitch in the French Enlightenment, of which Condorcet is perhaps the extreme case. Because what we may call "the logical construction of the world" proceeds for Condorcet by the public criterion of mathematics and is concerned with nothing but the truth as universally applicable to all human beings, it is by its nature socially and politically enlightening as well and will lead to the extirpation of religious, moral, and political differences, the causes of discord among human beings.[1] The replacement of philosophy in the old sense by science in the new sense is now understood as the foundation of the modern pursuit of happiness, a pursuit that will be crowned with success in the human race at large, if not quite in every individual human being. The blessedness of the sage is gradually redefined as the industry of the engineer. It is no longer necessary to be wise in order to be happy, and in fact, there is no necessary connection between happiness and scientific genius.

At this point, a striking bifurcation takes place in the fate of the Enlightenment. Scientific and technological progress leads to an extraordinary amelioration of human ills and a steady increase in material comfort. But the philosophers divide into two camps. Perhaps we may mention Karl Marx and August Comte as the most prominent of the nineteenth-century thinkers who associate happiness with rationality. In the camp of what I am calling sad reason, one finds such thinkers of the first rank as Schelling, Kierkegaard, Schopenhauer, and Nietzsche. There is general agreement that the nineteenth century is an uneasy combination of belief in scientific and material progress, together with a deepening sadness on the part of the most perceptive and best-educated members of European society.

One could easily multiply quotations to verify this observation. I restrict myself to two representative examples. In 1818, Giacomo Leopardi writes in his notebooks that Enlightenment is actually barbarism and brings with it the debilitating consequences of the progress of reason, that is, boredom, unhappiness, and a knowledge of the illusory and empty character of human life, which latter is preserved by the imagination, the prime source of human happiness.[2] I cite Leopardi because he brings out very well, in anticipation of Nietzsche, the condemnation of reason, understood in the light of the scientific paradigm, as the source of sadness. The second example is Nietzsche himself, from whom I cite two brief passages. The first is from the notebooks of 1885: "The darkening, the pessimistic hue comes necessarily in the wake of the Enlightenment. Around 1770 one notes already a decrease in serenity."[3] The second passage makes explicit the responsibility of reason for late-modern sadness. A scientifically oriented rationalism is certainly visible beneath Nietzsche's assertion that "the world is not an organism but chaos."[4]

Despite the hundred years that separate us from Nietzsche, he is no longer a man of the day after tomorrow but the most contemporary of philosophers. And yet, there is a perceptible difference between his condemnation of sad reason and the two most powerful philosophical schools of our own generation. Nietzsche still speaks of "the gay science" and evokes, albeit in the register of nineteenth-century romanticism, the theme of the happiness of the philosopher. It would, of course, be impossible to say that Nietzsche returns in a straightforward manner to the tradition of Socrates. But neither does he simply repudiate that tradition, as has so often been suggested, sometimes by Nietzsche himself. There is a curious mixture of the traditional link between reason and happiness on the one hand, and the condemnation of reason as the source of sadness on the other. The connection between these two apparent opposites is that Nietzsche is very close to the conception of rationality as understood by nineteenth-century scientific materialism. The happiness that he claims to derive from understanding that the world is chaos is not something that he regards as the source of happiness for the majority of the human race.

In short, Nietzsche is a disgruntled product of the Enlightenment, one who confuses us by teaching almost simultaneously that the spirit is an epiphenomenon of the body and that art is worth more than the truth for life. These doctrines are not incompatible in the slightest, but they must be addressed to different audiences. I cannot go into the details here, but I believe that Nietzsche understood this. What I do not believe is that he managed to achieve a coherent articulation of his dual rhetoric. It must be said on his behalf that coherence is not plainly desirable on this delicate point. In the preface to the second edition of *The Gay Science*. Nietzsche celebrates his own return to physical and spiritual good health and associates traditional philosophy with "the sick body." The following observation is of special interest: "I have frequently asked myself if, speaking very generally, philosophy has hitherto been altogether nothing but an interpretation of the body and a *misunderstanding of the body*."[5]

This is a passage that could have been written by a contemporary philosopher of cognitive science. I think, for example, of Daniel Dennett, whose ready wit and apparent good humor illustrate nicely the differences and similarities between Nietzsche's hyperbolical endorsement of the deconstruction of the subject and that of our own generation, which has, so to speak, replaced metaphysics with neurophysiology. In reading these two quite different and yet closely related authors, I am struck in the first case by the forced rhetoric of happiness and in the second by what I am going to call the jocular self-assurance of someone for whom the scientific Enlightenment is a fait accompli.

I mentioned a moment ago that there are two dominant schools in contemporary philosophy. By the second school, I have in mind those who do not accept the rhetoric of the Enlightenment, but for whom reason is as destructive as Nietzsche portrayed it to be, or, to take a rather different example, as is intrinsic in the later Wittgenstein's deconstruction of rationalist theories in philosophy. I myself see an inner relation between Wittgenstein's disconnected analyses of the senselessness of traditional philosophical activity and, say, Derrida's publication in parallel columns of an essay on the Marquis de Sade and a commentary on Hegel's *Logic*. It is true that Wittgenstein seems to represent a traditional religious sense of seriousness that separates him from the jocularity of Dennett on the one hand and the playful seriousness of Derrida on the other. But religion to one side, the two main contemporary schools seem to agree that there is no connection between happiness and the life of philosophical reason. This is, of course, not the same as the explicit connection between reason and sadness. But the connection is implicit.

Let me be very careful here. I do not know whether Dennett is personally as happy as his literary style would suggest, and I know as little about the inner cheerfulness of Derrida. In the case of Wittgenstein, we have some biographical evidence, but this too is irrelevant to my point. What interests me is that the conception of reason is essentially the same among those contemporary philosophers who support the Enlightenment and those who call it into question or reject it entirely. The question is not whether contemporary philosophers are happy or sad, but whether their conception of reason makes it reasonable to speak of the happiness of the rational life. This is quite separate from the question of whether they approve or disapprove of the paradigm of reason that is their common heritage from the Enlightenment.

So much for my introductory *tour d'horizon* of the history of the transformation of happy into sad reason. I want now to have a closer look at the situation in classical antiquity, and in particular at the Platonic Socrates, who introduces in a decisive manner the thesis that philosophy is the blessed life and, in fact, that the unexamined life is not worth living. My intention is not to give a comprehensive analysis of these propositions but to indicate by appropriate examples why Nietzsche's criticism of Socrates as an enemy of life is not without warrant. This will help us to understand the similarities as well as the differences between ancient and modern views on sad reason, and therefore on happiness as well.

Very generally, the premodern philosophers have tended to affirm the link between reason and happiness, whereas the poets have given us a more eloquent description of sad reason. But this is only the surface of a more complicated situation. I want to illustrate this point with some references to Plato. In book 7 of the *Republic*,[6] Socrates explains that the central role of mathematics in the education of potential philosophers is that of a prelude to the study of dialectic. Mathematics, to be sure, points us in the direction of the Ideas or genuine natures of things, but mathematicians, Socrates says, "dream about being" whereas dialecticians perceive the beings as they genuinely are and reason directly about them without the use of hypotheses or axioms on the one hand or images on the other. Mathematics stands to dialectic or wisdom as does dreaming to wakefulness. This is a specification of an earlier passage in which Socrates says that, in dreaming, we take a likeness to be not a likeness but the thing it is like.[7]

In order that we may preserve our belief that the beautiful city is "not altogether a daydream," as Socrates puts it a few lines later,[8] the science of dialectic, and so the philosopher-kings, must be possible. Let us note first that even if the city is possible, it is not entirely clear that its citizens will be happy. I restrict myself to the guardian class. At the beginning of book 4, Adeimantus asks whether Socrates has made the guardians happy. Socrates replies that this was not his purpose, but that he has tried to make the city as a whole as happy as possible. He warns his interlocutor not to furnish the guardians with a kind of happiness that will impede their capacity to be guardians.[9] In a later passage, Socrates claims that the guardians will be happier than Olympic heroes because we have freed them of the adolescent view of happiness that comes from the possession of property, a family, and the other ostensible benefits of a private existence. Instead, "both when they remain in the city and go outside to war, they must guard together and hunt together like dogs."[10]

We must distinguish within the guardian class between the soldiers and the philosopher-kings. As these two classes overlap initially, however, all members partake of the nature of the noble hound.[11] Because Socrates cites the hound as proof of the possibility of the guardian nature, it cannot be simply a joke when he says that it is the sign of the dog's philosophical nature to bark at strangers.[12] The main point in these passages for me is the following: the conception of happiness shared by most human beings is for Socrates childish. Genuine happiness depends upon full citizenship in the philosophical city. One is tempted to say that happiness for the soldier class is a dog's life.

It is evident that Socrates is attempting to combine two elements that seem to conflict with one another: the patriotic courage of the warrior and abstraction from the body. Otherwise put, the city replaces the family in the guardian class altogether, but this seems to extend rather than to narrow the erotic activity of its members, at least until such time as they devote themselves to mathematics and, in the highest instance, to dialectic. Despite the numerous restrictions on mating, Socrates admits that the city will be destroyed by their inevitable violation.[13]

To summarize, the Socratic conception of happiness points us away from the body to the soul, but to a particular activity of the soul, namely, the vision of the pure forms. Those who are incapable of this vision must be content with the happiness of noble hounds. This is why Socrates says in the *Phaedo* that the philosopher strives to live in a way that is as close to death as possible, and that the truly philosophical life is the practice of dying.[14] According to the Platonic Socrates, mathematicians believe that geometrical figures and pure numbers are the genuine or original beings of which their spatiotemporal counterparts are images and reflections. But human life is an epiphenomenon of those counterparts, an epiphenomenon that corresponds to nothing in the original or genuine figures and numbers. More precisely, life is not an image of a triangle or of the Pythagorean theorem. Our everyday experience, including our experience of ourselves as mathematicians, corresponds to no mathematical originals. We are thus faced with a choice of interpretations. Either human life is a simulacrum, something less than an image and barely to be characterized as a dream, or else it constitutes a distinct type of originality, other than the mathematical forms and irreducible to them.

Both answers are to be found in Plato. In the *Republic*, there is no discussion of the pursuit of self-knowledge. The happiness of the beautiful and just city is dependent upon the antecedent knowledge of the philosophers that life is a dream from which we may awaken only through the dream of dialectic. We are fully awake only when we are not fully alive. And it is not easy to see that dialectic has any more to say about the pursuit of happiness than does mathematics. And in fact, when Socrates turns from everyday experience to reflection upon the nature and destiny of the life of the individual soul, he has recourse to myth: to poetry rather than dialectic.

Human existence is not a copy of Platonic Ideas. But neither is the personal soul an Idea; on the contrary, it is described as the erotic desire for the Ideas. It would be going too far to say that life has no shape at all. In the *Phaedrus*,[15] Socrates says that it is not possible for mortals to describe the Idea of the human soul but only to tell what it is like. He does so by narrating the myth of the winged charioteer and the noble and base horses, or in other words, the intellect and the two opposite forms of erotic spiritedness. It is extremely revealing that, in this myth, the soul is entirely silent on its ascent to the vision of the hyperuranian Ideas, except for the unsuccessful attempt of the base Eros at a lower stage of the journey to persuade its noble counterpart to have sexual intercourse with a beautiful youth. Eros is appetite and visual satiation but not rational discourse.

The alternative is evident: on the one hand, a quasi-mathematical dialectic; on the other, poetry. Equally clear is the dual task assigned by Plato to philosophical poetry. It must both explain human life and conceal the full import of that explanation from everyone but the philosophers. As to philosophical happiness, it hovers somewhere in the ambiguous region between the endless pursuit of wisdom and personal extinction in the vision of pure forms. It is a direct consequence of the definition of wisdom that there is no domain of genuine wakefulness in some place beyond the heavens that is the original of which our dreamlike existence is the image. In Socrates' myth, he tells how the bodiless divine souls rise to the roof of the cosmos and there view the pure Ideas. But our souls are not copies or instances of these divine beings; we are held back by our bodies and see only reflections of the Ideas, as though through a glass darkly. In order to see the Ideas themselves, we must be dead.

In the *Symposium,* the priestess Diotima tells the young Socrates that Eros is continuously changing its shape, that is, continuously dying and returning to life.[16] Accordingly, there is no Idea of Eros, but only a myth of the erotic ascent to the Ideas by the human soul. One could infer from the mythical status of the doctrine of Eros that the ascent to the Ideas is a dream. No one could suppose that the winged charioteer and his two steeds are the genuine reality of the human soul. The soul is patently not the dream-image of an actual charioteer and his horses. It would be more correct, but still unsatisfactory, to refer to the image of the charioteer as a dream-image of the soul.

In sum, a quasi-mathematical rationalism not only cannot explain the phenomenon of human existence but serves to empty it of independent substance and significance. From the standpoint of such a rationalism, if we try to reconcile Plato's myths of the soul with his doctrine of Ideas, the myths look like subterfuges or philanthropic attempts to conceal the bitter truth under a salutary veil of rhetoric. They look like noble lies. And the need to tell noble lies is the mark of the inner sadness of reason. This is why those who repudiate myth or for whom reason is equivalent to calculation and formal analysis move imperceptibly from the ideology of openness to the bravado of frankness and end up in a universal version of the sadness that is concealed by myth. The rationalist assertion of the illusion of wakefulness renders rationalism irrational.

I introduced this discussion of Plato with the proviso that it is intended only as an indication of the complexity of the relation between happiness and the life of reason in classical antiquity. Had I chosen Aristotle instead of Plato, the story would have been somewhat different, thanks to Aristotle's distinction between the theoretical and the practical life, each with its particular version of happiness. But it is not evident that the story would have been radically different for theoretical reason, which is directed to the contemplation of the natures of things, and so to formal structure. Suffice it to say that there is an initial association by the classical philosophers between reason and happiness, but that the association becomes problematic the more closely we examine it. In sum, Nietzsche was not simply mistaken in his assessment of Socratic rationalism. But he was not entirely correct. I will take up this point in the last part of the chapter.

I return to the moderns through the way station of Shakespeare and the famous lines in the *Tempest:* "We are such stuff as dreams are made on, and our little lives are rounded with a sleep." My thesis is that this passage serves equally well as a summary of the ancient and the modern rationalist traditions. It does so, of course, because, like all great poetry, it is not only universal in import but also ambiguous. From a modern perspective, we are struck by the fact that if Prospero offers us another world in compensation for our own, it too is a dreamworld, not the wakefulness of reason but the illusion of poetry. From this perspective, one can plausibly argue that Prospero, if not Shakespeare himself, is the direct ancestor of Nietzsche. It is also of more than symbolic interest that Shakespeare and Galileo were contemporaries, both having been born in 1564. For it is Galileo's distinction between primary and secondary attributes, and so between the worlds of reason and perception, that lies at the heart of the new science. And this distinction leads directly to the conclusion that we are such stuff as dreams are made on.

Here I want to revisit the modern period in the light of what we have just acquired from our quasi-Nietzschean inspection of the Platonic texts. This will enable me to formulate my view on the difference between the sad reason of the ancients on the one hand and the moderns on the other. The distinction between primary and secondary attributes in effect equates wakefulness with mathematics and human experience with a dream. In the words of E. A. Burtt, "In the course of translating this distinction of primary and secondary into terms suited to the new mathematical interpretation of nature, we have the first stage in the reading of man quite out of the real and primary realm." Burtt adds that "man begins to appear for the first time in the history of thought as an irrelevant spectator and insignificant effect of the great mathematical system which is the substance of reality."[17]

The modern scientific revolution thus reverses the magical powers of Prospero. Where he could create an illusory world that conceals human reality, Galileo and his followers created a reality that transforms the human world into an illusion. At the outset of the modern age, the sources of happiness are conceived in terms that guarantee the sadness of reason, as was clearly seen by Pascal. Nevertheless, modernity begins with the promise of happiness. This is the first stage of modernity to which Burtt alludes.

The second stage may be described as the dialectic between the peculiarly modern forms of happiness and sadness. I have already noted Nietzsche's observation about the decrease in serenity around 1770. I will discuss briefly a somewhat earlier sign of this decrease. David Hume is one of the first of the

Enlightenment philosophers to make clear the human consequences of the quasi-Newtonian rationalism that he himself espouses. His *Treatise of Human Nature* was published in 1739. Hume continues the tradition of British empiricism in the construction of human life from impressions and simple ideas, through the agency of the vividness of the imagination together with the will in its pursuit of pleasure and avoidance of pain. As to reason, "it is, and ought only to be, the slave of the passions." The "ought" is enforced by the fact that "truth is of two kinds, consisting either in the discovery of the proportions of ideas, considered as such, or in the conformity of our ideas of objects to their real existence."[18] Neither conception of truth is capable of investing the exercise of reason with a connection to goodness or of sustaining the belief in the value of a world that is the artifact of a vivid imagination. Little wonder that Hume is forced to seek relief from the melancholia induced by philosophy in the distraction of everyday life.[19]

I want to make two points about this passage in Hume. The first is that it represents a significant turn away from the traditional philosophical affiliation of reason with happiness. The second is that although Hume turns for solace to everyday life, not to poetry, his epistemology and ontology are nevertheless decisive stages in the process by which the imagination gradually assumes priority over reason. The subterranean link between Prospero and Galileo is represented in Hume by the connection between the imagination and world-building. The same connection exists in the nineteenth century between materialistic empiricism and idealistic romanticism. Both contribute to the preparation of the triumph of the poets in their quarrel with philosophy.

I lack the time to explore all of the implications of this triumph. The key point for us is as follows: The eighteenth-century celebration of happy reason is challenged by internal weaknesses and external attacks. These attacks range from Rousseau's association of happiness with sentiment and imagination to Kant's critique of Eudaimonism and his contention that we must strive to deserve to be happy, not simply to be happy. Those who share the orientation of later thinkers like Schelling, Kierkegaard, Schopenhauer, Nietzsche, Wittgenstein, and Heidegger tend to associate the life of reason, now understood as mathematical rationalism, with sadness, dread, senselessness, and so on. But those who follow the tradition of Frege, Russell, Carnap, and strict scientific materialism, regardless of their personal cheerfulness or their continued commitment to the Enlightenment, represent a conception of reason that is incapable of sustaining the link between the life of reason and happiness. In Max Weber's famous expression, they are advocates of the disenchanted universe.

My preliminary inference is then as follows: Tolstoy says, "All happy families are alike but an unhappy family is unhappy after its own fashion."[20] In the case of historical epochs, however, the fashion of happiness differs as well as that of unhappiness. There is a difference not only in rhetoric but in the conception of human existence that is reflected in, say, the wit of Socrates on the one hand and that of the twentieth-century skeptic or nihilist on the other. I am concerned primarily with the connection between the modern conception of reason and the deepening melancholy that pervades the nineteenth and twentieth centuries. This melancholy is inseparable from the modern sense of the nature of happiness, of which styles of wit and comedy are derivative consequences.

Stated concisely, the radical shift from the ancient to the modern perspective brings with it the expectation of imminent happiness in this life together with its progressive postponement. Despite Descartes' own optimistic estimate of the time required to master nature, each step forward seems to separate us by an equivalent amount from our goal. This has two consequences. First, happiness is gradually displaced by satisfaction, which is to be attained from the productive labor, spiritual or physical, by which we seek happiness. What I will call the unsatisfactory nature of a satisfaction of delayed gratification leads in turn to its replacement by resolution and authenticity, or sublimated sadness. One may see here the resignation of the ancient Stoic rather than the Socratic claim to happiness. As Leo Strauss says of Locke's doctrine of human labor, life is the joyless quest for joy.[21]

In this context, we need to cite once more the author of the "gay science," although this time in the vocal register of Zarathustra: "What does happiness matter? For a long time I have ceased to strive for happiness; I aspire to my work!"[22] Nietzsche, of course, is referring to the creative work of the artist, and in particular to world-construction, not to the labor of the marketplace or factory.[23] But the first kind of work is related to the second by a subterranean filiation that connects both to Hegel, who replaces personal happiness with satisfaction in the construction of actuality by conceptual labor. This is Hegel's rationalist revision of Hume's world-constituting imagination. Nietzsche in turn replaces logic by art. In the twentieth century, we talk of the art of logic but no less of "ways of world-making," as Nelson Goodman entitles a recent book.

The second consequence of the postponement of gratification is "the peculiar restlessness and dispersion of our modern consciousness," noted by Hegel,[24] or, as I would call it, the simultaneous stimulation and stupefaction of our spiritual faculties that is induced by the endless pursuit of happiness. In slightly different terms, the residents of modernity alternate between radical new proposals for the attainment of happiness and admissions of temporary failure. The result is that whereas we *anticipate* happiness, we experience sadness directly. This anticipation is easily confused with happiness, especially because of the intensity with which we throw ourselves into revolutionary enterprises. With apologies to the psychiatrists, I call this manic depression, and this, I suggest, is the peculiar feature of modern, and in particular of late-modern sadness.

My point is not at all that the ancients were happy whereas we moderns are suffused with sadness. Sadness is an essential element of human existence. I do not know how to eliminate it, and I do not know what we would be like without it. In particular, I am convinced that without an experience of sadness, we would never be happy, just as, if there were no evil, we would not know goodness. What I am suggesting is that the modern epoch begins, at least in its full rhetorical manifestation, as a dream of universal happiness, and so precisely as the promise that sadness will be abolished from the face of the earth. In this dream, wakefulness is to be obtained by replacing poetry, metaphysics, and religion with mathematics and experimental science as the correct instruments for the analysis and vindication of human life. The continuous rhythm of the traditional dialectic of happiness and sadness has thus been disrupted and accelerated simultaneously.

We are, then, faced with something of a paradox. Modern science, one of the greatest creations of the human spirit and an unquestioned source of endless, even miraculous, blessings, is widely perceived as the most important cause of the stultification of the human spirit. But the truly frightening aspect of this process is the apparent joy with which the elimination of the spirit has been greeted by the champions of scientific materialism. This ostensible joy, which is more accurately described as enthusiasm, is caused by the conviction that the body alone is intelligible. The unrestricted progress of scientific knowledge is thus made to depend upon a doctrine that eliminates as irrational the very rhetoric with which we celebrate it. We are asked to embrace the coming generation of happy machines.

None of this is intended as a repudiation of science and technology. What cannot make us happy is also incapable of making us sad. The question whether science and technology will lead us to paradise or extinction is philosophical, not scientific or technological. But the answer to this question cannot lie in a simple return to the ancient tradition of rationalism because, as I have also argued, the connection between reason and happiness in that tradition is itself problematic. There can be no question of repeating the past, nor is there any point in shifting from one philosophical school to another. What we require, as always, is to rethink the problem.

Two different inferences can be drawn from the historical evidence I have summarized up to here. The first is that there is no intrinsic connection between reason and happiness. The second is that whereas reason alone cannot make us happy, it can contribute to our sadness. As I have argued, reason saddens us by lending its authority to the presentiment that life is a dream. The response by Nietzsche that reason is also a dream is not satisfactory because it leaves us with no dimension of wakefulness. In fact, as I have indicated, Nietzsche arrives at this conclusion by accepting the model of reason that descends from the Platonic doctrine of formal perception to modern *mathēsis universalis*. But this model results in the elimination of life, not in its explanation, and certainly not in its justification. If life is a dream, however, what we dream is life itself, not mathematical equations. Otherwise put, we dream of ourselves as employing mathematical equations as one instrument among others for the investigation of the structure of the dream of life.

At this point it becomes obvious that it is senseless to speak of life as a dream because there is no other condition accessible to reason that could count as the original of which our dream is an image. In order to arrive at such a condition, we would have to shift from philosophy to religion and a belief in the next world. But religion is not my topic; if it were, it would serve to reinforce the sadness of reason: *credo quia absurdum est*. The image of the dream is seductive because it draws upon the brevity and uncertainty of human existence. But natural processes may also be brief and uncertain. We shall have to find some other criterion for the identification of illusions. Besides, brevity and uncertainty have no meaning in themselves; they are perceptions or beliefs of intelligences like our own.

But who are we? Or more properly, who am I? The Western philosophical tradition has its official beginning in Socrates' attempt to obey the Delphic oracle's command to "know thyself." In the opening scene of the dialogue *Phaedrus,* which contains Plato's most vivid account of the human soul, there is a passage of crucial importance for the present topic. Socrates explains to his young companion that he has no time to provide rationalizing analyses of mythical beings like the wind Boreas, the Centaurs, the Gorgons, and all the rest: "I am not yet able to know myself, in accord with the Delphic inscription. It seems laughable to me, when I am ignorant of this, to investigate what does not concern me. So I bid farewell to these other matters, persuaded by the customary stories, and investigate not these things but whether I myself am a monster more complicated and filled with greater desires than Typhon, or whether I am a gentler and simpler animal that has by nature a divine fate that is not puffed up like a wind" (229e6–230a6).

I am well aware that this statement by Socrates is playful, but that does not deprive it of an instructive seriousness. Socrates is not advocating the abandonment of natural science, and I am not inferring such a recommendation from his words. He is raising the question whether the procedures of natural science are appropriate to the search for an answer to the question of personal identity. And this question, as I showed earlier, also applies to his own conception of the highest form of reason. We are not only entitled but required to ask, What replies does philosophy give to the question Who am I?

The answers are not encouraging. It turns out, as we have seen, that the life of reason is being lived by an illusion, and that I am actually an image of an Idea, a stream of impressions, an instance of a transcendental structure, a monadic reflection of totality, or finally, my body, expressed in various ways but most recently in the language of neurophysiology. In short, philosophy, whether in its ancient, modern, or postmodern forms, tells us that the answer to the question Who am I? is No one. It seems that Odysseus, who gave this reply to the monster Polyphemus when asked that question, was the first epistemologist and deconstructor of the self. Something has gone badly wrong here. Philosophy begins its career as the pursuit of a life that is happy because it is in accord with reason. But reason leads to the conclusion that happiness depends upon our departing from this life as soon as possible, or, alternatively, that reason and happiness have nothing to do with one another.

I acknowledged at the start of this essay that many contemporary philosophers would reject the question about the link between sadness and reason as too large, too vague, and in short, unphilosophical. But this confirms the fact, if it required confirmation, that philosophy no longer promises us happiness in the life of reason. To this I add that it seems to guarantee the sadness of the life of reason. One might have said that whereas human life is sad, the philosopher escapes by withdrawing into his thoughts or in the satisfaction of the pursuit of truth. But even this argument, which is the counsel of despair rather than blessedness, loses its force if the truth itself is depressing. And what could be more depressing than to be told that life is a dream from which we can awaken only by entering into the oblivion of chaos?

It will come as no surprise when I say that I have no answers to these dilemmas. But there are one or two points that seem to me worth making. The first is that whereas life is unsatisfactory in many ways, it is not an illusion or a dream. There is no original of which our life is a distorted copy. But please note: The fact that life is not a formal structure does not mean that there are no formal structures. The Platonic doctrine of Ideas has to be supplemented by the recognition of the erotic nature of the soul, but without the Ideas or their formal equivalent, Eros quickly deteriorates into the will to power, and then into chaos. To say this in another way, if we begin entirely from within the stream of consciousness and attempt to construct our personal identities from impressions or sense data, we will fail.

It is easy enough to point to the various dislocations, confusions, and illusions that mark our individual lives. But these disruptions or decenterings are themselves identifiable only with respect to the individual person who undergoes them. I cannot demonstrate my personal identity by conceptual analysis because I am not a concept and because analysis dissolves; it does not unify. I am not my neurophysiological processes but the person who undergoes them and who studies them. But neither am I the transcendental ego or the absolute subject, however accurately these concepts may express the conditions of my cognitive experience.

I have argued that an excessive reliance upon a formalist paradigm of rationality leads to the impossibility of asserting rationally that reason is good; and if we cannot say this, then it is not likely to contribute to our happiness. In no way am I suggesting that we abandon formalism. But we require something more than a conception of reason as an instrument of the passions. As an example of what I have in mind, I shall take a brief look at the inner relation between formal or analytical reason and goodness. A perception of that relation may not make us happy, but at least it will not contribute to our sadness.

I begin my argument with some assistance from Aristotle. Goodness is a property that is not amenable to the precision of quasi-mathematical analysis. This does not mean, of course, that we are reduced to silence with respect to the question What is the good? On the contrary, the problem seems to be that we have altogether too much to say on this point. The striking fact is that whereas we disagree sharply in our definitions of the good, this disagreement is rooted in an everyday or prephilosophical understanding of its fundamental nature. Whereas some things are good for the sake of something else, we reserve the unqualified use of "good" for that which is choiceworthy in itself. On this point, Aristotle was certainly correct. We may express this choiceworthiness in religious, aesthetic, philosophical, or political terms, but in all cases we mean to say that it is both possible and reasonable to choose, or, in colloquial terms, that some things are better than others. In a word, we require *to metron*, "the appropriate," not arithmetical exactness.

In the *Areopagitica* Milton says that "reason is but choosing."[25] I think that the qualifying "but" is too strong; nevertheless, the assertion is useful. I want to claim that all rational analysis is grounded in the capacity to distinguish one element of formal or conceptual structure from another, and so one thing, deed, or speech from another, and that this capacity to distinguish is fulfilled at each step by a choice of the better and a rejection of the worse alternative. We call this sound reasoning, but I am suggesting that the adjective is not strong enough. By "sound" we mean "good" in an intuitively obvious sense. In judging, we choose what is choiceworthy. The appropriate is built into the correct.

This is not enough to get us to a satisfactory account of the good, but it is a necessary first step. When we say that something is more reasonable than something else, we are asserting a judgment about goodness. To participate in an activity that is governed by a set of rules is implicitly to accept those rules as definitive of good as distinct from bad behavior in that context. Less formally expressed, if I ask someone to "be reasonable," the request is unintelligible if it is taken to mean that it makes no difference what the person does. We can determine the procedures that are to regulate reasonable behavior, but the unspoken rule is that it is good to follow those procedures.

One might object that it is merely reasonable to follow them, but this objection is based, I think, upon the assumption that "good" means here "moral." On the contrary, I am in the process of claiming that there is a mediating step from the sense of good as reasonable to the moral sense. Morality itself involves a choice between alternatives, whether this choice is regulated by explicitly formulated rules or is left to our "good" judgment. In other words, we cannot be moral except by invoking the goodness of reason, namely, the application of the correct rule or the formulation of the sound judgment. In no case could it be moral to apply the wrong rule or to obey an erroneous judgment. This is a formal point and one that is independent of the content of any particular moral code or doctrine. It is also compatible with a morality based upon divine revelation because we must obey the correct revelation or make the proper interpretation of the divine command.

To come back to the general case, it is therefore evident that one cannot distinguish sharply between analytical reason on the one hand and evaluation on the other. To analyze is to distinguish, and thus it is not simply to identify elements as of such and such a kind, but more broadly to isolate structures as pertinent or irrelevant to our intentions in initiating the analysis. Still more broadly, when we are moved to utter the expostulation made famous by Wittgenstein, "Now I can go on!" we have not simply mastered a rule but acquired an insight into the rightness, that is to say, the goodness, of our journey.

My inability to define "good" by analyzing it into simpler and more immediately intelligible terms is no more a sign of the irrationality of the judgment "This is good" than it is a sign of the unintelligibility of set-membership or negation that neither can be defined in a noncircular way. On the contrary, if one could define "good" out of simpler terms, this would show that goodness is not a first principle. It might or might not show that goodness is an illusion, depending upon the nature of the hypothetical simpler terms. On my view, however, we do not need to worry about these hypothetical cases. I urge that it is our comprehension of goodness that leads us to praise reason, for such praise is tantamount to the assertion that reason is good. And this assertion is built into the analytical and synthetic modalities of formal reason, exactly as it is built into the process of practical judgment. Reason is not simply identifying but it is also choosing.

Assuming for a moment that you grant me this point, you might still rightly object that people choose bad things or make bad choices. But this is not a problem for the view I am defending. I reply that we come to identify bad things and bad choices on the basis of our perception of what would be good in those cases. We correct our mistakes, and thus we say, "Now I can go on!" It is of course true that human beings disagree as to which things in particular are good and which are bad. But the disagreement would be impossible if they did not agree that there is a difference between good and bad, and that we can reason about it in such a way as to construct arguments that are designed to persuade our opponents to accept our choices. No one disagrees with the superiority of correctness to error or of success to failure. As one might put it, we play language games to win, not to lose. And this is also true of the eccentric language game in which losing counts as victory.

As I hope is evident, I am not defending the thesis that formal structure is good in itself, if by "in itself" is meant "independent of human evaluation." At the same time, the association of the good with human evaluation is not an endorsement of a vitiating relativism. In the absence of an intelligent spirit to say, "This is good," the conception of goodness in itself is unintelligible. By the same token, an arrangement of formal elements constitutes a significant form if and only if it is accessible to identification by a discerning, that is, a judging, and so choosing, intelligence. A form need not be seen, but it must be visible. And the same is true of a significant absence or veiled presence. Correlatively, when philosophers urge us to be rational or to reason logically or to repudiate metaphysics, they do so in the conviction that they are advocating a good choice, not simply a rational one, because the notion of "simply rational" is meaningless if it excludes goodness. A simple rationalist is a simpleton.

To say that reason is good for life is, of course, not the same as to say that life is good. My point, however, is not that reason is an instrument for something else but that it is a direct expression of goodness. It remains to be proven that the expression of goodness is happiness. But such a perception of reason is no longer an obstacle to happiness. It helps us to correct the quasi-Nietzschean interpretation I gave previously of Platonic rationalism.

The connection between reason and the good is established by the structure of human experience as a process of choosing between better and worse. It is a false description of human nature, and therefore bad science, to say that we make these choices on a narrowly utilitarian basis, and it is simply unintelligible to be told that we are not making these choices at all but that they are being made for us by our blood-sugar level or the firing of cells in our brains. There is no ghost in the machine, not merely because there are no ghosts, but because we are not machines. Otherwise stated, if consciousness is an illusion, then illusion is worth more than the truth. More precisely, "illusion" becomes true for human beings, and scientific truth becomes an illusion. Once again we see the allegiance between Prospero and Galileo. It is this allegiance that symbolizes the connection between sadness and reason in the modern epoch.

There is a beautiful and very sad line by one of my favorite American poets, Allen Tate, which says, "We are the eyelids of defeated caves." Tate was a classical scholar as a young man, and it is not at all unlikely that he was thinking of Plato's allegory of the cave when he composed this line. The cave is, of course, the symbol of the human city; the eyelid as I understand it expresses the closing of the eye of the Enlightenment. Contemporary man resides neither within nor outside the cave, neither in the shadows nor in the sunlight. We are the eyelids of defeated caves, that is, the last vestige of the Enlightenment. But eyelids can open as well as close. Otherwise stated, Tate conceives of contemporary life as dreaming behind lowered eyelids. The question is whether the lids can be raised without revealing an entirely defeated cave. There is not much solace to be derived from the joys of creativity if reason has persuaded us in advance that our cave is empty or, at best, populated with phantoms.

Chapter 9 Transcendental Indeterminateness

This essay was published in the Italian journal Il cannochiale *(September 1990): 5–26. It addresses itself to a limited but crucial aspect of Kant's claim to have provided the conditions for the possibility of our thinking a world like the one we actually inhabit. I try to demonstrate that Kant's technical argument renders it impossible to explain judgments of sense-perception. Kant has been criticized by others for a failure to explain adequately how false perceptual judgments are possible. I go farther than this and claim that Kant is unable to provide an explanation of true perceptual judgments of an empirical kind, such as "This is a dog." Kant has not resolved the problem of how to combine the transcendental structure of cognition (perceptual and conceptual) with the empirical specificity of judgments about concrete objects (phenomena). As the reader will see, I connect this to a further problem in Kant, namely, how to reconcile transcendental purposiveness and empirical contingency.*

The essay emerges from my conviction that Kant's critical philosophy offers us a plausible general hypothesis as to the steps that need to be taken in order to overcome the separation between modern subjectivity, understood as an agent of representation, and the objectivity of experience. The

Kantian question could be rephrased as the query What does it mean to be a world? in which "world" in turn refers to the coherence and unity of human experience. Kant is unable to escape from the responsibility for explaining, not just the general conditions for objective knowledge, but how these conditions produce knowledge in particular cases. If the conditions do not work, this defect is not masked by calling them transcendental and assuring us that an account of empirical knowledge is not Kant's aim.

The Kantian hypothesis assumes from the outset the doctrine of representation, that is, of subjectivity as both separated from reality and capable of representing what it cannot present in the first place. The subsequent history of epistemology provides us with empirical evidence that if one begins with separation, no amount of technical ingenuity will overcome it. Instead, we set out on the endless process of inventing artificial bridges from the subject to the object. Kant, as it were, solves the problem of dualism by transforming it into an ontological structure. But the enterprise is itself necessary if and only if there really is a problem of dualism. I mean by this, if and only if the modern doctrine of subjectivity is plausible. I need to emphasize that I do not sympathize with those who try to remove the problem by dissolving subjectivity, if by this is meant an attempt to replace the phenomena of consciousness with talk about syntax on the one hand and brain synapses on the other. These desperate expedients are simply the latest consequences of the over-whelming success of the Kantian enterprise, that is, of the postulate that immediate experience requires transcendental foundations. What requires deconstruction is not the soul but transcendental philosophy.

It has often been observed that, in describing the transcendental structure of possible experience, Kant has difficulty in preserving the indeterminateness of empirical knowledge. This difficulty centers on the nature of perception.[1] Simply stated, the problem is how to combine a transcendentally imposed necessity with empirical contingency. In my opinion, there is a parallel difficulty that has not received extensive consideration: how to combine transcendental purposiveness with the empirical contingency of reflective judgment.[2]

In this essay, I want to consider these two problems together. My question is, then, What is the link between perception and judgment in Kant's model of possible experience? I shall conclude that Kant fails to provide a coherent account of this link. On the one hand, he includes determinant judgment within perception, thereby distinguishing it from sensation or the private modification of consciousness (which one could almost call private perception, bearing in mind paragraph 18 of the *Prolegomenon*). On the other hand, he speaks regularly of the "givenness" of the empirical object to judgment, whether determinant or reflective. The ambiguity is compounded by Kant's failure to explain the relation between the spontaneous formation of concepts by the understanding and the act of epistemic judgment.

In *The Critique of Pure Reason,* Kant introduces the term "transcendental" as follows: "I call all knowledge transcendental that concerns itself entirely, not with objects *but with our manner of knowing objects, insofar as this is to be a priori possible*" (B25).[3] A priori knowledge is produced (Kant uses the verb *ausmachen*) through the relation of the categories to possible experience, namely, to objects of sensation (which last is a modification of the pure forms of intuition), in accord with various syntheses that need not be rehearsed here. This relation of categories to sensation is governed by mathematical and dynamical principles (B187ff). The mathematical principles are constitutive and state that appearances in space and time have extensive and intensive magnitude. The dynamical principles are regulative and define the necessary connections underlying the relations of appearances (for example, causality) as well as the three modalities of experience: possible, actual, and necessary (B222ff).

The usual term for "object of experience" is *Gegenstand;* when this official use obtains, *Objekt* stands for any mental modification or representation "insofar as one is conscious of it" (B234f). In my previous terminology, a Gegenstand is then an object of public perception, whereas an Objekt is a quasi-object of private perception or sensation. Kant does not employ this terminology consistently; I take this as a sign of his failure to have thought through carefully the nature of perception.

As appearances (*phenomena*) subject to the transcendental machinery, the objects are constituted by the spontaneous activity of the understanding. But as objects of sensation (*Erscheinungen*), they are given to the receptive faculty of intuition. As we shall see in greater detail, only the former counts officially as an object of perception. Thus arises the problem of how to distinguish perception from judgment; in other words, all perceptions must be veridical. There cannot be a false perceptual judgment of an actual object of perception. We may be wrong with respect to illusions and fantasies of sensation, but this "error" cannot count as a judgment in the official sense of the *First Critique.* Neither can the referent of such a pseudojudgment be a genuine object (Gegenstand). Furthermore, the "veridical" judgment concerning the actual object of perception is itself both transcendental in its categorial structure and empirical or contingent with respect to the empirical concept and the content of sensation. Necessary a priori knowledge is restricted to the conditions of the possibility of objects of experience: to their transcendental superstructure or infrastructure. We can have only contingent, a posteriori, and (as I shall show) indeterminate knowledge of the actually existing empirical object.

The following citation is pivotal: "Conceptual knowledge [of Gegenstände], to which all a priori principles must finally always pertain, is merely possible experience. Hence the principles can have nothing as their aim but to be the conditions of the unity of empirical knowledge in the synthesis of appearances. This unity can be thought only in the schema of the pure concept of understanding. Its unity, as a synthesis in general, is contained in the category. The category is itself a function that is restricted by no sensible condition" (B223–24).

This, succinctly stated, is the general framework of possible knowledge, as adumbrated in the *First Critique,* and of the associated problems that will concern us here. I now turn directly to *The Critique of the Faculty of Judgment* in order to introduce the second of the two problems mentioned in the opening paragraph of this essay. This introduction having been made, I shall explore in detail Kant's treatment of perception, and then come back to his account of judgment. The two lines of analysis will unite in the conclusion that Kant fails to explain the relation between perception and judgment.

In the *Third Critique,* Kant says that "a transcendental principle is one through which is presented a priori the universal condition in accord with which alone things can be in general Objekte of our knowledge" (17).[4] Such a principle is that of the purposiveness (*Zweckmässigkeit*) of nature. Its concept covers "Gegenstände of possible empirical cognition in general, and it contains nothing empirical" (18). Thus the principle covers the same objects as are constituted by the understanding and regulated by reason. It is itself not constitutive but regulative only (222–23).

This is stated fully as follows: "The concept of a thing as in itself a natural purpose is thus no constitutive concept of the understanding or of reason, but it can be a regulative concept for the reflective judgment, that guides our investigation of objects of this kind in accord with a distant analogy with our causality according to purposes in general; it also guides our meditations concerning the last ground of these objects" (238). A purpose, understood transcendentally, is "the object of a concept, insofar as the latter is regarded as the cause of the former (the real ground of its possibility); and the causality of a concept with respect to its object is purposiveness (*forma finalis*)" (58).

The "distant analogy" is to everyday experience (my expression), in which we regularly attribute purposes to human acts and artifacts. Because the "artifacts" of nature are suitable for our cognitive faculties, we assume that this suitability is an intention of their maker, an intellect other than our own but which is unknown to us. This way of formulating the point is puzzling because it treats nature as independent of and given to our cognitive faculties, whereas, according to transcendental philosophy, we make objects in our capacity as empirical instances of the transcendental ego. Once granted that our concepts constitute objects from given sensations, there is nothing mysterious, no reason to demand an additional explanation about the fit between object and concept. The role of purposiveness in the systematization of knowledge, however, needs to be considered separately.

But first, a comment is required concerning the use of the expression *forma finalis* in connection with purposiveness. We see here a residue of the Aristotelian doctrine of form, which was no doubt transmitted to Kant by way of the Leibnizean scholasticism of the eighteenth century, which had a considerable influence on his thinking as well as upon his choice of terms. I shall later suggest another residue of Aristotelianism when I turn to Kant's treatment of the material content of the empirical object.

With respect to systematicity, Kant claims in paragraph 6 of the introduction to the *Third Critique* that "it is a command of our faculty of judgment to proceed according to the principle of the suitability of nature to our capacities of knowledge" (25) as far as we can in the integration of empirical knowledge within a hierarchically ordered unity of ultimate simplicity. At the same time, the presupposition of the faculty of judgment concerning purposiveness is indeterminate (*unbestimmt*) with respect to how far that purposiveness extends (ibid.). In non-Kantian but accurate terms, the hypothesis of purposiveness as a principle is a convenience to our psychological predisposition to organize empirical knowledge into a totality.

Exactly what Kant means by such a systematic hierarchy of nature is far from clear. I shall cite an additional passage to amplify the point, a passage in which Kant again makes references to the "undetermined" nature of the ostensible transcendental laws covering our experience of actual objects. "But there are so many forms of nature, and so many modifications of the universal transcendental concepts of nature, which are left undetermined [*unbestimmt*] by the laws given a priori by the pure understanding, because these only concern the possibility of a nature (as Gegenstand of the senses). There must therefore also be laws [for this manifold of forms] which indeed, as empirical, may be contingent to the insight of our own understanding, but which, if they are to be called laws [*wenn sie Gesetze heissen sollen*] (as is required by the concept of a nature), they must be regarded as necessary, out of the principle of the unity of a manifold, even if it be unknown to us" (16).

Why should there be laws organizing empirical knowledge which must be regarded as necessary? Kant is pointing to a dimension intermediate between the constitution of the intelligible world and empirical science itself. As is perhaps most obvious in his subsequent discussion of teleology and organism, Kant asserts that we cannot understand nature simply by describing the general laws of its possibility. But neither can we make do with empirical knowledge alone, which is radically contingent.

The task of fitting together contingent empirical knowledge within a comprehensive edifice is not accomplished merely by recourse to the aforementioned general laws, such as causality. We are able to regard empirical objects as fitting together because we employ the analogy with our own purposiveness to discover larger patterns within experience, such as the species-structure of genera or the laws of evolution. Kant uses the terms "law" and "rule" to refer to these systematizing aspects of experience. They are endlessly many because of the endless variety of natural objects. Hence they cannot be determined a priori by the transcendental principles of cognition. We must discover them one at a time, under the contingent circumstances of experience.

Our procedure in so discovering these rules or laws is intrinsically ambiguous. On the one hand, the laws are contingent so far as we can understand them because they are laws of actual empirical objects, and so, like the concepts of these objects, they are subject to change (*First Critique*, B755; I shall have occasion to discuss this passage again). On the other hand, as laws, they depend upon a pervasive property, namely, purposiveness. The property is itself ambiguous, since we attribute it to the objects, but this attribution is transformed into a principle by an act of heautonomy (22), that is, by placing ourselves under the obligation to obey what Kant calls "the *law of the specification of nature* with respect to its empirical laws" (ibid.).

We must obey this law because our judgment so commands, and yet what it commands us to do is to select from the "endlessly manifold ways" in which objects of experience can function as causes, the rule or law that regulates the object within a given empirical situation (19). We are commanded to find by reflection "endlessly many possible empirical laws" (20). I call this commandment the law of transcendental indeterminateness. Kant's transcendental deduction, when it finally arrives (paragraph 38), is anticlimactic and tells us nothing that we have not learned from the preceding paragraphs. The main point is that because the faculties of knowledge of all human beings are the same, the fit between the object and the concept is a priori the same for all (140).

The peculiar nature of the command, which is eventually articulated into a transcendental deduction, is plain from the following passage: "Now this principle can be nothing else but this. Since universal natural laws have their ground in our understanding, which prescribes them to nature . . . the particular empirical laws must be considered, with respect to that in them which is left undetermined [*unbestimmt*] by those universal laws, in accord with a unity of such a type, as if an understanding (although not our own) had given it to them for the sake of our faculties of knowledge, in order to make possible a system of experience in accord with particular laws of nature" (16).

This is one of those passages that divide Kant's readers into believers and skeptics. I must confess that I belong to the skeptics. Even if we make the "as if" assumption, it is our own understanding, in accord with the principles of transcendental philosophy, that must have assigned purposiveness to empirical objects. Kant of course means that we cannot know purposiveness in the same way that we know the categories or principles of pure understanding. But this should lead him to develop a more flexible doctrine of knowledge, not to talk as though nature had been after all created by a *deus absconditus* and presented to our cognition for consideration. Such a more flexible doctrine might begin from Kant's sound observation that there are no rules to determine the application of rules (3). What he calls reflective judgment is better understood as intuition, a faculty for which, unfortunately, Kant has little use.

On Kantian principles, it is we who present nature to ourselves as the product of the very acts by which we contemplate it. Purposiveness, which is a fact of experience, should then be regarded as a constitutive principle of the understanding.[5] But a more fundamental objection can be made to Kant's procedure. The expression "as if" (*als ob*) makes it evident that the entire transcendental doctrine, and not only the principle of purposiveness, is a hypothesis. Our experience has certain characteristics which we cannot prove to be universal. But we cannot understand our experience unless we assume that these characteristics are universal. Let us therefore assume them to be so. Elsewhere (when speaking of proofs for the existence of God) Kant points out that "what is supposed to serve as a hypothesis for the possibility of a given appearance must itself be completely certain with respect to its own possibility" (339). But the universality of purposiveness is not completely certain with respect to its possibility; on the contrary, this is what we are asked to assume. Kant's procedure is circular.

I want now to return to the *First Critique* in order to study Kant's treatment of perception. I need to do this in order to prepare for the subsequent consideration of the faculty of judgment, in the course of which I shall have something more to say about reflective judgment. Toward the beginning of section 1, I summarized the general framework for possible knowledge of objects of experience. Actual knowledge of such objects is a function of intuition and conception, which yield sensation or perception and judgment. I say "sensation or perception" because the exact status of perception is unclear, to say the least.

Perceptions are defined as follows in the section "Of Ideas in General" (B376). Kant is in the process of giving a summary of the stages of types of representations, culminating in the Ideas of reason:

> The genus is representation in general (repraesentatio). Under it is the representation with consciousness (perceptio). A perception that is related merely to the subject as a modification of its state is sensation (sensatio), an objective perception is knowledge (cognitio). This is either intuition or concept (intuitus vel conceptus). The former refers immediately to the Gegenstand and is singular; the latter [refers to the Gegenstand] mediately, by way of a characteristic that can be common to many things. The concept is either empirical or pure, and the pure concept, insofar as it has its origin merely in the understanding (not in a pure image of sensation) is called Notio. A concept made up of notions which transcends the possibility of experience, is the Idea or the concept of reason.

This passage establishes that there are two kinds of perception, which I shall designate as private and public. The private perception is limited to, and in fact seems to be identical with, sensation. It therefore corresponds to the "idea" of British empiricism, which is itself an impression. We are conscious of these "impressions," but they do not amount to knowledge. An objective perception, as knowledge, may be either an intuition or a concept. What Kant means by intuited knowledge is unclear, unless it is mathematical or geometrical knowledge. Discursive knowledge of empirical objects certainly depends upon concepts; the empirical concept is a perception, but not a product of the pure understanding. The "pure *Bild*" to which Kant refers may be the schema of the imagination, although at B179f Kant emphasizes that the latter is not a *Bild*, that is, not a "picture" based upon sensation but a rule for constructing an empirical object.

With respect to the empirical object (and disregarding purely intuitive knowledge), subjective and objective perception both contain sensation. The difference between the two is that in objective perception a concept is also present. The concept of the object is empirical, but it must be embedded in a structure of categories, and so of syntheses of the imagination as well as of pure or original apperception, in order to be possible at all, and hence to be actual as an element of intersubjective experience.

The distinction between subjective and objective (or private and public) perception is virtually the same as the official distinction between Objekt and Gegenstand, to which, unfortunately, Kant is often unfaithful. The dependence of objective perception upon synthesis is plain from many passages, among which I cite B234, from the proof of the second Analogy of Experience: "In other words, the *objective relation* of appearances that follow one another remains undetermined through mere perception. . . . Therefore experience itself, i.e., empirical knowledge of appearances, is possible only because we place the sequence of appearances together with all of its alterations under the law of causality." This is the basis for empirical knowledge of a Gegenstand. Any representation, insofar as one is conscious of it, may be called an Objekt, that is, a private perception; even these are subject to the synthesis of the imagination (B235).

Thus far, it is established that an objective perception, although distinct from a subjective perception, is not fully objective unless it is subsumed under the category of causality. One would be forced to infer from the passages just cited that this is a subsumption of sensation under an empirical concept, which is again subsumed under a category. Still more specifically, there are *no* objective perceptions without objects. But this leads directly to a fundamental problem.

Private perceptions may be dreams, illusions, or sensory errors; but they may also be proto-objective; "In themselves, appearances, as mere representations [that is, not as things in themselves], are only actual within perception, which is in fact nothing but the actuality of an empirical representation, i.e., appearance" (B521). There is no such objective actuality prior to perception. "Everything is actual that stands in connection with a perception in accord with laws of empirical process" (ibid.). Because it is the concept that connects the perception to experience, no explanation is given as to how the concept itself distinguishes between illusions and proto-objects within the domain of private perception.

In fact, the objective perception ought to be the basis for the application of conceptual structure. But Kant rules this out because there is no objective perception until such conceptual structure has been applied. If, then, subjective perception or sensation determines when concepts are to be applied, actuality is *not* distinguishable from a dream or illusion. That is, actuality is merely a conceptually structured subjectivity, and this amounts to subjective Idealism or even to solipsism. On the other hand, if the conceptual structure itself determines which subjective perceptions are to be made actual, the result is objective Idealism. It is altogether unintelligible how, on Kantian principles, concepts could distinguish actual from merely subjective or illusory objects of sensation. "Thoughts without content are empty; intuitions without concepts are blind" (B75). I conclude that Kant has not explained perception.

According to Kant, the preconceptualized content of subjective or private perception is governed by the Lockean or Humean psychological laws of association (B118f, A112–14). Addition of the concept results in a judgment. A judgment is the subsumption of a Gegenstand under a concept (B304). But the Gegenstand is itself the result of the subsumption of a unified intuition under a concept (B74ff). The understanding is a faculty of judgment and can make no use of concepts "other than that it judges through them" (B93f). "The judgment is thus the mediated knowledge of a Gegenstand, and so a representation of a representation of it" (ibid.). In other words, the unity of the perceived object is furnished by exactly the same operations (the schematized pure concept: B223f) as supply the object of empirical knowledge via a judgment. To constitute an object is to judge or determine it, hence to raise it from possibility to actuality by subsuming it under a universal, that is, the predicate of a judgment (B94).

This line of analysis leads to the inference that there is no difference between perceiving an object of experience and judging it. In its objective sense, perception is conceptual or judgmental. Since the perceptual object is inseparable from judgment, there is no possibility of distinguishing between true and false perceptual judgments. The inference can be strengthened by the following consideration.

We must distinguish between synthesis and unity. The imagination synthesizes the sensibility, that is, sensations, but it does not unify them (B152). Unity is either that of possible consciousness altogether or of an actual object of experience in particular. The former is equivalent to the original synthetic unity of apperception or transcendental unity of self-consciousness (B132); the latter is furnished by the network of categories, schema, and empirical concept

(B114). The imagination, in synthesizing sensibility, prepares the manifold for objective unification. It does not supply Gegenstände. According to Kant, the laws of association governing subjective perception yield nothing but "an unregulated heap" (A121) of appearances.

At the same time, this heap must yield (what the *Prolegomenon* calls) "what seem to me" to be objects, as well as what, through the mediation of concepts, actually are objects. Seeming or private objects, whether illusory or protoactual, lack unity; strictly speaking, the expression "protoactual" has no meaning. There are no merely subjective objects. As we have just seen, the shift from the subjective to the objective, or from the possible to the actual, is itself a shift to perception and knowledge. Because concepts without the sensations of intuition are empirically blind, and because there is nothing objective about sensation alone, nothing accounts for the combination of concepts and sensations. The only visible candidate, the laws of association, would, if elected, reestablish British empiricism, despite the elaborate transcendental machinery introduced by Kant.

In fact, I believe that this is exactly what happens, as I will show in the next section when I turn to the empirical concept. Before I do so, I want to make a remark on receptivity and spontaneity in Kant's account of perception. Kant regularly asserts that the empirical object is "given" to the understanding by way of the receptivity of intuition: "Gegenstände are given to us via sensibility, which alone furnishes us with intuitions; they are, however, thought through the understanding, from which arise concepts" (B34).

If the object is given to us by intuition, then it must possess preconceptual objective properties. The intuited Objekt must itself be potentially the Gegenstand; that is, the material content furnished by sensation is the object of experience *in potentia,* exactly as Aristotle maintains. On the other hand, if the swarm of sensation is held to lack preconceptual determinateness, and so not to be in each instance any particular protoobject, what is given to the concept is a kind of Aristotelian prime matter that makes no determinate contribution to the specificity of the object. The specificity comes exclusively from the *forma finalis.*

To summarize and conclude this section: Kant refers frequently to the givenness of the object of experience as a consequence of the "mere receptivity" of sensibility (B33). Givenness in this sense cannot be objective: "When I take away all thinking (through categories) from empirical knowledge, there remains no knowledge of any Gegenstand because nothing is thought through mere intuition; and that this sensation is in me, constitutes no reference of that representation to any Objekt at all" (B309). Kant also asserts that perception, understood as empirical consciousness that contains sensations, contains "in addition to intuition the matter for some Objekt in general" (B207). The net result is to reduce sensation to the role of prime matter, and so to identify perception with conception.

Judgments about empirical objects depend not merely upon sensation and categorial structure but upon an empirical concept as well. Objects of experience, considered solely as resulting from sensation and an empirical concept, are contingent. Kant's doctrine leads to the strange consequence that objects are necessary as possible but contingent as actual. Once again, the ostensible or pseudo-object of private perception is not really an object, and so it is neither possible nor actual (terms reserved for experience, and so for objects).

The contingency of the empirical object means that the empirical concept is also contingent. I need to cite at length a passage on definition from the *Methodenlehre:*

> To define, as the expression itself states, shall signify authentically only this much: to exhibit originally the circumstantially detailed concept of a thing within its limits. In accordance with such a demand, an empirical concept can indeed not be *defined,* but only *made explicit.* For since we have in it only some characteristics of a certain species of a sensible Gegenstand, it is never certain whether one designates the same object by that word, or whether by its use we think at one time more, at another time less characteristics. . . . We make use of certain characteristics only for so long as they are sufficient for making distinctions; new observations remove some and add others, so that the concept never stands between secure limits. (B755–56)

The same point is made more concisely with respect to intuition at B199: "The a priori conditions of intuition are thoroughly necessary with respect to a possible experience. Those of the *Dasein* of the Objekt of a possible empirical intuition are in themselves only accidental." Whatever exists contains sensation and is accordingly a posteriori (B218). In the *Third Critique,* Kant refers to the *forma finalis* as the locus of purposiveness. In the *First Critique,* such an expression, as applied to the very same empirical concept, would be entirely inappropriate. The Aristotelian *eidos* has become a discursive rule.

The insubstantial character of the empirical concept is well illustrated by the following passage:

> In the universal principles of morals there can be nothing uncertain, because the propositions are either entirely nugatory and senseless, or else they must flow from

nothing but concepts of reason. In the natural sciences [*Naturkunde*], on the other hand, there is nothing but an infinity of conjectures, with respect to which no one can ever anticipate certainty, because the natural appearances are Gegenstände that are given to us independently of our concepts, to which therefore the key lies, not in us and in our pure thinking, but outside of us, and so in many cases cannot be found. Consequently no secure conclusion is to be expected. (B508–09)

As this passage makes plain, the "givenness" of the object is to the pure concepts of the understanding, not to the empirical concept. All other problems to one side (such as the role of categorial synthesis even in the actuality of the empirical object), the immediately noteworthy point is that the empirical concept, as so given, lies within sensation. It is therefore useless in accounting for objective perception. The need to preserve the endlessly indeterminate nature of the empirical concept is directly connected to, and no doubt one of the main causes of, Kant's failure to explain perception.

As a collection of objects under a common characteristic, an empirical concept possesses generality. This generality is empirical, derived as it is from particular subjective perceptions (B118). The origin of empirical concepts is physiological in the style of Locke (B119). And yet this is not the whole story. Obviously Kant is aware of the impossibility of deriving even an empirical concept from a heap of sensations. I turn accordingly to B180, the main passage in which Kant discusses the role of the empirical concept in the production of the object of perception. This passage will give us the added element that ostensibly renders sensation into an object, however contingent.

At B180, Kant uses the example of a dog, which he contrasts with geometrical objects like the triangle. "The schema of the triangle can exist nowhere else but in thought, and denotes a rule of synthesis of the imagination in respect to pure *Gestalten* in space. Still less is a Gegenstand of experience or its image [*Bild*] ever adequate to the empirical concept, but this always refers immediately to the schema of the imagination as a rule for the determination of our intuition in conformity with a certain general concept."

In addition to sensation, then, empirical concepts require a schema of the imagination. Kant's explanation is, as usual, lacking in detail, but we must remember that the empirical concept emerges from sensation, not from pure understanding. As a generalization, it must be a product of the understanding, but I can find no passage in which Kant explains how the understanding produces empirical concepts. I think we must assume that the empirical concept is somehow produced by the reproductive imagination in cooperation with understanding (see B195). However this may be, the schema does not supply the image of the object or what we may call its phenomenological form; it is instead "the representation of a method for representing a concept in an image" (B179).

Not only the schema but the empirical concept as well is a rule (a mark of its owing its existence, at least in part, to the understanding). "The concept of dog signifies a rule, in accordance with which my imagination can sketch the *Gestalt* of a four-footed animal, without being restricted to any individual particular *Gestalt* which experience furnishes me, or any possible image which I can exhibit *in concreto*" (B180).

This is a remarkable passage in every way. We now have two rules, one a schema and the other a concept. The origin of the concept is unexplained. The rule instructs the imagination on the sketching (the very word suggests a vague, only partially filled-in perception of a blurred object) of a four-footed animal, that is, *not a dog,* and certainly not any dog in particular. The forms (*Gestalten*) of experienced dogs do not determine the sketch but presumably assist it in some general, indeterminate manner. These "forms" are presumably shapes within the heap of private perceptions; as a result, they cannot count as objects of experience, that is, as actual dogs. And yet, where else are we to obtain the phenomenological form of the dog; indeed, of this dog?

The imagination that produces the sketch is like a painter working from a discursive description of a dog in general rather than from a living model. In ordinary, pre-Kantian experience, we perceive dogs and then attempt to describe them. Kant reverses this procedure; the description precedes the perception. It is therefore entirely unintelligible from Kant's transcendental model of the conditions of the possibility of experience *how experience is possible.* On the contrary, if we follow Kant's model patiently and in minute detail, perception is shown to be impossible.

I understand that the indeterminateness of the empirical object is meant to reflect faithfully the difference between mathematical and natural science or between the transcendental and the empirical. But a satisfactory transcendental model must offer some explanation of how we succeed in perceiving such a thing as this dog here, Rex the beagle, who is sitting at my feet and wagging his tail. To say that my concept of beagles, or even of dogs, is indeterminate, is one thing. But it is something else again, and something entirely absurd, to say that my perception of a beagle is indeterminate in the Kantian sense of the term. Entirely apart from the inner contradictions in Kant's technical doctrine, he is refuted by the fact of perception.

On Kant's analysis, what I perceive as my beagle might also be a fox, a wolf,

or for that matter an elephant. This cannot be justified by a reference to
the Darwinian theory of evolution and the indeterminateness of species. The
population or gene-pool of dogs may be in the process of evolution, but any
given dog is just what it is, namely, a dog. In Kant's doctrine of perception, the
empirical world is in the process of being transformed into a text. Perception is
hermeneutics.

At B195 Kant says that space and time are necessarily applied to the Gegenstände of experience by the reproductive imagination, which "calls up the
Gegenstände of experience. . . . The possibility of experience is therefore that
which gives a priori objective reality to all our knowledge. Now experience rests
upon the synthetic unity of appearances, i.e., on a synthesis in accord with
concepts of Gegenstände of appearances in general, without which they would
not be knowledge, but a rhapsody of perceptions that would not fit into any
context in accord with rules of a thoroughly combined (possible) consciousness, and so also not to any transcendental and necessary unity of apperception."

In other words, empirical knowledge is not knowledge at all, but a rhapsody,
except to the extent that it is unified, and so objectified or incorporated within a
rule-governed structure of experience by the pure understanding. Either this
objectification transforms the rhapsody into a totally determinate world in
which only veridical judgments are possible, or else it has no bearing upon the
actual world, which remains a rhapsody, entirely apart from the a priori world
of pure possibility. There is no actual, objective, scientifically determinable
world intermediate between private rhapsody and a priori possibility. Such a
world would have to be perceived first and only then conceptualized; it would
have to be given in a pre-Kantian sense.

As is the case with most modern philosophers, existence or actuality is for
Kant ontologically posterior to, or lower than, Being or possibility. When Kant
claims that Being is a logical rather than a real predicate, he seems to use
"Being" (*Sein*) and "existence" (*Dasein*) as though they were synonymous
(B625–26). Elsewhere, as at B199, *Dasein* is used to refer to empirical or actual
existence. It can easily be shown that Kant makes a distinction between Being
and existence in his discussion of one hundred thalers, but we must remember
that both terms apply to "objects," not to the transcendental conditions for the
possibility of objects. I nevertheless believe that it is legitimate to apply the term
"Being" to the transcendental because the latter is for Kant the conceptual
articulation of possibility.

At B626, Kant argues that Being is not contained in the concept of a thing

(*Ding*), whether the thing be God or a hundred thalers. Being is merely the "position" of a thing as a possible object of experience. This position is represented by the copula in a judgment. As we have now seen at length, the object shifts from possibility to actuality through the contribution of perception. When Kant says that "the actual contains nothing more than the merely possible" (B627), he is referring to concepts or predicates, that is, to determining features of the object. Because categories do not contribute actual predicates, Kant must be referring to empirical concepts here. Putting to one side the various problems we have canvased to date, the statement just quoted overlooks the fact that, on Kant's own grounds, the actual must contain sensation in the form of perception, whereas this cannot be true of the possible.

To conclude this section: at B94, Kant says that "thinking is knowledge through concepts. Concepts however refer, as predicates of possible judgments, to some representation of a still undetermined Gegenstand." I have shown that, in the case of empirical concepts, the object is never determined. Logical possibility is then determinate or definite only with respect to general conditions for possible existence. Any particular possibility, such as a four-footed animal, is indefinite, and it remains indefinite upon actualization.

So much for Kant's treatment of perception. Let us now shift our focus to judgment, and under that general topic, we will return to the reflective judgment of the *Third Critique*. I begin with a very brief recapitulation. The *First Critique* teaches that knowledge is derived from intuitions and concepts (B93). Intuitions are sensible and "received" by the pure forms of space and time (to which I add parenthetically that they are actually "produced" as appearances within space and time). Concepts are produced by the spontaneity of thinking.

This spontaneity expresses itself in functions, namely, "the unity of the act by which various representations are ordered under a common representation." The common representation is the concept; in its pure form, the category, whereas the empirical concept is an amalgam of sensation, imagination, and understanding. "The understanding can make no other use of these concepts than to judge by them" (ibid.). Concepts are related to objects via intuitions. Because judgments are made of concepts, "a judgment is therefore the mediate knowledge of an object, and so the representation of a representation of that object" (ibid.).

I want to call attention to two unclear points in this account of judging. First, it is not clear whether concept-formation is identical with judgment. This lack of clarity holds good with respect to both empirical and categorial judgments. It is one thing to say, "This is a dog," and something else again to say, "Dogs are carnivorous." Analogously, it is one thing to say, "This is a body," and something else to say, "All bodies are divisible" (cf. B128–29). Granted that the understanding is a faculty of judgment and can make no other use of concepts than to judge with them (B93), are conceptualization and judging two acts or one and the same act?

This leads directly to the second point: It is not as clear as one could wish that the understanding and the judgment are two distinct faculties. At B94, Kant says, "All judgments are functions of unity underlying our representations. . . . We can therefore reduce all acts of the understanding to judgments, so that the understanding in general may be represented as a capacity to judge" (*ein Vermögen zu urteilen*). Does this mean that there are two capacities or faculties for judging, the *Verstand* and the *Urteilskraft?*

We might try to answer this question as follows. In the *Third Critique,* Kant distinguishes between two kinds of judging, determinant and reflective. The first corresponds to the judgments of the understanding (allowing "determinant" to apply in a weak sense to empirical objects), whereas the second corresponds to the judgments of the faculty of judgment. This answer, however, is blocked by the fact that Kant assigns both types of judgment to the faculty of judgment.

Kant does say that the principles of the faculty of judgment need not form a separate set between the theoretical principles of the understanding and the practical principles of reason, but may be attached to either of these (*Third Critique,* 3). This is because the faculty of judgment has no objects of its own but may function with respect to both natural objects and the desires relevant to morality. There is no doubt that Kant is here asserting three distinct faculties of understanding, judgment, and reason. But this does not explain the sense in which the understanding is a faculty of judging.

Such an explanation would be forthcoming if Kant were to say unequivocally that the understanding engages in determinant judging whereas the faculty of judgment engages in reflective judging. Perhaps the closest we can come to clearing up the point is by a modification of this reply. Reflective judgments fall within the scope of the faculty of judgment acting alone, and also when its principles are attached to reason. Determinant judgments are those which arise when the principles of the faculty of judgment adhere to the understanding. I am not entirely satisfied with this explanation, but I cannot think of a better one.

The same tripartition of faculties that underlies the *Third Critique* is to be found in the *First Critique* at B171. But Kant says there that they are the faculties of concepts, judgments, and inferences. This seems to contradict the identification of the understanding as a faculty of judgment. Kant goes on to say that the Analytic of Principles "will be solely a canon for the faculty of judgment, that instructs it in the application to appearances of the concepts of the understanding, which contain the conditions for a priori rules."

This supports the thesis that determinant judgment is the work of the understanding, but it conflicts with, if it does not in fact contradict, the assertions that knowing is judging (B93–4 and B223–24) and that the understanding is the faculty of knowing (B137). Even worse, at B106, Kant says that the capacity to judge is the same as the capacity to think. It is hard to see how this is not equivalent to identifying the faculty of understanding with the faculty of judgment.

In the *Third Critique,* the tripartition is explained as follows (15ff). The understanding deals with the faculties of knowledge and furnishes these with a priori constitutive principles. Reason regulates the understanding; it contains a priori constitutive principles only with respect to the faculties of desire (2). Judgment is concerned with the application of understanding; it does not constitute the object but applies the concept in the act of thinking the particular as contained within the universal. The universal is a rule, principle, or law. If it is furnished by the understanding, the subsuming judgment is determinant. If the particular is given, but the universal must be found, then the judgment is "merely reflective."

I take this passage to support the identification of determinant judgment as the work of the understanding, whatever follows about the independence of the faculty of understanding. But what precisely is the work of the reflective judgment? I am not the first to observe that Kant never explicitly and unambiguously states the answer to this question.[6] He mentions two tasks: the organization of empirical knowledge in a systematic hierarchy of increasing generality, and the formation of judgments of the aesthetic, sublime, teleological, and even moral type, which are valid for all persons and which, in the first three cases, concern the pleasure occasioned by the correspondence between the object and the cognitive faculties of the subject.

The main point for us is that the reflective judgment is regulative, and that the principle of purposiveness is imposed by the subject upon itself (this is heautonomy: 22). Purposiveness lies in the concept (considered as *forma finalis:* 58) as the condition of the possibility of the object of our knowledge (17). The fit between the object and the concept, that is, the representation of the object, "is immediately bound up with the feeling of pleasure" (26–27). The judgment of purposiveness is not constitutive; accordingly, reflective judgment does not participate in, but depends upon, the perception of the object. Only perceived objects can be fitted into a hierarchy of empirical knowledge.

This point is worth emphasizing: Nothing in the *Third Critique* casts light upon the mechanics of perception. At the beginning of paragraph 36, Kant says, "The concept of an Objekt in general can be immediately combined with the perception of a Gegenstand [here Kant uses his official distinction between the two German terms], which latter contains the empirical predicates, and thereby a judgment of experience is produced" (138).

This is the process of object construction as described (however unsuccessfully) in the *First Critique*. The concept of an object in general is a category. The perceived object is structured in advance of the application of the category, as is necessary in order for it to be indeterminate or open to endless interpretations. It is to this perception, namely, as it obtains within a judgment of experience, that the feeling of pleasure, pain, or satisfaction "is immediately attached" (ibid.). The feeling serves in place of the predicates as the basis for a reflective judgment, which accordingly makes no contribution to, or modification of, the perceived object.

The reflective judgment, as occupied with the discovery of the endlessly many rules that fit epistemic judgments into a systematic hierarchy, fulfills a hermeneutical function that is analogous to the interpretation by the understanding of the empirical object. If the structure of the object completely determined it, there would be no reflective judgment, and determinant judgment would be equivalent to conceptual constitution.

In this event, experience as we know and live it would be impossible. Kant wishes to account for the structure or coherence of experience, that is, for the conditions of the possibility of experience. He must accordingly provide a structure that leaves the content of experience contingent. The traditional defense of Kant, according to which the critical philosophy is not concerned with experience as such, but only with its transcendental conditions, itself requires an explanation of the possibility of experience. I have argued that Kant's model fails to provide this explanation.

A contingent world must possess a structure that gives it both order and intelligibility without suppressing that contingency. The transcendental conditions either remove contingency or fail to provide a structure to it. These alternatives are evident from our study of his doctrine of perception, which both identifies perception with epistemic judgment and leaves the empirical object indeterminate. Kant is in a position to offer us a refutation of British empiricism only by rendering experience necessary; this is precisely the implication of his *Opus postumum*.

Kant's failure to solve the problem of the relation between form and content led directly to German Idealism, which is a development of his own doctrine of form as act. But German Idealism succeeded only in preserving the dualism of form and content within a comprehensive activity styled "absolute" rather than "transcendental." This is the background of the rise of Historicism (including the variant of Historicity), and so of the triumph in our own generation of difference over identity. We are still trying to understand how that triumph is not also the affirmation of comprehensive chaos. To be told that the affirmation of comprehensive chaos is in fact wisdom is to bring out the intrinsic Hegelianism of Nietzsche's teaching. A Nietzscheanized Hegelianism may replace the dualism of form and content with that of noble and base nihilism. But we still require a criterion for that distinction, a criterion that is nowhere in view.

Chapter 10 Freedom and Reason

This essay originated as a lecture that was delivered in earlier forms on a number of occasions. The present text was published in a Festschrift for Professor Manfred Riedel of Erlangen University: Inmitten der Zeit, *edited by Thomas Grethlein and Heinrich Leitner (Königshausen and Neumann, 1996), 161–78. The central purpose of the essay is to distinguish three types of freedom, named after Plato, Kant, and the post-Kantians. The first type associates freedom with the apprehension of a formal structure; in so doing, however, it transforms freedom into necessity. Although I do not discuss Spinoza here, he is perhaps the best modern example of this conception of freedom. Kant associates freedom with spontaneity, but he defines spontaneity as the activation of law. This conception of freedom has two outstanding characteristics. First, the rational structure that is the expression of freedom is now understood as an activity of the mind (Gemüt). In other words, the mind is free through the thinking, and so actualizing, of structures which are not the same as but dependent upon the process of cognition. Second, necessity is now conceived as a product of spontaneity. When the conceptual productions of spontaneity (such as the axioms of geometry or the laws of logic) are themselves seen to be contin-*

gent, possibility comes to dominate over necessity, and freedom begins its long decay into what one could call historical libertinism. Post-Kantianism is the story of that long decay. The most important episode in the story of post-Kantianism is Hegel, who attempts to combine the Kantian doctrine of form as activity with a modern version of the Platonic doctrine of (spiritual) eros. But this doctrine of eros has been detached from independent forms and reconceptualized in light of the new psychology introduced by Descartes in the Passions of the Soul. *Eros is now understood as desire for self-satisfaction. In short, Hegel attempts to unify ancient and modern philosophy by defining freedom as the synthesis of classical form and modern subjective excitation. Desire is satisfied through the production of intelligible structure, the order of necessity. Freedom, exactly as in Spinoza but as anticipated by Plato, is the cognitive grasp of that structure. One could summarize post-Kantianism as the result of the collapse of produced intelligible structure into the activity of production, which activity itself collapses from the spontaneity of the mind to the chaotic will to power of desire. The history of philosophy seems to suggest that there is no way in which to define freedom through concepts, rules, or, more generally, the apprehension of ontological or intelligible structure. The attempt to "rationalize" freedom turns it inevitably into necessity, and this in turn is reification of existence. We are today witnessing what may be the last form of this attempted rationalization in the philosophies inspired by neuroscience and artificial intelligence.*

I begin with an informal statement of three different theses concerning the relation between freedom and reason. According to the first thesis, freedom is a consequence of the subordination of the intellect to independent formal structure. One finds a version of this thesis, for example, in Plato's *Sophist* at 253c6ff, where dialectic, or the science of the combination and separation of forms—also referred to as division in accordance with kinds—is identified by the Eleatic Stranger and the young mathematician Theaetetus as the science that characterizes the free man.

In the *Symposium* and *Phaedrus,* Plato assigns to Socrates the primary role in the promulgation of quite a different doctrine, namely, that one rises to the intellectual apprehension of the Ideas or pure forms by various purifications of the love of the beautiful. The word "free" never occurs in the main accounts of erotic ascent, for the obvious reason that Eros is a form of compulsion.[1] In fact, there is no fundamental difference on this point with the passage in the *Sophist,* in which the compulsion of formal analysis replaces that of contemplation.

The second thesis is conveniently illustrated by Kant's association of freedom with spontaneity and autonomy. Reason is spontaneous rather than receptive;

more precisely, *Verstand* produces concepts spontaneously whereas *Vernunft* produces the idea of a spontaneous, extraworldly, or noumenal cause of a series of conditions within the spatiotemporal or phenomenal world. It thus supplies the Idea of freedom "as a capacity of absolute spontaneity."[2] Reason is spontaneous because it produces concepts and Ideas by its own activity and from itself alone, not from supernatural inspiration or by generalization upon sensuous impressions. It is autonomous because it acts or expresses itself as a law or rule; this is what distinguishes spontaneity from radical contingency or chaos.

We do not need to concern ourselves with the details of Kant's doctrine. Suffice it to add that the practical reason is free because it actualizes as a moral rule or law that supplies the unconditioned origin of a chain of conditions required by theoretical reason but unobtainable for it.[3] According to Kant, we know a priori that we are free because we know that we are bound by moral laws.[4] The moral law is the analogue in the domain of practical reason to the concept and the Idea in the domain of theoretical reason. The upshot of the second thesis, which we may refer to for convenience as Kantian, is that it modifies the Platonist thesis but does not reject it entirely. Freedom continues to be understood with respect to the apprehension by reason of necessary or binding forms; but by "forms" is now meant rules or laws rather than looks or (in an Aristotelian expression) essences.

I shall call the third thesis about the relation between freedom and reason post-Kantian. It arises as a historical consequence of the weakening and eventual dissolution of the Kantian connection between spontaneity and autonomy on the one hand and necessity on the other. In Kant, spontaneity actualizes as necessity, in the form of concepts, categories, rules, laws, and regulative Ideals. As the force of these spontaneous emissions weakens, whether because of advances in physics and mathematics or simply by virtue of the unrestrainable fecundity of the human imagination, the bond between necessity and possibility dissolves. In other words, history presents us with alternative concepts, Ideas, rules, and laws, each attempting to define necessity. Necessity accordingly loses its ontological status and becomes a matter of contingency or choice. The difference between necessity and possibility dissolves.

It is not necessary to follow here the various discussions in Kant of freedom or the variations on these discussions introduced by Kant's immediate successors, of whom the most important is Fichte. The upshot of the decay of the Kantian into the post-Kantian thesis is as follows. The transcendental ego is replaced by the historical consciousness, whose structure of development is initially said to be absolute. Soon, however, the absolute is itself dissolved by temporality or historicality; freedom is in effect the same as spontaneity, but spontaneity now means contingency or chance and so can no longer be distinguished from chaos.

Interestingly, one finds in the twentieth century the analogue to the eighteenth- and nineteenth-century development of transcendental or absolute historicity, and its devolution into temporality, in the evolving doctrines of Martin Heidegger, or as one could also put this, in the shift from Heidegger's doctrine of Being to the post-Heideggerian doctrines of difference. It is also present in the gradual emancipation of the imagination, together with the tendency to equate necessity with the logical principle of noncontradiction, while at the same time the creation of logical principles is attributed to the imagination.

In sum, the post-Kantian thesis regards itself—or is easily regarded as—the reversal or deconstruction of the Platonist thesis. Freedom now means freedom *from* reason, just as spontaneity means freedom from rules or laws. In the main part of this essay, I want to prepare a different way of understanding the post-Kantian situation. I am going to provide evidence in support of the contention that post-Kantianism is in fact a deteriorated, decadent, or in a sense borrowed from Nietzsche, a reversed version of Platonism. I want to suggest that the Platonism of the late modern and contemporary anti-Platonists has been overlooked because of a failure to treat with equal attention the two elements of Platonism, namely, the doctrine of the Ideas and the account of Eros.

I am well aware that Eros is today a "hot topic," especially among heterodox classicists. On this point, the situation is entirely different from what it was in 1968, when I published my study of Plato's *Symposium*. But the contemporary treatment of Eros seems to proceed independently of the so-called technical or ontological signification of the doctrine of Ideas. Conversely, those who take their bearings by ontology or by its Anglo-Saxon equivalent, conceptual analysis, tend more or less to ignore Eros and to identify Platonism with the doctrine of the Ideas.

The heart of the matter is to see that the several advertisements in the Platonic dialogues for a science of dialectic or diaeresis are never honored with actual examples, except for the patently ironical cases of the sophist and the statesman, neither of which, of course, is an Idea. Correlatively, the doctrine of Eros praises the ultimate stage of the contemplation of pure forms, but at the price of the disappearance of our historical or political selves. To whatever extent the notion of freedom makes sense in this constellation of doctrines, it is surely only as the subordination or moderation of desire to the order of intelligibility. In the extreme but accurate formulation, freedom means not merely freedom from contingency but from human existence altogether.

Stated with maximum simplicity, post-Kantianism is Platonism because its eventual repudiation of subjectivity, humanism, and anthropomorphism is a hyperbolical version of the disappearance of the personal soul in the culmination of erotic ascent. It is, however, a deteriorated or decadent Platonism because the Ideas are now dissolved into the passions of Eros. In the age of difference, Eros no longer has any limits. It is no longer possible to distinguish between ascent and descent. Heracleitus's assertion that the way up is the same as the way down, which is false for Platonism, is true for post-Kantianism. I have already noted that the post-Kantian defines freedom as freedom from reason. To this I may now add that post-Kantian freedom is indistinguishable from the chaos that Nietzsche tells us is at the heart of all things.

In somewhat broader terms, my suggestion is that modern philosophy can be understood as the process by which the Platonic Ideas are transformed into manifestations or productions of Eros, rather than preserved as external objects of erotic desire. The corollary to this transformation of the Ideas is the secularization of Eros or its demotion from divine or daimonic status to its modern status as physiological passion. The Platonic distinction between the corporeal or pandemic and the psychic or heavenly Eros disappears. Interestingly enough, whereas reversed Platonism understood as the demotion of Eros leads to the suppression of the distinction between the human and the bestial, the philosophical disregard of Eros results in the suppression of the distinction between human beings and machines. The question whether machines can think would look quite different if one were to ask whether machines are erotic.

Although post-Kantianism is, as it were, reversed Platonism, it is a consequence of an internal dialectic in the Kantian thesis, by which expression, let me emphasize, I do not refer simply to Kant but to a pervasive theme in modern philosophy that culminates in Kant. In the next section of this essay I am going to discuss Descartes' *The Passions of the Soul,* in accordance with my terminology a Kantian text, which will illustrate the beginning of the transformation of the Platonic doctrine of Eros into the common ancestor of the two predominant schools of post-Kantianism, one terminating in the celebration of difference, the other in neurophysiologically oriented approaches to the so-called artificial intelligence, the contemporary version of "man the machine."

In section 3 I will turn to Hegel, whom we may fairly consider as the last stage of the modern expression of the Kantian thesis, but also as the preface to the emergence of post-Kantianism in its full bloom of nineteenth-century positivism, historicism, and nihilism. I will then conclude with three summary remarks that may serve to introduce subsequent discussion.

By encouraging us to be as the masters and possessors of nature, Descartes initiates the process of overcoming the separation of the human from the divine, a process that culminates in Hegel. What Descartes means by mastery is, of course, quite different from what Hegel means when he tells us in his *Logic* that he has thought the eternal essence of God as it is, prior to the creation of the universe.[5] We are primarily concerned here with Descartes' doctrine of human nature, of which he says in *The Passions of the Soul* that he offers us a new analysis, one that begins with an explicit rejection of the analysis provided by the ancients.[6]

Descartes says that the investigation of human nature is not especially difficult because each of us feels the passions within us: "One has no need to borrow from elsewhere any observation in order to discover their nature."[7] Descartes takes for granted the regularity of human nature as well as the direct accessibility of the soul, or *ego cogitans*, to itself. He does not explain why the ancients were prevented from acquiring this relatively easy science. We may infer from his own procedure that the obstacle lay in their distinction between the heavenly and the vulgar or pandemic Eros or, more prosaically, in their failure to replace poetry by neurophysiology.

The point is quite clear in what is for us the decisive case of Eros. In the *Symposium,* a dialogue to which Descartes explicitly refers,[8] Diotima says that Eros is an intermediary between mortal and immortal who practices the hermeneutic art of interpreting human needs and divine commands. Hermeneutics, as we may put it, thus binds the cosmos into a whole.[9] In contrast, Descartes secularizes Eros by designating love (*Amour*) as one of the six basic or physiological passions, which are all subordinated not to pure forms but to a derived passion of the soul, which Descartes calls *generosité* as well as *magnanimité* and *megalopsuchia*.[10]

At this stage of the analysis, it is essential to recall a crucial tenet of the Cartesian teaching, namely, the independence of the soul from the body. I note in passing that Descartes never actually explains how these two substances interact, despite his notorious claim that the locus of interaction is in the pineal gland. What counts for us is the fact that Descartes argues simultaneously for the mechanical nature of the body and the thesis that passions in the soul are caused by actions, that is, motions, in the body, but also for the thesis that the actions of the soul are all volitions and that these are free.[11]

He therefore argues simultaneously that knowledge of the motions of the body makes possible modification of the passions of the soul, and that the will is free or able to initiate thoughts in the soul and motions in the body. Depending upon which aspect of the Cartesian teaching one pursues, the result is mechanism on the one hand and Idealism on the other; this is the double historical heritage of Descartes.

In Descartes' teaching, mechanism is subordinate to freedom of the will. Whereas love and hate are subordinated to *generosité*, a species of admiration or self-esteem,[12] *generosité* is itself produced by knowledge of the fact that nothing truly belongs to one or is reason for praise or blame, except the free will. In the last analysis, freedom or the action of the soul controls mechanism or the passions of the soul. Let us now consider briefly Descartes' treatment of love, *generosité*, and the free will.

Descartes writes, "Love is an emotion of the soul, caused by the movement of the spirits [he refers here to the animal spirits that are conveyed by the circulation of the blood to the pineal gland], which incites the soul to join itself voluntarily to those objects which appear suitable [*convenable*] to it."[13] I note here a serious ambiguity in the Cartesian doctrine. The will is influenced by the emotion or passion of love on the one hand, and on the other is hard to distinguish from thinking or judging, by which we determine that objects are suitable to us. We see in Descartes not simply the elevation of the will, but its mingling with the intellect; this is the preparation for German Idealism.

This to one side for the moment, Descartes goes on to consider a common distinction between two kinds of love. These are benevolence, "which incites us to want [*vouloir*] something good for that which we love," and concupiscence, "which makes us desire that which we love."[14] This distinction applies to the effects of love but not to its essence because benevolence follows immediately upon union with the object of desire. Conversely, we desire to possess whatever we regard as a good. Because desire is a passion and because generous persons "are entirely masters of their passions,"[15] it is again unclear whether the person marked by *generosité* is moved primarily by desire and hence by passion or by the will.

There is also an ambiguity with respect to the distinction between benevolence and concupiscence. Love is defined for Descartes uniformly as a movement toward union with the suitable or useful. The erotic madness of Platonism is thus replaced by a mixture of psychic and corporeal motions that are regulated by self-interest or sober calculation. This calculation is again of two kinds: with respect to the good and the bad, as represented by inner sense or reason, and with respect to the beautiful and the ugly, as represented by our external senses.[16] The good is that which is *convenable,* that is, suitable or useful to our nature. The beautiful is that of which we approve because it gives pleasure (*agréement*). Finally, Descartes distinguishes both these species of love from desire, "to which one often attributes the name of love."[17]

The Cartesian analysis of love thus turns out to be unclear and indistinct. In looking to the future, love seems to be the same as desire, which is itself both specific (= concupiscence) and generic. The generic term "desire" is defined by Descartes as "an agitation of the soul, caused by the spirits, which disposes it to will for the future those things that it represents to itself to be suitable" (*convenables*).[18]

We see again the ambiguous relation between desire and will. These are officially distinguished as follows. Desire is a passion that refers to the future. Will refers to the "consent with which one considers oneself at present as joined to that which one loves."[19] This contradicts the previous passage, according to which the will is directed to the future. It is unclear whether desire engenders will or whether, as Descartes elsewhere contends, the will is entirely free and thereby enabled to control all other passions through the master-passion of *generosité.* As to the desire that modifies the will, or at the least influences it, this is presumably not one species of love in particular, but all or any of them. To the aforementioned mixture of will and intellect, we must add desire, an addition that is again crucial for all of subsequent philosophy. Descartes denies the tripartition of the soul as introduced by Socrates in the *Republic.*

The good is for Descartes the suitable or the useful, whether in itself or with respect to its effects; love in general and sexual love in particular are thus subsumed under self-interest, which replaces Platonic madness; the corollary of self-interest is self-esteem. It therefore comes as no surprise when we learn that for Descartes, what depends upon us alone will provide "a complete satisfaction" (*une entière satisfaction*),[20] an expression that partly anticipates the Hegelian *Befriedigung.*

Descartes holds that no soul is too weak to acquire "an absolute power over the passions" and hence over the desires that move us to act, provided that our soul is well guided.[21] This guidance comes from knowledge of good and evil as well as of the truth, which is then employed by the will to make correct resolutions.[22] Descartes speaks of the will as though it were a rational agent, but he also speaks of rationality or judgment as though it were an instrument of the will. One can try to excuse these ambiguities by noting that the ego cogitans is a simple substance, and so that it is not really possible to distinguish the various cognitive faculties. One might then say that the will is the expression of the last step in the process by which the ego cogitans acts on the basis of desire and judgment. But this merely reformulates the original ambiguity; it does not remove it. Genuine freedom depends upon the autonomy of the will; desire and judgment are indissolubly connected to the body and thus to the external world or to nature.

According to Descartes, the will is free and need never be restrained, whether by the passions or (except indirectly) by the motions of the body.[23] Descartes thus contends that we can act on the basis of complete independence, moved only by rational calculation of what is useful (good) on the one hand and pleasant (beautiful) on the other, that is, useful and pleasant for oneself. The recognition of this independence arouses in us the aforementioned master-passion of *generosité*, which prevents us from desiring passionately whatever does not depend solely upon ourselves. The sole legitimate cause of *generosité* or self-esteem, is "the use of our free will, and the rule that we have over our volitions . . . this makes us in a certain way similar to God, by making us masters of ourselves."[24]

Generosité, or sober, dispassionate self-esteem caused by admiration for the freedom of the will to desire only that which is in its own power, thus replaces the Platonic Eros for the Ideas that are entirely independent of and other than ourselves. For Plato, the Ideas regulate the soul, and freedom is the same as contemplation of the Ideas. For Descartes, the separate Platonic Ideas are replaced by the innate ideas of geometry and algebra, which in turn yield to the mastery of the will. Knowledge, and so reason, are instrumental to freedom.

I can briefly illustrate the difference between Plato and Descartes by comparing their discussions first of intellectual love and second of admiration or wonder. There is a Cartesian equivalent of the ecstatic Platonic love for the Ideas, namely, the joy of intellectual love, of which Descartes says there can never be too much (contrary to his advice concerning the joys of the body).[25] This love of knowledge, however, is not purely theoretical; it is connected with self-perfection, independence, and so with *generosité* by joining us to those goods that are useful because they increase our power.

As to admiration, Descartes calls it "a sudden surprise of the soul" arising from the consideration of "objects that seem to it to be rare and extraordinary."[26] Admiration is useful because it makes us "apprehend and remember things we previously ignored."[27] But often it happens that we admire too much and so lapse into wonder *(Estonnement)*, which deranges the reason: "It is good to be born with a certain inclination to this passion, because it disposes us to the acquisition of the sciences; but we ought always to try afterwards to get rid of it as soon as possible." The only way to do this is to acquire knowledge of many things.[28]

I note a residue of Platonism in the previous set of passages: an inclination toward the derangement of reason, or in other words a trace of divine *mania,* is advantageous to the acquisition of knowledge. But there is, I believe, a difference from Platonism. In the *Theaetetus,*[29] Socrates says that wonder (*thauma*) is the origin of philosophy, a point also made by Aristotle in the *Metaphysics.*[30] According to Socrates, however, wisdom is inaccessible to human beings; philosophy is therefore continuously associated with ignorance, or the need to know, and so too with wonder. Dialectic is not the Cartesian *mathēsis universalis,* nor even the Aristotelian *prōtē philosophia,* but what one might call a regulative Ideal.

Descartes' treatment of love, self-esteem, or *generosité,* and freedom of the will culminates in his praise of mastery and independence. The only apparent exception to this is his assertion that love of children and friends can lead us to sacrifice ourselves (he is silent about wives and husbands). We can therefore love others more than we love ourselves.[31] But Descartes also explains that love is caused by knowledge of the goods that we possess, which possessions perfect us.[32] Love of children and friends thus turns out at bottom to be self-love. Furthermore, "those in whom the will is by nature able most easily to master the passions and to arrest the accompanying movements of the body, are without doubt the strongest souls."[33] The person of extreme *generosité* or self-mastery and self-esteem is accordingly also free of the love of friends and children that may lead to self-sacrifice.

Descartes represents the initial stage of what I am calling the Kantian thesis concerning the relation between freedom and reason. Although the exact formulation of the relation between reason and the will is, in my opinion, never satisfactorily clarified by Descartes, it is obvious that he does not intend to equate the will with the imagination, and in particular not with the imagination in the late-modern and contemporary sense of the fantasy. Knowledge is the instrument of freedom, but freedom is defined by Descartes in terms of knowledge. This is a crucial element in Descartes' Platonist heritage. The Platonic Ideas are replaced by the forms of geometry, the ratios of algebra, and the rules of sound reasoning, at the basis of which is a quasi-Platonic intuition of pure form.

On the other hand, Descartes deviates from Platonism in his constructivism, which itself turns upon the imagination.[34] Number, figure, and so on are not really distinct from body but only imagined to be so.[35] Or, as Descartes puts it in the *Regulae,* whereas the nature of geometrical forms is independent of our cognitive activities, we choose the problems that we wish to resolve, and so too the particular configuration of numbers and forms that are useful starting points for those problems.[36] I discuss this point elsewhere[37] and have no space to pursue the details here. Suffice it to say that Descartes fluctuates between direct apprehension of mathematical forms by the *lumen naturale* and their production by the combined activity of intuition and imagination. Finally, freedom is associated for Descartes with formal intelligibility, not with morality. In Kant, the freedom of the will or practical reason is limited or expressed by the ought of the moral rule.[38]

Thus in the Cartesian teaching, reason, will, and passion are closely connected by, if not quite identified with, the desire for freedom, understood as independence and mastery. This desire leads the soul to replace Platonic Ideas with abstract objects that are in part or altogether its own productions. The desire in question is motivated finally by self-interest rather than by erotic madness. There is no extinction of the historical or political person in Cartesian wisdom.

To this I add the following observation: Despite the internal structure of the ego cogitans, Descartes has no doctrine of negativity to correspond to the indeterminate striving of the Platonic Eros, which is an ancestor of Fichte's *Streben* and Hegel's negative activity and which may be understood as the struggle of the parts of the soul, intellect, spiritedness, and desire, a struggle that receives its dialectical structure from the directedness toward the independent Ideas. From this standpoint, whereas Plato's *psuchē* is a direct ancestor of the Hegelian *Geist,* the Cartesian ego cogitans is not. Cartesian mastery amounts to the regulation of all passions by *generosité,* or prudent self-esteem.

In addition to the absence in Descartes of a dialectic of the soul, the forms of mathematics, even if produced by the soul, are secure and definite; and so they provide the gateway to the mastery of nature. In other words, Descartes emphasizes the positive side of work or production, even within the transformation of the passions into the satisfaction afforded by recognition of one's independence. In the *Symposium,* Diotima refers to the indeterminateness of the erotic soul, which she calls a juggler, poisoner, and sophist that is neither immortal nor mortal but that waxes and wanes in the same day, just as all living things are continuously dying and being reborn.[39] Plato's account of the soul is thus much closer than is that of Descartes to what Hegel calls "the peculiar restlessness and dispersion of our modern consciousness."[40] From this standpoint, one could call Plato a modern, as could not be said of Aristotle.

This observation provides the decisive clue to the sense in which Hegel's attempted reconciliation of ancients and moderns within the circle of the Absolute is not only the last stage of the Kantian thesis, but the immediate preface to the post-Kantian thesis concerning the relation between freedom and reason. Stated with extreme concision, but not misleadingly, I think, the transition from Hegel to the post-Kantian thesis is a process of two steps. First, the conceptual structure of Hegel's circular Absolute is replaced by the historical contingency of Nietzsche's eternal return of the same. Second, the sameness of Nietzsche's eternal return is replaced by the difference of the post-Heideggerian Nietzscheans of contemporary Paris.

Looking now to the other end of history, one may also designate the evolution of Hegelianism as a very general process of two steps. First, Plato's Idea, which is independent of thought, is replaced by Aristotle's *eidos,* which actualizes in the activity of thinking. Second, the activity of thinking is transformed by the Christian doctrine of spirit, and in particular by the entrance of eternity into temporality. As is already visible in Descartes, and much more so in Kant, the identification of form as the principle of intelligibility, and so as the regulating principle or actual expression of freedom, is replaced by the formation process.

The negative activity of the Platonic psyche is thus transmitted to the forms themselves by a series of stages within the second step; these stages culminate in Hegelian dialectico-speculative logic. Platonic Eros, Aristotelian actualization, and Christian subjectivity: these are the crucial historical roots of Hegel's culminating exposition of the modern or Kantian thesis of the relation between freedom and reason. The crux of the matter is visible in Hegel's insistence upon the identity of the cognized form in itself (*an sich*) with the form as cognized within consciousness (*für uns*).[41] The intelligible world is a production of divine thought, but this thought can be "recollected" by the human intellect. In Aristotle's *Metaphysics,* we think the forms of beings by actualizing them in our thought, but we cannot think the divine intellect, or *noēsis tēs noēseōs.* In Hegel's system, there is no final separation between the divine intellect and the forms of the beings, or between the sage's intellect and thought thinking itself.

It is easy to see that the Platonic Eros is present in the "pure simple negativity" of Hegelian substance understood as subject or life. What Diotima refers to in her ironical terminology as the magical and sophistical transformations of Eros is expressed in Hegel's romantic idiom as "the seriousness, the pain, the patience and work of the negative" that arrives eventually at the fully developed totality of truth.[42] Eros is associated in Plato with playfulness and pleasure, whereas in its sublated Hegelian rendition it is associated with the seriousness and pain of labor. This is a crucial difference between the pagan and the Lutheran temperament. Hegelian satisfaction is not the same as Platonic blessedness, nor is the route the same to these two goals. As Hegel strikingly puts it, "Death is the most frightening, and to hold fast to death is what requires the greatest force. The beautiful, which lacks force, hates the understanding, because the latter expects of it that of which it is not capable." And again, the life of the spirit "wins its truth only by finding itself within absolute disruption" (*Zerrissenheit*).[43]

In my opinion, texts like these support the inference that what Hegel calls "the unhappy consciousness" cannot be restricted to a single period of historical development. The attainment of freedom is a preservation as well as an overcoming of the disruption in the Absolute. With respect to the anticipation of post-Kantianism, I call attention to the famous ending of *Thus Spoke Zarathustra:* "Do I think about *happiness?* I think about my *work.*"[44] The satisfaction of desire is for Hegel not simply painful but self-lacerating. The destruction that Zarathustra tells us must precede creation[45] applies to the worker himself. The union of subject and object in the satisfaction of desire "is in general *destructive,* as with respect to its content it is self-addictive."[46] The restlessness of addiction, I suggest, does not cease with wisdom but is reproduced as the interior motion of the concept, by which one moment is continuously transformed into the others.

We saw previously that, according to Socrates, philosophy originates in wonder. In Descartes, the claim is preserved but modified in such a way as to justify the inference that wonder must be mediated by desire for the suitable and the pleasant. In Hegel, desire is, if anything, even more important than in Descartes. I want to illustrate Hegel's understanding of the origin of philosophy by discussing a passage from the *Differenzschrift* of 1801. The remark that interests me is one in which Hegel anticipates the later notion of absolute disruption. In it, he speaks of the form of philosophy as produced by "the living originality of the spirit, which has shaped it through its own production and activity, the disrupted harmony [*die zerrissene Harmonie*]." As a harmony, this disunion (*Entzweiung*) has itself a particular form, namely, "the source of the need of philosophy, and as formation [*Bildung*] of the age, it is the unfree given side of the shape of philosophy."[47]

The main point of this passage is that philosophy emerges from desire, which itself bears the structure of the separation of the subject and the object. This separation is located within the subject in two senses: as defined by desire and as overcome through conceptual satisfaction. This is why Hegel alludes to the disrupted harmony of the spirit. Each such disruption or disunion has a particular historical form that is expressed most fully in the dominant philosophy of the time. Thus the particular way in which each epoch conceives of the separation between the subject and the object, and so how it conceives of its primary task, both defines the age and restricts the spirit or constitutes the unfree dimension in the origination of philosophy. This dimension is the pursuit of freedom through the historically conditioned negative work of desire.

Once again we see the subterranean presence of Eros as the mediator (the hermeneut) between reason and freedom. I remind the reader of the general situation. Plato possesses the concept of negativity, but as applied to the soul only and not to the Ideas. Descartes takes the decisive step of replacing the independent Ideas with new objects of desire, which are prepared by abstraction with the assistance of the imagination and subordinated to the will. But he lacks the concept of negativity as overcoming, and so emphasizes self-independence as limitation (that is, detachment from what is not within our control). In Hegelian language, Cartesian dualism shows that the truth of nature remains exterior to the subject. This is a dualism that Hegel continues to see in the Kantian distinction between the noumenal and the phenomenal. Hegel believes himself to have overcome Platonist dualism by investing with negativity the form of the desired object as well as of the desiring subject. Form is now a derivative of the formation process.

One should nevertheless not overlook the interplay in our passage between form and disruption. To repeat: Hegel shares the traditional view that intelligibility depends upon order or structure, whether established by looks, rules, or processes. He employs three different words in our passage to express intelligibility: *Form, Gestalt,* and *Bildung.* The structure of the particular philosophical discourse of a given epoch is a result of the spiritual activity of "shaping" (*gestalten*) through negative work the type of cultivation (*Bildung*) that is peculiar to spirit in that epoch. But these senses of "form" are united by an underlying sense of formation: of activity that is primarily negative or transformational. I note that at the very end of the greater *Logic*, Hegel emphasizes that the culminating synthesis is *Bewegung* and *Tätigkeit.*[48]

The disruption or disunion that characterizes the spirit at each historical epoch is negative or deconstructive. Although negation has a "positive" goal in the sense of completeness or of the overcoming of the separation between each determination and its opposite, completeness is nevertheless not static. It is not a Platonic heaven or harmony of eternal elements, each of which is forever itself and nothing else. The negative excitation of the subject is also to be found within the formal elements, and for two closely related reasons. First, the attempt to think each separate element as separate is impossible and demonstrates their interconnectedness in themselves. Second, as intelligible, the elements of intelligibility are already within thinking or subjectivity.

I come now to the conclusion of this brief inspection of Hegel's sublation of Eros. "The genuinely free will," says Hegel in the *Encyclopedia,* "is the unity of the theoretical and the practical spirit"; as such, it is both immediate individuality and the universal determination of freedom, which latter the will possesses as object and purpose "insofar as it thinks itself, knows this concept, is will as free intelligence."[49] Freedom is for Hegel in effect rationality; he thus refers to "the rational will" (*die vernünftige Wille*) which unfolds into actuality or objective spirit.[50] In nontechnical language, freedom is the unification of the subject and the object in an existence that thinks, and thereby exemplifies in its existence, the truth. Not only is the true the whole, but freedom is as well.

It is obvious that in his account of freedom, Hegel intends to overcome the Kantian dualism of theoretical and practical reason. In order to accomplish this, Hegel must unify reason and the will, in a way that is closer to Descartes than to Kant. One could also say that the existential origin of will and reason is for Hegel desire, as is implicit in the famous struggle for recognition between individuals who are initially defined by that struggle as master and slave. Desire is the origin of history, and it is thanks to this origin that the negative excitation of Eros is transmitted to both subject and object, an excitation that underlies and is the engine that accomplishes the unification of the theoretical and practical spirit.

For my present purposes, the most important difference between the Platonic *psuchē* and the Hegelian *Geist* lies in the aforementioned separation in Plato between the erotic soul and the Ideas. The soul, or Eros, has no intrinsic stability, no definite structure. (I note parenthetically that the tripartite structure of the soul in the *Republic* is in fact compromised by the presence of Eros in all three parts.) The soul is not itself an Idea, except in the most general sense that we can discern its nature or power. Instead, this power is activated and directed by the Ideas. The Ideas give shape and a kind of fluid stability, paradoxical as that expression may seem, to the soul, which is defined as a soul of a certain type by the degree of erotic ascent of which it is capable. The object of love, in other words, determines a rank-ordering of souls or human lives; this would be impossible for Eros alone because in itself it is polymorphous perverse or unsatisfiable. We are what we love, and the most capacious souls love everything.

As was already evident from the reference in the *Sophist* to dialectic as the science of free men, for Plato, only the philosopher, and perhaps not even the philosopher, is or can be free in the fully rational sense of the term. In keeping with the softer virtue of modernity, the situation is somewhat easier in Hegel; although only the wise man could be said to be genuinely free, there is also a secondary sense of freedom that is available through participation by obedience to rational laws in a rational state.[51] But what looks softer from one standpoint is harder from another. Freedom depends for its actualization, whether in the life of the wise man or in the quotidian existence of the citizen, upon the achievement of wisdom. The concept must actualize in world history as well as in the thought of Hegel and his disciples. There can be no as-yet-unrevealed categories or moments in the intelligible structure of the whole. And this is so regardless of what stance we take on the much-disputed question of the end of history.

In my opinion, the Hegelian teaching is doomed to deteriorate into post-Kantianism, the third of my three theses, regardless of whether or not wisdom is genuinely achieved. If it is not, or if Hegel's successors deny that it is, then the results must be something very much like what actually happened in the course of the nineteenth century: a disillusionment with speculative philosophy, a return, ostensibly to Kant, but in fact to positivism, or else a rapidly accelerating descent into the maelstrom of history. But suppose that Hegel was in fact wise or universally believed to be so. The circularity of the concept, and so of the satisfaction of desire, guarantees perpetual boredom, as was well understood by Alexandre Kojève, who diagnosed the satisfaction of the sage as depending either upon lovemaking or the Japanese tea ceremony, in other words, upon the mindlessness of bestiality in one case and of hyperaestheticism in the other.

I have suggested that there are three main theses in our philosophical tradition concerning the relation between freedom and reason. The Platonist thesis identifies freedom as the desire for, and knowledge of, the formal structure of intelligibility, which structure is independent of and so regulates both desire and cognition. I identify the second thesis as Kantian in order to give prominence to the crucial premiss of the modern epoch, namely, that the structure of intelligibility is conditioned and hence, in senses that vary from one philosopher to another, constituted or produced by one or both of the activities of desire and cognition.

On the Platonist thesis, it is difficult if not impossible to understand how freedom is rendered accessible by the reason to which it is attributed. On the Kantian thesis, freedom is inseparable from the implicit or explicit axiom that we know only what we make. As a corollary to this axiom, the Kantian thesis holds that freedom is the satisfaction of desire by reason. Reason accordingly tends to be understood primarily as practico-productive; as an aside, I note that this is the basis of the gradual emergence and rapid acceleration of the conceptions of theory construction, interpretation, hermeneutics, and perspectivism.

On what I am calling the Kantian thesis, which I have illustrated by the historical examples of Descartes and Hegel, the two end points of the modern epoch, there is a delicate balance between freedom understood as spontaneity and freedom in the sense of autonomy. The Platonic forms are gradually replaced by ratios (for example, Cartesian equations), rules, or rule-guided formation processes; in general, one can say that freedom is law-abiding. But we ourselves must formulate these laws if we are truly free, and herein lies the problem. If autonomy is spontaneous, how can we certify the validity of the laws? It is easy enough to say that their validity lies in the principle of human freedom, but to say this is to place freedom both outside and above reason. This is in many ways an attractive claim, but it has the serious difficulty that it engenders the conception of reason as the decisive obstacle to freedom. The consequence of making freedom prerational, however, has been to make it irrational; the post-Kantian thesis thus emerges from the inner disintegration of the Kantian thesis.

I close with three brief observations that may serve as the basis for further discussion. First, the theses that I have discussed here are not intended to be an exhaustive account of all doctrines of freedom. I have restricted myself to the two fundamental attempts to relate freedom to reason, and to the third that emerges from the enervation induced by their conceptual inadequacies. Second, as I consider the history of Western philosophy, I become progressively more convinced that an excessive desire for freedom is self-vitiating. In the vocabulary of this essay, Eros is incapable of defining itself by means of its internal resources alone. Otherwise put, those who produce their objects of love are suffering from the delusion induced by narcissism.

Third and finally, freedom cannot be identical to wisdom in the sense of the contemplation or discursive grasp of intelligible form. The reason we desire freedom is not that it is rational but that it is desirable. Each of us, of course, can give reasons why we prefer freedom to bondage. But these reasons are not accounts of intelligible structure; they are justifications of desire, and their rationality depends upon the degree to which our desires are justified. In that sense, the connection between freedom and reason amounts not to a philosophical system or to a postphilosophical deconstruction of systems, but to the attempt to philosophize and so to live a philosophical life. I once referred to the space in which that life transpires as the absence of structure. I close with the supplementary remark that absence is always defined by presence.

Chapter 11 Interpretation

and the Fusion of Horizons:

Remarks on Gadamer

This essay is a revision and extension of my contribution to the volume of the Library of Living Philosophers devoted to the thought of H. G. Gadamer. The original text is entitled Horizontverschmelzung *[The Philosophy of H. G. Gadamer, edited by Lewis E. Hahn (Chicago and La Salle, Ill.: Open Court, 1997), 207–18]. The German word refers to a central conception in Gadamer's hermeneutic, namely, the "fusion" of the two horizons of the creator of a work of art (or by extension the author of a text) on the one hand, and the audience (or reader) on the other. What is retained from the original version of my essay is the attempt to analyze how Gadamer's fusion of horizons would work in a particular case, here, the act of performing and the associated act of appreciating the performance of Beethoven's "Hammerklavier Sonata." I suggest that Gadamer's valuable analysis requires modification on one or two points in order to preserve the integrity of the work of art from the multiplicity of perspectives implicit in the diffusion of the creator's intention through the perspectival interpretations of the endlessly possible audiences to which it is presented. In the new version, I add a discussion of the Heideggerian presuppositions underlying Gadamer's hermeneutics, in particular, the doctrine of time contained in*

Being and Time. *I try to show that the ambiguous ontological status of the artwork in Gadamer's analysis is exactly analogous to the ambiguous status of the present in Heidegger's ontology of temporality. This theme is discussed more generally in chapter 2 of the present book.*

The expression "fusion of horizons" (*Horizontverschmelzung*) is the central concept of the universal hermeneutics developed by the German philosopher H. G. Gadamer in his influential book *Truth and Method*. It will be the main topic of this essay, but in order to set it into the proper context, I need to say something about Gadamer's overall enterprise. In so doing I will try to clarify the meaning of hermeneutics and discuss the sense in which it is intended to be universal. This discussion will culminate in a fundamental criticism of Gadamer's hermeneutics. In the second half of the essay, I will elaborate on that criticism. It should be understood that my criticism is in no way intended to diminish the philosophical importance of Gadamer's work, with which I am in considerable sympathy. My intention is to contribute to the fruitful modification of hermeneutics in general and to Gadamer's hermeneutics in particular. Gadamer has carried out the extremely valuable task of adapting the Heideggerian hermeneutic of Being to the science of interpretation as employed by the *Geisteswissenschaften*. This adaptation deserves the most careful consideration, and, as a student of Heidegger might be willing to allow, sympathetic disagreement is an aspect of care.

The term "hermeneutics" means something like "the art of interpretation" and first came to prominence in connection with the attempt to arrive at an authoritative understanding of the Bible, although it was soon extended to the documents of classical antiquity, in particular to those of a literary, philosophical, historical, or juridical nature. The term "interpretation" suggests that the understanding of a text is not directly accessible, and so that there is more than one possible explanation of its meaning and more than one way in which to evaluate its importance. At the same time, however, the possibility of interpretation is based upon the assumption that there is a meaning and even a value intrinsic to the text that is the goal of our investigation. A successful interpretation is one that explains this meaning and confirms this value.

The goal of biblical hermeneutics was thus originally to ascertain the word of God, just as philological hermeneutics aspired to determine the intended word of the author of a disputed text. It was obvious from the outset that practitioners of both forms of hermeneutics disagreed with one another about the explanatory or veridical status of their interpretations, but this disagreement was attributed to the obscurity of the text or the incompetence of the inter- preters. It was not associated with the absence or irrelevance of the author's intentions or with the impossibility of attributing a meaning to the text which our interpretations seek to explain. Hermeneutics is therefore rooted in the commonsensical procedures of everyday life by which we attempt to discern the meanings of the wide range of speeches that are addressed to us either directly or indirectly. Someone may speak to us ambiguously, as in the case of the pagan as well as the biblical prophets, and we may misunderstand the sense of an oracle or revelation; but this misunderstanding is usually revealed by the course of events. If the misunderstanding is never revealed, we assume that it might have been; otherwise, we would normally say that the utterance in question was not a genuine speech but nonsense or gibberish.

To make a long story short, the contemporary view that an author's inten- tions are irrelevant to the sense of a text and, more radically still, that there is no fixed or objective sense intrinsic to a text is itself a product of the gradual triumph within the modern epoch of historicism. By this term, I refer to the thesis that all meanings and values are historical creatures, and so that residents of a later historical epoch can never understand the intentions or meanings of residents of an earlier epoch except through the historical spectacles of the later time. These spectacles alter the perspective of the older views; in effect, they become versions of our own views. Views are thus replaced by viewpoints, which are said to be determined by one's historical standpoint. The old-fash- ioned notion of the common accessibility of views is replaced by the neutrality of points. In other words, the ostensible privacy or subjectivity of the content of one's viewpoint is joined to a generalizing or mathematicizing of the activity of looking, which in turn leads to the subsequent devaluation of subjective con- tent; one viewpoint is worth neither more nor less than any other. Each is a point on the continuum of history.

The difference between the prehistoricist and the historicist epochs can be easily illustrated by considering the different senses given to the term "perspec- tive" by Leibniz and Nietzsche. For Leibniz, who was not a historicist, a pers- pective is the viewpoint of a particular intelligence or monad upon the sense of the intelligible universe as a whole. The very particularity of the viewpoint is thus defined by the intelligibility of the whole. For Nietzsche, who was at once a critic and an exponent of historicism, every doctrine about the intelligibility of the whole is itself a perspective. Even more radically, what we call a viewpoint of an individual person is itself a kind of continuously shifting congeries of subviewpoints or perspectives associated with shifts in physiology and psychology in the individual viewer or speaker. Despite Nietzsche's attempt to defend a doctrine of rank-ordering and a conception of nobility, his hermeneutical teaching contributed to the dissolution of values into abstract geometrical points, or to *pointillisme,* which he often stated in physicalist language as the expression of power. Value is redefined as the accumulation of points of force. This is Nietzsche's version of nineteenth- and twentieth-century materialism.

Nietzsche is the effective originator of universal hermeneutics in its radical sense, by which I refer to the thesis that we cannot understand the meanings of our own discourses or those of our immediate interlocutors, let alone those of authors of another time, because there are no meanings but only perspectives or interpretations, and indeed, not even coherent or intrinsically meaningful interpretations but only continuously changing creations of meaning and value. This is expressed by Nietzsche in a famous passage in his notebooks when he says, "World-interpretation, not world-explanation."[1] In other words, the world is itself an interpretation. Whether or not he would accept this attribution, I count Derrida and his contemporary disciples as practitioners of universal hermeneutics in the radical sense because they hold that reading is writing. And again, whether or not Derrida would admit it, I understand this axiom to mean that each attempt to read a text produces another text that is superimposed upon the original. The result must therefore be that it is not possible to read a text but only to write something that is itself unreadable.

Gadamer, on the other hand, is a practitioner of what I shall call a conservative version of universal hermeneutics. Although he falls under the rubric of historicism, he shares with his teacher, Martin Heidegger, the desire to articulate an ontology of historicity, or what might ironically be described as the permanence of transience. I shall illustrate the general shape of Gadamer's historicism with the assistance of a series of quotations from *Truth and Method.* First, Gadamer rejects the view I infer from the Derridean thesis that reading is writing. This view is to be found in the words of a Parisian intellectual of an earlier period, Paul Valéry, according to whom there is no standard of appropriateness in the interpretation of an artwork and for whom each encounter with the work has the status and right of a new production. Gadamer, quite rightly in my opinion, rejects this thesis as "hermeneutical nihilism" (90).[2]

His own view follows directly from the conviction that "it is the *origin of the historical consciousness* to which hermeneutics owes a central function in the human sciences" (157). Four pages later, Gadamer refers to what he calls Hegel's decisive truth that "the essence of the historical spirit does not rest in the restoration of the past [as Schleiermacher believed] but in the mediation through thinking with the contemporary world" (161). This is the original of Gadamer's conception of *Horizontverschmelzung,* or the fusion of horizons. We are, however, not quite ready to tackle this notion head-on. To continue with the general portrait, Gadamer accepts the thesis just cited from Hegel, but he is a Heideggerian, not a Hegelian, in his ontology. The heart of the matter emerges from a passage in which Gadamer is explicating Heidegger's view on eternity and temporality. He says that Heidegger's thesis on the horizon of time does not mean that human being (*Dasein*) is radically temporalized and can experience or possess nothing as always existing or eternal, but that *Dasein* "always understands itself by starting from within its own time and future" (94f).

The reference to the future is to the possibilities that confront us in the present moment, from among which we choose partly on the basis of how we have been shaped by the past and partly by an unusually obscure openness to an indeterminate and silent call of conscience that compels us to accept one possibility rather than others as our authentic choice. It should be noted that the ontological status of the present in Heidegger's account of the horizon of time is unusually tenuous.[3] The determinate content of the present comes primarily from the past. This will reappear in Gadamer in the form of his account of tradition, preunderstanding, and prejudice, by which last he means not bigotry or thoughtlessness, but the established views of one's time and milieu.

Gadamer thus holds that we have access to permanently enduring meanings, but only from within the perspective of our own time. And this perspective is itself decisively conditioned by the various interpretations that have been made of the original artwork whose meaning and value we are attempting to assess. Gadamer holds that it is unacceptable to speak of the "mind of the author as a possible measure of the significance of an artwork," just as it is an unsatisfactory abstraction to refer to "a work in itself, sundered from its ever-renewed actualization through being experienced" (xix).

By "ever-renewed actualization," Gadamer means fundamentally the exhibition or performance (*Darstellung*) of the artwork by successive interpreters, and so the manner of reception of the work by successive audiences. Gadamer's technical term for this history of interpretation through performance is *Wirkungsgeschichte* (283ff). To return to the concept of the fusion of horizons: The interpretation of an artwork is the activity through which we assimilate the original work, or in other words the historically conditioned production of the artist, as modified by its *Wirkungsgeschichte,* into our own viewpoint, which has itself been preshaped by the prejudices and traditions of our historical generation.

It sounds initially quite reasonable to speak of the act of interpretation as a fusion of the horizon of the artist with our own standpoint. But in what sense does the fusion of the artist's horizon with our own make accessible to us the meaning and value of the work of art? We might very well agree with Gadamer that it is an abstraction to speak of the work of art in itself apart from the interpretations to which it gives rise. But it can hardly be wrong to speak of the work of art in itself when we are attempting to interpret its polyvalence or to assimilate its significance into our own terms. If we cannot speak of the work of art in itself, how can we know which of its purported interpretations or performances are actually of the work in question?

What is for me the central difficulty with Gadamer's doctrine is that in fact he never does speak of the artwork in itself, but only of its ontological nature as play and its historical occurrence within performances. Thus Gadamer says that the mode of being of art is "performance that embraces play in the same way as image, and communion in the same way as representation" (144). He also says that "the being of all play is continuous redemption, continuous fulfilment, energeia that has its end in itself" (100f). Even further, for speech, by which Gadamer means the discursive expression of our interpretation, the subject of play is not subjectivity but play itself (99). Now whether assertions like this are true or false, helpful or misleading, they certainly do not take us to the heart of the concrete nature of the individual artwork. Something is being performed in the recitation of a poem or the playing of a symphony by an orchestra. This something may well be described ontologically as play, but such a description tells us nothing about which performances accurately exhibit the original and which do not.

It looks to me very much as though the fusion of horizons is between an ontological manifestation of play as play, the concrete determinations of which are a historical blend of the viewpoint of the author or creator and those of his successive interpreters, and the historical viewpoint of the contemporary performer as it is itself interpreted by an audience. The only concrete content of this fusion is, then, a series of historical viewpoints. But viewpoints of what? What about Shakespeare's *Hamlet* or Beethoven's Hammerklavier Sonata? Do these mean anything? Did their creators have anything in mind when they produced them? Is there a difference between an appropriate and an inappropriate performance of either work? Are some interpretations better than others?

Despite the fact that Gadamer is himself an interpreter of great subtlety and erudition, it is not easy to find anything in his theory that would help us in adjudicating the previous questions. He would no doubt reply that this is because theory is ontology and precisely not practice, which depends upon the exemplification of theoretical principles by the particular interpreter of the particular work of art. But my question is whether the theory is in fact a sound explanation of the practical activities of the skilled interpreter. Let me emphasize that I find Gadamer's model of the hermeneutical act to be of great interest, and I agree with much of what he says. My objection is directed at an ambiguity, or perhaps a lacuna, at the core of the model, a lacuna that must be filled if the model is to retain its efficacity.

To state the difficulty as strongly as possible, the lacuna in Gadamer's model seems to make impossible the task of assigning any identity at all to the original artwork. All of the concrete content that we associate with a work of art is in Gadamer's treatment derived from historical fusions of perspectives. But this means that the present content is already a historical artifact, that is, a modification of the past. Otherwise put, a perspective must be a viewpoint of *something*. It cannot be just a perspective of some other perspective. In Gadamer's analysis, however, it is difficult if not impossible to find any single element within the fusion that is not itself the product of a fusion. The artist's intention, the actual phenomenon of the artwork, and the responses of the audience, all of them historically conditioned, are the constituents of the fusion that we call the interpretation of a work of art.

Now in one important sense, I think that this way of looking at the situation is obviously correct. Even the performance of an avant-garde work is set within a historical context, for example, that of the performance of artworks itself. But that is quite different from the actual existence of the historically conditioned work of art as some particular work that serves as the basis for distinguishing between valid and invalid performances as well as legitimate and illegitimate receptions. This particularity cannot be supplied by the ontological definition of the work of art as play for its own sake. I might note that this is as true of hopscotch and the finger painting of kindergarten children as it is of the poetry of Shakespeare and the music of Beethoven.

Universal hermeneutics is plainly a rival of philosophy in the grand sense of that term, and it is not by chance that it was developed under the influence of Martin Heidegger, the most important twentieth-century spokesman for the view that the grand tradition has come to closure or that we live, or ought to be living, in the postphilosophical epoch. I should add at once that it is probably too strong to say of Gadamer himself that he intends to replace traditional philosophy with hermeneutics. He has often stated that he is a Platonist. But to borrow his own thesis that the effect of a work of the human spirit upon its successive audiences is a part of its meaning, it is in a Heideggerian sense that the universality of hermeneutics has come to be understood. Furthermore, Gadamer goes a considerable distance toward making hermeneutics not simply "a universal aspect of philosophy" (451) but its foundation, since the task of hermeneutics is to explain how we understand interpretations of our lives as lived totalities. Hermeneutics is thus for Gadamer the foundation of the natural as well as of the human sciences. Once again I say that I am in substantial, but not complete, agreement with Gadamer. I certainly agree that philosophy is rooted in an interpretation of everyday life and hence of life as a lived totality. My reservation is with respect to Gadamer's analysis of the act of interpretation.

I want next to make a bit more precise my previous reference to the dependence of Gadamer's doctrine of hermeneutics on Heidegger's *Being and Time.* Gadamer cites this work in *Truth and Method* as the inspiration for his investigation (366). He is referring in particular to part *A* of chapter 5, in which Heidegger develops his doctrine of the existential structure of human being (more precisely, *Dasein*), which he calls *Verstehen.* By *Verstehen* is meant the openness of human existence in the world as an activity of directedness toward some project or purpose. This openness is not a "what" or state of objective facts, "but Being as existing."[4]

To exist in Heidegger's sense is thus to be directed by a purposiveness that emerges from our understanding (*Verstehen*) of the significance of our acts. The source from which this purposiveness emerges is the particularizing by our local situation of the possibilities that are genuinely available to us in light of the preformation that we have assimilated from the past. The development of this understanding is called *Auslegung*,[5] the word that Nietzsche substitutes for *Erklärung,* or explanation. Interpretation for Heidegger is not, however, a product of the will to power or a modification of chaos by a transient human perspective. It is the working out of the existential possibilities that have been projected to us in the openness of our understanding; and this in turn is an ontological expression of the historicity of human being.

In other words, Heidegger may be understood as attempting to transform Nietzsche's doctrine of world-interpretation from a myth into a *logos* or philosophical account of the whole. The world is a horizon of meanings projected by *Dasein,* but the project is ordered rather than arbitrary and it is grounded in Being, not chaos. World-interpretation is thus fundamentally the interpretation of human purposiveness, but by purposiveness is not meant adherence to a natural teleology. Each human being produces an interpretation of life that is based upon the ontological structures or categories of existence but is not limited or determined by them. The stories that we tell in order to make sense of our lives are interpretations, but the structure of interpretation is accessible to explanation. In this sense, *Being and Time* is an explanation, not an interpretation.

This is obviously the prototype for Gadamer's doctrine of human historicity and the historical structure of the exercise of *Verstehen,* an exemplary instance of which is the interpretation of works of art. But just as Heidegger dissolves the present into the past and the future or, more famously, criticizes the traditional doctrine of Being as presence (*parousia*), for which he substitutes what could fairly be called a doctrine of Being as absence, or as presence only through concealment, so Gadamer dissolves the presence of the artwork into the past of the historical perspectives of its creator and the future of the interpretations to which it will be subjected. The present moment within which the artwork is performed for a particular audience is itself an unstable fusion of the past and the future. The permanent being of the work of art is its ontological existence as play; but as a work of art in itself, and so as an intentional production of an author who wished to communicate some set of meanings to all audiences, regardless of the particular manifestations or perspectives to which these meanings may be subjected, the artwork has no presence. It is absent—or present only as concealed by the various fusions of historical horizons that forever prevent us from grasping it in its own terms.

This completes my preliminary survey and criticism of Gadamer's doctrine of universal hermeneutics, with its two central notions of the fusion of horizons and *Wirkungsgeschichte,* or the history of a work's reception. I want now to begin again and take a somewhat more concentrated look at the concept of the fusion of horizons. As noted, I have great sympathy with Gadamer's effort to elucidate the sense of "understanding" that is appropriate to the interpretations by which we find meaning and value in our lives. He is certainly correct is his view that this type of understanding goes beyond the apprehension of facts, rules, inferential patterns, and formal structures. It is more like the process by which human beings come to an understanding with one another.

I also agree with Gadamer that this process is secondary to the process of "understanding oneself *in der Sache,*" that is, in the course of events. Understanding of this sort is for him grounded in the preunderstanding that is articulated by Heidegger as the interpretive structure of the everyday existence of *Dasein* (278). This also seems plausible to me, although I prefer the version of preunderstanding that is to be found in the writings of Plato and Aristotle. My reason for this preference is that I reject the modern doctrine of historicism upon which Heidegger's adaptation of the Greeks depends. In other words, I hold that we can understand artworks as well as texts of other kinds from epochs other than our own and that we can submit them to new interpretations only because of this antecedent understanding. This is, of course, in no sense to say that works of art, or products of the human spirit, have exactly one correct meaning which is itself fixed for all time. Life is indeed an interpretation. But of what?

I therefore reject Gadamer's ontology, but not at all his interest in how we interpret works from the past. Gadamer has a valuable point to make about interpretation, but unfortunately he makes it in such a way as to prevent its accomplishment. The manner in which he fails is as important as the excellence of his intentions because it is, I believe, exemplary of the general, not to say universal, breakdown today in the conditions of understanding and evaluating not only works of art but ourselves. In the second half of this essay, I shall be primarily guided by the question of what contribution if any is made by Gadamer's ontology to the actual experience of judging or interpreting a work of art.

To begin again, Gadamer explicitly rejects the thesis that the interpretation of a work of art is the creation of a new work of art. His is the more moderate thesis, according to which every interpretation is necessarily a modification of the original. There is obviously something very plausible in this claim. We cannot help but appropriate a work of art on the basis of our experience. How does this appropriation affect the nature of the artwork? Or differently stated, what is the nature of an artwork that allows us to appropriate it in our own terms without substituting a new work for the original? What I call here appropriation is a virtual equivalent to the German *Verstehen* employed by Gadamer.

Gadamer adopts the nineteenth-century philological tradition according to which *Verstehen* designates an understanding of texts that is rooted in sympathy or a refined sensibility (*Einfühlung*) that is closely associated with cultivation (*Bildung*) and the experience (*Erlebnis*) that comes only from a life informed by these spiritual attributes. In Gadamer's discussion, *Verstehen* is expounded not only with the aid of these terms but also with *phronēsis* and *sensus communis*. These words have various roots and canonical sources; all express modalities of *Weltweisheit*, or worldly wisdom, as praised by Goethe, which is perhaps closer to the heart of Gadamer's sense of *Verstehen* than the philological tradition. We cannot practice *subtilitas legendi* if we have no experience of life or insight into the human soul.

One could therefore say that for Gadamer, a critical aspect of human intelligence is the blending of prudence and aesthetic sensibility. The universality of hermeneutics is largely if not entirely rooted in this prudential sensibility or worldly wisdom, which is itself a product of native talent and *Bildung* or, in other words, tradition. The ontological foundation of hermeneutics is essentially the articulation of the structure of judgment and understanding in the sense just defined. My criticism of Gadamer is that the exercise of sound judgment or worldly wisdom in the judgment of artworks has nothing to do with his historicist ontology, which in fact interferes with, if it does not entirely prevent, our apprehension of any actual work of art. Gadamer's ontology leaves us with no stuff or content of an actual work upon which to direct our sound judgment.

In an important and much-cited passage, Gadamer says, "The human relation to the world is strictly and from the ground up discursive [*sprachlich*] and thereby intelligible. Hermeneutics is, as we have seen, therefore *a universal aspect of philosophy* and not simply the methodological basis of the so-called *Geisteswissenschaften*" (451). This is directly preceded by a still stronger statement that is italicized in the original: "*Sein, das verstanden werden kann, ist Sprache*" (450): "Being that can be understood [in the sense of *Verstehen*] is speech." Gadamer does not mean by this that the world is all words. His remark is connected to a famous passage in *Being and Time*, in which Heidegger says, "Only for as long as *Dasein is*, i.e., the ontic possibility of the understanding of Being, is there [*gibt es*] Being."[6] In other words, Being is that which is to be interpreted or understood in the sense of *Verstehen*. It is that which transmits sense and value to beings. And the source of *Verstehen* is *Dasein*.

So just as for Heidegger Being in the ontological sense of the term is accessible to us as the interpretation of *Verstehen*, the same is true for Gadamer with respect to the work of art. But the ontological structure of historicity is intended to sustain a concern with immanent history or the medium of the human production of works. The ontology, to put it colloquially, would simply be spinning its wheels if it did not show us how to interpret a work of art. Perhaps Gadamer would allow the suggestion that he wishes to determine how human beings take a stand within history toward their existence understood as historicity. Just as Heidegger says that we take such a stand by a resolute choice of an authentic possibility, so Gadamer says that we judge examples of play by a fusion of horizons. It is not the task of ontology to identify particular possibilities or to choose the right ones for us. But it is the task of *Verstehen* to interpret works of art. Gadamer's ontology is therefore obligated to tell us how to do this; and this requires some method for attaching our interpretations to the correct artworks, which in turn depends upon the existence of these artworks independent of their interpretations. Gadamer in effect equates the existence of the artwork with its interpretations. But this is faulty ontology in addition to its uselessness for the activity of criticism.

I do not therefore minimize Gadamer's concern with the "ontological application of hermeneutics" (part 3 of *Truth and Method*). But his primary goal is to establish the conditions for the understanding of textual productions of the human spirit, including artworks of all kinds from the discursive to the musical, the visual and the ornamental. What unites these "texts" is their making possible an interpretation of life as lived. The question of artistic interpretation is thus a paradigm for the historical appropriation of the Western tradition. It is the question of how we can understand one another and in particular the works of the past, given that we are historical beings who derive our multiple senses primarily from our own epoch but who are able to dwell within epochs of the past and to be understood by residents of the future. I will now restate my criticism of Gadamerian ontology. The hermeneutical structure suffers from the same defect that marks Heidegger's historicist ontology. The present dissolves into the past and the future. The doctrine of the fusion of horizons substitutes the structure of temporality for the presence of the artwork. In fact, no artwork, or at least no identifiable artwork, is present.

The identity of the present as the future is most obvious in Gadamer's previously mentioned conception of *Wirkungsgeschichte*. Because the meaning of a work of art is essentially modified by its reception, there cannot be any stable or definitive meaning in the present. But the role of the future is not as pronounced in Gadamer's exposition as it is in the Heideggerian original. The importance of the future is muffled by Gadamer's emphasis upon the present as the residue of the past. According to Gadamer, "*Verstehen is itself to be thought as not so much an activity of subjectivity as (self-) insertion into an event of tradition* in which past and present continuously mediate one another" (274f).

This has two main senses. First, we can grasp the determining moments of the historical process of encounter between a work of the past and an interpreter of the present. To say only this, however, would be to transform hermeneutics into a pure ontology of historicity. Second, therefore, Gadamer wishes to argue that the very historicity of Being, and so the discursivity of human existence, enables us to incorporate our temporal prejudices or perspectives into an interpretation that is true both to the general and the particular or local circumstances of the work. Gadamer simply takes for granted here the stability of the present as independent of future episodes of *Wirkungsgeschichte.* He misses the radical elimination of the present by Heidegger even as he falls victim to it.

Gadamer is also less radical than Nietzsche, as is evident from his tacit transformation of "perspective" into "prejudice." The term "prejudice" is used here not in its pejorative sense but rather as signifying the views at which we have arrived through education, formal and informal, in the standards and tastes of the tradition. We are preformed by prejudgments that, so to speak, articulate the horizon within which we judge the work of art and that assist us in the act of critical appropriation.

Interpretations are always carried out by actual persons who reflect one version or another of the standards of their time. To interpret is, of course, to grasp and to appreciate, but also to accommodate to one's own views. Gadamer makes this point in general terms as a criticism of Leo Strauss's thesis that one must think the thoughts of an author exactly as the author thought them (506ff). According to Gadamer, if Strauss's thesis could be applied to a work of art, we would have to understand it entirely as of its own time. But this, says Gadamer, is to deny the claim of the work to be true for *me,* and not just for me personally but for persons from all moments in the tradition. Gadamer apparently means by this that it is in the nature of an artwork to accommodate itself to the varying perspectives from which the standards of the tradition may be applied. The history of the effect of the work on its subsequent audiences is thus a genuine part of the meaning or significance of the work itself (109ff. et passim).

One might object to Gadamer that to understand a work is to grasp its significance for any time, and that this significance is what makes the work accessible to interpreters of different epochs. From the standpoint of this objection, the core of the work is valid for human beings by virtue of their common humanity, and it is this core that makes possible the assimilation to the perspective of one's own epoch. Localism, in other words, is then a concrete exemplification of the universal. To understand a work in *my* terms is precisely to understand it in the author's terms, that is, as the very work that it is.

Gadamer meets this objection in part by his doctrine of the fusion of horizons. He claims at an early stage of his discussion that the timelessness and the temporality of an artwork must be brought together in the act of interpretation (115). I remind the reader that "timelessness" means enduring accessibility to reinterpretation; it is therefore a pseudonym or mask for the permanence of the future. This follows from the contingency of all past performances or interpretations with respect to all future possibilities. Even assuming that Gadamer had explained a plausible sense in which the actual artwork is present to the interpreter, each "present" interpretation is a transient placeholder for future modifications. This is why I say that, for Gadamer, the actual content of the present is the possibility of the future. Gadamer himself, however, takes "timelessness" to refer to the present as a modification of the past.

The insertion of the critic into an event of tradition is in fact an entering into the work itself, the existence of which includes the role it has played for the various audiences constituting that tradition. In other words, the various senses attributed to *Hamlet* by representative readings from Shakespeare's time to our own form a part of the significance of the play for us. It is precisely the significance of a work of art that it evokes diverse interpretations, each of which is a function of a different set of prejudices and points of view; each thus elicits a different stratum of meaning from the play or actualizes another possibility that is intrinsic in Shakespeare's creation.

On this view, there is no object-in-itself of historical knowledge. The being of a work of art is the understanding to which it gives rise. To understand is thus, so to speak, to come to an understanding with the work and only secondarily to understand the thoughts of its producer (269, 278). The work, in yet another formulation, must meet us halfway and accommodate to what we bring to it; it does not simply transfer its meaning to a passive recipient. As a particular example of this thesis, one may note Gadamer's discussion of the performance of a musical composition, and his claim that there is no such thing as *the* objectively correct performance (109–12). Because the being of the artwork includes the moment of performance, it follows that we understand that work, say Beethoven's Hammerklavier Sonata, not simply by studying the score but by listening to a wide variety of performances from different periods and schools of interpretation.

There are a number of difficulties with this example. Simply because performers understand a piece of music differently at different times, it does not follow that the composition has no intrinsic nature. We could not tell that several different performances were of the same composition if its nature depended upon the particularities of each performance. Gadamer must therefore want to say that the nature of the work is flexible or open to various interpretations, but not entirely or even essentially dependent upon them.

Beyond this, we recognize interpretations that differ perceptibly from the intention of the composer in a way that is hard to justify simply by recourse to the score because the manner in which music conveys a sense is too controversial to allow for expert agreement on its authentic understanding.

One might play a Haydn symphony in a style appropriate to Brahms or Mahler, and to the connoisseur this would be a falsification of the music, even if each note were played as written. The sense of the piece would have been distorted or destroyed. But *what* sense? Perhaps an analogous example is the performance of the text of *Hamlet* in modern dress or even with emphases and gestures that turn the speaking of Shakespeare's text into a comedy. But if the notes are played or the lines are spoken as written, what is to stop us from calling the obviously inappropriate performance the result of a "fusion of horizons" or from insisting that we have correctly interpreted the original by inserting our own viewpoint into that of the composer's or playwright's historical period?

It is hard to say whether a piece of music has a discursive sense analogous to that of a play. Perhaps a literary text can be falsified in two senses, one in which the author's meaning is incorrectly explicated by the critic and another in which the work is incorrectly performed or (as in the case of poetry) recited. I find it dubious to suppose that the same is true of a musical score. Whatever the composer's intentions, the nature of music allows for a much broader latitude of interpretation than is the case with discursive works. However this may be, Gadamer evidently holds that to enter into a work of the spirit from another epoch is to understand it through the act of assimilating it into an interpretation that is in accord with, but as mine (or the critic's), not the same as, the spirit of the historical horizon of the creator. To understand is to interpret the work, not in its terms or ours, but in a fusion of the two.

No one would wish to reject outright Gadamer's emphasis upon the partially open or evocative nature of a work of art. But there must be a work of some definite sort about which we can say accurately that it is open. A work of art cannot be sheer openness or pure possibility; to take this line is to define presence as absence. Gadamer in effect asserts that the encounter between the horizon of the interpreter and that of the artist or, more precisely, the artwork leads to the genesis of a third horizon by way of a fusion of the first two. But if the work itself is essentially a possibility, it cannot function as an element in the fusion. The three horizons in question are the temporal versions of possible determination, past, present, and future. But past and present collapse into the future because their content is open to modification by subsequent interpretations. There is no stability here, other than that of the three tenses or modalities of time, because there is no work in itself in which these tenses and their associated interpretations can be grounded.

As a proof-text for the views I have just elaborated, I cite the passage in which Gadamer introduces the notion of fusion of horizons: "In truth the horizon of the present is grasped in continuous formation, insofar as we must constantly test all our prejudices. To such a testing there belongs not as the least element the encounter with the past and the understanding of the tradition from which we come. The horizon of the present, therefore, does not form itself without the past. There is as little a present horizon for itself as there are given historical horizons that are to be acquired. *Verstehen is rather always the process of fusion of such ostensibly independently existing horizons*" (289).

Once again I call attention to the absence of any reference to the future. It is almost as if Gadamer wishes to avoid noticing the implications of his own insistence upon the transience of the present and therefore emphasizes the stability of the past. It can of course be objected to me that the present just is transient or that it is in the nature of time that each moment is ceasing to be what it was even as it turns into what it is not yet. I reply to this objection that transience is an unstable synthesis of past and future that cannot be held together by temporality alone. It is a fundamental mistake to try to explain the unity of the present in terms of two types of absence, past and future. But this is the theoretical implication of Gadamer's account of the openness of the past to revision in the present. The present is in fact not present; it is rather ceasing to be what it once was even as it comes to be what it is not.

I believe that I can make this point more simply as follows. There is a difference between the synthesis of time within which we grasp the meaning and value of works of art and the meaning and value themselves. When I say that the structure of time is the past, present, and future, I am not referring to a temporal event. Tradition comes to us from the past, but it is not identical with the past as a dimension of temporality. The content of the present is not the present moment, which in any event is not itself present *as* a moment but rather as an unstable fusion of past and future. And whatever the future may bring, it will not be identical with the temporality of the future. In short, we have to distinguish between the synthesis or fusion of time and the unity of the senses by which we understand that fusion. Time has a content that is not just more time.

To say that thinking and judging are situated within the temporal structure of consciousness is one thing; the claim that the sense or significance of a particular perception is a fusion of past senses or significations is something else again. When I perceive that two and two are four, I am prepared to do so by my previous experience and education, including my prejudice that the laws of addition for natural numbers are confirmed by an extension of my intuition of elementary examples. I also anticipate that what I have learned in the past will continue to hold true in the future. But the truth or falsehood of the statement that two and two are four does not itself arise as a fusion of memory and anticipation. This fusion instead constitutes the horizon of the present within which I judge that two and two were, are, and always will be four, altogether independent of the prejudices I have acquired and which enable me to see the correct sum.

How I am prepared or enabled to understand something is one thing; what I understand is something else. This is an elementary distinction, often invoked in the refutation of psychologism. I have no doubt that Gadamer is familiar with it, but I am nevertheless not certain that he accepts it. But perhaps he would claim that mathematical truths constitute a special case that is not pertinent to the issue of human truth, and in particular to the question of the interpretation of works of the spirit. In other words, Gadamerian hermeneutics applies to the significance of the formation of mathematics as a human activity, but not to the truth or falsehood of individual mathematical propositions.

Let us therefore set mathematics aside and consider the relation between a theory of interpretation and the interpretation of a work of art. A theory of interpretation is an explanation of how we interpret works of art. A particular interpretation may be open to a wide range of variations, but all of them must fall under the authority of the explanation; otherwise the theory is falsified. It follows immediately that there must be something invariant about an interpretation, something that is identifiable as a variable and to which the theory applies. But this in turn requires that there be something invariant about the nature of a work of art, which is after all precisely what is being interpreted.

Now let us translate all this into the language of horizonal fusion. A work of art can be interpreted in various ways. But something underlies this variety that is not itself merely a variable. If I want to modify previous interpretations of Beethoven's Hammerklavier Sonata in the light of my own structures of preunderstanding, I cannot succeed if I am instead interpreting a sonata by Mozart or Haydn. Are we to believe that the Hammerklavier is identifiable merely by tradition, which is in any case in the process of continuous modification? Or is it not rather the case that traditions of interpretation spring up precisely from the creation of the Hammerklavier Sonata?

We must first identify the Hammerklavier Sonata and then interpret it. By "identify" I mean that we must locate it by apprehending the specificity of its nature as this particular artwork. Its identity cannot be a matter of interpretation. But this entails that the Hammerklavier Sonata possess a nature and therefore a meaning that is not itself an interpretation. And this is so even if it is the *nature* of the sonata to provide us with a musical *interpretation* of human existence. The theory of the sonata form will not suffice to enable us to identify the Hammerklavier Sonata in particular. This is essential because it is also true that a theory of interpretation will not suffice to enable us to identify any particular interpretation *as* an interpretation. Interpretations, like works of art, must have a specific nature, by which they can be identified.

Now nothing in the immediately preceding remarks has anything to do with the fusion of horizons. I have been speaking within the fusion of temporality, but what I have said is not itself a fusion of temporality. If anyone should happen to read this essay a hundred years from today, their understanding will take place within a horizonal fusion of a metaphorical sort, thanks to which my views will be transmitted through tradition and memory to the minds of my future readers. But it is my views that they must understand, regardless of how they choose subsequently to vary them, if they are to be truly said to have understood my arguments. My views may well be based upon interpretations of the views of my predecessors, but this does not alter their identity; it rather contributes to that identity. The interpretations by my future readers may well contribute to the significance of my views by bringing out implications that were invisible to me. But that will not change the identity of my views. It will not transform them, for example, into the views of Heidegger or Wittgenstein or some other philosopher.

In short, a horizonal fusion of the sort envisioned by Gadamer can take place only if there is some identifiable artwork with an intrinsic nature and meaning independent of those modifications subsequently to be made by its interpretations. If this is not so, there will be no fusion of horizons but rather a dissolution in which the original artwork is lost by the very act of interpretation. Gadamer identifies the being of the artwork with the understandings to which it gives rise. But the result is to dissolve the difference between a work of art and its interpretation.

I think that there is indeed a connection between the nature of art and the process of interpretation. It may even be right to say that artworks are themselves interpretations of human experience. I would further grant that part of the task of understanding a work of art is to interpret it. But if the sum of interpretations *is* the being of the work of art, then it would seem that the artwork is not only superfluous but nonexistent apart from its interpretations. And this is nonsense. It is, after all, also true that there are interpretations of the sense of philosophical doctrines, including interpretations of Gadamerian hermeneutics. These interpretations differ, but it can hardly be the case that Gadamer's theory of hermeneutics is just the unending sequence of its interpretations. There is an *art* of interpretation, but the quality with which we exercise that art is determined by the success with which we expound the meaning or value of the work we are interpreting.

I am therefore not myself offering some ontological account of the nature of art but rather insisting that each work of art must be identifiable apart from and as the object or basis of our interpretations of it. It is not a pronouncement on the ontological essence of music to say that the Hammerklavier Sonata must possess a nature that suffices for us to distinguish it from other sonatas, and furthermore to discriminate among valid and invalid interpretations. If an incompetent pianist plays the Hammerklavier in the style of Mahler or Poulenc, there may occur a fusion of horizons between the performer and the composer, but has any contribution been made to the being of the Beethoven sonata? or has that being been falsified and so obscured or damaged?

I assume that Gadamer, and many of my readers as well, would want to object that there is a difference between identifying a work of art and understanding it. They might want to say that the identification of the exact score of the Hammerklavier is entirely distinct from understanding it. I would agree with this. My point is that we cannot understand the Hammerklavier unless we can identify it, and we cannot identify it if to do so is to interpret it. Otherwise stated, we are not interpreting the Hammerklavier Sonata if we have not correctly identified it. We are instead creating our own sonata, which we cannot even say is quite similar to Beethoven's, since his sonata does not exist apart from our interpretations of it.

The main point that I have been defending here is difficult to establish with respect to music, which is why I have been using the example of the Hammerklavier Sonata. I do not at all want to make things easy for myself when I say that we cannot interpret what we do not understand. Where such understanding is absent, we are improvising or creating or perhaps spouting nonsense. There are different kinds of understanding, and I for one am not well prepared to explain the nature of musical understanding. But actually my argument is in no way contingent upon such an explanation. It depends instead upon the existence of a piece of music the nature and value of which we can pursue in a responsible manner. And only in this way will we be able to investigate the nature of musical understanding. If there is a fusion of horizons, it depends upon something independent of the fusion itself, namely, upon some understanding of the nature of the work we are attempting to appropriate. And this condition carries with it the requirement that works of art have some nature or being that is independent of how we appropriate them. There must be something to appropriate or there will be no interpretations.

Interpretation is the act of restating a commonly accessible truth which we have antecedently understood in a local representation of our own. The restatement of truth does not transform its universality but allows it to function within a modified context. Interpretation, or the transfer of universality from one local representation to another, is the process by which we arrive at an understanding of the universal significance of locality in human life. Without this understanding, the local is meaningless, and history is reduced to rubbish.

Chapter 12 Is There a Sign
of Freedom?

This essay takes up the problem of freedom from what I referred to in chapter 10 as the post-Kantian standpoint. It was written to be presented at a colloquium in honor of the sixtieth birthday of Professor Josef Simon of Bonn University. The proceedings of the colloquium were published as Zur philosophie des Zeichens *(Berlin: Walter de Gruyter, 1992). My essay appears in German translation on pages 59–78 under the title* Kann die Freiheit ein Zeichen Sein? *Professor Simon is a distinguished member of the school of hermeneutical philosophy descending from the later Nietzsche via French deconstruction. The main point of disagreement between us is Simon's contention that consciousness is syntactic or, alternately expressed, that all thoughts are signs of other signs. I deny the major premise, and in particular I argue that freedom, a central concern of Simon and those who sympathize with his approach, is not itself a sign but that conversely there are signs of freedom. Underlying Simon's philosophy of signs is a form of late Kantianism, according to which the world (in the Kantian sense of that term) is a product of consciousness in general and the imagination in particular. I have been criticized by Tilman Borsche, one of Simon's students, for taking a pre-Kantian attitude. The charge is correct, al-*

though whether this constitutes a failure on my part seems to me to be the issue under discussion, not the axiom by which it is regulated. In this essay, I provide another example (see also the previous chapter on Gadamer) of my version of ordinary language philosophy. The positive corollary to my denial that the given is a myth is that signs terminate in referents which are either intended by the user of the signs or recognized through that use. And these referents derive their intelligibility from the coherence of everyday life. If this were not so, philosophy would be purely spontaneous; there could be no external criterion by which to choose between competing philosophies, but only standards of inner coherence and finally of taste. It is for this reason, incidentally, that I reject the modern emphasis upon originality in philosophy, an emphasis that is an erroneous importation from art, and thanks to which philosophy has become indistinguishable from poetry, albeit often from bad poetry dressed up in empty and pompous technical terms and quasi-mathematical symbols. But mathematical rhetoric is as much rhetoric as the stream of signs signifying other signs.

One last point. Some will object that philosophy is a departure from or deepening of ordinary experience, not a submission to it. I reply that the ordinary is shot through with the extraordinary, and that there is no access to the latter except via the former. Without reference to the common world, which is, incidentally, antecedent to "proof" and can only be described or analyzed, one man's extraordinary vision is another's hallucination.

There is more than one way in which to honor the work of a thinker. I shall try to recognize the contribution of Josef Simon, not by a summary of his achievements or even by a textual analysis of his work, but by addressing the theme which he has so subtly articulated in the two books *Wahrheit als Freiheit* and *Philosophie des Zeichens*. In the course of a single essay, I cannot pretend to do more than to indicate how Simon's thinking has assisted me in stating the difficulties I see in contemporary philosophy of language.

It seems to me that the best way to proceed is to restrict myself to the first step in the problematic of the philosophy of signs. Perhaps Simon would agree that the first step is decisive in any inquiry. As I shall try to show, one can already discern the goal in the beginning: not of course the last step, since as Simon and I agree, there is no end to philosophy (35).[1] We may not agree as to the best way in which to formulate the first step, but such disagreement, if it exists, is the occasion for further discussion. Philosophers are not courtroom lawyers seeking to refute the arguments of their opponents but judges united by a common dedication to the pursuit of truth.

The first step is for me a decision concerning Simon's thesis in *Philosophie des Zeichens* that consciousness is syntactic ("das Bewusstsein ist syntaktisch": 51). This thesis appears in more extended form on page 199, from which I now cite: Simon is discussing the Nietzschean assertion that grammar is the schema of a "power of imagination that is aligned toward thinking" ("[eine] *auf Denken ausgerichtete* Einbildungskraft"). We look through this schema, but we cannot go beyond it: "on the basis of the structure of a particular, historically developed grammatic, we *think altogether* and *at the same time* in a *determinate form*" ("Aufgrund der Struktur einer besonderen, historisch entwickelten Grammatik *denken* wir *überhaupt* und *zugleich* in einer *bestimmten Form*"). A few lines later: "For there is no 'thinking in general' that does not follow a determinate grammatic which, as determinate, is also presupposed" ("Denn es gibt kein 'Denken überhaupt,' das nicht einer bestimmten, als bestimmte aber doch auch wieder nur *vorausgesetzen* Grammatik folgte").

This passage makes three points. First, thinking and language are coextensive. Second, language is in each manifestation historical or contingent; accordingly, Simon would reject transcendental categories or ontologically separate regulative forms. Third, contingent or historical grammar is the schema of—that is, it articulates—the imaginative exercise of thinking. This third point is expanded on page 218, as follows: "Becoming a sign, if not 'immediately'" [as in the case of natural signs (102) or simply because of agreement that a sign is not problematic for the time being (193–96)], "then as understood through interpretation, that is, in transition to another sign. This transition, in the *intention* of "better" versions as contrasted with the 'given' one, is not arbitrary but free. It occurs through the power of imagination" ("Zeichen werden, wenn nicht 'unmittelbar' dann durch Interpretation verstanden, d.h. im Übergang zu anderen Zeichen. Dieser Übergang ist in der *Intention* 'besserer' Versionen gegenüber den 'gegebenen' nicht willkürlich, aber frei. Er geschieht durch Einbildungskraft").

In this passage, Simon, if I understand him right, links his doctrine of interpretation to the Kantian doctrine of the imagination, which is both productive and free in the sense that it can transcend any existing linguistic horizon in the production of a new integration of phenomena. As is obvious from Simon's overall development, however, he rejects transcendental categorial structure; accordingly, the imagination cannot avoid arbitrariness, as in the case of Kant, merely through the unity of "Urteilskraft," but rather, as we shall see in the concluding section of this chapter, it must rely upon the "Energie" of its interpretation: Here Simon is a Nietzschean.

Simon's latest work may thus be understood as a development of themes from an earlier work, *Wahrheit als Freiheit.* I have no space here to consider that work in any detail but wish to mention one of its main conclusions. Simon identifies truth with freedom and defines freedom as a right of the individual (392).[2] Stated with maximum brevity, truth is understood as an activity or way of life rather than as an objective structure or ontological entity. It coincides with the subjective reflection upon the limitations of objective definitions of truth. This subjective reflection is semantical: semantics replaces ontology. In *Philosophie als Zeichen,* we have Simon's lapidary presentation of semantics as a comprehensive doctrine of signs. Freedom is accordingly understood as the freedom of interpretation, or of the imaginary production of new signs.

My own view on these points is somewhat different. I deny that language and thinking are coextensive. I can therefore accept that every language is a historical creature, without granting that all thinking is governed by historical grammar. Finally, I would distinguish between what the Greeks call *noēsis* and *dianoia* on the one hand, and between *Einbildungskraft* and *Fantasie* on the other. It is the *Einbildungskraft* that freely produces signs, but in obedience to, or as regulated by, *noēsis* and *dianoia.* Only in this way can we distinguish between *Einbildungskraft* and *Fantasie.*

The question now arises: How can I best develop, in the form of an essay, this difference between Simon and me? Although I have made use of historical references, in part because Simon makes them and in part to clarify the issue at stake, I prefer to proceed more directly by turning "zur Sache selbst." I want to suggest, by a simple consideration of everyday experience, the fundamental distinction between thinking and speaking, but also the distinction between signs and things. To put the last distinction somewhat more precisely, I shall contend that things may serve as signs, but that this semiotic function is not ontologically fundamental.

As a preliminary remark, I might say that if thinking and language are coextensive, then not only is the world a text but ontology becomes the writing of fiction. I will indicate later why I regard this as impossible. Furthermore, the propensity of consciousness to adapt itself to a syntax is not a proof of the identity of thinking and language. On the contrary, the ability of consciousness to adapt itself to *any* syntax rather suggests that thinking occurs, transcendentally, so to speak, in a prelinguistic dimension.

To state only the decisive point, if thinking is entirely discursive, we could never begin to think because we would be unable to begin to understand the language we use. We should have to know a language in advance in order to begin to understand it. This "transcendental" point is made over and over again in ordinary experience, as we see what people are talking about and, even more important, as we see what we are to say next. It must be a prelinguistic intelligence that understands the first statement of a historical language. But it is the same prelinguistic intelligence that fits thinking to appropriate linguistic expression at every stage of experience.

So much by way of introduction, in order to make clear my own orientation. I turn now to a development of the first step.

One of the characteristic disruptions of our age is that of signs or signifiers from their referents. It was once taken for granted that a sign points to something which, although it may function in turn as another sign, is, as pointed out, an identifiable entity and so a terminus of reference. Smoke is a sign of fire, although fire may serve in turn to indicate danger, negligence, warmth, illumination, and so on. Smoke and fire are identifiable elements in a network of intelligibility, each having a nature that allows it to serve as the beginning or the end of an inference.

The link between signs and referents was weakened by the insertion of a concept as intermediary between the two. It was accordingly claimed that the name "smoke" signifies, not fire, and not even smoke, but the concept *smoke.* A concept, however, is a human artifact; it has no natural but only conventional senses. The name "smoke" then signifies whatever we wish or intend it to signify. Wishes and intentions are not entities but signs of something else, something that varies from person to person, something that is modified by circumstances.

A wish or intention is finally a sign of desire, and desire is, so to speak, polymorphous perverse. The concept, which was itself intended to fix the sense of the name and so to determine with greater precision the referent, serves instead to negate the referent and to multiply the sense of the name. The triumph of semiotics is the defeat of philosophy. Whereas philosophy was originally understood as the attempt to satisfy desire, it has come to be nothing more than a pseudonym for desire. As a concept, philosophy is what we wish it to be, and hence it is nothing.

This process of disintegration is initiated by thinking itself, which moves by an inner necessity from intuition to analysis. We wish to determine with precision what it is that we have seen. Unfortunately, the process of analysis replaces the initially coherent view with a multiplicity of partial perspectives. We respond to this multiplicity by the activity of synthesis, but synthesis is productive rather than recuperative. The intellect makes to stand together that which it has antecedently separated. The configuration is determined, not by the initial intuition, which we reject as "impressionistic" or "pretheoretical," but by what we have established as a result of our analysis.

This is not to say that intuition disappears. On the contrary, "intuition," which means literally a "seeing into," is closely associated with analysis, which takes us *into* the structure of something by identifying its elements. This identification is not a random dissolution; the elements of structure are arranged in a *construction*. They stand apart as elements by virtue of standing together in a totality. Intuition shows us what to analyze; analysis provides us with the elements of a synthesis.

One might therefore suppose that synthesis returns us to intuition at a higher level, that it is articulated intuition: a seeing into the nature of something without relinquishing its identity as this something here. We know from our experience that such is not uniformly, or perhaps ever, the case. What happens instead is that the analytic refinement of our orienting intuitions serves to replace them with something else. The ensuing synthesis is itself a temporary stage of analysis.

We normally regard this process as a deepening of our understanding, an increase in maturity or sophistication; and often we are right to do so. But there are difficulties as well. To take a simple example, an initial belief in God is eventually subjected to elaborate analysis. The intuition of an all-powerful and merciful creator is replaced by a series of concepts of divine attributes. We are driven by the intuition itself to break it into its components, to see it more closely and hence more precisely. The original intuition is replaced at first by a conviction that its content will coincide with the results of our analysis, and then by absorption into those results, which in turn gives rise to the attempt to reunite the elements obtained by analysis into a new, "higher" synthesis.

The higher synthesis is a product, an artifact of our analytical ingenuity. What we mean by the name "God" is a function of our conceptual sophistication, which accordingly modifies what is understood as spiritual maturity. This sophistication is then attributed to God, who is said to speak *ad captum vulgi,* that is, to speak through his prophets to the understanding of the many and hence to imply something quite different to the few. We attribute esotericism to God.

Cogent reasons for this self-concealment or duplicity may be offered, but they are not our concern here. The point is that God bifurcates or multiplies; the many have their concept of God, and "we" have ours. But "we" is already a multiplicity of "I's." The road is open to an understanding of God as a personal concept. The intuition of monotheism with which we began is replaced by polytheism. The gods are expressions of individual desire. "God" means what we want it to mean. God is dead because we no longer desire him. There are no gods but only signifiers signifying other signifiers. The disrupted harmony is replaced by disruption.

Nothing that I have said thus far should be taken as a repudiation of analytical reason. My point is rather that the necessity and the desirability of analysis is a multiplying or disruptive factor as well as an indispensable force of refinement and precision. Philosophy divides us in the process of unification. This is necessary because initial desire is itself a sign of disruption or disunion.

Neither have I intended in these opening remarks to repudiate the importance or for that matter the omnipresence of signs. Wherever there is intelligence, or the perception of concatenation, signs necessarily exist. One thing points out another to the attentive observer, and, whereas there are, of course, numerous "natural" signs, there are perhaps even more artificial inferences drawn by the imagination as it considers the various patterns of its experience.

To say this in another way, and to come closer to the heart of my present reflections, signs are both compulsory and free. Thunder and lightning compel us to think of rain; we disregard these signals at our risk. But we are free to conceive of thunder and lightning as signs of divine anger. I believe that an important conclusion follows from these simple distinctions. Thunder is, or may be, a sign of something else, just as a certain darkening of the horizon together with an intensification of chill and a scent of moisture may conjointly be a sign of impending thunder, and so too of an increasing divine anger. But thunder is not "merely" or "entirely" a sign. It has an intrinsic identity, by no means rigid or mathematically precise, and of sufficient flexibility to include something of the meteorological symptoms mentioned above as its semiotic auxiliaries.

To say this with a desirable imprecision, which may after all be exactly the kind of precision we require in such discussions, thunder is just that sort of thing that signals the coming of rain. The brightly shining sun, high in a light blue sky punctuated by fleecy white clouds, is no more a sign of rain than it could plausibly be imagined to be a sign of the anger of the gods. We are free to imagine the sun and its lucid horizon as signaling a variety of events, but some events are excluded by the nature of sunlight and clear skies.

In general terms, we are free, but not completely free, to interpret things, processes, or events as signs. However we may wish to distance ourselves from the traditional doctrine of Platonism, nature, with all deference to its flexibility, intervenes. In order to appreciate this point, it is hardly necessary to go to the metaphysical extreme of introducing Platonic Ideas. But an equal restraint must be exercised with respect to concepts. Thunder is not a sign of the concept "thunder," but neither is it a sign of the concept "rain." Thunder is a sign of rain.

We go wrong when we reflect upon, or analyze, the process by which we express the connection between thunder and rain through the medium of language. I have already mentioned my disbelief in the contention that thinking is identical with speech. Suffice it to say that the process by which we express discursively the signaling of rain by thunder is quite distinct from the natural connection between thunder and rain. Just as that natural connection is linguistically mute, so is our thinking as it grasps that silent point of intelligibility. If this were not so, the point would itself be a product of the discursive imagination, hence not a point but an unravelling web.

The English word "thunder" is a conventional symbol for the natural phenomenon of thunder. It is also a conventional symbol for the concept "thunder," which is something distinct from the natural phenomenon. I regard it as a fundamental error to take the word as a sign for the concept and to infer from the conventional status of both that signs are free inventions of the human imagination.

The word is a symbol, but not a sign. We agree, when speaking English, to call the natural phenomenon by the sound "thunder." But we might have agreed to employ some entirely different sound, if, that is, the English language had developed differently. What we cannot plausibly, or as I shall say, reasonably, agree upon is to regard the natural phenomenon of thunder as some other natural phenomenon, say sunshine. This has an obvious bearing upon the connection between the word and the concept, but here there is much greater flexibility.

The reason for the greater flexibility is that we have now shifted from the observation of natural phenomena to the domain of the interplay between reason and the imagination. The concept "thunder" would be worthless if it did not derive its initial stratum of meaning from the properties of the natural phenomenon. We must see, hear, and, by extension, touch and even taste the properties of the meteorological context of thunder. But nothing prevents us from associating, via the imagination, these properties with things, processes, or events which are not present to the senses.

These associations, when they are accepted by a wide enough circle of native speakers of English, come to be regarded as a stratum of the meaning of the concept "thunder." No one can say in advance what the outermost limit of these associations will be. It does not, however, follow that the concept "thunder" is entirely indeterminate or, as many would today put it, a mediate stage in an indefinite sequence of signs, no one of which has a fixed core of sense except as embedded in a purely conventional or historical linguistic perspective.

Let me repeat: English is a historical language, and the concepts associated with its words are historical or perspectivally modifiable entities. But thunder is a natural phenomenon; just as it cannot be confused with sunny skies, so too the plausible perspectives or strata of meaning which may be added onto the semantic core of the concept "thunder" are also limited. Even those who insist that thinking is inseparable from discourse cannot persuade us that discourse is inseparable from natural phenomena.

I must now make two qualifications of the very simple remarks just concluded. The first is that we are often required to apply our imagination to the task of identifying natural phenomena. Examples of this sort abound in contemporary physics or in any science in which model-construction plays a major role. The second qualification is that even imaginary or artificial entities impose a limit upon the semiotic perspectives from which they may be viewed or within which they may be interpreted. These two qualifications, taken together, insulate my earlier formulation against the objection that the observation of natural phenomena is not restricted to sensation and intellectual perception.

The properties of matter are initially accessible to the senses, which are in turn subjected to cognitive interpretation. As the study of nature deepens, the imagination plays an ever more important role in interpretation. I grant this, although I must caution that we tend to use the term "imagination" too loosely. An insight into the probable consequences of accessible phenomena is not the same as a fanciful invention or the application of a private perspective. But even fanciful invention has its limits, regardless of whether or not we are able to formulate plausible rules by which these limits are determined.

We cannot know in advance every insight or every plausible, that is, convincing or useful, construction of the imagination. This does not alter the fact that, in each case, insight or imagination does its work on an existing situation: a thing, process, or event of such-and-such a kind, whatever that kind may be. And this is why I regard it as misleading to say that insight and imagination operate upon signs. It has to be made clear that insight and imagination are operating upon words and concepts, not things, processes, or events, and certainly not upon natural phenomena.

We extend the concept "thunder," but not the nature of thunder. Thunder, of course, like any natural phenomenon, may in principle be modified by the application of scientific technology. But these modifications proceeed on the basis of natural laws, if that is not too old-fashioned an expression. And in this case, thunder is not a sign of rain-making by seeding clouds, just as the atom is not a sign of the atomic bomb.

One could perhaps maintain that what I have called natural phenomena, or things, processes, and events, are themselves signs in the sense that their interpretations are inexhaustible. No one could ever say that the possible interpretations of thunder, for example, have been exhausted, even though thunder must itself serve as the basis for assessing the plausibility of candidate interpretations. I am prepared to acknowledge this point, on which I agree with Simon, in the following way. Each suggested interpretation of the concept "thunder" must be evaluated on its merits; in particular, it must be decided whether the suggested interpretation fits the facts of the nature of thunder in such a way as to extend the associations which we are prepared to make with the phenomenon.

But it is the nature of thunder that rules here; no interpretation that asks us to deny the properties of the phenomenon itself will be acceptable. As I have noted, new properties—for example, those studied by statistical mechanics in the case of air currents, drops of moisture, and so on—may be discovered. But they are not inventions or fanciful interpretations. They are *discoveries;* we learn something about the nature of thunder that we did not know. Thunder is itself not altered by new interpretations; what is altered is the concept "thunder."

The claim is frequently made today that scientific theories are themselves interpretations in the sense of perspectival and hence historical linguistic productions. Stated with maximum simplicity, on this view, the ostensibly natural phenomenon of thunder is in fact a linguistic and so a historical artifact: a sign, possessing no determinate or final nature, but open to endlessly novel interpretations. If this claim were taken literally, it would amount to the thesis that the world is a text, or that sensuous and cognitive experience of the world is in fact the reading of a book with no determinate content and no identifiable author.

I do not regard this claim as one that requires extensive refutation; on this score, I am, no doubt, regrettably immune to contemporary hermeneutical fashion. My reasons for this recalcitrance are as follows. First, there is a fundamental and immediate difference between experiencing a thunderstorm and reading about one. If it is necessary to specify further, we hear the sound of thunder and we are both chilled by the associated air currents and drenched by the ensuing rain. Not even Marcel Proust could undergo these physical sensations merely by the act of reading.

I understand that this initial reason will be regarded as naive by sophisticated proponents of textual postontology. But naivete is not self-evidently a philosophical vice, especially when it comes to protecting oneself against inclement weather. Let me, however, pass on to my second reason. An interpretation is in every instance the giving of an account, or what the Greeks called *logon didonai,* and this means that an account is given of something in particular, or of what Aristotle called a *tode ti,* a this thing here, which is also a *toionde ti,* a thing of a certain kind.

If this were not the case—if, in other words, interpretations were actually of indeterminate signs—then there would be no basis for comparing interpretations or for accepting some as plausible and others as absurd. It is not simply the case that interpretations of signs would be temporary or subject to further questions; there would be no interpretations at all because there would be nothing identifiable to interpret. I can fortunately state this point in slightly more up to date terminology. If reading is interpreting, then writing is clearly impossible. Each attempt to "read" a text would result in the superimposition of a new text onto the old; one could not even read what one had oneself written.

Texts are as stable as natural phenomena; their semiotic capacity is a function of this stability rather than a theoretical advance that exposes stability as a metaphysical illusion. I therefore agree with Simon in one way that we can never arrive at a referent which loses forever the capacity to function as a sign (via its concept, I add). In this sense, there is no "final" replacement of a sign by a referent. On the other hand, each replacement of a sign by a referent is final: it is always *this* referent that is designated by *this* sign. Every instance of reference, whatever ambiguities it entails, is always sufficiently precise so as to occur: to serve as the ground for subsequent disambiguation.

I want to reiterate an earlier point which, in my opinion, goes to the heart of the matter. We must not confuse language, to which signs belong, with things. There is no doubt that our conceptualization of things is linguistically permeated, and in that sense historical or perspectival. But things are not brought into being by our talking about them. Thunder is not a sign of a rainstorm except to some sentient entity or to a creation of a sentient entity, such as a thermostat.

Because it is the distinction between things and concepts that makes possible signs, or, in other words, because signs are interpretations (and in the case that interests us, interpretations by human beings), I am able to agree with Simon that the human animal is *free,* and precisely as a maker of signs. This freedom depends upon the independent existence of what are called in semiotics "referents," but which I prefer to call things. But my freedom is law-abiding, and in two senses. First, it takes its bearings in every case by this thing here of such and such a kind. Second, freedom always actualizes as itself law-abiding. The laws cannot be given in advance, except perhaps in the most general and platitudinous sense. They appear together with the exercise of freedom itself; in the given case, together with the new sign or novel interpretation.

I am unable to discuss here whether these two criteria of law-abidingness are the same as or whether they deviate from Kant's doctrine of freedom. My intentions are not philological but philosophical. I am defending the thesis that philosophy is impossible unless the free projection of interpretations (or the multiplication of signs) regulates itself both by what has been and by what has just come to be. An interpretation of thunder is not an interpretation of sunshine. And the extension of the concept of thunder, as, for example, to include the role of sign of the wrath of the gods, brings into play additional laws bearing upon the nature of gods and the consequences of their anger. We are in one sense, of course, free to conceive of the gods as we like. But in another and perhaps deeper sense, we are regulated by considerations, largely but not entirely visible only when the new interpretation presents itself, of the nature of the elements of that interpretation itself.

I want now to cite a passage from *Philosophie des Zeichens:* "The *freedom* of interpretation (not its arbitrariness) is the fundamental natural right because it grounds in the understanding of signs as such. *Everything* that we understand is sign and sign-interpretation. The freedom of interpretation is the *presupposition* of each interpretation" ("Die *Freiheit* der Interpretation (nicht die Beliebigkeit) ist das fundamentale Naturrecht, weil sie im Zeichen-verstehen als solchem gründet. *Alles,* was wir verstehen, ist Zeichen und Zeichen-interpretation. Die Freiheit der Interpretation ist die *Voraussetzung* jeder Interpretation": 294–95).

If it is not yet evident, let me spell out where I agree with Simon and where I seem to disagree with him. In the German text, Simon underlines the word "*Alles*"; I think this goes too far. The text does not distinguish clearly between signs as linguistic artifacts and things, including linguistic artifacts but not restricted to them, which may (but need not) serve as signs. When I understand that thunder is a sign of rain, it is thunder that I understand, thunder to which the concept "the sign of rain" belongs. It is therefore true that thunder is a sign of rain, not because thunder is a sign, but because it may serve as a sign. This "service" is its accommodation to discursive intelligence.

I take this to be a crucial distinction. If thunder were a sign, it would be a linguistic artifact in the sense of a discursive interpretation, relative to a certain transient stage of linguistic history, as articulated by local common sense, the current stage of natural science, available schemes of conceptualization, and so on. But that is not at all what thunder is. It is instead what we think about thunder, or a large portion of what we think about thunder. As such, it could be modified in various ways by further thought, and so, by further exercise of the imagination. But none of this would have the slightest effect on thunder (at least not until we translated our thinking into appropriate technology).

We are, further, not *entirely* free to interpret signs or, perhaps more accurately, to employ things as signs, for reasons which I have now stated at some length. One would therefore have to qualify Simon's contention that "the freedom of interpretation is the *presupposition* of each interpretation." If freedom of interpretation is the fundamental natural right, it remains true that natural right is defined by nature, not by freedom. The nature of things provides us with the right to interpret; and by "right," I mean here that things do not exclude this capacity on our part. This right is structured by the kinds of things we choose to interpret, what we choose to say about them, and how these statements can be rendered intelligible both to ourselves and to our fellow human beings.

My qualifications of Simon's text could perhaps all be derived from his parenthetical distinction between freedom and arbitrariness. I am as it were providing the commentary to the words "not its arbitrariness." But I have a further observation on this text. Let me first add an additional citation. Earlier (262), Simon says, "Everything is a sign, inasmuch as everything is Being for *another* (and not object for a subject)" ("Alles ist Zeichen, indem alles Sein für *anderes* (und nicht Gegenstand für ein Subjekt) ist"). This text has a variety of meanings; I limit myself to just one of these, while disregarding the distinction between "another" and a "subject."

I take Simon's general contention to be that all understanding is the interpretation of a sign, and that "*every* interpretation of the interpretant as *something* (as an existent under a determination) can arrive only at a pragmatic end, for a [certain] time, for which a given understanding allows itself to be sufficiently understood *through it*" ("*Jede* Interpretation des Interpretanten als *etwas* [als Seiendes unter einer Bestimmtheit] kann selbst nur ein pragmatisches Ende finden, zu einer Zeit, zu der ein gegebenes Verstehen sich nur *durch sie* hinreichend verstehen lässt": 279). In other words, to be is to be a sign; to be understood is to be interpreted; and interpretations are historical artifacts. I can now state my point. Whereas there may be signs of freedom, in the secondary sense that those who produce interpretations, and accordingly multiply signs, are free to do so, *freedom is not itself a sign;* accordingly, it is not itself an interpretation.

If I have understood Simon rightly, it is as crucial for him as it is for me to say that there can be no legitimate interpretations of human being which deprive it of its freedom. Human beings may be temporarily enslaved, for as long a time as a given ideology of tyranny holds sway over the imagination of a people or nation. But this is an illegitimate interpretation of human nature; and yet, it conforms to what Simon calls "Naturrecht."

My question is then, How do we repudiate tyranny as a false interpretation of human being? Why is Hitler not as free as Jürgen Habermas or for that matter Kant to offer an interpretation of human nature? Does not the tyrant's interpretation serve a purely pragmatic end for a time during which it and it alone provides a wide circle of users of a common language with their understanding of human existence?

I can state my question more abstractly as well. Because freedom is not an *etwas* or a *Sein für anderes,* it cannot be a sign on Simon's own terms. But this can be expressed in a still more fundamental way. Freedom is the source, the *Urgrund* of the law-abiding spontaneity (and I borrow this expression from Kant) of interpretations. There is, then, a sign *that* we are free, but no sign of freedom itself as the source of signs. And the signs *that* we are free are perverse in the sense that they may be produced by dictators as well as by philosophers.

I suggest that freedom of interpretation cannot be the fundamental natural right for this reason: it leaves open the pragmatic abolition of freedom and, in particular, the suppression of the freedom of interpretation. The problem is already prefigured in Kant's doctrine of spontaneity.

To say that freedom actualizes spontaneously *as* law does not alter the fact that the status of the given law, precisely as spontaneous, is contingent. I do not want to pursue this question as a topic in Kantian scholarship but mention it only as a background to these present concerns. The equation of Being with signs and of understanding with interpretation gives priority to spontaneity. And I deny that spontaneity can serve as the effective ground of freedom. To the contrary, it cannot effectively distinguish between freedom and slavery.

This problem emerges clearly on page 94 of *Philosophie des Zeichens* when Simon says of the *Wahrscheinlichkeit* of an interpretation, "This likelihood defines itself in dependence upon the energy that has been applied to it, for there are no absolutely definitive interpretations. There is only the relation of the consequences to the effort applied" ("Diese Wahrscheinlichkeit bestimmt sich in Abhängigkeit von der Energie, die dafür aufgewendet wird, den es gibt keine absolut definitiven Interpretationen. Es gibt nur das Verhältnis des Erfolges zur aufgewandten Mühe"). I discern here an oblique reference to the doctrine of the *Wille zur Macht,* or what might be called a hermeneutical version of the thesis that might makes right. For my part, I hold that it is not *Energie* but *energeia* or the presence, however defective and despite all chiaroscuro, of what we interpret that is the criterion of probability.

It does not follow from my modest Aristotelianism that interpretations be regarded as absolute. To the extent that I accept the Aristotelian thesis of the unification of intellect and form, this unity is one of orientation, not of epistemic precision. In slightly different terms, *energeia* is a limitation on spontaneity, just as one might say that categorial structure is the Kantian limitation on spontaneity. I must, however, add that the analogy with Kant is not with respect to the categories but with respect to the need for a criterion of order and intelligibility.

Let me emphasize that I am not denying spontaneity to human beings; it is part of our nature to be spontaneous, but we regulate our spontaneity by other properties of our nature. This comes down to the same thing as to say that we are not signs. We may serve as signs, that is to say, we may extend our natural understanding by imaginative or spontaneous interpretations; but these interpretations are evaluated on the basis of our natures, not vice versa. We do not determine who we are by spontaneous interpretations.

Spontaneity is like a gap or fissure in human nature from which emerge the signs and interpretations of the surrounding terrain. I do not wish to press the analogy, but one could compare this gap to the nothingness (*to mēdamōs on* or *nihil absolutum*) which, very far from representing a false concept or hypostasizing of negation, is the necessary background for the visibility of determinate beings. There is nothing to be said "about" nothingness, yet without it nothing could be said at all.

In the same sense, there is nothing to be said about freedom. What we talk about are the signs of freedom, for example, our efforts to construct arguments to demonstrate that we are free. In my view, however, it is freedom which allows the arguments to be formulated. Arguments are signs, linguistic artifacts, interpretations of the gap or disjunction between consciousness and ontic being. So long as the gap remains open, there is no end to the production of signs and interpretations; and here I am in agreement with Simon.

I should like to suggest by way of conclusion that the production of signs and interpretations, and so philosophy, precisely as a product of the gap, is also dependent upon that within which the gap occurs. Something does in fact come to be from nothing, but only because Being and nothingness are coordinates. As it happens, and as does not seem to be widely understood in our own generation, this is a fundamental truth of Platonism in the original, not the traditional or "metaphysical" sense of the term. Eros is the gap: this is why Diotima calls Eros the interpreter (*hermēneuon*) between gods and mortals (*Symposium* 202e3).

Chapter 13 Philosophy and
Ordinary Experience

This chapter was delivered as the Bradley Lecture in Political Theory at Boston College in 1996 and again in December of that year to a seminar on political theory led by Harvey Mansfield at Harvard. It has not been previously published. The essay is based upon material developed in a graduate seminar of the same title at Boston University, also given in 1996. The problem I address is that of the beginning of philosophy and the standard, if any, by which we may distinguish legitimate from illegitimate philosophical doctrines. The difficulty is to steer between the Scylla of reducing philosophy to everyday language and behavior, thereby eliminating it in favor of a conventional standard idiom, and the Charybdis of attributing to it an extraordinary origin, a procedure that has the almost immediate consequence of depriving philosophy of a commonly accessible subject matter. Both of these extremes result in the transformation of philosophy into poetry, that is, into adherence to artifacts of speech, whether these are ordinary or extraordinary. Otherwise stated, either we become policemen who enforce the public idiom, itself a historical creature, or else we dissolve the public altogether into an infinite regression of outbursts of linguistic "originality."

This essay is connected to chapter 8, "Sad Reason," by its discussion of the quarrel between the ancients and the moderns.

I propose to deal with the question of the relation between philosophy and ordinary experience. This sounds quite straightforward, but I am afraid that it is actually an unusually difficult problem. It is a striking fact of our century that philosophy has become increasingly concerned with ordinary experience, ordinary language, everyday life, or the life-world, to cite four often-used expressions. This concern is evident in both wings of the two major contemporary philosophical movements, which are popularly if inaccurately designated as the analytical and the continental or phenomenological schools. Interest in everyday or ordinary language has clearly been stimulated by a widespread perception that modern philosophy, or perhaps even Western philosophy altogether, is at a crisis point.

The crisis is variously defined, but a common element in these definitions is the view that philosophy as traditionally understood in the West has somehow failed, whether through old age and its accompanying decadence or because of some intrinsic theoretical error. Even though there has been no diminution in the advance of technical philosophical innovation, it is nevertheless true that the most influential thinkers of the twentieth century, Husserl, Heidegger, and Wittgenstein, have each advocated a decisive turn away from the theoretical constructions of metaphysics, ontology, and epistemology, and thus a return to everyday life in the attempt to rediscover the origin of philosophy or to purify philosophy of the historical incrustations that have obscured its vision and cut it off from its source.

There are two main versions of contemporary interest in ordinary language and experience. In one version, despite the criticism of theoretical or technical constructions, the approach to everyday life is made by means of a technical apparatus at least as complex as those it seeks to replace. The emphasis upon method, technique, and artificial terminology is at least as strong in these ostensibly trans- or postscientific philosophies as in the most systematic of the doctrines of the modern Enlightenment. I shall refer for convenience to this approach as *transcendental*. By this I mean the attempt to construct a theory or model that expresses the structural conditions or ontological presuppositions for the existence of ordinary experience. As particular examples I cite Husserlian phenomenology of the *Crisis* period, Heidegger's ontology of the everyday in *Being and Time*, and Wittgenstein's *Tractatus*.

The second version of the attempt to recover the everyday as the origin or standard of philosophical discourse deviates, at least in principle, from theoretical construction and comprehensive model-building and takes its bearings instead by how we actually talk and live in our everyday, pretheoretical lives. Whereas those whom I am calling the transcendentalists approach ordinary experience in a scientific spirit, and so as detached or neutral observers whose task is to give an objective theoretical account of the structure of the ordinary or life-world, representatives of the second school attempt to grasp the ordinal nature of the ordinary from within, that is, as speakers of the everyday language or as motivated by the values of ordinary experience. The assumption here, whether explicit or not, is that the philosopher has access through his or her very humanity to the sources of normative discourse or, more generally, to the standards, purposes, and values that underlie and regulate our theoretical reflections and technical productions.

Perhaps the best-known example of this way of approaching the problem is the later Wittgenstein, as most famously represented by the *Philosophical Investigations*. One may also mention the ordinary language philosophy of persons like Ryle and Austin, and the attempt by Leo Strauss to return to the pretheoretical dimension of human nature as expressed in the speeches and deeds of the classical Greeks and the biblical Hebrews. Perhaps it would also be fair to classify pragmatists like James and Dewey in this camp. Thinkers of this tendency, whether explicitly or implicitly, assume the constancy of human nature as underlying historical change. For example, neither the later Wittgenstein nor ordinary language philosophers, so far as I am aware, characterize the ordinal function of everyday discourse as historical in its very root. Whereas people speak differently at different times, and despite the differences that separate one language from others, it is apparently always true that philosophy *ought* to be judged by how we currently speak; that is, by prevailing standards of intelligible discourse. If these standards are capable of radical transformation from period to period, from country to country, and from one stratum of society to another, then of course there is no such thing as ordinary discourse in an ordinal or normative sense, but only local, historically relative dialects.

The position just sketched generates many complications, such as the basis for the distinction between truly ordinal "ordinary" language and the multiplicity of dialects, both everyday and technical. If, however, these complications cannot be plausibly explained, then all attempts to "deconstruct" traditional philosophy on the basis of "what we normally mean when we say" so-and-so are doomed to failure. In other words, if ordinary language is itself a historical creature, then the best that can be said for contemporary ordinary language philosophy (and in this context I include the later Wittgenstein's teaching) is that it may hold some paradigmatic status for the evaluation of philosophical discourse in our own time. But even this is dubious because the attribution of historicity to ordinary discourse, including the standards, purposes, and values of ordinary action, deprives it of paradigmatic status. The enforcement of local linguistic behavior as regulative for philosophy is an expression of the tastes and power of the enforcers.

At first glance it would seem that Leo Strauss clearly distinguished his attempt to return to human nature from all forms of historicism. Strauss was primarily concerned with the natural or pretheoretical expression of political life, but it was a necessary presupposition of his argument that man is by nature the political animal, or in other words that the ordinal or regulative aspect of ordinary experience is political. Even the philosopher, whose fundamentally theoretical way of life detaches him from political custom, remains a citizen and is therefore required to justify the philosophical life before the bar of justice. One has only to reflect upon Strauss's adoption of Greek antiquity as the privileged moment in the exhibition of human nature (to say nothing here of his assessment of the biblical Hebrews) to see that he was not entirely free of what he called historicism. It is perhaps not intrinsically self-contradictory to claim that there is a natural basis for the evaluation of speeches and deeds, but that this basis is only, or especially, visible at a certain historical time. One could very well argue that some times are more propitious than others for the discovery of nature. But if nature is accessible at all, it must be accessible in principle at any time during which human beings are sufficiently developed to look for it.

In particular, it may be true that human nature was more accessible in Greek times than it is today. But it is on the basis of our own experience that we recognize it in the testimonials and records of the ancient Greeks. We do not perceive human nature by reading Plato and Aristotle; on the contrary, it is our perception of human nature that makes Plato and Aristotle intelligible to us. Life teaches us how to read, or in other words how to decide which books are in accord with our understanding of how to live. Commentaries on Plato and Aristotle thus serve a secondary or pedagogical role. If the historical mode of expression of human nature is decisive for its intelligibility, then human nature is fundamentally historical. In order to produce the conditions that would enable human beings to live in accord with nature, we would have to reinstitute classical Greek everyday existence, and so, the Greek polis.

The phrase "to live in accord with nature" is intrinsically ambiguous and cannot, incidentally, be applied to Plato in the same sense as it applies to the

Stoics or for that matter to Aristotle. The main point for present purposes is that everyday life is not relative to a particular political organization. If it makes any sense to have recourse to ordinary experience as the ordinal principle of theoretical discourse, it cannot be the case that this principle obtains only in the ancient Greek polis. To hold that it does is like the claim that ordinary English is visible exclusively among upper-class graduates of good English public schools and Oxbridge colleges.

I leave the example of Leo Strauss with the following observation. Let us assume with Strauss that Plato and Aristotle make the nature of political things more transparent than later writers because they stand at the beginning of the Western tradition and see things more directly because their vision is not occluded by the history, or the ideological distortion of the history, of subsequent philosophy. At best, this allows us to claim that Plato and Aristotle provide us with the best understanding of Western political life. But Strauss wants to claim that Western political life is somehow exemplary; more precisely, some part of it is exemplary rather than all of it. He must therefore appeal to a paradigm, or understanding of human nature, that is capable of allowing us to compare the merits of the Greeks and the barbarians, or Western and Eastern visions of society, and even further of free societies and tyrannies, democracies and aristocracies, and so on. The Greeks must submit to this paradigm; they cannot represent or constitute it.

That paradigm is philosophy. In order to do its work, philosophy must be available, whether or not it is perceived, in any historical period in which human beings are concerned with the question of the best life. In fact, the Greek experience sustains my contention because Plato and Aristotle arrived at their political understanding under the corrupt circumstances of the late fifth and fourth centuries, not while living in well-regulated cities of the kind they describe in their theoretical works. But the key point, to repeat, is that ordinary experience transpires under all regimes and in all historical epochs, if it transpires at all. And this is entirely compatible with the assertion that under some regimes or in some historical epochs, it is easier to reflect upon and discuss openly the theoretical implications of the ordinary or everyday.

Let me now try to say something more specific about what is to count as ordinary experience or everyday life. To begin with, I am in greater sympathy with the second of the two approaches that I have described above. Since I used the term "transcendental" to designate the first tendency, let me employ the term "immanent" to designate the second. I am not especially fond of these terms, but some way of referring to the two tendencies is helpful. I count myself among the immanentists. It is our view that human experience cannot be understood as we actually live it, if we adopt in advance a purely theoretical, detached, scientific, or ontological standpoint. We speak of ordinary or every-day experience or life, not in order to trivialize it or because we deny that remarkable speeches and deeds occur within it, but in order to contrast it with the speeches and deeds of modern experimental science and the technical modification of nature on the one hand, and theoretical accounts of its formal structure on the other.

For representatives of immanentism, the ordinary or everyday is the medium within which theoretical discourse emerges; it is the horizon of the extraordin-ary. Ordinary language is accordingly not itself homogeneous but takes on a variety of forms that correspond to the different modalities of experience that are ordinarily available to us. We speak ordinarily of the beautiful, the true, the good, the useful, and so on, but also of our desires, hopes and fears, intentions, goals, and the like. Ordinary language is sufficiently flexible to issue in the whole range of technical dialects that correspond to specialized attention to one way or another of carrying out the tasks of human existence. But it is suffi-ciently common to all these tasks to enable us to discuss their various merits and flaws, to evaluate them on a variety of grounds, and in general to attempt to determine their position within the totality of our conception of a happy or good life.

The turn to technical languages is motivated either by intellectual curiosity or the need to resolve some puzzle or to rectify some inadequacy in ordinary discourse and experience. But the curiosity or wonder that we often call the love of truth is itself an event within ordinary experience; no technical language is required in order to discover or engender it. So too with the technical satisfac-tion of perceived needs or desires. These latter are events of everyday life, not artifacts of *technē*. It is true that the advance of technology produces new objects of desire, and so that we speak of "artificial" desires. But speech of this sort also transpires in ordinary rather than technical language. What one might call second-order desires, such as the desire to be an astronaut, are intelligible as desires with reference to the first-order desires thanks to which we engage in technological, scientific, or purely theoretical investigation in the first place.

No claim is being made here for the infallibility of ordinary experience or for the internal consistency of its desires, intentions, values, and so on. What I am trying to identify is not a standard of infallibility but rather a basis for intel-ligibility and accordingly a guide to the rank-ordering of ways of living and talking. Ordinary experience includes the understanding of mistakes and limitations as well as of successes and powers. It provides us with fundamental ends, but not with an absolute ordering of those ends and certainly not with a deductive demonstration of the completeness of any enumeration of those ends. Ordinary experience is not a first principle; it is just ourselves, that is to say, the speeches and deeds with which we exhibit the regularity that underlies and encompasses our pursuit of the extraordinary. It is thus not intrinsically a historical epoch that existed prior to the advent of science and modern technology, like the state of nature of seventeenth- and eighteenth-century political philosophers, but a continuous dimension of human life.

Everyday life is articulated by customs and beliefs that are in continuous historical transformation. But these transformations are exhibitions of the flexibility of human nature, not of its nonexistence. It is with respect to what ordinarily endures that we identify changes in custom and belief, for example, as different ways of pursuing glory or enjoying the beautiful. If this were not so, we could never perceive changes as changes of a particular kind; in fact, we would not perceive that we were changing but only that we were responding spontaneously to the stimuli of existence. The same is true of common sense. It is of course true that the content of commonsense judgment changes from one age to the other. But what we mean by common sense does not change. No one can define common sense with mathematical precision because it would be *senseless,* that is, a violation of common sense, to try to do so.

I would also say that it is common sense that tells us when to abandon it, that is, to accept counterintuitive or extraordinary technical results. In the same way, one cannot say that our preformal logical intuitions are infallible, but this does not prevent logicians from appealing to what is intuitive or counterintuitive. To make a different but related point, there is no logical justification of logic. Nor do we abandon logic because it contains inner limitations or because we are sometimes misled by its exercise. It is our common sense that enables us to see when and how logic is to be employed, even though the actual exercise of logical reasoning is dominated by *technē.*

What does it mean to justify a theoretical pursuit or the use of extraordinary language? There are, of course, purely formal standards by which we prefer one technical discourse to another: logical consistency, simplicity, completeness, richness of consequences, and also such intangible but well-founded criteria as profundity and beauty. How did we arrive at these formal standards? Certainly not on technical grounds because the standards must themselves be accessible in order that we be able to distinguish preferred examples of technical exercise from their inferiors. I suggest that these standards are furnished to us by ordinary experience. Let me try to elaborate this suggestion by discussing the general case of which it is a striking example.

In the present essay, I am interested in one particular property of ordinary language as the expression of ordinary experience. I am referring to the discursive medium within which we compare the merits and defects of rival theoretical doctrines, and specifically of rival philosophies. It will be best to begin with a simple example. Consider the case of the materialist who insists upon reducing mental or spiritual experience to the motion of atoms in the void. The materialist of my example accordingly claims that consciousness and, in particular, self-consciousness, is an illusion. What actually transpires are fluctuations in our blood chemistry, the firings of nerve cells and other modifications of our neurophysiological structure, and so on. Now such a philosophical doctrine cannot be stated without contradicting itself existentially. Only conscious and, in particular, self-conscious beings are in a position to deny the reality of the appearance of self-consciousness. Life may be an illusion from the standpoint of scientific materialism, but scientific materialism is itself a product of that illusion and is endorsed by those who are under its spell. But that is enough for us to reject this simple version of scientific materialism. It flies in the face of everyday experience. The Cartesian appeal to the *cogito* is thus not a metaphysical argument or first principle but the evocation of ordinary experience.

Now let me move on to a more complicated illustration of what I have in mind. How do we understand philosophical doctrines? What, for example, does it mean to give a "clear and distinct" elucidation of Hegel's *Science of Logic?* Here there can be no question of a simple comparison of Hegel's discourse with the obvious facts of everyday life. Hegel states explicitly that he repudiates commonsense reasoning and that we must ascend to the level of the absolute in order to grasp the truth as he exhibits it. But the absolute is not some neutral terrain, like a heavenly lookout tower from which we may view without obstacles the splendors of conflicting philosophical discourses. On the contrary, according to Hegel, the absolute is precisely the truth that is revealed by his dialectico-speculative logic. Are we then to conclude that in order to understand Hegel, we must become Hegelians?

If this were a necessary inference, then it would clearly be impossible to present an elucidation of any sort, let alone one that is clear and distinct, of Hegel's logic to the intelligent and sympathetic, but as yet uninitiated student. Furthermore, it would be impossible for Hegelians to engage in philosophical disputation with non-Hegelians about the merits of their master's doctrine. Even worse, however, how could the Hegelians know that their master's philosophy is true? What precisely would it mean for a philosophy to be true if it were intelligible only to those who accepted it? And how would we know that our acceptance is based upon genuine understanding of the doctrine rather than upon an illusion of some sort?

Questions like these could easily be multiplied, and of course they apply to the entire enterprise of philosophy, not simply to Hegel. We do not explain a philosophical doctrine, to ourselves or others, simply by repeating it. The translation of one doctrine directly into another, better-known doctrine, say, of Hegel into the language of Wittgenstein or Heidegger, is in the first instance a departure from Hegel and an arrival at Wittgensteinian or Heideggerian ways of looking at things. But even if such a transition could be made without begging the question of the sense of Hegel's teaching, we would have accomplished nothing so far as the pedagogical task is concerned. For we would now have to explain the teaching of Wittgenstein or Heidegger, which must first be understood in order to determine the accuracy of the translator's rendition of Hegelianism into a foreign tongue.

Considerations of this kind might lead us to hold that philosophy is impossible. But this is as much contradicted by experience as the claims of naive materialism. In the first place, philosophical doctrines exist in great plenty, and there is a reasonably large number of human beings who have been engaged for more than two millennia in the task of defending one or another of these doctrines. One might regard all this activity as a mass psychosis, but in order to take this tack, we should have to insist that the entire dispute is unintelligible, and this is simply not the case. In order to establish the unintelligibility of philosophy, one must philosophize.

What actually happens is not that, say, Platonists translate Plato into Heideggerese in order to explain the views of their master to Heideggerians, but rather that both Platonists and Heideggerians have recourse to some third mode of discourse that is neither pure Platonism nor pure Heideggerianism. This third mode cannot itself be the language of some third philosophical doctrine, say Thomism or Husserlian phenomenology, because that leads to an infinite regress of unintelligible chatter. Neither is it the simple patois of the man in the street. Nor can we call it the language of scholarship without considerable qualification, since scholarship tends to reflect theoretical presuppositions of its own and, even assuming that there is such a thing as "objective" scholarly discourse, it remains for us to determine the source or ground of its objectivity. How do we know when an ostensibly objective analysis of a Hegelian text is accurate? If through a knowledge of Hegel, then the scholarship is superfluous.

But in any case, the accuracy of the scholarly account can be established only by an understanding of Hegel, and it is a vicious circle to hold that we acquire knowledge of Hegel through accurate scholarship.

Odd though it sounds at first hearing, I am inclined to suggest that the question of how we understand a philosophical text is in principle the same as that of how we understand academic gossip or cocktail party chat about philosophical research. There is no doubt that special training is required to understand philosophical texts and even to gossip intelligently about the latest research in the field. But the training has its roots in the ordinary language of everyday life. There is a dialect of ordinary language that is accessible to every person of sufficient intelligence and training, a dialect that does not consist solely or even primarily in the subdialect of the discipline of philosophy but that allows us to understand that subdialect (or those subdialects) by providing us with general conceptions of the common human experience that gives rise to, and is the source of the meaning and value of, philosophical doctrines.

My thesis is not simply that there is an ordinary language, reflective of the common stratum of human nature and accessible under certain historical circumstances without itself deteriorating into a historical artifact. I also claim that this ordinary language is retained as the basis or foundation of all technical dialects. It is this basis that serves as the fundamental paradigm for the plausibility or implausibility of theoretical discourse and in particular of philosophical doctrines. It is not satisfactory to evaluate philosophical doctrines on purely technical or formal grounds because these grounds cannot establish their own validity or authority.

This in turn leads me to the following claim. Philosophy is extraordinary speech, but extraordinary speech derives its first and most important level of significance from ordinary experience or everyday life. In saying this, I have no intention of reducing philosophical to ordinary or everyday discourse, or even to the subdialect of ordinary discourse within which the communication of technical philosophy and its basis in everyday life is established. But I do wish to render intelligible the difference between philosophy and rhetoric or poetry. If there is no ordinary basis to philosophy, that is, if there is no paradigm common to all philosophies, not as determining their entire inner discourse but as enabling human beings to judge these doctrines to be plausible or implausible, thereby providing an indispensable basis for their intelligibility, then the choice between one philosophy and another is purely arbitrary. If there is no common world that is the originative reference of philosophical speculation, but it is rather the case that each philosophical doctrine creates its own world, then of course there is no such thing as philosophy, but only the production of unique works of discursive art. And these works of art are not intelligible, in the first instance not to any external audience, but also not to their creators, since there is no standard by which to distinguish between a true and a false interpretation of one's own creation.

Let me now terminate this line of my argument. I hold that we are capable of distinguishing between better and worse ways of acting and speaking, and that this capacity cannot be explained on the hypothesis of radical linguistic perspectivism or historicism; it cannot be explained as the mastery of technical subdialects or idioms that render superfluous the ordinary language with which we began. There is a common human nature that is initially and decisively accessible to us as we refine our ordinary discourse into the dialect that is appropriate to the mode of theoretical investigation we wish to pursue. This dialect is not yet the technical subdialect of the particular theoretical activity; it is the transition and so the link between ordinary and extraordinary language. At the level of the transitional dialect that is closest to ordinary language, we gossip about contemporary philosophical research. At the level that is closest to technical discourse, we "interpret" philosophical doctrines or explain them, at first to ourselves and then to our students.

I will now restate the main thesis of this essay. If philosophy is understood as a thoroughly extraordinary event or activity having nothing to do with ordinary experience or sound judgment, then there is no basis on which to distinguish between genuine and specious philosophical speeches. If philosophy is a radical departure from everyday life, if it claims that ordinary life is an illusion, or an accident of our neurophysiological structure, or the detritus of outmoded scientific theories, or that it is for some other reason irrelevant to philosophy, then philosophy is indistinguishable from poetry or, if you prefer, from arbitrary rhetorical assertions. And I deny that this latter alternative is feasible because such arbitrary assertions cannot be understood by anyone other than their authors, and perhaps not even by them, if the doctrine of radical perspectivism is accepted. My own thesis may be wrong, but it is feasible because it is intelligible. This may seem like a small virtue, but in the postmodern epoch, one should be thankful even for small virtues. Stated more generally, conceptions of philosophy are feasible if and only if they may be debated in the common language of ordinary experience. Let me emphasize that the detailed doctrines of the philosophy do not have to be expressible in everyday language. But the general claims or overall assumptions must be so expressible, for otherwise philosophy is impossible.

Postmodernism has already infected mathematics and natural science, to the amazement and outrage of many practitioners of those disciplines. I am not surprised in the slightest by this development, which I predicted more than a quarter of a century ago in a book entitled *Nihilism*. This prediction, which I do not claim as original to me, was based on two closely related points. The first is that modern science from its very advent is rooted in a repudiation of the stability, seriousness, and intrinsic significance of ordinary experience. If human life is an epiphenomenon of the motions of atoms in the void, then it would seem to be a dream. And what might at first appear as the dream of freedom from God and nature soon deteriorates into the nightmare of the obsession that chaos is the heart of all things. But if chaos is the essence of Being, as Nietzsche insisted, then "everything is allowed," including the replacement of truth by rhetoric. The second point is that the main current of modernity accepted very soon mathematics as the paradigm of rationality. Because mathematics is intrinsically silent on its own excellence or lack thereof, it was inevitable that all doctrines about the value or significance of human activity, including the pursuit of scientific Enlightenment, would come to be identified as irrational.

To come at the same point from a slightly different angle, the traditional understanding of philosophy as love of wisdom, and so of the rationality of the love of the noble, was effectively vitiated by the redefinition of the noble as freedom of the will, or the ability to pursue what is suitable, fitting, and so admirable to oneself. This redefinition takes place in Descartes' *Passions of the Soul*, where he also defines love as a physiological passion rather than a spiritual appetite for the noble. Despite the light disguise by the rhetoric of Stoicism, one finds in this insufficiently studied text a decisive step in the modern revolution. If one combines it with that other Cartesian doctrine of the *mathēsis universalis*, the way is open to the emancipation of the imagination as the faculty that prepares rhetorical or ideological justifications for a reason that cannot reasonably defend itself. At the end of the twentieth century, imagination has gone a considerable distance in the process of assimilating reason entirely. It would be ironical indeed, but in my opinion not impossible, if humanism were forced to rely upon the technological spirit for its salvation, since technology is practically necessary even to the prodigies of difference.

For reasons like the ones I have now given, it seems to me that unless one can arrive at an adequate account of the relation between philosophy and ordinary experience, it must remain an open question, not whether philosophy is dead, or whether we live in a postphilosophical epoch, but rather whether philosophy has ever existed or ever could exist. Let me try to clarify this last assertion by means of a brief discussion of the question of a philosophical foundation. As the term is used today, "foundationalism" designates the attempt to ground philosophy in an absolute first principle, preferred method, or by claimed access via direct intuition to some privileged domain of being. Such a ground might be ordinary or extraordinary. The question arises: am I a foundationalist?

To begin with, I have no first principle in any traditional sense, such as that all is matter or, alternatively, that all is idea. Second, I have no preferred method but am content to proceed as circumstances require. Third, it is not my view that philosophy originates as the intellectual perception of Platonic forms, Aristotelian species, or for that matter the will of God, although I want to leave open the possibility that one or more of these perceptions might be subsequently discovered to play a crucial role in philosophical activity. But that would have to be defended by careful argument and more precisely by the detailed analysis of ordinary experience. The search for the foundations is not the same as foundationalism.

The antifoundationalist might at this point call my attention to the grounding or regulative role played by ordinary experience in my conception of philosophy. My reply is that I have not turned ordinary experience into an infallible criterion of philosophical truth. Instead, I have identified it as the ambiguous matrix of philosophical investigation. It is on my view a necessary but not sufficient condition for a philosophy to be worthy of serious consideration that it offer a plausible response to the needs elicited in human beings by the everywhere compelling features of everyday life. It is the satisfaction of these needs that justifies a philosophy in transcending ordinary experience. But we must never forget that satisfaction is not abandonment.

In our everyday life, we understand texts and discuss them with each other, and we are able to communicate with persons whose native language is different from our own, either through interpreters or by learning the language ourselves. How do we manage this, if not by recourse to a common level of linguistic understanding? No doubt the language of this level is too rich to be codified in a set of rigorous rules, and it is filled with equivocal terms. But equivocity is essential to ordinary understanding because it allows us to decide which of a word's several senses applies in the particular case. Problems arise, not from equivocity, but from a lack of sound judgment. As to sound judgment, it does not arise from some other intellectual activity but manifests itself in its judgments. This is not quite to engage in circular reasoning, but I agree with Heidegger about the hermeneutical circle. It is self-evidently true that in order to understand, we must first understand. The question is not whether this is circular, but whether it is empirically correct. I claim that it is verified by the fact that we understand. For example, readers of my text who belong to diverse linguistic communities will understand me well enough to pose plausible objections to every major point I am making in this essay. How will they accomplish this, unless I am correct in my basic thesis that we speak a common language, the language of our humanity?

I want to repeat that the same situation obtains with respect to modern science, which, despite its constructive dimension, cannot be said to manufacture a multiplicity of independent worlds without ceasing to be the discovery and explanation of common laws and principles of nature. By extension, even those who wish to narrow or eliminate the difference between philosophy and science must admit that science is the clarification and mastery of everyday life. Scientific discoveries, methods, models, and so on, are no doubt "extraordinary" in the sense that they are radical refinements of, or often deviations from, the kinds of reasoning that characterize ordinary experience. But it is ordinary experience that science seeks to explain. The extraordinary and the counterintuitive are not pathways to private creations but rather to the elements and principles of the ordinary or common world.

I trust it is now clear that there is an intrinsic connection between ordinary experience and human nature. I hold to the Socratic thesis that the human animal is by *nature* philosophical. This means that every normal person is open to philosophy in some form or another, and primarily through the medium of sound judgment about ordinary experience. But it does not mean that every human being is a philosopher in the highest or even the intermediate sense of the term. Philosophy is like running or swimming; everyone can do it, but some do it better than others.

As a corollary to the preceding assertion, I also hold that the philosophical impulse is visible in ordinary life in either of two ways. I would prefer to argue from the visibility of the perception of nobility in everyday life, a perception that is all too often lost by the time one has been deformed by advanced education. Rather than tilt at windmills, however, I will take the low road and speak of human desire. It is my view that the two roads, properly negotiated, soon come together into a single highway. However that may be, no desire, including the desire for freedom, can be satisfied without knowledge. Furthermore, not all desires are satisfied in the same way; different kinds of knowledge are required for the satisfaction of different kinds of desires. As we progress in the task of satisfying these desires, we soon come to experience that some desires conflict; we must arrive at a decision about the hierarchy of these desires. Which ones supervene over others? And this in turn leads to the following question: Is the satisfaction of desire its own end, or is there some end that we aspire to achieve through the satisfaction of desire? From here it is a short step to the question of the most desirable life, that is to say, the good life. Desire is thus the middle term between knowledge and the good life.

Those who claim that human beings are simply engines of desire, or that desires have no rank-ordering and no purpose beyond themselves, seem to me to be in the same position as those who claim that translation is impossible or that reading is in fact writing. They are contradicted by everyday life, as, for example, in their pride, their ambition, or even in their pursuit of the truth. Just as Socrates shamed Callicles by raising the example of the catamite, so we should be able to bring a blush to the cheeks of a Foucault or a Baudrillard. But if their cheeks are immune to shame, why is that a plausible argument for following in their footsteps? We cannot assess the extraordinary recommendations of half-crazed intellectuals except by recourse to the sound judgment of ordinary experience, unless of course we are preserved from harm's way by the divine gift.

This is a brief sketch of what I mean by saying that human beings are philosophical by nature. That some apparent human beings are quasi-bestial, or defective, or that we fall short of the task of satisfying our desires in the most efficacious manner, is irrelevant; or rather, it is also a part of human nature. I have not claimed that all human beings must recognize the philosopher as the highest type or, if you prefer, philosophy as the paradigm of the good life. I am rather claiming that all human beings desire the good life, whether or not they desire truth, that is, whether or not they understand that true knowledge is the basis for the satisfaction of desire. The philosopher can attempt to persuade the nonphilosopher of the superiority of one way of life to another because both are residents of the common dimension of the ordinary existence in which the need for philosophy arises.

I want next to clarify what I mean by "the good life." I would never claim that only philosophers live the good life, or conversely, that in order to live the good life, one must be a philosopher in the full sense of the term. What I rather claim is that the good life always participates in philosophy. We are all philosophical by nature in the sense that we aspire to wisdom and need the love of wisdom in order to guide and regulate our desires. Whether the individual person is a poet, a scientist, a statesman, a minister, a businessman, or a laborer, we share as human beings in the desire for the satisfaction of desire. Let us call this the root desire. This root can also be called the desire for the good life, whatever we happen to mean by "good." Here I allow of relativism, which is in accord with the facts of experience. But I repudiate relativism by adding that the pursuit of the good leads us inevitably to reflection on the nature, ranking, and value of desires. It is this reflection that I call the origin of philosophy, and it originates as a disjunction within ordinary experience, but a disjunction that is addressed to that experience.

The desire to philosophize cannot be initially problematical, despite the extraordinary difficulty of sustaining it by satisfactory theories, interpretations, or even opinions. We are not brought to philosophize by arguments; on the contrary, the arguments, as it were, are brought to us by the desire to philosophize. This is nowhere more visible than in the efforts of the great antiphilosophers like Jehudah Halevi, Kierkegaard, and Wittgenstein to free us from the grip of philosophy, an effort that requires the most intense philosophical thinking on their part. All discussions of the origin of philosophy are accordingly appeals to the deepest experience of the interlocutors. But there is nothing obscure or mystical in such an appeal; it is verified by our ordinary experience.

Most if not all of what I have said thus far is compatible with what I shall call a middle-of-the-road Platonism. It is now time, however, to lay another card on the table. The road down which my Platonism travels is not that of a return to the wisdom of the ancients; I am instead advocating the transmission of ancient wisdom into the contemporary terrain. In less metaphorical language, one does not need to jettison the modern Enlightenment in the effort to rediscover the origin of philosophy within ordinary experience or *doksa*. I am not advocating the recuperation of *phronēsis* at the expense of, but rather in order to preserve, *ratio* and *technē*. And I want to say that it was Leo Strauss who first called my attention forty-five years ago to the powerful passage in Nietzsche entitled "Advice whispered into the ear of the conservative." "Man is not a crab," Nietzsche observes; he cannot travel sideways or backwards but must go forward into the depth of nihilism in order to emerge on the other side. If I endorse this maxim, it is not because I am a nihilist but because we are now in the midst of nihilism. The unity of theory and practice is today palpable as the question of how to inch our way forward through the darkness. Equally urgent is the question of the theoretically correct rhetoric.

In the first part of this essay I introduced the distinction between the love of the noble and the desire for the pleasant and useful. I went on to employ the rhetoric of desire because it is a more accessible road to the love of the noble. It is not difficult to formulate a noble justification of the attempt to satisfy human desire; such a justification lies at the heart of the modern epoch. The radical defect in the modern pursuit of satisfaction consists in the separation of *mathēsis* from *phronēsis*. By equating *phronēsis* in effect with prudential rhetoric, and I say "in effect" because this is the consequence whether or not it is the intention of the aforementioned separation, the founders of modernity transformed their revolution from an act of noble reason to an assertion of the will. To make the same point in a different way, the separation of *mathēsis* from *phronēsis* had as a direct result the separation of satisfaction from nobility. Satisfaction inevitably came to be defined in the light of the body rather than the soul; efforts like that of Hegel to reunite satisfaction with the soul, alias the spirit, were soon diluted into nineteenth-century historicism and the eventual triumph of custom, that is to say, of multiple perspectives, or of difference, and so of the body.

In view of the contemporary triumph of the body over the soul, it seems to me unlikely that what we require today is a radical new theory or system designed to reverse the status quo by powerful metaphysical or ontological arguments. The body is too simple for fundamental ontology, but it is not immune to reason. It can, of course, be easily hypnotized by complex rhetorical speeches; but the remedy for these is not a still more complex speech. I am suggesting that it is rather an invitation to return to everyday discourse in order to sort out what is in the best interests of the body; perhaps that will lead to the discovery of the best interests of the soul as well.

Whether from a theoretical or practical standpoint, then, it seems to me that the time has come for a return to ordinary experience. In saying this, I am not breaking new ground but endorsing a common tendency of our century. For that very reason, however, I need to emphasize the way in which that return is to be negotiated. The return I contemplate is not quite that of the Husserlian phenomenology of the *Lebenswelt*, which presupposes the theoretical apparatus of Kantian transcendental philosophy. I do not recommend an *Ausschaltung* or switching-off of our existential immersion in the value-saturated stream of everyday life, since it is precisely this value-saturated character that I take to be our starting point. That is to say, I want us to perceive from the inside what surrounds us and constitutes the essence of our human experience. Neither am I advocating a return to ordinary language analytical philosophy, another contemporary movement with which I feel some sympathy, but which seems to me to adhere to an excessively narrow view of the ordinary as ordinal or regulative, while at the same time falling victim to the nominalism and conventionalism of so many philosophies of language.

At the beginning of this essay I pointed out that my thesis was deceptively simple. If I have accomplished nothing else by what has been said thus far, I suspect that I have at least demonstrated that point. My position will no doubt become still more precarious when I confess that I have no systematic method for engaging in the analysis of ordinary experience. And yet, this is not as bad as it seems. For there could be no systematic analysis of ordinary experience unless ordinary experience were a system, unless, in other words, it possessed a determinate and unequivocal structure. But this is not at all my thesis, nor is it true.

A word of clarification is required at this point. When I say that ordinary experience is not a system, I am referring to the rich heterogeneity of actual human life. This heterogeneity is not completely random; it is shaped by the structure of space-time, the law of causality, biological nature, and the whole variety of historical, political, and social traditions, institutions, customs, and so on. I am sure that a phenomenological description of the structures of each of these dimensions of the *Lebenswelt* can be of great interest. But these descriptions still leave us on the outside of actual human life. We may be watching how people live, but we are not living, and therefore we are not ourselves animated by the operations of intelligence, love, and desire that are the life-pulse of the process of understanding life.

It should be evident by now why my conception of ordinary experience is not the same as the endorsement of the paradigmatic status of Greek political existence. In the first place, ordinary experience occurs within all political organizations, whether ancient or modern. An appeal to ordinary experience is thus not an invitation to return to one period or another of European history. But second, it is evident to common sense that we *cannot* return to some way of life except perhaps via the only road that is open to us: through the future. Third, however, I am by no means of the view that classical antiquity was entirely superior to modernity. Let me now try to say why.

I seem to have learned from Leo Strauss that the fundamental difference between the ancients and the moderns comes down to a question of courage. Strauss taught me that the modern revolution was due to a combination of philanthropy and excessive daring. There is much debate about the doctrines of Leo Strauss, a debate into which I shall not enter, except in this entirely personal reminiscence. My own view is that philanthropy and daring were not only necessary but noble attributes of the fathers of modernity. The question of whether this daring was "excessive" is a much more difficult one. It may be that excessive daring is indispensable for the initiation of a revolution. Perhaps the emancipation of mathematics from eros on the one hand and *phronēsis* on the other could be construed as a theoretical error. But whatever its cause and however debilitating in the long run its consequences have been, I hold that the error can be corrected without repudiating the Enlightenment.

I am, in short, a moderate defender of the possibly excessive daring of the Enlightenment. My basic and simple argument on behalf of the Enlightenment may be found in an essay, "A Modest Proposal to Rethink Enlightenment," published in my book *Ancients and Moderns*. I shall not repeat that argument here, except to say that it is in basic accord with Nietzsche's "Advice whispered into the ear of a conservative." But this essay is not about the Enlightenment. My point is a general one, and it is intended to cast light on the equally general question of the origin of philosophy in ordinary experience. This origination is not a historically conditioned event. It does, however, take on different local forms, depending upon the historical epoch in which it occurs. And these local forms are sometimes better, sometimes worse. It is here that we must pick and choose. But the choice is never a simple matter of the ancients or the moderns. That is a simplicity with which I have nothing to do. Excessive caution is as stultifying as excessive daring if erected into a universal principle; that is why I appeal to *phronēsis* to adjudicate between the two. It is a theoretical mistake to choose caution as one's attorney, just as it would be a theoretical mistake to identify daring as the judge.

In the last part of this essay, I want to give a single extended example of the kind of investigation that the philosopher might pursue with respect to ordinary experience. The example is that of what we normally call subjectivity. The term itself has many ambiguities, like all philosophical terms, but some clarification is possible. We are often told that the ancients had no sense of interiority, subjectivity, or self-consciousness. This is surely absurd; as a single counterexample I call attention to the Socratic expression *eneblepsen eis eme*, "I looked into myself" (*Euthydemus* 275D). Whenever Socrates considers within himself what he should say next, he is encountering his subjectivity. Needless to say, he would not employ that term, and one will not find a full-blown theory of subjectivity or self-consciousness in ancient philosophy. The Socratics in particular tended to regard thinking in its theoretical manifestation as a kind of transparent operation that takes its shape from the form of what it thinks. In the case of practical judgment, however, this is hardly possible. The admonition to know oneself comes as close as one needs to the sense of subjectivity I have in mind.

Subjectum means in Greek *hupokeimenon,* that which stands underneath and so supports. The modern "subject" is normally defined in tandem with *object.* The *subjectum* in the modern sense stands beneath or sustains that which it "throws" before itself. An *objectum* is thus a *projectum;* hence the appropriateness of referring to modern philosophy as a "project." But none of this terminological lore should prevent us from seeing that the ancients, or, more precisely, the Socratics, were as much concerned with the liberation of the subject as the moderns. One may disagree as to the nature of liberty and the percentage of the human race that has access to it. But there can be no such thing as the pursuit of the noble if one is by nature a slave. This is a commonsense inference from everyday life; everything crucial about the philosophical enterprise depends upon how this inference is assessed.

My own assessment is to agree with the modern view that it is in crucial cases nobler to be excessively daring than overly cautious in the pursuit of the liberty of the subject. In such cases, excessive daring may actually be more prudent than excessive caution, if prudence is in the service of the health of the body and the virtue and wisdom of the soul. Please note that excessive daring is here a metaphorical, perhaps even a hyperbolical expression; I want to make a point that is difficult to state with exquisite precision. It is therefore not my view that excessive daring leads to the jettisoning of *phronēsis* or the unleashing of the imagination. The question at issue is the degree of courage that is required in order to avoid stagnation. In other words, it is a question of the degree that is required by philosophy, from which the love of the noble is enriched and sustained.

I accept the modern "project" as a liberating enterprise of the person or self who is "sub-jected" to the ostensible order of nature. I do not mean by this that I entirely reject the ancient notion of a natural order. But on my view, nature is at odds with itself, and human being constitutes the locus of this *Entzweiung* or *Zerrissenheit,* to employ two pertinent Hegelian terms. For this reason, the liberation of the subject is itself a project of nature and not a repudiation of nature *tout court* by man the maker. The mastery of nature is therefore in accord with one aspect of nature. There is no such thing as a life in complete accord with nature because the natural order is our enemy as well as our friend.

As the previous point could also be stated, the liberation of the subject is not a project of the *ego cogitans,* which is an essentially solipsistic abstraction from what I called above, with the assistance of Socrates, "looking into oneself." Inwardness or interiority is not here peculiarly Kiekegaardian or Christian but rather it is the natural correlative of outwardness or exteriority. And this dualism is the fundamental structure of ordinary experience. There are neither materialists nor idealists in everyday life.

On my view, then, the modern revolution is not at all the repudiation of nobility on behalf of utility or pleasure. In short, I regard the modern revolutionary enterprise as more noble than the classical understanding of noble resignation. But I believe that modern thinkers, in their eagerness to break with the past or at least to subordinate it to the present, not to mention the future, have jettisoned concepts and terms that are essential to the best statement of their own enterprise. Whereas the students of Socrates gave excessive weight to caution and too little weight to courage, the moderns imprudently minimized the role of caution by surrendering to an excessively courageous view of mathematics. In so doing, as I have already argued, they lost the ability to verify the nobility of mathematics and, more broadly, of their own revolutionary project. And this, of course, is the primary example of the defective manifestation of excessive courage.

And so at last to my peroration. Because science cannot certify itself as noble, we fall into rhetorical justifications of science, justifications that cannot be valid or rational, given the criteria of validity and rationality that are acceptable to scientifically oriented philosophers. The ultimate consequence of this situation is a steady deterioration in the certitude of the rationality, and so the legitimacy, of the modern revolution altogether. The revolution begins in a flurry of rhetoric, a rhetoric designed to repudiate rhetoric, and deteriorates into the rhetoric of nihilism. The way out of nihilism is not by a return to the past, but instead by a reconsideration of ordinary experience, and so to the rediscovery of the starting points of philosophical investigation.

This essay has been rather more programmatic than directed toward the clarification of a single, well-defined point. It was, however, my intention to argue that we cannot clarify single, well-defined points if we possess no illumination from the horizon. Stated differently, I have indeed been trying to clarify a single, well-defined point, but in the only way possible for a point of the sort I am making, namely, by what will look to the lover of systems as excessively random skirmishes. Given the comprehensive nature of ordinary experience, its investigation is in a certain sense necessarily random; the divine gift of philosophy can come literally anywhere. But the randomness of the starting points is balanced by the fact that all lead us into a common medium, something that is more like a nutrient than a structure. Let us just call it the stream of life.

My invitation to begin with the ordinary or everyday is not an invitation to conservatism. It should be clear by now that the way in which we are to begin with the ordinary is itself extraordinary. The ordinary plays a regulative role in our investigation only in the sense that it requires clarification, explanation, even justification. But the clarifications, explanations, and justifications that we give are not themselves ordinary and could not be philosophical if they were. Philosophy is a revolutionary activity.

Plato is the great paradigm of philosophy as revolution, that is, as the attempt to transform the conditions of human existence. The fundamental metaphor of the Platonic revolution is medicine: the human soul is by nature ill, as is almost melodramatically evident from the fact that Socrates refers in the *Republic* to the just or beautiful city as "fevered" and "luxurious" (2. 372e3–8). This fever can be brought under control but not extirpated by the rule of philosophers. Aristotle's separation of theory from practice (and so too from production) is at bottom the effort to preserve the philosopher from the fevers of political life, but perhaps more importantly, to preserve the people from the revolutionary speeches of the philosophers. This is a fundamental difference that lies at the heart of the origin of philosophy, and so in the ancient epoch, not the modern. It would take us too far afield to work out the details; I will end with a simple suggestion. The entire complex puzzle of the relation between philosophy and ordinary experience is contained within the disagreement between Plato and Aristotle.

Chapter 14 Nothing
and Dialectic

The material in this chapter was delivered as an invited lecture to the Metaphysical Society of America during their 1995 meetings. It is a concrete representation of my thesis, presented in the prefatory note to the previous essay, that the ordinary is shot through with the extraordinary. I have discussed the problem of nothing on numerous occasions. It is a topic that is easily burlesqued and very seldom faced up to in its full depth and seriousness. I offer yet another version of the problem because I have not yet seen any evidence that my criticism of the traditional approach—in which the problem of nothing is transformed into the technical analysis of something—has been understood, let alone refuted. This problem cannot even be stated in the discourse of analytical rationalism without some deviations from the standard rules of syntax and indeed, semantics. So long as we believe the problem to be spurious or itself rooted in a grammatical error, and so resolvable by recourse to technical artifacts such as sets and rules for negation, we shall be deluded by artifacts. The theory of predication is not equipped to explain what we mean by "nothing" because it was designed to avoid the problem by instructing us to talk about a technical surrogate. But negation and privation themselves rest upon the antecedent

intelligibility of nothing. That intelligibility cannot be captured by a positive con-
cept; the term "positive" already begs the question because it is intelligible only in
contrast with "negative," which is not itself explicable in positive terms. A fuller
exposition follows directly.

I have been thinking about nothing for nearly forty-five years; prior to
thinking about it, I worried about it a lot. It was upon first reading Plato's
Sophist that my worrying was temporarily quenched by thinking. The first
thing I thought was, "What am I worrying about?" It would be gratifying to
be able to report that this devotion to thinking put a permanent end to my
worries. Unfortunately this is not possible. At least with respect to nothing,
thinking and worrying are very closely connected. The attempt to distinguish between thinking and worrying is not without its interest. But I have
other fish to fry here. I want first to review the problem of thinking about
nothing in the usual ways and then to reflect briefly about unusual ways to
approach the same question.

First, I want to explain what I mean by "the usual ways" of thinking about
nothing. These ways are all descended, as far as I can determine, from the
procedure introduced by Plato in the *Sophist*. This procedure amounts to the
replacement of worrying about nothing by thinking about nonbeing. The
replacement is motivated by the thesis that it is impossible to think about
nothing; stated positively, every thought is about something. The suggestion is
then made that, when we believe ourselves to be thinking about nothing, we
are actually thinking about something, which we can call nonbeing as a first
approximation. The Eleatic Stranger argues in the *Sophist* that we have to go
one step farther; what we call nonbeing is itself actually otherness. On the
Stranger's analysis, if I say, "This is not a cow," I mean that the animal to which I
refer is something other than a cow, say, a horse. Again, if I say that the cow
is not brown, I mean that it is some other color. Note that these examples
illustrate two different operations, the denial of identity on the one hand and
predicate negation on the other. One might well ask, What is the correct
analysis of the denial of existence? For example, if I say that Sherlock Holmes
does not exist, do I mean that someone else does in fact exist? This is a question
that once interested ordinary language philosophers; the sensible answer is that
Holmes exists as a fictional character in the stories of Arthur Conan Doyle. I
accept the answer, as far as it goes. But it tells us nothing about the deeper
problem of the intelligibility of "not" within the fictional world, or in what
sense the fictional world is "not" the real world.

The main problems inherent in the Platonic solution are easy enough to spot. First, what does it mean to say that although we believe that we are thinking about nothing, we are actually not doing so at all? How can we understand a command not to engage in activity that is unthinkable and unspeakable? We have to understand what it is to think about nothing in order to understand the command not to think it. Commands of this sort resurface in twentieth-century analytical philosophy, for example, in Bertrand Russell's logical atomism. Russell tells us that when we suppose ourselves to be thinking about certain things, say, the street called Piccadilly in London, what we are actually thinking about is a series of classes of material events. More concisely, analytic philosophy begins for all practical purposes with the assertion that ordinary language is muddled and even incoherent, and that we must replace many of its expressions with technical artifacts produced by a process of logical and conceptual analysis. Unfortunately, this procedure no more explains why we think that we are referring to a street in London when we speak about Piccadilly than does the Eleatic Stranger's suggestion explain why we suppose ourselves to be thinking about nothing rather than something.

By and large, philosophers enjoy telling us that we should not be talking in the ordinary manner if we hope to understand the truth. This advice antedates the advent of modern science, but it intensified under the influence of technological progress. Even the so-called ordinary language philosophers had unusual notions of the language required for the analysis of genuinely ordinary language. In my opinion, the relation between ordinary or everyday language on the one hand and technical language on the other is exceedingly complex; it can neither be ignored nor resolved by a few technical definitions. To mention only one difficulty, a lot of ordinary language is extraordinary; one could even say that it is quite ordinary to speak in an extraordinary way. The only instance that currently concerns me is our ordinary speech about nothing. I really don't believe that we have much trouble talking about nothing. Here is a famous dialogue that exemplifies such speech: "Where did you go?" "Nowhere." "What did you do?" "Nothing."

I wish now to consider briefly the usual manner of explaining thinking or talking about nothing. I have claimed elsewhere, and continue to believe, that the great philosophical tradition from Parmenides to Heidegger, and in our own time the various philosophical analysts and, so far as I am familiar with them, the postmodern heirs to Heidegger, all continue to obey Father Parmenides' injunction against thinking "the altogether not," which type of thinking they replace with thinking about what Hegel calls "determinate negation."

Stated quite generally, every theoretical analysis of the structure, nature, or power of nothing by means of concepts, descriptions of formal structures or for that matter of processes, or the attribution of predicates designating properties or powers is an analysis of something, and hence of something other than nothing. But this is obviously not the same as the definition of nothing as otherness.

Philosophers enjoy talking, and it seems to them to be impossible to talk about nothing. Furthermore, they enjoy solving conceptual puzzles and promulgating theories. These two types of hedonism combine to encourage philosophers to replace the unthinkable and unspeakable with the thinkable and the speakable. Unfortunately, the unthinkable is not much impressed with this shift, nor does it dissolve in face of accusations that it is nothing but a grammatical error or a hypostatization of an apparent substantive or something of that sort. The accusation is absurd in any case, because it is not we ordinary language speakers who hypostatize the specious noun "nothing" but the philosophical technicians who transform it into negation. We ordinary speakers are well aware of the fact that nothing is not a referential term in the usual sense; we use it not simply even though, but precisely because, there is nothing "about" which to talk or think. To paraphrase Gertrude Stein's alleged remark about Oakland, that "there is no there there," in the case of nothing, there is no about about.

Why is it widely believed to be impossible to talk about nothing, when we do it all the time? There seem to be two reasons for this. The first is the influence of what Heidegger calls the doctrine of presence. Whatever one may say of Heidegger, he is surely right to emphasize the importance of the concept of presence in traditional philosophies of being. He exaggerates and perhaps distorts this influence, but he is not inventing it out of whole cloth. The second reason, no doubt not as ancient as the doctrine of presence but still no youngster, is the doctrine of reference. In my view, claims that we cannot talk about nothing because there is no about about, or in other words because the term "nothing" does not refer, are question-begging. One of the most interesting things about nothing to my mind is that it shows us the illegitimacy of comprehensive doctrines of reference. I will not now debate the intricacies of the doctrine of presence. I want to make just one remark about it. There is a good bit of evidence in the Platonic dialogues that their author was aware of the gaps in presence. The passage in the *Sophist,* precisely because it shows us a philosopher, not necessarily to be identified with Plato, trying to get rid of nothing-talk, is perhaps the most important bit of evidence on this score. But one could also point to the discussions of eros and the human soul; eros is constantly ceasing to be what it was and coming to be what it is not, or being continuously reborn and perishing. This shows that human life is not pure presence. On the other hand, it is certainly not pure absence.

To make a possibly startling suggestion, I suggest that we can talk about things without referring to them, if "to refer" means to point out something that is separate from the speaker, something standing opposite to us and which we illuminate or somehow pick out with our words, as when we name things or indicate their properties, relations, and what have you. For example, assume for a moment that Aristotle is correct to say that the intellect "is" somehow the beings. He means by this that when we think something, our intellectual capacity actualizes as the thinkable form of the thing in question. Now neither I nor anyone else can give you a plausible discursive or conceptual analysis of what Aristotle means by this, but I believe that he describes pretty closely our direct experience of thinking; in fact, I doubt that anyone has described it better. The reason for this is that all explanations of thinking generate conceptual apparatus that tends to stand between us and the beings we are thinking, or attempting to think once the conceptual machinery is in place.

Let us for one moment adopt the hypothesis that in thinking, we become what we think. In this case there is no reference to something outside of and apart from ourselves. A doctrine of reference, very far from connecting us to the beings or things in the world, serves to separate us from them. Or rather it starts from the assumption that we are separated from them and offers to intercede on our behalf by hooking us up to these external entities by means of references. Note that concepts refer by virtue of senses or meanings; there is no other way to pick out something from the jumble of experience just by pointing to it. One requires a sense in order to refer successfully, even if the sense is as primitive as a name applied by the act of pointing.

It is not my intention to develop this suggestion here. I want only to establish that a doctrine of reference requires a coordinate doctrine of sense; and once we generate a doctrine of senses or meanings, we have effectively separated ourselves from direct apprehension of, or what Russell, whom I cited earlier, calls direct acquaintance with, beings or things or however you like to call them. I will not even insist that we never require a doctrine of reference; my point is only that comprehensive doctrines of reference are defective. In particular, they mislead us when we try to understand how it is possible for us to think nothing. Please note that if thinking were uniformly becoming what one thinks, then it would seem once more to be impossible to think nothing. But this, I believe, is an illusion induced by allegiance to doctrines of reference. If our intellect becomes nothing at all, and if it is possible to think this emptiness, not by an act of reflection or doubling of the intellect but by virtue of the very nature of the intellect as that which thinks, then it is possible to account for how we think about nothing. I take it for granted that we do so; otherwise we could not be assured that we are wrong to suppose that we are doing so.

There is one other preliminary point I need to make. Should one speak of nonbeing or not-being when one is attempting to avoid reference to nothing? Does it make any difference? Here is a concise statement of my view on the matter. It is possible to distinguish between the syntactic devices of propositional negation on the one hand and predicate negation on the other. I did so earlier in this talk. "Is-not p" differs syntactically from "is non-p," and we normally explain the difference as one between propositional and predicational negation. But I am not interested in forms of negation; as will be shortly evident, negation is of interest to me only because it is used, in all of its forms, as a fruitless dodge against talk about nothing. I shall be arguing that negation is intelligible only via the intelligibility of nothing, and this is as true of verb negation as it is of predicational negation. The case of existential negation is, however, of special interest; once otherness is rejected, the usual explanation of existential negation is by way of class membership or the denial that the value of a certain variable is that of an instance of a certain concept. "Socrates does not exist" thus presumably means that there is no instance of a human being who is Socrates. My question focuses upon what we understand when we say "*no* instance," but I will just mention here that to say that there is no instance of a human being named Socrates itself means that Socrates does not exist. The analysis is quite circular.

Now I want to start again: *palin eks archēs,* as Socrates says. I will speak in somewhat greater detail about the usual manner of treating talk about nothing. Since the most vociferous critics of nothing-talk are self-styled analytical philosophers, I will formulate my remarks in terms of a consideration of analysis. But this cannot be done without reference to synthesis and, as I am going to argue, talk about analysis and synthesis is empty verbiage without talk about intuition.

To analyze is to take apart some compound into its constituent elements. But we cannot construct compounds, totalities, or wholes merely by analysis. Construction of this sort is synthesis. Intuition functions in conjunction with both these activities. Analytical thinking in itself does not tell me what compound to analyze, or more precisely what entity is in fact a compound; but neither does it explain to me when my analysis is completed. These two tasks are carried out by intuition. By the same token, synthesis does not function at random, and it is not analytical thinking that tells synthesis which wholes or totalities or compounds to produce.

Kant thus goes too far when he says that every analysis is preceded by a synthesis, although he is certainly on the right track and moving in the right direction. Some analyses are no doubt preceded by syntheses, but even if one is a Kantian and holds that there are transcendental syntheses by which the field of cognition is produced in advance of every act of judgment or discursive thinking, it remains true at the immanent level that synthesis will not tell us which transcendentally constituted entity to analyze. It is what I call intuition that does this.

As a supplement to these brief terminological remarks, let me say that one cannot analyze where there is no compound, and so no structure. Consider the case of thinking. One of the most important aspects of thinking is knowing what to say next. This knowledge is not rule-governed but is rather spontaneous. If one were making a model of the mind, would one leave a gap in one's hard-wiring and label it the spontaneity aperture? Once something is said, we can then analyze it in various ways, although I repeat that analysis is not the only operation that we employ in understanding what has been said. But the capacity of spontaneity has no structure any more than there are rules for deciding how to carry out a conversation, as, for example, "If the interlocutor says *A*, then say *B*." More generally, what model is there of the human soul or spirit that corresponds to the subtlety, complexity, and spontaneity of its operations? Is there a set of synapses corresponding to the subtlety function or the irony operation, analogous to the aforementioned spontaneity aperture?

It will not be necessary to develop this point further. Suffice it to say with Kant and Wittgenstein, both of whom are preceded by the Eleatic Stranger in Plato's *Statesman,* that there are no rules for the application of rules. But this means that there is no analysis of the capacity to apply rules. And these cases correspond to the absence of structure, or alternatively to the presence of an excessive fluidity in the formation and transformation of structures. Most cases of this sort are commonplace, although in my opinion self-styled partisans of analysis often fail to draw the proper inferences from them. As a teacher of mine used to say, the depths are contained in the surfaces, and only in the surfaces. Unfortunately, he never told us what is the surface of nothing.

If it is a trivial truth that analysis needs to be supplemented by synthesis, and that both require the guidance of intuition, then it is entirely arbitrary to speak of "analytical philosophy" or to define philosophy as "conceptual analysis" or by any more or less equivalent expression. Please note that I am not denigrating analytical thinking but pointing to its limits. To be sure, philosophy is analytical, but it is also synthetic and intuitive. No doubt all three of these powers function together in the activity of thinking, but if we are going to pick one out for special emphasis, then I claim the sovereignty of intuition over both synthesis and analysis. If philosophy is to be designated by an honorific term, that is, by the adjective derived from the most important of its functions, then it should be called "intuitive philosophy."

It will be prudent at this juncture to say another word about intuition. I have used it to designate the faculty by which we see the point of an analysis, or grasp a synthesis that from some appropriate standpoint is suitable for analysis. Intuition is the power by which we discern the point of an argument, and also of a joke. When someone dazzles us with a brilliant deductive argument, it is intuition that leads us to say, "I see what you mean!" and the absence of intuition that elicits the contrasting response: "I don't see your point." In the construction of scientific models, it is largely by intuition that we perceive analogies or isomorphisms that underlie our formal constructions. Stated more generally, analysis and synthesis are the taking apart and putting together, respectively, of formal elements. By "formal elements" I mean elements of the structure of intelligibility of an entity, whether that structure be understood in the old-fashioned sense of an essence or a Platonic Idea or in the modern sense of a mathematical or logical representation of the nature of the entity. By intuition I mean among other things the power to identify something as a candidate for analysis or synthesis. With respect to formal structure, then, intuition is very much what Descartes calls it in his *Regulae:* it is the power to take in a formal structure as a whole. But when we see the point of an argument, the beauty of a formal structure, the relevance of a totality to our analytical curiosity, and so on, we are not only viewing the elements in their configuration as a totality. We see something about this totality, something that is true of the totality of forms but is not itself a form.

This is easiest to see in the case of what we call values. A certain geometrical structure may be beautiful, but the perception of its beauty is not identical with the perception of its formal structure or algebraic equation or discursive definition. A mathematical theorem may be deep, but what we mean by "deep" is not a physical or spatial dimension of the theorem or the logical extension of its consequences, even though we are referring to these entities when we speak of depth. I have asked numerous mathematicians what they mean by a "deep" theorem, and I have invariably been told that a theorem is deep if it has powerful implications. When I ask what they mean by "powerful," I am told that they mean "deep." If this is not a circular definition, then I will convert to logical positivism immediately.

One might suppose that the circle can be avoided by speaking of utility, but this is a fruitless dodge. Useful for what? The generation of more theorems? But how distinguish between deep and superficial theorems? If it is not useful to produce superficial theorems, then what we need are deep theorems. If deepness is to be defined on the basis of the current level of agreement among mathematicians as to what is fruitful or profound, then we either rely upon convention, which reduces mathematics to the level of a historical or sociological process, or we are forced to invoke intuition. I hope that I do not need to multiply examples or introduce variant cases to cover all kinds of situations in which we are obviously neither analyzing nor synthesizing. But neither is the cognitive motor idling as we decide what to do next. It is simply false, and incompatible with his own best work, for Wittgenstein to say that intuition is an unnecessary shuffle.

Please note that in speaking of intuition, I am not talking about going into a trance, having a mystical experience, transcending spatiotemporal limitations, or arriving at a viewpoint *sub specie aeternitatis*. I am not opposed to these activities, but they do not arise at the present level of discourse. Neither am I suggesting that intuition is purely silent understanding, or that one either cannot or need not attempt to explain discursively the content of what one has intuited. I am saying that at every point of discursive thinking, and so a fortiori with respect to synthesis and analysis, we make an intuitive judgment or perceive the significance of a formal structure, a significance that is not itself a formal structure. And I flatly deny that the intuition is itself analyzable into an equivalent set of synthetic or analytical statements that render the intuition superfluous. On the contrary, such analyses are guided at every significant point by intuition itself.

Another objection that is sometimes put to me is that in speaking of intuition, I mean nothing more than understanding. To this objection, my reply is, "Fine. And how do we understand? When do we know that we have understood any particular point?" In my opinion, epistemologies that seek to eliminate intuition also eliminate understanding; their description of the process of knowledge is that of a race of sleepwalkers bumping about in the dark, all the while taking things apart and putting them back together, with no awareness of when they have accomplished anything worthwhile. No wonder that persons of this sort often believe themselves to be computers.

For the past few minutes I have used the very important example of values in order to illustrate a more general point about intuition, or if you prefer, understanding, and that is the peculiar fact that all of our analytical and synthetic activities are performed in the service of deep convictions, themselves neither analytical nor synthetic, about the utility, interest, value, beauty, or depth of formal structures of various kinds. Analytical and synthetic thinking are both in the service of a thinking that is connected to formal cognition but not reducible to it. The value of a form is not its structure. But neither is it a separate structure. If I am asked to explain the beauty of a geometrical figure, I do not merely draw the figure on the blackboard; but neither do I draw some other figure. I can recite a series of formulae or chant an ontological mantra while pointing at the ostensibly beautiful figure, but I will look pretty silly. Now of course not all values are like beauty; I can certainly explain why I regard something as good or profound or interesting or useful. But my explanation, even though it is made up of synthetic and analytical propositions or, more precisely, of propositions that are both synthetic and analytical, is guided at every step by the intuition or understanding that what I am saying is sensible, to the point, plausible; indeed, true.

I can never explain why what I am doing makes sense merely by repeating what I am doing. Neither can I grasp the sense of what I am doing merely by describing what I am doing. To claim simultaneously that there are no senses or meanings, and that the correct explanation of thinking is by way of conceptual analysis, is to contradict oneself. What is presumably meant by this claim is that there are no ontologically distinct meanings but only sentences or propositions. But this is inadequate because the meaning of a sentence can and must be distinguishable from its verbal or logical form. Otherwise, the only meanings would be syntactical. On the other hand, senses or meanings can't be semantic structures because a structure doesn't mean anything; it simply is. It is intelligence that discerns, that is, intuits, the meaning of semantic structures, just as, I cannot resist adding, it is intuition that discerns the meaning of signs, such as arrows on street signs; and it is intuition that tells us which way they beckon us to go.

I am in the process of arguing that understanding is intuitive in that it is not directed primarily at formal structure, whether in the ontological or linguistic senses of that expression. To understand is to see the nonformal significance of form. I cannot simply keep producing formal sequences by way of explanation of the meaning of some initial formal sequence. At some point, and sooner rather than later, I have to see what the analysis is getting at. And although once

I have seen it, I can state it to one degree or another of precision, I will be understood only by those who see what I am getting at. In other words, the analysis is not an animate object with intentions of its own; it is not getting at anything. It is instead being produced by the analyst, who believes himself or herself to be getting somewhere in the manipulation of formal structures. Now it is often extremely difficult to explain "what" we are getting at, and the reason for this is that it is no explanation at all simply to produce more formal structure. But much of the time, especially in what are popularly called analytical contexts, we are so fascinated by the heaping-up of intricate structures that we do not notice the *absence* of structure in our intuition of the point, value, or sense of the whole business.

I want to hammer this point home in the balance of my essay by returning to the problem of nothing. The problem of nothing is not that we don't know what we mean by that term or others like it. The problem is that we cannot explain what we mean in a noncircular way. And the reason for this is that all explanations are of something; they are rooted in some kind of formal structure, some ontological presence, as the Heideggerians like to say. Our ability to talk about nothing is the most forceful example of the nonformal nature of the understanding that I call intuition, which is of course in no way to deny that intuition also functions with respect to form, although it cannot be reduced to the synthesis or analysis of formal elements.

I begin with the apparently simple and straightforward case of logical negation. Standard introductory texts on logic normally introduce negation in what can only be described as a circular manner. This is virtually self-evident in the case of definitions that rely upon truth tables, but it is equally true in other cases as well. Consider the following passage on the introduction and elimination of negation from a recent text that employs considerable rigor from the outset while attempting to explain what is involved in straightforward language: "A philosophical consideration arises from the perspective that rules of inference, not truth-tables, constitute the primary way of explaining the meanings of connectives. The version of -I which uses explicit contradictions is unsatisfactory from this point of view, since negation occurs in the formula $q \wedge -q$ to which the introduction rule for negation is applied, and so we would be explaining negation in terms of itself." The author uses instead rules asserting that if -q is inferred from q, we may then infer % , the sign for "absurd," and so too with respect to the inference of -p from p and %. He concludes his discussion of the introduction and elimination of negation as follows: "Of course, whether the formulation of -I in terms of % is an improvement depends on whether absurdity can be understood independently of understanding negation."[1]

The obvious answer to the author's indirect question is that absurdity cannot be understood apart from negation because it blocks further inferences; and this is to say, "One cannot continue in this line of inference," which in turn depends upon the sense of "not." Otherwise put, one can transfer the problem of the meaning of "not" to the metalanguage and formulate rules for the introduction of the negation-sign within the formal calculus, which sign then serves as a syntactical function carrying no sense beyond its defined operation. However, nothing is gained by transforming one's logic into a senseless game. The philosophical problem persists in the metalanguage. There is no way in which to introduce negation into logic that does not depend upon a prior understanding of the concept of negation. From the standpoint of how we understand nothing, then, nothing is gained by distinguishing between a metalogical appeal to falsehood and the logical function of negation, because falsehood is not understood apart from our understanding of "not true," and this in turn depends upon our understanding of nothing. We must then ask what it means to understand the concept of negation.

A concept is a human construction by means of which we grasp or apprehend some sense. For example, the concept of logic arises from our grasp of what we mean by inference, and this in turn arises from our grasp of the expression "this follows from that," and so on. But what do we grasp when we understand the concept of negation? The procedure followed by logic books seems to imply that we are grasping the substitution of a truth-value by its opposite, for example, "1" by "0" or "T" by "F." But truth-values designate truth, and truth in this context refers to a state of affairs expressible in a proposition. Are there negative states of affairs? Even if we agree with the Russell of logical atomism that there are negative facts, the problem remains of explaining the negativity of the fact in question; and this cannot be done with purely positive concepts. In fact, we recognize a concept as being positive by tacitly distinguishing it from negativity, and so finally from nothing.

Or, to take another example, one sometimes finds set-theoretical definitions of "not" or "nothing" as the conceptual basis for negation; for example, as the set containing the set containing the null-set. But the problem here is that we are employing an extensional definition of the absence of extension. Furthermore, "not" is not a set. Perhaps one can employ a set-theoretical definition of "not" in the metalanguage of one's set-theory, but only by entering into the same circle that we noticed a moment ago in the case of introductory logic books.

There are two closely related problems at work here. The first is that the concept of "not" or, more broadly, of "nothing" is itself unintelligible except upon the basis of our understanding of nothing. And as Plato showed at considerable length, where there is nothing, there is nothing to understand. The second difficulty is that those who are naturally gifted at logic and mathematics tend to look for syntactical or notational devices in order to eliminate "metaphysical" questions. They prefer to have something rather than nothing; but to borrow a witticism that Bertrand Russell employed in another connection, this is to prefer theft to honest toil. One makes no progress by excluding senses and restricting oneself to syntax because a syntax without sense is literally senseless, and so useless as an analysis of genuine philosophical problems. It is doubly defective because it means nothing.

Let me emphasize this last observation. The point is not simply that syntax requires supplementation by semantics. I am asserting that syntax is inseparable from semantical correlations and is unintelligible as syntax without these correlations. Even a pure calculus requires discursive definitions of legitimate formations of expressions, transformations of one expression into another, the conditions of inference, and so on. But I would go farther than this. My own view is that although logic and mathematics do not begin with metaphysical assumptions, they tacitly presume such assumptions, which must sooner or later be made explicit. Examples are the assumption that being and existence are synonymous, or that to be is to be countable or nameable, and so that what is neither of these is nothing. But hence it is assumed (no doubt truly if in a way inaccessible to analysis) that we understand nothing. I must repeat that this is different from understanding some concept or another of nothing because the term "nothing," when used as a concept, appears to refer to something, and in this case there is nothing to which to refer. If I understand a concept that directs me to something, whether a symbol for absurdity, a set, or some discursive instruction for performing a syntactical operation, then I may be in a position to play a formalist game but I have understood nothing of nothing while believing myself to have understood something.

Some might feel there is an inconsistency in my presentation. In the first part of my essay, I made the suggestion that thinking is nonreferential to the extent that we think by "somehow" becoming the thing thought. This is incidentally Aristotle's commonsense revision of the so-called Platonic theory of Ideas. But my exposition of analysis, synthesis, and intuition rests upon the usual distinctions of sense and reference, and so of meanings and concepts. There is, however, no inconsistency here. The usual manner of treating nothing-talk is itself committed to the sense-reference apparatus in one version or another. In criticizing the usual manner, I am therefore not merely permitted but required to show the inadequacy of this apparatus. In so doing, I do not commit myself to it but indicate incoherences that derive from its acceptance.

To continue now with the main line of argument, let us assume that we think by way of concepts. If I say that I understand nothing of nothing because there is literally nothing to understand, I am invoking some concept in order to express this conclusion. But what concept? Even if I were employing a concept and hence some definite linguistic entity in order to negate the thesis that one must understand nothing, the term "nothing" in the immediately preceding clause is not itself the concept doing the negating but the concept being negated. I am in effect carrying out a rule of approximately the following sort: "Apply falsehood [and so negation] to the proposition 'in order to understand negation, we must understand nothing.'" Please note that we are not following a rule to apply the concept of falsehood [and so negation] to the assertion that we must understand the concept of negation, as we would have to be if "nothing" were a muddled reference to negation. This would be doubly absurd because we must understand that concept in order to use it. What understanding, then, are we negating by its means? Those who regard the term "nothing" as referential, but as referring to a concept and so to something, are insisting not only that the complete absence of reference is unintelligible, but that one can assert or establish this unintelligibility by a syntactical analysis of assertions to the contrary. To carry out this explanation, however, they must refer to the absence of all reference as a reference *to which they are not referring.*

The strange thing is that we do understand something of nothing, just as we understand something of indeterminateness or unlimitedness, to mention two prominent examples. We can formulate a concept of these by way of negation; thus the indeterminate is that which lacks, that is, has no, determinateness, and determinateness can be defined in an apparently straightforward manner. But indeterminateness owes its intelligibility to negation, and as we have seen, the situation in this case is unique. But is it desperate? I believe that the situation is desperate if and only if we insist upon noncircular definitions of a formally rigorous type. We need at this point to turn away from logic, which is based upon the interdefinability of logical particles, particles, incidentally, that are selected from a multiplicity of candidates by an appeal to intuition. In so turning away, we must ask ourselves how we speak of nothing in everyday language. And such a reflection shows us almost immediately that the so-called analysis of ordinary language that labels this speech as incorrect is itself gratuitous and incorrect.

In a quite obvious sense there is no problem in referring to nothing; we do it by contrast with something. In another and deeper sense, however, the reference in question is not to nothing but to a collective representation of everything, which is distinguished from the total absence of reference. How do we do this? There is no answer to this question that can be devised from the usual procedures of dealing with senses, references, logical particles, concepts, and so on, no answer that is not circular, that does not assume that we understand nothing. I call this mode of thinking intuitive simply to distinguish it from analysis and synthesis. But I do not believe that the problem is soluble simply by shifting to, or invoking, intuition.

I want to take one more step in my illustration of how the usual manner of discussing nothing terminates in a dead end. We often refer to something in particular that is not present where we expected it. For example, I walk into a room where I was supposed to meet John and after inspecting its occupants I conclude that "John is not here." On the usual analysis, this sentence is supposed to mean that of all the persons present, none of them is John. But this cannot be stated without the use of negation. "For all x, if x is a person in this room, then x is not John." Or alternatively, "There is not at least one x such that both x is a person in this room and $x =$ John." This is not an advance on the initial assertion of ordinary language because it leaves unanalyzed the sense of "not" that validates the operation of negation. But even more peculiar is the statement "John does not exist." This cannot be represented by the logical form "There is no x such that x exists and x is John" since "exists" is a quantifier, not a predicate (at least in standard first-order logic). If to exist is to instantiate a concept, what concept are we invoking in denying John's existence? Much ink has been spilled on negative existentials, none of it terminating in a satisfactory analysis because there is no analysis of the "non" in nonexistence, to say nothing here of the fact that existence is not a concept. If it were, what would we say about concepts, and in particular the concept of existence? Is a concept an instance of itself?

"Where is John?" "Nowhere." Or again: "What lies on the other side of the universe?" "Nothing." The simple fact is that ordinary language, when correctly used, is metaphysical in precisely the sense in which we are assured by linguistic therapists that it is not. In ordinary language, we invoke nothingness constantly and in countless ways, none of which can be explained as a reference to a concept, that is, to something that refers to something. The so-called syntactic or correct analysis reduces ordinary language to gibberish. The correct philosophical procedure at this point is not to keep searching for a referent to terms like "not" and "nothing," but to *give up an excessively rigid allegiance to the doctrine of reference.* We do understand sentences employing words like "not" and "nothing," and what we understand is that these words do not refer; they are not the names of concepts or sets and certainly not some ontological structure. This understanding is the extreme case of intuition. It has *nothing* (and I emphasize the term) to do with synthesis or analysis, except in the crucial sense that synthesis and analysis play a vital role in the discursive thinking that leads us up to the threshold of nothing. Nor is any of this affected by the fact that the statements we use in order to paraphrase what we understand are themselves constructed with the assistance of synthesis and analysis. The paradigm-case of intuition is also the paradigm-case of the difference between Being and language; that is, it is the limit case, because here Being is nothing.

If it were true that one could identify something only by its predicates, then one could never identify anything because we are in no position to know that we have grasped the essential predicates. The truth is that we do not identify anything by exclusive reliance upon predication. What happens instead is that we grasp an entity by its look or pattern as a whole; this is what Plato and Aristotle call *noēsis,* and what I call an application of intuition. And only after we have apprehended the entity as a unity with a definite internal articulation are we able to proceed to the task of picking out what are for us its defining properties or, as we call them by their linguistic equivalents, predicates. *Noēsis* is not a part of the analysis of identity and predication. It is not an analysis at all, but neither is it a Kantian synthesis. It makes no difference for my present purposes, however, whether we argue from Platonist or Kantian premises. The point is that no one identifies things like cows, trees, or persons by uttering predicational statements. We cannot build up the unity of a perceived or cognized object by glueing together predications. We require a pattern in accord with which the glueing process can begin, continue, and end at the proper point of identification. I have to leave it here at this extremely concise claim. Those who disagree are invited to explain how we identify things via predication. The usual result of these attempts is to dissolve the world into a contingent product of unintelligible linguistic operations; and from here, the step to the chaos of deconstruction and postmodernism is a very short one. In fact, it has already been taken by someone with no interest in predication:

Nietzsche, who, despite his lack of interest, is the hidden God of all philosophies of language that begin with a theory of reference and predication.

And now at last a word about dialectic. Dialectic is more interesting than standard modes of reasoning in all cases where the issue is one of existential process. It is also an essential corrective to all forms of logical atomism, including that of the Eleatic Stranger in Plato's *Sophist*. But in my opinion it adds nothing to the task of explaining how we understand nothing because it functions in such a way as to incorporate nothing into being and thereby to transform it into a moment or constitutive element of becoming. In so doing it transfers our attention from the moment to the dialectical compound. That is to say, dialectic attempts to explain nothing as something by transforming it into determinate negation. We need to reflect more carefully, and without metaphysical prejudices about language, reference, and so on, on our everyday speech about nothing. I have been arguing here, not that nothing is an obscure metaphysical mystery (although it may well be), but that it is a familiar participant in our daily lives and discourses. It is ordinary language that shows us that we can understand without referring to something. In that sense, ordinary language is metaphysical.

What we require in the case of nothing is neither logical analysis nor Hegelian dialectic, but a sober attention to ordinary discourse. The kind of investigation of ordinary language that I have in mind is obviously not grammatical or syntactical in the usual senses of the term, although grammatical and syntactical considerations can certainly be brought into play, so long as they are not tied indissolubly to the standard doctrines of reference and predication. If the term had not been preempted by Hegel, I might have suggested that we call the relevant investigation dialectical. The term is appropriate to the extent that it captures the give and take between speech and silence, with the leading role taken by speech, in any effort to understand the absence of structure, and in particular, of course, the absence of everything. As things stand, however, I see no advantage and much disadvantage in adopting the term to my own purposes.

Nevertheless, Hegel is a valuable ally in our inquiry because he grasps the "presence" or activity of nothing as a differentiating factor, which he designates by a variety of effective names, such as the infinite labor of negativity. He is a distraction, however, to the extent that he tries to assimilate nothing into the process of becoming that is the actual content of the Concept. A successful dialectic, one that is capable of meeting the challenge of the intelligibility of our everyday allusions (as distinguished from references) to nothing, will have to move outside the rationalist tradition, to which Hegel and Heidegger as well as Plato and Aristotle belong (and presumably all logicians and mathematicians), a tradition wedded indissolubly to the notion of finite negation. This is because, as I can only hope to have hinted in this brief essay, finite negation also invokes the intelligibility of the "altogether not" that Parmenides was apparently the first to forbid us to mention.

Here then is my conclusion, which is also intended as an invitation to participate in a subsequent reflection for which this essay was merely a propaedeutic. Dialectic may be characterized as the weaving together of something and nothing in discursive thinking. In this characterization, "weaving" should be understood as an active process, not as a static result or web. The various truths of Hegelian dialectic concerning nothing, which may be summarized in the assertion that every determination is a negation, point to a deeper truth that nothing cooperates with being in the presentation of something. There is a fundamental parity of function between being and nothing, and we should not attempt to reduce either to the other. The fact that we cannot talk about nothing except via speech that is both about and itself something does not alter the fact that we understand the referential character of this speech, not because it actually succeeds in hitting its target but because it fails. The primordial thinking of nothing is of the emptiness of thought. Only afterward do the explanations begin, and it goes without saying that they begin in and through speech.

As it turns out, I have been advocating a kind of analysis that might be called metaphysics or dialectic, depending upon one's terminological preferences, but a mode of analysis that is rooted in a sensitivity to how we actually speak, and not at all to the dogmas of the therapists of language.

Chapter 15 Kojève's Paris:
A Memoir

*This is a radically revised and expanded version of a short essay commis-
sioned by* parallax *for a special issue on Kojève's Paris. I want to emphasize
that what follows is a memoir, not a scholarly analysis. It is nevertheless my
hope that some readers will find it of philosophical interest. I have been
thinking about Kojève for almost forty years, both in himself and in
relation to another great teacher, Leo Strauss. Strauss used to endorse
Nietzsche's remark that the student's duty to his teacher is to kill him. This
advice, which was not understood by many of those who later came to be
called Straussians, is intended to free the neophyte for the arduous task of
philosophy, and so for the task of doing justice to the nature of one's teacher.
It is, of course, not intended to legitimate a shallow, narcissistic expression
of independence or presumed originality.*

*It is a striking fact that, although Kojève was the more "original" of my
two teachers, in the sense that he espoused a fully developed philosophical
system as Strauss did not, there are many Straussians but very few if any
Kojèvians. Much of the protestation about Strauss's disciples is hypocritical
in that it overlooks the equivalent phenomenon associated with all charis-
matic teachers. Nevertheless, it is worth asking why Kojève's influence was*

of a different kind from that of Strauss. The answer, I think, is that Strauss seemed to represent the revitalization of something old, whereas Kojève claimed to manifest the conclusion of the philosophical tradition and seemed thereby to license the initiation of a postphilosophical epoch. One could not follow Kojève's exoteric or pedagogical doctrine without departing from it or generating something new; there was no question here of reiterating forever the closed circle of Hegelo-Kojèvian wisdom. The closure of the circle meant that such reiteration would be sterile in a new historical age, an age devoted perhaps to the repetition of fragments of the Hegelian system as though these fragments were themselves novelties, or else an age in which philosophy is to be replaced by eros and aestheticism, both disguised by the rhetoric of a postphilosophical discourse. In a word, Kojèvians could not rise to the level of the master by repeating his logos, which was or claimed to be a systematic endorsement of the lapsing into silence of that logos. Strauss, on the contrary, whatever his private thoughts, articulated a philosophical program in political terms that was explicitly intended to be followed or enacted. One might call Straussianism in this sense the mirror image of Wittgensteinianism in the sense of the invocation to dissolve positive teachings of a systematic sort. Heidegger's disciples present a more complex problem because they attempt to enter a new epoch of thinking by repeating the deconstructive mantras formulated by the master.

These introductory remarks are intended only to hint at the complex problem of the nature of the philosopher as educator. I should like to encourage others to stop judging Kojève by the criteria of Hegel philology, just as one should not judge Strauss, Wittgenstein, or Heidegger by their pedagogical rhetoric alone. The rhetoric becomes intelligible only when one has understood the underlying philosophical doctrine. And one cannot understand this doctrine without grasping the intentions of the teacher. This is why a laudatio *of one's teachers can never be a simple tissue of pious flattery. If I may paraphrase Strauss (or Nietzsche), one keeps alive in philosophy only what one has sacrificed on the altar of truth.*

In 1960–61 I was a Fulbright Research Professor at the Sorbonne. My sponsor was Jean Wahl, a kindly gentleman who was one of the first, and perhaps the first, to redirect French philosophical attention to Hegel in the late twenties with his lectures on the unhappy consciousness. Wahl was interesting because of a certain amorphousness in his nature. By education and age, he served as a symbol of the Paris of the previous generation. At the same time, he possessed a childlike openness and imaginative predisposition for novelty that hinted at things to come. One could not confuse him with the traditional masters of erudition like Gueroult or Gouhier, who exemplified in a higher degree the classical formation of France between the two world wars but who at the same time were speaking in muted voices to partially closed ears. Unfortunately, Wahl was no longer in his prime when I met him. Our contacts were limited and of a social rather than a philosophical nature. In short, even though Wahl was administratively or politically the most important philosopher at the University of Paris (or so I was told), he was no longer in a position to lead the way into the next generation.

Despite the presence of interesting younger individuals (among them Paul Ricoeur), the Sorbonne was essentially in the hands of the old guard, a cadre of cultivated historians with an academic view of philosophy. Those who were interested in philosophy as a living enterprise had to look elsewhere: the École des Hautes Études, the Jesuits, the salons, and above all, the Quai d'Orsay, where Alexandre Kojève held court.

My affiliation with the Sorbonne as a Fulbright professor was, to be perfectly honest, a technical device that made it possible for me to carry out my primary motive for coming to Paris. I carried a letter of introduction to Kojève from Leo Strauss, with whom I had studied at the University of Chicago as a graduate student in the Committee on Social Thought (an organization that deserves its own memoir). In 1960 I was thirty-one years old, or what Raymond Aron described to me, upon our first meeting, as "a bright young man—but not too young!" He was sufficiently polite to refrain from qualifying the degree of my brightness. This ambiguous compliment was accurate enough with respect to my age, which permitted me to admire the striking personalities of contemporary Paris without becoming their disciple. I had, so to speak, been inoculated against the pathos of Old Europe by growing up in the United States, and against discipleship by the spectacle of the circle (or rather circles) rotating around my old teacher at Chicago.

As this is a memoir of Kojève's Paris, I need to say something about those Parisians of the time who were most important or striking to me. My wife and I arrived in Paris on the day before the now-famous colloquium at Royaumont on dialectic, to which we had been invited by our friend Jeanne Hersch, a professor at Geneva and a well-known member of the philosophical world of Paris. I was officially introduced to this world by Jacques Lacan, a dour, gray-faced man in a black suit who was speaking that day on what I vaguely remember, probably incorrectly, as the mirror image. I understand that his talk, which continued for some three hours, was an epoch-making event in post-modernism, and so in the annals of the influence of Kojève, whose famous lecture-course on Hegel Lacan had followed.

Like so many other Parisian celebrities of the day, Lacan, according to my information, had been deeply influenced by Kojève's analysis of the master-slave dialectic. To anticipate, when I once asked Kojève about Lacan, he replied, "Il gagne beaucoup d'argent." To return to the lecture, it was delivered in a stuffy, overheated room filled largely with central European specialists in dialectic, all wearing identical dark suits with widely spaced chalk stripes and all puffing away on unbearably strong cigarettes. My wife left after a quarter of an hour; I stayed for another thirty minutes or so, trying desperately to keep breathing, both literally and figuratively, in the thick atmosphere of my colleagues' cigarettes and the lecturer's unassimilable rhetoric. I found Lacan pretentious, obscure, and dull, a perception that will perhaps outrage the readers of this memoir but which I must confess I have retained for thirty-five years. This is obviously not intended as an informed scholarly judgment; every effort on my part to replace initial impressions by careful study of the key texts has met with failure.

This was perhaps the most important event of the conference from a historical standpoint, but it was only a passing moment for me. There were in attendance a wide assortment of individual types, ranging from the foolish to the profound, each with its special contribution to the education of a (not too) young American. How well I remember one Parisian mandarin in his midthirties, to whom I was introduced by Jeanne Hersch as someone who shared his interest in Heidegger. The gentleman in question refused to look at me and treated me to five minutes of intricate tooth-picking (his own, of course) with the fingernail of his right thumb as I muttered the usual inanities. I had previously witnessed the dental ritual only as practiced on film by Brigitte Bardot, for whom I took it to be a signal of sensuousness. In the case of my present interlocutor, who had been, I was told, an assassin for the Greek communist party, it seemed more like a symbolic execution.

It was only later that I came to understand the aforementioned gentleman's obvious dislike of someone about whom he knew virtually nothing. His behavior was inspired in large part by an anti-Americanism that was unfortunately not atypical of Parisian intellectuals of his generation in the 1960s. This is a topic that offends some French scholars when I mention it, but I cannot sympathize with their irritation, especially after having been subjected while living in France to countless episodes of rudeness and quite banal criticism of the United States. On one point at least, a memoir is exactly like a scholarly essay. One must tell the truth. It would be absurd for me to have to say that many of my best friends, in particular my wife, are French, and that I have had some of the most satisfying philosophical experiences of my life in their company. It also has to be said that the strong point of the French character is not that of taking criticism well.

The fact remains that in 1960, the influence of Marxism in general and of Sartre and de Beauvoir in particular was extremely strong in Paris. The anti-Americanism of these persons is a matter of public record and does not rely upon anecdotes or personal memories. One should bear in mind associated phenomena such as de Gaulle's insistence upon keeping the Americans from tarnishing the lustre of French glory, as well as the disdain felt at that time by most French philosophers toward the philosophical movements of the English-speaking world. At the deepest level, this philosophical condescension toward Americans in particular was in no small part due to the influence of Kojève but above all to that of Heidegger. I should say that at this period in my life, I was philo-European and entirely prepared to share in the criticism of the philosophical doctrines of my compatriots. What I was not prepared to accept was ignorant and malicious criticism of my country.

This unpleasant situation encouraged me to spend much of my time with Russians, Polish and Lithuanian Jews, and priests, all in their late fifties and sixties and all happily immune to the vulgar consequences of current fashionable ideologies, even when they shared in their intellectual formulations. The general view of virtually everyone with whom I came into contact was that America should be regarded at best by analogy with the Romans, whereas the French, of course, were the classical Greeks. I also encountered this view in Great Britain, but with a slight variation, according to which the English assumed the role of Hellenic mentors to the American Romans. In Germany and Italy, strikingly enough, I found widespread admiration for the United States, ambiguously expressed at times ("You won the war! We must be like you!" I was told in Tübingen by a prominent surgeon) and too often connected with the desire to receive invitations from wealthy American universities.

To restrict myself to Paris, the French at that time showed nothing of the desire to accommodate their superiority to the largesse of American academic institutions, nor did they wish to turn their own philosophical faculties into bastions of pragmatism and Anglo-Saxon analytical philosophy, as did some of the brightest younger Germans. These latter were understandably motivated by a revulsion toward the philosophical views of the generation between the two world wars, and in particular toward Heidegger, who was widely acknowledged to be a Nazi as well as an unsavory personality in other respects, and whose influence was held largely responsible for the destruction of German civil and spiritual society.

In France, on the contrary, Heidegger was (and is) held in high repute. The first half of his famous observation that, metaphysically speaking, America and Russia are the same, and that these two countries constitute a pincers between the two tongs of which Germany is impaled, was endorsed by Kojève himself. It is a curious phenomenon that France and the United States are the two countries in which defenders of Heidegger's personal character have held out the longest against the evidence. To explore in detail why this might be so would take me too far afield. Suffice it to say that Heidegger provided a rallying point in the United States for many of those who rejected, or who were rejected by, the dominant analytical movement in academic philosophy. With respect to France, it should at least be noted that Jean Beaufret, one of the most influential philosophy professors in Paris (he taught at the lycée Louis le Grand), was a close friend of Heidegger and shared his political and social ideology. As the case of Derrida is enough to exhibit, however, it is hardly possible to connect Heidegger's influence in France with a proclivity toward anti-Semitism. That this influence should take the political form characteristic of the left rather than the right is also a matter that deserves attention.

It is surprising to recall how much of the viewpoint on America held even by intellectuals and artists was apparently shaped by Hollywood and the comic strip. The fantasies of political conviction also played a considerable role here. I will rest content with a single anecdote from a slightly later period. In 1963–64 I was a postdoctoral fellow at the Humanities Research Institute at the University of Wisconsin. One day we were visited by Nathalie Sarraute, a prominent French novelist and a Jew. She was seated next to me during lunch, presumably because I spoke French. When Sarraute learned that I was also Jewish, she informed me that there were a number of public beaches in New York City where Jews were not permitted to swim. I was unable to shake her conviction on this point, which she had acquired in Paris.

I want to expand the previous remark about Hollywood films. These were extremely popular with French intellectuals and students, who would stand in long lines in the rain in order to see a Robert Mitchum or Jerry Lewis film, very much as New Yorkers did for the films of Ingmar Bergman and Federico Fellini. These American films were discussed in great detail and highly appreciated; yet paradoxically enough, they served as an important basis for the largely pejorative view of American life. A similar attitude prevailed toward "le Coca" (Coca

Cola, of course), which Parisians consumed in vast quantities, even as they castigated Americans for preferring it to wine. And the same story could be told about popular music. At a more serious level, the undeniable fact of racism in the United States was put to unfair use by Parisians, who seemed not to notice that blacks were conspicuous by their absence from fashionable districts such as the eighth and sixteenth arrondissements.

I will add a word about anti-Americanism when I discuss Kojève. To return to Royaumont, another amusing aspect of the event is that I was one of four native speakers of English at the conference, the other three being G. R. G. Mure, John Findlay, and Leslie Beck. For the first time in my life, I was classified as an Anglo-Saxon. I maintained cordial relations with these men after the conference, to one degree or another, but that is part of a different story. It figures in this memoir as a background detail or preparation for the *parousia* of Kojève. These charming and articulate Anglophones helped to mediate my entrance into continental dialectic, as well as providing me with living examples of what British philosophy had been like prior to the triumph of ordinary language analysis. Mure, who belonged to the era of Collingwood and Joachim, was especially bitter about the advent of analytical philosophy, which he attributed to the loss of an entire generation of gifted young men in the First World War. One does not have to accept either his dislike of analytical philosophy or the precise form of his explanation for its rise to power in order to see that there is a connection between World War One and the changing of the guard in European intellectual life. The age of analysis and the age of *Angst vor dem Tode* are the theoretical and practical consequences of the destruction of a historical epoch.

It was at Royaumont that I first encountered a number of figures who played a peripheral role in my Parisian education, among whom perhaps the most hospitable was Lucien Goldmann. Goldmann had an ambiguous reputation in Paris as a kind of lackey for Georg Lukács. His work was never as highly regarded on the Continent as it came to be for a short time among the Americans and English. I found him both open and polite, despite his obvious fanaticism: an intriguing combination. He invited me to his apartment, where, after his wife had served us coffee and pastries, Goldmann inquired in a high, squeaky voice, "Alors! Quelle est votre position philosophique?" I could think of nothing better to say than "Je suis platonicien" or something of the sort. "Platonicien!" Goldmann screamed, and proceeded to speak for two hours at machine-gun-like speed, largely about Kasavubu, Mobutu, and Lumumba, leading figures in the contemporary crisis in the

Congo. I liked him quite a bit but found his views to be conventional historicism and in no way comparable to the sharpness of Lukács' formulations. I single him out for comment because he was spirited and prepared to discuss philosophy with a young American.

But the most important discovery at Royaumont by far was for me the remarkable personage of Father Gaston Fessard, S. J. Fessard is not only important in himself; he was one of Kojève's closest friends, perhaps his closest friend in Paris. To look ahead for a moment, the structure of my year in Paris was soon fixed by Monday mornings at the Quai d'Orsay, in conversation with the reincarnation of Machiavelli laced with Hobbes and Cagliostro, and Thursday afternoon at the Jesuit House with a man of God whose extraordinary intelligence and beautiful spirit won my immediate and permanent love.

Five men above the rest impressed me during that first year in Paris: Alexandre Koyré, Gabriel Marcel, Raymond Aron, Fessard, and Kojève. In singling out these five, or rather in acknowledging that the force of their intelligence and personality singled them out, I do not wish to overlook such interesting individuals as Paul Ricoeur, Jean Hyppolite, Father Dominique Dubarle, Henri Lefebvre, and others whom I either observed or met briefly. I did not meet Merleau-Ponty, who died before Kojève had the opportunity to introduce me to him. At that time I had no personal access to Emanuel Levinas, nor did I have any clear idea of his philosophical views, but I attended his public examination for the advanced doctorate and found him to be an imposing figure toward whom his examiners showed unusual deference. I never saw Erich Weil but once asked Kojève for an opinion. The answer was restricted to a negative judgment on Weil's book, *Hegel et l'état*.

In writing this memoir, I have had occasion to consider once more a question that has puzzled me for many years. Has the level of philosophical splendor in Paris radically decreased from the period of 1960 to the present decade? Is there more rhetorical posturing, or only rhetoric of a different kind? I am not the greatest admirer in America of postmodern speech patterns, but I prefer them to the Marxist rhetoric of the early sixties. Derrida, Deleuze, and Michel Serre at their best are not radically inferior to Lukács (not a Parisian, of course, but very much present in 1960), Goldmann, and Althusser. In this context, I can only suggest that Marxists and postmodernists are responding in almost exactly opposite ways to the same fundamental crisis, namely, the apparent failure of the Enlightenment in the first half of the twentieth century. One should not make a comparative judgment between the 1960s and the 1990s on the basis of popular adaptations of legitimate political rhetoric, but rather with respect to the seriousness and profundity of the formulation of the fundamental problem by the best representatives of the two periods.

One way in which to make my point on this issue is to say that I consider Nietzsche and Heidegger to be deeper thinkers than Marx. On the other hand, Marx, despite his revolutionary intentions toward old Europe, incarnates something of its breadth and lucidity that are not present in Heidegger, and that are obscured in Nietzsche by his tendency to bombast and vagueness of conceptual expression. Kojève is unique in my experience because the unconvincing veneer of Marxism—one might almost say of Spenglerian foolishness—that defaced his speeches and writings was balanced if not entirely dissolved by a Slavic openness to which was joined the best-stocked and best-functioning brain that I have had the pleasure of observing.

I interpolate a remark about the style of this memoir. It is, precisely, a memoir, not an essay in systematic metaphysics. Kojève is the main theme, but in my symphony his appearance is anticipated in a variety of introductory figures. He thus plays the same role in this memoir that he and his close friends, Leo Strauss and Gaston Fessard, have played in my life, which has been inevitably an effort to come to terms with the present by way of a *recherche du temps perdu*.

If we put to one side the excessive or vulgar rhetoric of Marxism on the one hand and of postmodernism on the other, I believe we can say that neither moment in Parisian philosophical culture, the 1960s or the 1990s (and these are, of course, artificial end points, defined by my experience, not by the world-spirit), predominates over the other. Both are equally serious and equally necessary moments in a more comprehensive dialectic, alluded to above, and which I represent as the fate of the Enlightenment. Postmodernism looks weightier to us today because it is *our* moment. This increases the dangers that it poses for us, which are by now widely recognized to be the dissolution of the subject and the object, or the replacement of the text by incoherent scribbling. These are dangers, but their dangerousness does not cancel the seriousness of the failure of traditional rationalism, a failure that may be properly held responsible for the worst excesses of postmodernism.

So far as I am able to tell, a similar story can be told about the domain of philosophical scholarship. Despite much grumbling by present-day academicians about the radical deterioration in higher education, especially in the humanities (grumbling that one hears in Germany as well as in England), it is my impression that scholarship is flourishing in contemporary Paris, in large part because of the salutary influence of Pierre Aubenque, who was the center of an unusually wide and highly competent circle of scholars for a number of years (he retired quite recently). The excellence of this scholarship is for me occasionally muted by a Heideggerian bias, but one must also say that the influence of Heidegger was instrumental in the revivification of the study of the history of philosophy in Paris. On balance, I could not say that scholarship has radically declined in Paris during the last thirty-five years. There are some lacunae, but I am not sure that these can be blamed on the deterioration of the times so much as on the ebb and flow of human affairs.

Nevertheless, something is missing. I infer this in part from what will be regarded by many as a preference for the old-fashioned philosophical culture of pre–World War II Europe. However this may be, there was a largeness of spirit in the "stars" of the previous generation that has too often been replaced by narcissism and sometimes even madness in their contemporary successors. Eccentricity has replaced greatness of soul, and rhetorical posturing too frequently pretends to be originality of thinking. I believe that the main reason for this deterioration is obvious: a widespread rejection of the traditional paradigm of the philosopher as a person of universal *Bildung*. There has been a shift in our conception of wisdom, as is perhaps most obvious in the English-speaking world, where the term has acquired a pejorative, ironical sense. It would take me too far afield to discuss the reasons for this shift. Let me instead try to describe briefly the *Stimmung*, or attunement of the spirit, characteristic of the older view. A moment ago I used the expression "greatness of soul." If taken strictly in the Aristotelian sense of *megalopsuchia,* the term is misleading. Nor would it be precise enough to speak of an aristocratic bearing, although this contains an element of what I have in mind. The best representatives of the European formation between the two world wars were stamped by a blend of courtliness and freedom; to be a philosopher was for them to hold strong views that one could defend with competence and elegance, but views that were held by a free spirit rather than holding or binding the spirit in the grip of an ideology, or even worse, a pose of freedom.

I grant at once that this is inadequate, but at least it points in the right direction. Let me try one more formulation. The manners, the well-bred humor, the irony modulated by good-natured playfulness were an expression of a nobility of the intelligence and spirit, not of the aristocracy of class or wealth. There is today instead a rejection of nobility, a celebration of technique rather than universality, and most striking of all, the transformation of the praise of freedom into an ideology that narrows rather than enlarges the view. The earlier complex of characteristics was sustained by its roots in the European cultural heritage. Having been uprooted from that soil, the contemporary spirit has withered in its freedom. I want to emphasize that this "paradigm shift" is not due to science and technology in themselves but rather to a different and narrower conception of the relation between philosophy and science. One has only to compare the philosophical writings of Cantor, Brouwer, and Gödel with contemporary philosophy of mathematics, or of Bohr, Heisenberg, and Weizsäcker with recent work in the philosophy of physics, to appreciate the difference.

Needless to say, I have been attempting to describe two general types or paradigms, not the many exceptions to both. And no doubt even within the highest exemplars of the older model, there were blemishes. The most pertinent example for the present occasion is Kojève himself. Before I turn my thoughts directly to Kojève, let me say a few words about the other four thinkers who particularly impressed me as products of a now-dead civilization.

Of these four, I have the least to say about Koyré because I saw him the least, not because I do not estimate him highly. He was a gentleman and a scholar, lucid, erudite, rational, and polite. The one thing that seemed to be missing was philosophical *mania*. I was not surprised to learn that although it was Koyré who had invited Kojève to lecture on Hegel at the École des Hautes Études in the early thirties, relations between the two men were currently poor. Kojève mentioned to me that Koyré thought him to have appropriated the latter's doctrine on the connection between Christianity and the origin of modern science, but I suspect that the peculiar personality of Kojève and his infinitely greater charisma generated a feeling of rivalry in a dimension in which Koyré could not compete.

Some readers may be surprised that I include Gabriel Marcel in my list of five, and it has to be said at once that I know very little about his philosophical productions. The only passage that stays in my mind is a comment somewhere on the French Revolution. Marcel accepts without qualification liberty and fraternity but notes that equality is a difficult conception. Or so I remember it. My homage is to the man and his vivid personality and keen intelligence as well as to his great generosity to younger philosophers. I saw him privately once or twice and attended his salon on a few additional occasions, where I was invited to give a paper. I could not say that I felt any sympathy with Marcel's political views, the articulation of which played a major role in his salon. His circle consisted largely of the conservative wives of rich Catholic bankers and industrialists. I shall always remember ascending the steps to his apartment on the

Rue de Tournon shortly after de Gaulle had given Algeria its independence. The hallway reverberated to the sound of Marcel's voice as he read from his weekly editorial (I do not recall for which paper): "General de Gaulle, Je ne vous aime pas!" Impossible to reproduce in print the passion and the emphasis with which this line was delivered. And yet, Marcel was a friend of Fessard and Aron, and that in itself speaks well for him. He was also immune to contemporary ideological prejudices and, despite his advanced age, surprisingly quick-witted and fresh in the face of novel ideas. He is today largely forgotten, and I want to remember him here as a superior human being of great cultivation.

Raymond Aron presumably needs no introduction to readers of this memoir. I shall restrict myself to a few personal impressions of this unusual man. It goes without saying that he was highly intelligent, extremely witty, and spiritually vivacious. He was one of the regular auditors of Kojève's seminars on the *Phenomenology* during the thirties, and the two men remained on terms of close friendship. Unlike many Parisian intellectuals, including, unfortunately, Kojève (but not Fessard), Aron was politically sane. His record of opposition to Marxist corruption of political and philosophical thought is outstanding in its courage and lucidity. It is today, but it was even more so in the sixties. It should also be noted that Aron regarded Kojève as the most intelligent human being he had ever met, a judgment that he repeats in his memoirs. Aron was a philosophical spirit, but whereas I found him to be more animated than Koyré, he seemed to me to suffer from an analogous limitation. Aron was too sensible to succumb to philosophical *mania*. He was more reminiscent on this point of Leo Strauss than of Kojève, although the comparison between Strauss and Aron is faulty in various ways. Strauss had penetrated more deeply than Aron into the surface of the depths; in a way not entirely unlike Kojève, however, he had arrived rather early at exaggerated political views (a judgment shared by Aron).

Of the five men whom I have singled out for special comment, Father Fessard was in my view the greatest human being. That he is today virtually unknown in the English-speaking world, even among his fellow Jesuits, is not unexpected, given the peculiar style and content of his writings, which were invariably a mixture of philosophy and theology. He was a controversial figure in his own order and in particular in France, where he belonged to a generation of outstanding spirits that included Henri de Lubac and Teilhard de Chardin. The controversy centered upon Fessard's intention to rewrite Catholic theology with Kierkegaard, Hegel, and even Marx furnishing the philosophical foundation in place of Saint Thomas. Fessard was also famous in France for the pamphlets he had written against the Nazis during the Second World War under the pseudonym Monsieur *X.* Of his religious and theological disputes I will mention only his long polemic against the worker-priest movement. He was in no sense a Marxist but at the same time was regarded by Kojève as potentially the greatest authority on Marx in France.

Fessard is the highest instance in my experience of someone who combined the virtues of the priest and the philosopher. I had been educated to believe that such a combination is in principle impossible. Fessard taught me otherwise by his personal example. In lucidity and quickness of intellect, the ability to take in at once views alien to his own beliefs, and in that peculiar combination of profundity and childlike simplicity that marks thinkers of the first rank, Fessard surpassed everyone I saw in Paris with the single exception of Kojève. One could say that Fessard accepted Christ, whereas Kojève accepted only himself. But both men exerted every sinew of their spiritual being to give a *logos* of their faith.

I come now, or rather return, to Kojève himself. My remarks will again be entirely impressionistic, as the sociologists say; those who require a scholarly analysis of his writings will have to look elsewhere. The problem with most of what I have seen of the scholarly exegeses of Kojèvian "texts" is that they treat Kojève as a fellow scholar who must be judged by objective standards of academic Hegel scholarship (as though these standards are well known and securely possessed by them). Those who take this route inevitably criticize Kojève for his arbitrariness, and even go so far as to conclude that he was himself a sort of café-philosopher or farceur, of considerable ability but not in the last analysis to be taken seriously.

Now there can be no doubt that Kojève contributed extensively to the legitimacy of this assessment. His interpretation of Hegel is arbitrary and philologically unsound, despite the fact (somehow unexplained by his ortho-dox academic critics) that it remains the best in the sense of the most philosoph-ical single book ever written about Hegel, so far as I have been able to deter-mine. Kojève was indeed something of a farceur, although hardly a café philosopher. He detested intellectuals as well as professors and spent most of his leisure time, as he told me, with priests. He was in addition the second most important man in the French government, second only to de Gaulle himself. "De Gaulle decides on relations with Russia and the *force de frappe,*" Kojève once told me. "I, Kojève [his usual manner of self-reference], decide everything else." This at first outrageous assertion was in principle confirmed for me in direct conversation with such paragons of sobriety as Raymond Aron and

André Philip, head of the French legation to the General Agreement on Tariffs and Trade.

Kojève was what I have described elsewhere as the Mycroft Holmes of the French government. His desk was located in the Ministry of Foreign Economic Affairs, where he advised the minister, Robert Marjolin, who had been his student during the thirties. But he was also France's chief adviser to the GATT legation, and he traveled regularly to the United Nations, where he spoke for his government on economic affairs. In addition, he had a network of disciples in the French civil service. All this despite the fact that he had never studied economics formally and certainly had no academic training in political science, let alone direct political experience. He was conversant with Tibetan dialects, quantum mechanics, Russian mysticism, art history, and a wide range of other topics. And he was the most respected and feared individual in the Parisian philosophical world. I give this condensed list of his accomplishments because they are incompatible with the view, partly created by Kojève's own behavior, that he was a shallow, vain poseur, not to be compared for philological *Spitzfindigkeit* or understanding of Hegel with the solid representatives of the academic establishment. It should also be stated that Kojève was admired in the highest degree by people like Leo Strauss and Jacob Klein, who were not exactly generous in the praise of their contemporaries, but also by such figures as Stuart Hampshire and Sir Isaiah Berlin; as it happens, I was in a position to arrange a meeting between Berlin and Kojève, and Hampshire once told me of a reading group in London of which he was a member and which devoted much time to the study of Kojève's commentary on the *Phenomenology*.

I trust that these remarks will give an indication of why it is important to think carefully about Kojève's nature. We are now ready for the full orchestration of the main theme. But permit me a preliminary indulgence in the lighter side of my memoir. Although I saw Kojève on many occasions and for relatively long periods of time, I have great difficulty in remembering the exact features of his face. This cannot be due to a defective visual memory. For example, I saw Karl Löwith only once, for a period of forty-five minutes, yet I recall his appearance vividly. The reader may find my suggestion frivolous, but I believe my difficulty in conjuring up Kojève's face is because there was something in his skeletal configuration and gait that reminded me of T. S. Eliot. My contact with the great poet was quite brief and entirely trivial. As a graduate student at the University of Chicago, I was employed for a time as a waiter at the faculty dining club (known as the Quadrangle Club). One afternoon, Robert Maynard Hutchins, Julian Huxley, T. S. Eliot, and a specialist on dental caries, the vice president of the university, whose name, I think, was Ralph Wendell Harrison, walked into the club and took a seat in my section. I was petrified with fright. Hutchins, a very tall, splendid, and arrogant looking man, did nothing to reassure me when he opened the episode by pointing to his coffee cup. "Do you see that cup? Keep it filled at all times!" I skip directly to the climax. The four guests had ordered Wiener schnitzel, and I brought out only three portions. As long as I live, I shall hear Hutchins shouting across the hall toward me, "Waiter! More Wiener schnitzel!"

Let the Freudians make of this what they will. I admit everything. As for Eliot, he sat through the entire meal in silence, hunched over his various plates, and in particular with his striking profile dangerously close to immersion in the soup, ignoring even my sotto voce request if I might give him more coffee. Eliot's face I remember perfectly. Kojève was somehow a Slavic version of T. S. Eliot. And yet this is absurd; I was not afraid of Kojève, nor was he grim and silent. Even as I write these words, his features begin to emerge from the foggy memories of the past. His cheekbones were rather high and his cheeks somewhat hollow; his nose was nothing like Eliot's but much straighter. He wore heavy, horn-rimmed glasses and smoked constantly, waving a cigarette holder as he talked. His pace was heavy and his arms long; it was here that the resemblance to Eliot struck me, as also with the spectacles. Or so I remember it. This is how his image shakes itself loose from what is for me its Doppelgänger.

To turn now to his personality, I want first to speak of the difference between philosophers and professors. Kojève was widely regarded in Paris as a man of unusual arrogance, and in some superficial sense this is no doubt a correct assessment. Kojève did not suffer fools gladly. If he was uninterested in someone, he could be abrupt and even rude. This is no doubt a fault, but it does not take us to the heart of the matter. The Platonic dialogues make it evident that Socrates, with all his Attic urbanity, could be merciless to the pretentious and the vainglorious. Simply by his presence, Socrates constituted an existential challenge to those who prided themselves on their wisdom or knowledge. I am not implying that Kojève was at the same level as Socrates. But his superiority to his contemporaries was equally obvious.

Socrates is described in the dialogues as seeking out promising youths in order to interrogate them. With rare exceptions, Kojève sought out no one; people sought him out. If the auspices were good, Kojève was direct, open, friendly, and attentive to his visitor's views. I have been told that spontaneity is a characteristic of the Slavic temper. Perhaps so. More plausible to me is the argument that professors suffer from the vanity induced by decades of captive audiences and the pursuit of professional honors. The professorial soul is narrowed by a lifetime of dedication to a special field of study or the application of a particular technique. But Kojève was a civil servant, and professors might also be philosophers. Let us say simply that the combination of Slavic spontaneity and freedom from the customs of the academic life allowed Kojève's philosophical nature room in which to expand. One entered directly into conversation with him, and by this I mean that the conversation, and not the ceremony of society, was the medium of social intercourse.

There was, however, also an unsatisfying, even disconcerting side to Kojève, one that is most obviously visible in the defects of exaggeration and desire to *épater le bourgeois* that mar his written texts (he did not himself publish books; this was done for him by others, who edited his lecture notes or manuscripts). Whereas Kojève was entirely cordial and attentive to his favored visitors, and conversations with him were never lectures but genuine exchanges, he rarely failed to radiate the aura of supreme self-confidence and superiority to everyone, which may or may not have been warranted, but which marred that superiority. I have no objection to Kojève's perception of his own worth, and neither would I expect someone of his remarkable nature to conceal his virtues behind a false veil of humility. My point is that Kojève made something of a production of concealing his superiority by an almost constant play of irony, sometimes expressed verbally but often restricted to a slight smile, a wave of the cigarette holder, or a twinkle in the eye.

As I have already indicated, Kojève regularly spoke of himself by name, introducing some heterodox pronouncement or another with the formulaic "*X* says so-and-so, but I, Kojève, say . . . " He often stated his superiority by referring to himself as a god, although once he qualified this assertion by adding that his secretary laughed when he made the claim. More irritating, however, was his habit of reminding me that "Americans play with balls, whereas I, Kojève, play with people." To be honest, I found this all very amusing and impressive at the time, and it is entirely irrelevant to me whether Kojève was letting me into his confidence or playing with me. The premise of our conversations was that whereas it went without saying that he was the teacher and I the student, the reason he was allowing me to converse with him was that I deserved to be his student.

I am dwelling on this point because I think it is important to an understanding of Kojève's nature. It has nothing to do with my own amour-propre but with the degree to which Kojève was a genuine philosopher or, perhaps more precisely, with what it means to be a genuine philosopher, rather than a famous professor or statesman. There are two ways in which highly gifted individuals play with people. The first is by attempting to assimilate them into the game and thereby to raise them beyond their usual level. The second is to keep reminding them that one is playing with them. Kojève was a gamester in both ways, but whereas the first was his virtue, the second was his vice. In my opinion, this way of playing was an expression of Kojève's dissatisfaction with his own limitations, not in comparison to his interlocutors and certainly not to me, but to the world-historical figures to whose eminence he aspired, among whom the outstanding individual was, of course, Hegel.

As is well known, Kojève held that history in the philosophical sense of the term had come to an end with Hegel, and that nothing remained for his successors but the task of clarifying certain points in the absolute system and playing their various roles in the achievement of the universal world-state. In one famous formulation, these roles would culminate in lovemaking and the performance of the Japanese tea ceremony. This is not the place for a scholarly exegesis of Kojève's interpretation of Hegel or world-history. This is a memoir, and the nature of a memoir permits me to speak of something more important than absurd philosophical doctrines. I take Kojève's theses on the end of history (and so too of philosophy) to be his version of the response by Leo Strauss to the dilemma facing those who aspire to philosophy yet fall short of the highest level of intellectual and spiritual power. According to Strauss, philosophy is the continuous investigation of the very few plausible solutions to the fundamental problems, and not the convinced advocacy of one solution to each problem. Again I say: perhaps so. But the greatest philosophers did not restrict themselves to examining plausible answers to fundamental questions. They answered those questions, and they did so even when the answer took the form of further questionings. I mean by this that one cannot raise the fundamental questions if one does not know the foundation, and it is this knowledge that is the essence of philosophy. If one knows the foundation, then the answers to the fundamental questions become less important than the correct expression of the questions themselves. But one has to be able to describe the foundation.

Kojève once said to me that he and Strauss were the two genuinely original thinkers of their time because whereas others asserted the originality of their own views, Kojève upheld the teaching of Hegel and Strauss defended Plato. Taken at face value, the words mean little or nothing; Hegelians and Platonists are, so to speak, a dime a dozen. I think Kojève meant rather to say something like this. He and Strauss had understood the impossibility of philosophy in the grand or traditional sense but responded differently to this recognition. For

Strauss, the impossibility of determining the correct answers to the fundamental questions left us with the task of attempting to find the questions. For
Kojève, the same impossibility is the foundation of human freedom. We are free
to invent our own answers to the questions that are seen to be fundamental
because they motivate the very problematic of the philosophical nature. For
Kojève, the invented answers are his interpretation of Hegel, in the broadest
sense of a quasi-Hegelian interpretation of the totality of human history. The
questions, or rather the question, that the interpretation answers is the demand
of human desire.

One of the most important lessons I owe to Kojève, although he did not intend
it, is that realism and rationalism carried to their logical extremes produce a
reductio ad absurdum. To look at the same point from a different perspective,
in 1960 the political situation was still central to philosophers who saw a
mediating role for Europe between Russia and the United States in the shaping
of the future. I referred above to the conviction of the French and British that
each could play Athens to the American Rome. Kojève's version of this belief
was a variant on Gaullism. Both saw the American ruling stratum as Anglophile
and so as not only intrinsically naive but influenced by the inferior culture of
the English. Let us say that from this perspective, the Americans were Goths or
Vandals and the English Romans. Kojève accepted this, as is evident from his
frequent repetition of the previously mentioned Heideggerian thesis that there
was no metaphysical difference between the Russians and the Americans. For
de Gaulle and Kojève, it was France that had to play the decisive role in the
balance of powers, and in order to counteract the British influence with the
Americans, France had to lean toward Russia.

This was also Kojève's version of anti-Americanism, to repeat, based upon
realism carried to absurdity and so transformed into cynicism and ideology.
Nevertheless, it was rooted in the perception of the real historical and political
world and based upon the assumption that there is a link between theory and
practice that can be exploited by the philosopher in a positive manner. In other
words, Kojèvian politics were sufficiently close to Gaullism to be rooted in
traditional European political thought. Kojève, with all his talk of the end of
history and the postphilosophical man, was still attempting to purify and so to
preserve modern Europe. His postmodernism was at best a regulative ideal and
at worst a rhetorical fantasy designed to shock. In the generation of thinkers
whom he influenced, however, the realism and traditionalism of Kojève's thinking disappeared along with Gaullism; what remained was exaggerated rhetoric.
The responsibility of actual political power was replaced by the irresponsible

inculcation to destroy; at this point, Heidegger's Nietzscheanism proved centrally influential.

Kojève transcended not only his contemporaries, but his students as well. I will add my voice to the others who have called him the most intelligent person they have ever known. If I seem to have emphasized the weak elements in his personality, it is not because of any wish to diminish my teacher and friend, but in the effort to understand him. The most important lesson that a philosopher can bequeath to his students is that of his own nature. The philosopher's books can be read in libraries, but the nature of the philosophical spirit, which alone gives meaning and value to those books, is accessible only through direct contact. One cannot understand what it is to be a philosopher without grasping how human frailties are transposed by the philosophical eros into strengths. Where this transposition does not occur, there is also a valuable lesson to be learned.

The last degree of intellectual and spiritual freedom was missing from this superior being, in my opinion because he was at bottom a skeptic in the modern sense of that term, and very close to nihilism. Lacking a genuine system or the Socratic capacity to exist philosophically in the absence, even further the impossibility of systems, Kojève was driven to construct a pseudosystem of ever-increasing intricacy and, oddly enough in a thinker who hated academics, of scholastic rigidity.

Let me try to restate this speculation. Because he was not a philosopher in the classical sense of that term, Kojève turned his energies to the second-best life, namely, that of the statesman, a life that the eccentricities of history enabled him to live at an international level. As I surmise, he turned his attention to the serious game of instituting a philosophico-political revolution, or of demonstrating his divine nature by becoming one of those whom Nietzsche calls the commanders and lawgivers of mankind, in other words, the genuine philosopher—but not through genuine philosophy in this case. I say "not through genuine philosophy" because Kojève himself did not conceal the fact that his interpretation of Hegel, and so of European history, was moved by the practical goal of influencing that history, not by what was for him the impossible goal of achieving a theoretical understanding of nature that is not confirmed in history itself.

To this speculation of mine, one could reply that for a Hegelian, theory is indeed confirmed in praxis, and so that Kojève was acting in a straightforwardly Hegelian manner by attempting to bring about the advent of what he called the homogeneous or universal world-state, the paradigm for the recently notorious "end of history." I have already stated explicitly that I am writing a memoir, not a scholarly study. My speculation has no other ground than my meditative reflections on Kojève as a man and a thinker, reflections that have continued for more than thirty-five years. I have come to the conclusion that my initial intuition, formed during the year of my study and weekly contact with him, was correct: Kojève's system was unworthy of his intelligence and even of his illuminating commentaries on the *Phenomenology*. Not only this, but I believe that he knew its unworthiness, or at least suspected it, or knew it once but had allowed himself to forget it in the pleasures of his own success.

In short, Kojève presents us with the strange spectacle of a philosophical spirit of unusually high capacities who is spending his time in amusing himself as the only alternative to the impossibility of genuine philosophy. I want to say immediately that, with all of its posturing, Kojève's play was much more illuminating than the serious work of almost all professional philosophers I have had the opportunity to know personally. I repeat: Kojève was a genius, not a charlatan. But he was a defective genius. He was too self-conscious, in the good and the bad senses of that expression, to lose himself genuinely in a system, and (to repeat), not self-conscious enough to exist without a system.

Kojève's irony and playfulness affected his personal dealings, even with those whom he genuinely liked. On one point, however, he was without equal. This extraordinary intellect was cold and aloof toward many a Parisian celebrity who courted his attention, but to students who came to him from Strauss and who somehow met his standards of acuity, he was open, direct, gentle in applying his corrections and gracious in accepting plausible criticism. This openness and lack of pretentiousness or even of formality (beyond the minimal requirements of bourgeois civility) may be due to his Slavic nature, but I have found it in the truly superior and highly cultivated individuals of the western European nations as well. Let me simply add that I felt more at ease with Kojève than with any other person except Father Fessard. Kojève's openness and receptivity would periodically cloud over when he seemed to remember that he was, after all, a god, and so called upon to make some shocking remark. This was never the case with Fessard, who was also well aware of his remarkable personal gifts, but who was saved from vanity by the correlative perception of the distance between himself and his deity.

In bringing these remarks to a conclusion, I want to leave the reader with a positive impression of Kojève. He was one of those rare individuals who taught us as much through his faults as through his virtues. One cannot emancipate the philosophical spirit without risk. This is as true of the gifted few as it is of the many, although the risks are enacted at different levels and even in different registers. In reflecting upon Kojève throughout my adult life, I have been helped to understand that there is no unity of theory and practice, or, stated more cautiously, that there is no theoretical unity of the two. This is the exact opposite of what Kojève intended to teach me, but I remain permanently in his debt.

Notes

1. 13:14: All citations from Nietzsche are from the *Kritische Studienausgabe*, edited by Giorgio Colli and Mazzino Montinari (Munich: Walter de Gruyter, DTV, 1980). Numbers designate volume and page; bracketed numbers contain the date and, where appropriate, the fragment or section number.

2. 5:48.

3. 5:57.

4. 11:142 [1884; 25 (491)].

5. 11:543 [1885; 35 (76)].

6. 9:569 [1881; 11 (329)].

7. *Vom Nutzen und Nachteil der Historie für das Leben,* 1:333 [1874; 10].

8. 7:708 [1873].

9. 13:194 [1887/8; 11 (415)]; cf. *Götzen-Dämmerung,* 6:127 [1889; *Streifzüge* 24].

10. 13:227 [1887/88; 14 (21)].

11. For a fuller discussion, see my "Poetic Reason in Nietzsche: *Die dichtende Vernunft,"* in *The Ancients and the Moderns: Rethinking Modernity* (New Haven: Yale University Press, 1989), 209–34.

12. 13:333 [1888; 14 (152)].

13. 9:635ff [1881; 15 (7)].

14. *Sämtliche Briefe, KSA,* ed. Colli and Montinari (Munich: Walter de Gruyter, DTV, 1986), 2:60 [11 June 1685].

15. 11:544 [1885; 35 (76)].

16. Consider here *Die Philosophie im tragischen Zeitalter der Griechen*, 1:864 [1873].

17. *Über Wahrheit und Lüge im aussermoralischen Sinne*, 1:880, 883 [1873].

18. Ibid, 876.

19. Ibid, 877.

20. 7:199 [1870/71; 7 (156)].

21. Plato, *Theaetetus* 153a1–3.

22. 1:28; 4:21f; 7:23ff (cf. 5:16–18); 7:45–47 (the image of the cloud is replaced by that of the wind at 94f).

23. *Olympians*, 7. 94f.

24. *Pythians* 3. 103ff.

25. *Olympians*, 12. 5ff.

26. *Pythians* 10, 61–66.

27. *Olympians* 9. 35ff; *Pythians* 1. 41; 7. 71ff.

28. *Nemeans* 6. 4ff.

29. *Nemeans* 7. 20ff.

30. *Nemeans* 5. 17–19, cf. *Isthmians* 1. 63.

31. *Theogony*, 27f.

32. (Bern/Leipzig: Verlag Robert Noske, 1935). Numbers in parentheses in the text refer to pages in this edition until otherwise noted.

33. Cited from Marcel Detienne, *Homère, Hésiode et Pythagore* (Bruxelles: Collection Latomus, vol. 57, 1962), 48.

34. *Republic* 3. 389b2ff, 3. 414b9f, 5. 459c2-d2.

35. 3. 377d4ff.

36. *en pharmakou eidei:* 389b3–4.

37. 3. 677c4ff.

38. 316e5–317b3.

39. *Theaetetus* 151a1–3.

40. *Sophist* 235c8ff.

41. *Les maîtres de vérité dans la grèce archaïque,* 2d ed. (Paris: Francis Maspero, 1973), 73, 77.

42. See my "Nietzsche's Revolution" in the previously cited *Ancients and the Moderns*, 189–208.

CHAPTER 2. THE LIVED PRESENT

1. I want to acknowledge the assistance of my colleague Dan Dahlstrom, who read an earlier version of this essay and made valuable comments that led to a number of revisions.

2. *Essai sur les données immédiates de la conscience,* in *Oeuvres* (Paris: Presses Universitaires de France, 1959), 148, 91.

3. *The Inordinance of Time* (Evanston: Northwestern University Press, 1998). Professor Gallagher was kind enough to send me the manuscript of this book prior to publication, and I am quoting from the typescript, 44.

4. *Lebendige Gegenwart* (The Hague: M. Nijhoff, 1966). Numbers in parentheses refer to pages in this work.

5. *Sein und Zeit* (Tübingen: Max Niemeyer Verlag, 1977), paragraph 65 (pp. 323-30). Numbers in parentheses in the text refer to this edition.

6. Ibid, paragraphs 67–68.

7. The concern in question is *Besorgen* or inauthentic *Sorge;* see page 337 inter alia.

8. *Phenomenology of Perception,* tr. Colin Smith (London: Routledge and Kegan Paul, 1962), 427.

9. *Husserlian Meditations* (Evanston: Northwestern University Press, 1974), 159.

10. This is granted even by "Platonism" with respect to everyday life; see *Philebus* 39D-E. But to grant it is not to make it bear the weight of a complete doctrine of human temporality.

11. *Being and Time,* 329.

12. As I noted previously, this seems to be Husserl's view as well. Sokolowski says that the togetherness of retentions and the central impression (of the present) "is not in time because it is the condition for time" (*Husserlian Meditations,* 158). But this makes Husserl a Kantian.

CHAPTER 4. THE GOLDEN APPLE

1. *The Guide of the Perplexed,* tr. S. Pines, with introductory essays by L. Strauss and S. Pines (Chicago: University of Chicago Press, 1963), 11–12.

2. One should not overlook, however, a lapse into bad habits on page 20: "Only as the dialogue progresses does Socrates actually 'do' philosophy, as we like to say." Perhaps this is an esoteric dig at his "analytical" mentors.

3. I agree with Ferrari in general that Derrida's strictures about the deconstructive nature of the treatment of writing in *Phaedrus* are largely unfounded. See especially Ferrari's remark on page 204 to the effect that Socrates investigates good writing as well as good speaking. For a more elaborate criticism of Derrida, see my *Hermeneutics as Politics* (New York: Oxford University Press, 1987).

4. The reference is to two polemical articles attacking Leo Strauss on moral, political, and scholarly grounds, and published in *The New York Review of Books.* This is Burnyeat's contribution to the morning devotions of doctrinally sound late-modern intellectuals.

5. I refer to Seth Benardete, whose books are too idiosyncratic to serve as proof texts for the study of Strauss's methods despite their own frequent brilliance. But why should we turn to students at all, when the master has left a plethora of texts? The fact that none is specifically on *Phaedrus* is obviously irrelevant to the point at issue.

6. See my essays on Nietzsche in my books *The Quarrel Between Philosophy and Poetry* (New York and London: Routledge, 1988); *The Ancients and the Moderns* (New Haven: Yale University Press, 1989); and *The Mask of Enlightenment: Nietzsche's* Zarathustra (New York and Cambridge: Cambridge University Press, 1995).

7. See *Hermeneutics as Politics,* 153–55.

8. See ibid., 43.

9. See my essay "The Role of Eros in Plato's *Republic,*" in *The Quarrel Between Philosophy and Poetry.*

10. For a qualification of the analogy between the dialectician and the philosophical lover, which does not alter the point of the passages cited above, see 223ff.

11. Including Charmides; cf. *Symposium* 222b1 with *Charmides* 155d3ff.

CHAPTER 5. THE PROBLEM OF SENSE PERCEPTION IN PLATO'S *PHILEBUS*

1. For a more extensive treatment of the following point, see chapter 2 of this book.

CHAPTER 6. FORMS, ELEMENTS, AND CATEGORIES

1. *De Anima* 3. 430a14–15.

2. *Posterior Analytics* 2. 6, 92a6ff; 7, a37–92b1 and b12ff. In chapter 8, Aristotle presumably shows how one can exhibit the essence of a fact that has a cause separate from itself, but this procedure is question-begging, since it rests upon knowledge of the middle term. As Ross points out in his commentary to the *PA*, 93b21–25 together with 10, 94a11, make clear that there is no demonstration of essence, which must be *hupothesthai . . . ē allon tropon phanera poiēsai*. Cf. 19, 100b10ff. The *archai* must be known by *nous*. I believe that this is also true of *ousia*.

3. *Metaphysics* A2, 982b28ff.

4. *Posterior Analytics*, 2. 19, 100b7; *Nicomachean Ethics* 6, 1040 b31ff.

5. *Posterior Analytics* 1. 22, 83a18–23,83b11–16.

6. *Categories*, 4. 1b25ff; 5. 2a11ff.

7. Ibid., 5. 2a19ff.

8. *Posterior Analytics*, 2. 3, 90b33.

9. Ibid., 2. 13, 96b13ff. Cf. *Categories* 3. 1b10ff. This seems to be the sense of the distinction between *kath' hauta* elements of an *ousia* and predicates or *sumbebēkota* at *Posterior Analytics* 1. 4, 73a28ff and 73b8ff

10. *Posterior Analytics* 1. 22, 83a32ff.

CHAPTER 7. *TECHNĒ* AND THE ORIGINS OF MODERNITY

1. The quote is from *The Assayer*, the passage is cited in Gary Hatfield, "Metaphysics and the New Science," in *Reappraisals of the Scientific Revolution*, ed. D. Lindberg and R. Westman (Cambridge: Cambridge University Press, 1990), 130.

2. Stillman Drake, *Galileo at Work* (Chicago: University of Chicago Press, 1981), xxi.

3. Hatfield, "Metaphysics and the New Science," 130.

4. Ibid., 132.

5. Hatfield grants that Kepler was motivated by a theoretical or ontological Platonism; see page 109 in the cited essay.

6. See Alexandre Koyré, *Metaphysics and Measurement* (Cambridge: Harvard University Press, 1968), 13–15.

7. See my book *The Quarrel Between Philosophy and Poetry* (New York: Routledge, 1988), esp. chaps. 1, 3.

8. Cf. the discussion of ugliness and disease in *Sophist* 228a4ff. with the comparison between philosophy and medicine in *Gorgias* 464d2ff. and 500e4ff.

9. *Il principe,* in *Il principe e Discorsi* (Milan: Feltrinelli, 1960), 101.

10. *Les passions de l'ame,* ed. G. Rodis-Lewis (Paris: J. Vrin, 1955), 170.

11. See, for example, *Phaedrus* 246d6ff., as well as *Statesman* 271c3ff.

12. I am indebted to David Lachterman for calling this passage to my attention.

13. *Discours de la Méthode,* ed. E. Gilson (Paris: J. Vrin, 1947), 61f.

14. *Instauratio Magna,* in *Works,* ed. Spedding, Ellis, and Heath (Boston: Brown, 1861), 1:415. See 406, where Bacon says that human beings tend to underrate their strength.

15. *Les passions de l'ame,* 177.

16. *Discours,* 62.

17. *Epistles,* 2:314c4.

18. *Wissenschaft der Logik* (Leipzig: Felix Meiner Verlag, 1951), 1:20.

CHAPTER 8. SAD REASON

1. *Esquisse d'un tableau historique des progrès de l'esprit humain,* ed. Prior and Belavel (Paris: J. Vrin, 1970), 15.

2. *Zibaldone di pensieri* (Milan: Mondadori, 1988), 1:136.

3. *Kritische Studienausgabe* (hereafter KSA), ed. Colli and Montinari (Berlin and New York: Walter de Gruyter, 1980), Bd. 11, p. 571.

4. KSA, Bd. 13, p. 37; compare p. 333.

5. *Die fröhliche Wissenschaft* in KSA, Bd. 3, p. 348.

6. 4. 533b6f.

7. 5. 476c5-7.

8. 7. 540d1ff. Cf. 6. 499c1-5.

9. 4. 419a1ff.

10. 5. 466c7ff.

11. 2. 375a2ff.

12. 2. 376a5ff.

13. 8. 546a2ff.

14. *Phaedo* 67d12ff.

15. 246a1-6. The same situation obtains in the *Timaeus,* 35a1ff, where Timaeus speaks of the construction of the world-soul *eis mian idean.* Nothing is said here of the individual soul because the life has to be lived; it cannnot be constructed in advance because there is nothing out of which to produce activities other than the process of activity itself, which is precisely the process by which we construct our lives as we live them, and not as a copy of something else.

16. *Symposium* 202d11ff, 203d7f.

17. The quotation is from *The Metaphysical Foundations of Modern Physical Science,* as cited by H. Floris Cohen, *The Scientific Revolution: A Historical Inquiry* (Chicago: University of Chicago Press, 1994), 94.

18. *A Treatise of Human Nature* (Oxford: Clarendon Press, 1955), 399, 415, 448.

19. Ibid., 268-69.

20. *Anna Karenina,* trans. by Rosemary Edmonds (London: Penguin Classics, 1954).

21. *Natural Right and History* (Chicago: University of Chicago Press, 1953), 250.

22. *Also sprach Zarathustra* in KSA, *Bd.* 4, p. 295. See also p. 408.

23. See the *Nachlass* for 1870/71 in KSA, *Bd.* 7, p. 140. "The value of *Arbeit* is a mad modern fancy of the stupidest sort. It is a dream of slaves."

24. *Wissenschaft der Logik* (Leipzig: Felix Meiner Verlag, 1951), 2:20.

25. *Areopagitica*, in *Complete Poetry and Selected Prose of John Milton* (New York: Modern Library, n.d.), 697.

CHAPTER 9. TRANSCENDENTAL INDETERMINATENESS

1. A satisfactory discussion of the secondary literature would require an essay twice the length of the present essay. Let me simply mention here that the best discussions I have found of the problem of the perceived object are Gerold Prauss, *Erscheinung bei Kant* (Berlin: Walter de Gruyter, 1971); Robert Pippin, *Kant's Theory of Form* (New Haven: Yale University Press, 1982); and Hansgeorg Hoppe, *Synthesis bei Kant* (Berlin: Walter de Gruyter, 1983). Also helpful are Henry Allison, *Kant's Transcendental Idealism* (New Haven: Yale University Press, 1983), and R. E. Aquila, *Representational Mind* (Bloomington: Indiana University Press, 1983). Rather than state my various disagreements with the solutions offered by these scholars to the problems of empirical knowledge and perception, I restrict myself to acknowledging the benefit I have received from studying their works, especially the first three. This is also the place to acknowledge the kind assistance of Professor Pippin, who read several earlier versions of the sections of this essay dealing with perception and made many extremely helpful comments.

2. There is a thorough discussion of the ambiguities in Kant's treatment of reflective judgment in Paul Guyer, *Kant and the Claims of Taste* (Cambridge: Harvard University Press, 1979). Here is Guyer's version of the problem I shall be discussing: "The present argument connects pleasure to the perception of systematicity in virtue of the contingency of such perception, or the fact that systematicity is not guaranteed by the laws of the understanding; but the principle of reflective judgment, that nature itself is systematic, was apparently designed precisely to guarantee that such a perception would occur, or would at least not seem to be contingent. Thus the principle of reflective judgment seems to be incompatible with the only way in which that faculty can be linked to the feeling of pleasure" (83). I would rather say that the principle is given by the subject to itself in order to justify the perception of systematicity, a justification that cannot be sustained by the transcendental account of the understanding (and of determinant judgment). In other words, perception is ambiguous; we perceive both purposiveness and contingency. The connection with pleasure seems to me to be arbitrarily introduced by Kant. It is quite distinct from the question of the perception of purposiveness.

3. All citations from the *First Critique* are designated in the traditional manner by page numbers from the A and B editions, as printed in the *Philosophische Bibliothek, Bd.* 27a (Hamburg: Felix Meiner Verlag, 1956). Translations are my own.

4. Page references for the *Third Critique* are to the edition of K. Vorlander in the *Philosophische Bibliothek, Bd.* 39 (Hamburg: Felix Meiner Verlag, 1954). Translations are my own.

5. Guyer, *Kant and the Claims of Taste,* 46, makes a very similar point: if purposiveness is necessary, why is it not constitutive?

6. See, for example, the previously cited work by Guyer.

CHAPTER 10. FREEDOM AND REASON

1. In the *Symposium, eleutheron* occurs at 181e6 in the speech of Pausanias, who says that husbands of freeborn women constrain them in order to prevent their seduction. At 218c2, Alcibiades says that he decided to "say freely [*eleutheros*] what I think" to Socrates, namely, to offer him sex in exchange for assistance in becoming the best possible human being; Socrates restrains this freedom. In the *Phaedrus* Socrates says at 243c8 that those who have spent their lives with lowborn sailors have never seen *eleutheron erōta,* that is, love of free or highborn persons. At 256b3, Socrates says that the triumph of philosophy and the better part of *dianoia* binds the evil part of the soul and frees (*eleutherōsantes*) the virtuous part.

2. *Kritik der reinen Vernunft,* B74–75 and B93; B430, B561, B573ff.

3. *Kritik der praktischen Vernunft* (Hamburg: Felix Meiner Verlag, 1952), 57.

4. Ibid, 4.

5. *Wissenschaft der Logik* (Leipzig: Felix Meiner Verlag, 1951), *Bd.* 1, p. 31.

6. *Les passions de l'âme,* introduction and notes by G. Rodis-Lewis (Paris: J. Vrin, 1955). Title to *Première Partie* and Article I, p. 35. In citations from this text, Roman numerals refer to article numbers and Arabic numerals to page numbers.

7. Ibid., I, 65.

8. XC, 130.

9. 202d8-e7.

10. LXIX, 115; CXLV, 170; CLX, 180; CLXI, 184: *Generosité* is "la clef de toutes les autres vertus." The six primitive passions are admiration (of which *generosité* is a species), love, hate, desire, joy, and sadness (LXIX).

11. II, 66; XVII, 79.

12. CXLIX–CLI and CLIII, 175–78.

13. LXXIX, 121.

14. LXXXI, 123.

15. CLVI, 180.

16. I cannot develop the point here, but there is another ambiguity, even a contradiction, in Descartes' treatment of love. In XC, 129, Descartes claims that "la jouissance de ce qui agrée" is "le plus grand de tous les biens qui apartienent à l'homme." But otherwise he says that *agréement* has to do with beauty; this joy could not be as great, or as great a good, as the intellectual joy to which there is no limit and which I will mention in the text of this lecture.

17. LXXXV, 126–27.

18. LXXXVI, 127.

19. LXXX, 122.

20. CXLVI, 172.

21. L, 105; CXLIV, 169.

22. XLVIII, 103; XLIX, 104.

23. XLI, 96.

24. CLII, 177.

25. XCI, 164f.

26. LXX, 116.

27. LXXV, 119.

28. LXXVI, 120.

29. 155d1–5.

30. *A*, 982b12.

31. LXXXII, LXXXIII, 124–26.

32. XCI, 131; CXXXIX, 164–65.

33. XLVIII, 105.

34. *Regulae* 5, 7, 12.

35. *Regulae* 14.

36. Crapulli edition, Rule One, p. 3, lines 2–11; Rule Six, p. 18, lines 3–25.

37. "A Central Ambiguity in Descartes," in *The Ancients and the Moderns* (New Haven: Yale University Press, 1989).

38. *Kritik der reinen Vernunft* B576; *Kritik der praktischen Vernunft*, 65.

39. 203d7f, 207d6–e5.

40. *Wissenschaft der Logik*, Bd. 1, p. 20.

41. *Phänomenologie des Geistes* (Hamburg: Felix Meiner Verlag, 1988), 63ff. Cf. *Logik*, Bd. 1, 14 and 18, and for the unification of *an sich* and *für sich*, 42.

42. *Phänomenologie*, 14f.

43. Ibid, 26.

44. *Also sprach Zarathustra*, in *Kritische Studienausgabe*, ed. Colli and Montinari (Berlin: Walter de Gruyter, 1980), *Bd.* 4, 408.

45. Ibid, 75: "Immer vernichtet, wer ein Schöpfer sein müss."

46. *Encyclopädie* (Hamburg: Felix Meiner Verlag, 1969), p. 350, paragraph 428.

47. In *Jenaer kritische Schriften* (Hamburg: Felix Meiner Verlag, 1979), 1:10.

48. *Logik*, 2:499.

49. Page 387, par. 481.

50. Page 387, par. 482.

51. Cf. *Enzyklopädie*, p. 416, par. 539: "In der Tat, ist jedes wahrhafte Gesetz eine Freiheit, denn es enthält eine Vernunftbestimmung des objektiven Geistes, einen Inhalt somit der Freiheit." *Grundlinien der Philosophie des Rechts* (Hamburg: Felix Meiner Verlag, 1955), p. 67, par. 57: the Idea of freedom is genuinely actual only as the state.

CHAPTER 11. INTERPRETATION AND THE FUSION OF HORIZONS

1. *Kritische Studienausgabe* (Berlin: Walter de Gruyter, 1980), ed. Colli and Montinari, *Bd.* 12, p. 39.

2. Numbers in parentheses associated with citations from Gadamer refer to *Wahrheit und Methode*, 4. Auflage (Tübingen: J. C. B. Mohr, 1975).

3. On this point, see chapter 2 of the present volume.

4. *Sein und Zeit*, 14th ed. (Tübingen: Max Niemeyer Verlag, 1977), 143.

5. Ibid., 148.
6. Ibid, 212.

CHAPTER 12. IS THERE A SIGN OF FREEDOM?

1. Numbers in parentheses refer to pages in *Philosophie des Zeichens* (Berlin: Walter de Gruyter, 1989).
2. The number in parentheses refers to a page in *Wahrheit als Methode* (Berlin: Walter de Gruyter, 1978).

CHAPTER 14. NOTHING AND DIALECTIC

1. Graeme Forbes, *Modern Logic* (Oxford: Oxford University Press, 1994), 104. For typographical reasons, I have had to supply a different symbol for "absurd" than the one used by Forbes.

Index